WINCKELMANN AND THE NOTION
OF AESTHETIC EDUCATION

Winckelmann and the Notion of Aesthetic Education

JEFFREY MORRISON

CLARENDON PRESS · OXFORD
1996

Oxford University Press, Walton Street, Oxford OX2 6DP
Oxford New York
Athens Auckland Bangkok Bombay
Calcutta Cape Town Dar es Salaam Delhi
Florence Hong Kong Istanbul Karachi
Kuala Lumpur Madras Madrid Melbourne
Mexico City Nairobi Paris Singapore
Taipei Tokyo Toronto
and associated companies in
Berlin Ibadan

Oxford is a trade mark of Oxford University Press

Published in the United States
by Oxford University Press Inc., New York

© Jeffrey Morrison 1996

All rights reserved. No part of this publication may be reproduced,
stored in a retrieval system, or transmitted, in any form or by any means,
without the prior permission in writing of Oxford University Press.
Within the UK, exceptions are allowed in respect of any fair dealing for the
purpose of research or private study, or criticism or review, as permitted
under the Copyright, Designs and Patents Act, 1988, or in the case of
reprographic reproduction in accordance with the terms of the licences
issued by the Copyright Licensing Agency. Enquiries concerning
reproduction outside these terms and in other countries should be
sent to the Rights Department, Oxford University Press,
at the address above

British Library Cataloguing in Publication Data
Data available

Library of Congress Cataloging-in-Publication Data
Morrison, Jeffrey.
Winckelmann and the notion of aesthetic education / Jeffrey
Morrison.
—(Oxford modern languages and literature monographs)
Includes bibliographical references.
1. Aesthetics, Modern—18th century—Study and teaching.
2. Aesthetics, Modern—19th century—Study and teaching.
3. Aesthetics, German—18th century. 4. Aesthetics, German—19th
century. 5. Winckelmann, Johann Joachim, 1717-1768—Aesthetics.
6. Goethe, Johann Wolfgang von, 1749-1832—Aesthetics.
I. Title. II. Series.
BH181.M57 1996   111'.85'092—ds20   95-46832
ISBN 0-19-815912-9

1 3 5 7 9 10 8 6 4 2

Typeset by Alliance Phototypesetters
Printed in Great Britain
on acid-free paper by
Bookcraft Ltd,
Midsomer Norton, Bath

*For my mother,
Mrs Jean Helen Morrison,
and for Sylvia.*

Acknowledgements

During the work on the thesis which forms the basis of this book I was able to travel widely thanks to the generosity of the Provost and Fellows of The Queen's College, Oxford where I held a Laming Junior Fellowship. I am grateful to the Winckelmann-Gesellschaft (Stendal), the Ecole Normale Supérieure (Paris) and The British School at Rome for their support during my various periods of research abroad. On a personal note, I would like to thank my friend Dr David Constantine for the inspiration and the supervision which he provided over several years.
I would also like to thank Mr Francis Lamport for making me want to study and teach German.

Contents

ABBREVIATIONS x

1. ITALIAN TRAVEL IN THE EIGHTEENTH CENTURY: THE ROMAN SCENE AROUND 1750 1

2. JOHANN JOACHIM WINCKELMANN AND ROMAN INGARDEN ON THE RECEPTION OF WORKS OF ART 34

3. JOHANN HERMANN VON RIEDESEL 69

4. JOHANN JACOB VOLKMANN 169

5. CONCLUSION: JOHANN WOLFGANG VON GOETHE 206

BIBLIOGRAPHY 249

INDEX 271

Abbreviations

WINCKELMANN

Werke	*Sämtliche Werke: Einzige Vollständige Ausgabe*, ed. Joseph Eiselein, 12 vols. (Donauöschingen, 1825–9; repr. Osnabrück, 1965)
Briefe	*Briefe*, ed. Walther Rehm, 4 vols. (Berlin, 1952–7)
KS	*Kleine Schriften, Vorreden, Entwürfe*, ed. Walther Rehm (Berlin, 1968)
GK	*Geschichte der Kunst des Altertums*, ed. Ludwig Goldscheider (Vienna, 1934)

INGARDEN

OK	*Untersuchungen zur Ontologie der Kunst* (Tübingen, 1962)
EKW	*Erlebnis, Kunstwerk und Wert* (Tübingen, 1969)

RIEDESEL

Sizilien	*Sendschreiben über seine Reise nach Sizilien und Großgriechenland 1767*, ed. Kasimir Edschmid (Darmstadt, 1939)
Levante	*Randbemerkungen über eine Reise nach der Levante 1768*, trans. L. M. Schultheis, ed. E. E. Becker (Darmstadt, 1940)

VOLKMANN AND SOURCES

Nachrichten	*Historisch-kritische Nachrichten von Italien*, 3 vols. (Leipzig, 1770–1)
Lalande	Jerôme de Lalande, *Voyage d'un François en Italie*, 8 vols. (Venice, 1769)
Richard	Jean-Jacques Richard, *Description historique et critique de l'Italie*, 6 vols. (Paris and Dijon, 1766)

GOETHE

Werke	*Werke*, 142 vols. (Weimar, 1887–1919)
IR	*Italienische Reise*, ed. Peter Sprengel, paperback edn. (Munich, 1986)

I
Italian Travel in the Eighteenth Century:
The Roman Scene around 1750

EACH of the instances of aesthetic education with which this book is concerned took place in Rome. The Roman visit was often a precursor to further travels, and many excursions were made to other towns and cities within reach, or even further afield. Equally the journey to and from Rome provided an opportunity for extensive study. However, Rome was, in each case, the main focus of the traveller's attention. Although Riedesel wrote at length about Sicily, Goethe about the whole of Italy, and Volkmann about the whole of Europe, each of them underwent their aesthetic education substantially in Rome. Their examples provide obvious confirmation of Winckelmann's assertion that Rome was a 'Hochschule für alle Welt' in the field of the arts.[1] This belief was not peculiar to him and the dominant position of Rome in the contemporary European imagination was reflected, not only in the number of people visiting, but also in the fact that most guidebooks and travelogues of the period devoted a large part of their coverage to Rome.[2] It is important to identify the reasons for the intense focus of interest on Rome in the mid-eighteenth century. It was not stimulated by the arts alone; other factors were influential. The relative convenience of foreign travel allowed Rome to feature more prominently in travel plans. This convenience must be measured in terms of speed rather than creature comfort; any foreign travel was still an adventure. Most contemporary travel accounts contain detailed descriptions of the tortuous route across the Alps or the Apennine hills; or else we hear of the dangers of using coastal roads in Italy.[3] The seafaring traveller was subjected to equal risk; there was still

---

[1] *Briefe*, i. 16. This is one of many assertions of this kind by Winckelmann based upon his belief that Rome was 'eine unerschöpfliche Quelle von Schönheiten der Kunst' (KS 225).

[2] Volkmann's *Nachrichten* are typical of the contemporary guidebook. The second of his three volumes is devoted entirely to Rome.

[3] If the journey was not dangerous it was simply gruelling. Winckelmann observed that 'die Wege durch die Gebürge dermaßen schrecklich [sind], daß wir einen ganzen Tag über zwey deutsche Meilen zugebracht haben' (*Briefe*, i. 189). Wolgang Leppmann's *J. J. Winckelmann: Eine Biographie* (Frankfurt am Main, 1971), 129–31 describes the poor

a considerable threat of piracy, or of simply running aground in adverse weather. This risk had not been reduced by the time of Goethe's sea journey from Sicily back to the Italian mainland in 1787, when he was caught in a storm.[4] At least the large number of travel publications during this period meant that travellers were able to predict practical difficulties and so reduce their potential spoiling effect.

A second spur to travel was the increasing wealth of the middle classes. Money enabled the bourgeoisie to aspire to a form of educational tour which had previously been the reserve of the aristocracy. Bourgeois aspirations in travelling were often of a purely social kind, although some travelled in order to be educated. All travellers had a certain novelty value and so were often well received in Italy:

> Die Eigenschaft, *forestiere* zu sein, als Fremder Rom zu besuchen, genügte gewissermaßen als gesellschaftliche Einführung auch bei Römern von Stand; zu Grunde lag wohl die meist zutreffende Anschauung, daß jemand, der Rom besuchte, entweder über Mittel verfügte, oder Bildungszwecke verfolgte, oder endlich beides vereinigte.[5]

But what were the 'Bildungszwecke' which could be uniquely realized in Italy, and in Rome?

Italian travel was not a phenomenon new to the eighteenth century. Indeed there is a large stock of earlier travel literature, some of which contained recommendations for the most useful employment of time during a visit. In many respects little had changed since the sixteenth century. Ludwig Schudt reproduces a passage from Nathan Chytraeus' *Deliciae* (1594) to summarize the expectations of the traveller in the seventeenth and eighteenth centuries:

In iteneribus observanda
DEUM in primus invocat quotidie profecturus, praecibus itinerum, quas mox subjiciam.
I. Regio in qua consideranda nomina   Vetera
                                        recentia saepe mutata
II. Ditio hominum   Superiorum
                     nostrorum

---

state of accommodation on the route south and the sanitary precautions that were necessary. For those travelling on to Greece the problems redoubled. See David Constantine, *Early Greek Travellers and the Hellenic Ideal* (Cambridge, 1984), 6.

4 See the entry in the *Italienische Reise* for 14 May 1787 (IR 294–8).
5 Friedrich Noack, *Deutsches Leben in Rom 1700 bis 1900* (Berne, 1971) (repr. of the edn. pub. Stuttgart, 1907), 62.

III. Nomen urbis, & ratio nominis, si extet. Item conditor, amplificator, aut instaurator alicuius loci.

IIII. 1. Flumina eaq; aut prope distātia allabentia deducta
2. Mare alluens, aut portus.
3. Montes.
4. Sylvae, nemora, vel si quid aliud insigne.

V. Opera & haec vel
   Publica
      Sacra
         Basilicae
         Monasteria
         Templa
      Profana
         Palatia, arces, fora, armamentaria, propugnacula, turres, & ratio munitionis
   Privata
      Ut quae in civium aedibus sunt insignia, veluti horti, picturae, fontes, statuae.

VI. Ratio gubernationis, ad quam pertinent
   1. Curia, in qua Senatores, & familiae civium honestae.
   2. Scholae, ut ratio educationis, & institutionis pueritae. Item viri docti, & Bibliothecae.
   3. Vulgi mores, quo pertinent, ratio victus, & vestitus; item opificia.[6]

The author of this programme envisaged a traveller with a very wide range of interests, stretching from geography through history and politics to the arts. Presumably not many people were qualified or perhaps interested enough to cover all of the subjects suggested by this itinerary. None the less it gives an idea of the pattern of contemporary interests. In fact many later guidebooks have a very similar basic structure to that described by Chytraeus, even if they reveal a particular interest in the visual arts. The full title of Volkmann's guide to Italy confirms this, since he offered *Historisch-kritische Nachrichten von Italien, welche eine genaue Beschreibung dieses Landes, der Sitten und Gebräuche, der Regierungsform, Handlung, Oekonomie, des Zustandes der Wissenschaften, und insonderheit der Werke der Kunst nebst einer Beurtheilung derselben enthalten. Aus den neuesten französischen und englischen Reisebeschreibungen und aus eignen Anmerkungen zusammengetragen.*

Even if the general scheme suggested above held true for most travellers we must still investigate the specific motivation of members of the Winckelmann circle in visiting Rome. In advance of this we must also

[6] Ludwig Schudt, *Italienreisen im 17. und 18 Jahrhundert* (Vienna, 1959), 139.

consider in detail the other factors which made Italy and in particular Rome the preferred goal of most travellers. It was clearly rather more than the simple matter of access mentioned earlier.

Over a very long period there had been a historical focus upon Rome as a political and religious centre for Western culture. Corresponding attention was paid to its aesthetic appeal; the architecture of the city and its store of art treasures offered the most striking testimony to the city's enduring power and influence. The Roman Empire, Roman Catholicism, the Latin language as the language of learning, a powerful artistic tradition: each of these factors individually or, more tellingly, in combination, became major cultural determinants for the whole of Europe. Even the Reformation was unable to weaken the hold of Rome upon the collective cultural curiosity of Western Europe.[7] Ironically, it may even have contributed to Protestant fascination with Italian travel. This general cultural interest was not, however, historically specific. How are we to account for the sudden deepening of interest in the mid-eighteenth century? From his twentieth-century point of view, Noack points out that at the beginning of the eighteenth century the appeal of Rome was not as powerful as it became later in that century: 'Rom war damals noch nicht völlig das geworden, was es heute für das deutsche Geistesleben ist, und in Deutschland war die Empfänglichkeit für die Eigenart Roms nicht entwickelt.'[8] There is a very firm indication here that the crucial transformation in attitude towards Rome may have begun to take place during the period of Winckelmann's residence in Rome, although it could not wholly be attributed to him. Many other factors came into play.

The political organization of Rome had a major impact upon the shape of travellers' responses to the city and so upon the prospects for aesthetic education. The attitude of individual popes to the arts was important. Similarly the attitudes of the leading Roman dynasties, which provided the finances for art collection, could have a profound effect upon the arts, although for political or dynastic reasons their views often echoed those of the ruling pope. There does appear to have been a remarkable coincidence of interest in the arts during the period in which we are interested. Most of the great collections date from the seventeenth and eighteenth centuries.[9] The first public gallery was established

---

[7] See Fritz Blättner, 'Winckelmanns deutsche Sendung', *Deutsche Vierteljahresschrift*, 21 (1943), 23–66. The introductory section 'Die Romanitas und das Deutsche' (pp. 23–8) surveys Italian influences in Germany during the period in question.

[8] Noack, *Deutsches Leben*, 18.   [9] Ibid. 3.

ITALIAN TRAVEL IN THE EIGHTEENTH CENTURY 5

in 1734 under Clement XIII, though most of the work on it was not completed until the reign of Benedict XIV.[10] The latter was also responsible for the establishment of a variety of academies and he took an active interest in their activities.[11] In the end financial necessity limited his power to promote the arts. Other members of the higher echelons of the Church were also responsible for the new emphasis upon the arts. Cardinal Albani, Winckelmann's major patron, was crucial in this respect and, besides creating one of the major collections of the period and providing employment for architects and painters in the construction and decoration of his villa, he was also behind one of the *salons* in Rome. This was presided over by his long-standing mistress, Countess Cheroffini.[12] However, the cultural situation was not without its uncertainties. Winckelmann was able to find employment in the Vatican under Clement XIII, and yet this pope's reign marked one of the few dark times for the arts in Italy during the Enlightenment. The covering of male genitalia on statues and the strict control of the publishing industry (and the movement of books generally) were two of his policies. The nagging fear of investigation by the Inquisition was also constantly present for those active in the arts.[13] As a result many individuals found themselves in ambivalent positions. Justi points out that Archinto, before he became a cardinal, worked as Governor of Rome and was responsible for a very severe form of justice. This was not felt to be incompatible with patronage of the liberal arts; Winckelmann at least chose to ignore any conflict with his own liberal political outlook in order to accept Archinto's patronage.[14]

Even if Rome did not have the perfect political climate it contained so much work from classical Rome and, according to contemporary evidence, from classical Greece, in addition to many masterpieces of the Renaissance, that it still acted as a powerful magnet to Northern Europeans. To use Rehm's term, there developed alongside the conventional Church an 'aesthetische Kirche', which drew converts in large

---

[10] Ibid. 56–7. Progress in the Capitoline museum was matched by neglect in the Belvedere courtyard, where works of art were kept in appalling conditions.

[11] See Carl Justi, *Winckelmann und seine Zeitgenossen*, 3rd edn., 3 vols. (Leipzig, 1923), ii. 160–79 for a general survey of this pope's work. Justi makes very firm connections between the policies of the individual popes and the contemporary cultural climate.

[12] See ibid. 383, 396; iii. 40, 359; Winckelmann, *Briefe, passim*.

[13] Winckelmann had a copy of Voltaire removed from his luggage on arrival in Rome (*Briefe*, i. 194). His fear of the Inquisition reached a peak in 1767. See *Briefe*, iii. 288, 291, 311.

[14] See Justi, *Winckelmann*, ii. 121–31.

numbers.¹⁵ The dichotomy between the two churches is illustrated by Blättner. He refers to the new responsiveness to art, in the wake of Winckelmann: 'Das geschah im päpstlichen Rom, das ihn nährte, hegte und ehrte, vor den Augen erstaunter Römer, die als Kardinäle und Prälaten der Kirche in den ausgegrabenen Statuen nie mehr gesehen hatten als eine ferne dekorative Kulisse im Hintergrunde von St. Peter.'¹⁶ The movement of art out of the background in Rome and into the foreground of cultural life was accelerated not just by the presence of certain powerful individuals but also by the constant discoveries of ancient art within Roman territory. In addition the contemporary discoveries at Pompeii and Herculaneum added immediacy to the desire to travel to Italy and so inevitably to Rome. In the same way Naples, Magna Graecia, and Sicily were beginning to attract more attention from the travelling public which would inevitably pass through Rome. All of the great Italian sites also acted as an intermediate focal point for those travellers whose ultimate interest was the exploration of Greece and Greek art.¹⁷

Attention was drawn to the abundant attractions of Rome by the increasing number of travel reports and art surveys which were published. These were not a completely new phenomenon, but more were published from the middle of the eighteenth century onwards. Likewise, there was an increase in the number of works on educational and aesthetic theory available to the traveller. Clearly these texts awoke some new expectations of the arts although, as we shall see, they could not entirely replace more conventional notions of gentlemanly education. The travel literature in question written by, for example, Zeiller, Lassels, Addison, Misson, Spon, and Sandrart was by no means uniform in approach.¹⁸ To take different examples from the period, by way of an extreme contrast, it would be difficult to find many similarities in the attitude to travel in Sterne's *A Sentimental Journey*, and Cochin's *Voyage d'Italie*, the former focusing upon the psychology of the traveller, the latter purporting to be an objective account of works of art seen in

---

¹⁵ Walther Rehm, *Griechentum und Goethezeit: Geschichte eines Glaubens*, 3rd edn. (Berne, 1952), 16.

¹⁶ Blättner, 'Winckelmanns deutsche Sendung', 39–40.

¹⁷ The increasing appeal of Southern Italy, Magna Graecia, Sicily, and Greece is documented by Constantine, *Early Greek Travellers*.

¹⁸ There are numerous useful surveys of the travel literature of the period. Among those with an emphasis on Italian travel are: William E. Stewart, *Die Reisebeschreibung und ihre Theorie im Deutschland des 18. Jahrhunderts*, Literatur und Wirklichkeit, 20 (Bonn, 1978); William Edward Mead, *The Grand Tour in the Eighteenth Century* (Boston, 1914); Paul Franklin Kirby, *The Grand Tour in Italy 1700–1800* (New York, 1952); H. Neville Maugham, *The Book of Italian Travel* (London, 1903); Schudt, *Italienreisen*.

Italy.[19] The example of Sterne, who scarcely reported on Italy, is included deliberately to indicate that Italian travel reports formed only part of a large complex of travel literature which undoubtedly encouraged the desire to travel. The collective or individual impact of such works had the effect of awakening renewed interest in Rome by the middle of the eighteenth century. Batten, discussing travel literature in general and not necessarily work on Italy, indicates that while many travel books were learned studies of geography or history, they also had another function: 'Travel books, however, were not merely treatises, since they also provided an imaginative experience for the reader who happened to have a "kindred heart".'[20] The ability of the international book trade to awaken and then sustain interest in art and so to create a generation of 'kindred hearts' throughout Europe is important here. The surest indication of the influence of such literature is given by Batten, who points out that in eighteenth-century Britain travel literature came second only to the novel, in terms of book sales.[21]

Many other reasons have been suggested for the sudden resurgence of interest in Rome during this period. Rüdiger indicates that Germany had been exposed to modern Italian art and literature for quite some time, and that this would have had a considerable influence upon contemporary travellers.[22] Spengler points to a form of compensation reaction in Germany at having missed out on the Renaissance as a result of political instability at home in the sixteenth century and the subsequent effects of the Thirty Years War.[23] Again, from a German point of view, travel to Rome can be seen as the most concrete evidence of a reaction against the prevailing taste for French culture. What Vallentin calls 'die geistfeindliche Gefrorenheit der französischen Hofkultur und Literatur', was, in his view, replaced by a more profound engagement with the arts amongst travellers to Italy. He identified closer ties between those with a mutual interest in the arts; this group then gathered in Rome away from any social pressures and could focus its attention more clearly on their

[19] Charles-Nicholas Cochin, *Voyage pittoresque d'Italie, ou Receuil de notes sur les ouvrages de peinture et de sculpture, qu'on voit dans les principales villes d'Italie*, 3 vols. (Paris, 1751); Laurence Sterne, '*A Sentimental Journey*' with '*The Journal to Eliza*' and '*A Political Romance*', The World's Classics (paperback series) (Oxford, 1984).
[20] Charles L. Batten, jnr., *Pleasurable Instruction: Form and Convention in Eighteenth-Century Travel Literature* (Berkeley, 1978), 7–8.
[21] Ibid. 1
[22] Cf. Horst Rüdiger, *Winckelmann und Italien: Sprache, Dichtung, Menschen*, Schriften und Vorträge des Petrarca-Instituts Köln, 8 (Krefeld, 1956).
[23] Cf. W. E. Spengler, *Der Begriff des Schönen bei Winckelmann: Ein Beitrag zur deutschen Klassik* (Göppingen, 1970), 77.

shared interests.²⁴ This break with prevailing French culture was never as clean as the above statement suggests. The 'Hofkultur' travelled south with its representatives from throughout Europe (such was French cultural dominance), and the cultural expectations which it engendered often interfered with the prospects for aesthetic enlightenment. Equally the by then conventional literary/critical expectations, based upon the French classical model, often accompanied the traveller southwards and hindered appreciation of antique art. Kreuzer points out the dependence of Winckelmann upon French critical terminology, which is loaded with often inappropriate implications.²⁵ So French cultural dominance was perhaps not replaced as quickly as Vallentin suggests.

A further difficulty in understanding fully the attraction of Rome resides in the fact that the desire to travel to Italy was quite clearly a European, rather than a specifically German phenomenon. My bibliography so far may have indicated as much. Eberlein describes the confused genesis of the new classicism, produced by a large number of nationalities working in a large number of fields and responding to a wide range of different stimuli:

> Aber so einfach und klar ist die fein verästelte Genesis des neuen Klassizismus doch nicht, der sich allenthalben um die Jahrhundertmitte verspüren läßt und Deutsche, Italiener, Franzosen, Engländer bewegt. Archäologie und Reiseforschung, Architektur und Baulaune, Reizmüdigkeit, Sammelmode, Vedutenwesen, Weltbürgertum, Aristokratensnobismus und moralisierendes Sentiment, all das wirkt zusammen, bestärkt durch die Ausgrabungen in Herculaneum und Pompeji, die aber erst 1756 zur Sensation werden. Rom ist damals der wichtigste Umschlagplatz für 'les sentiments, les sensations et les idées', das Zentrum des Fremdenwesens 'le rendez-vous de toute l'Europe', und einer seiner erfolgreichsten gesuchtesten ciceroni war doch Winckelmann.²⁶

Eberlein manages also, whilst confirming the nature of the melting-pot that was Rome, to point to one of the most direct determining factors in

---

²⁴ Cf. Berthold Vallentin, *Winckelmann* (Berlin, 1931), 16.
²⁵ Cf. Ingrid Kreuzer, 'Studien zu Winckelmanns Aesthetik: Normativität und historisches Bewußtsein', *Jahresgabe der Winckelmann-Gesellschaft*, 1959 (Berlin, 1959), 16–25.
²⁶ K. K. Eberlein, 'Winckelmann und Frankreich: Zur Geschichte des deutschen Kultureinflusses im französischen Klassizismus', *Deutsche Vierteljahresschrift*, 11 (1933), 592–610 (597). Cf. also M. Fontius, 'Winckelmann und die französische Aufklärung', *Sitzungsberichte der deutschen Akademie der Wissenschaften zu Berlin, Klasse für Sprache, Literatur und Kunst*, 1 (1968), 1–27 and W. Heise, 'Winckelmann und die Aufklärung', *Schriften der Winckelmann-Gesellschaft*, 1 (1973) ('Beiträge zu einem neuen Winckelmannbild'), 32–8.

shaping experience of Italy. The importance of the single powerful personality, as guide or tutor, in refining a traveller's responses to such things as classical art is not to be underestimated. We need only reflect on the in many respects parallel strivings of Piranesi and Winckelmann in such a role. And they only represented the highest level of available tutors. Many lesser, but none the less influential figures such as Clérisseau were also at work and we shall examine his influence upon Robert Adam in due course.

The motivation for renewed interest in Rome is then multidimensional. It is tempting to use a vague terminology in describing the overall appeal of the city. We could perhaps follow Rehm's example, taken from a discussion of the desire to visit Greece, and talk of the 'spirit' which the thought of the place awakened. According to this approach, if the location is remote geographically, politically, and due to religious circumstances this adds a greater poignancy to the desire to visit. Rehm cites Humboldt in this connection because he actively promoted the idea of remoteness, suggesting that 'nur aus der Ferne, nur von allem Gemeinen getrennt, nur als vergangen muß das Alterthum uns erscheinen'.[27] But the aims of the mid-eighteenth-century traveller could also be more concrete. Antiquity was more than an intellectual construct for most travellers, and correspondingly it was important for them to go and see the most striking remnants of the ancient world in Italy. Proximity to the ancient world was their aim, and it was clearly possible. The journey to Rome had certainly become less hazardous and so there was the prospect of immediate satisfaction on the aesthetic level and otherwise. There was certainly a strong sense of consumerism among Italian travellers; like many a modern traveller some of them wanted to 'do' Italy, and publications like Volkmann's were there to help them towards this goal.

It might be useful to examine what individuals specifically required of Rome. Travellers did not, for the most part, gravitate towards Rome on some vague impulse, but had specific aims in mind. The example of Robert Adam is useful here. He belonged to the broad circle of scholars and artists which included Winckelmann and, although he may have been more directly influenced in his artistic preferences by Piranesi, his motivation for visiting Rome and his experience of it were broadly similar to those of most of Winckelmann's pupils. He worked most closely with Clérisseau, whom we know to have belonged to the inner circle of

---

[27] See Rehm, *Griechentum*, 1 for the general atmosphere and p. 5 for the quotation from Humboldt.

Winckelmann's friends.[28] Robert Adam's comments on Italy are contained in letters to his family at home.[29] These are interesting above all because they were written from an unusual perspective. The Adam family were not aristocrats, but had considerable wealth which derived in the last instance from lucrative government building contracts, won by their architect father. Their money and their associations with noblemen gave them access to high social circles but their sense of the novelty of this social world and of their own unbelonging in it never wore off. This is reflected in the constant references in Robert's letters from Italy to questions of social integration and to a (we have no reason to suspect insincere) desire to conform to the norms of a gentlemanly tour. They give a particularly self-conscious insight into the ideas which motivated many travellers to 'push forward for the city of Rome' (Fleming, 117).

It is interesting to measure Robert Adam's attitude to Italy against some general characterizations of the traveller of the period. Each of the first three examples given below is disparaging in tone. This choice was made deliberately in order to allow any subsequent positive deviations to stand out more clearly. The first comes from Ludwig Curtius, who deals with the prevailing attitude towards classicism, an attitude which the traveller is presumed to carry with him to Rome:

For the cultured upper classes in the eighteenth century the classical era was no more than an object of study for antiquated pedantry or something of a random collector's piece, nothing more than a decorative background for operas, processions, and garden parties. It could, of course, also serve to provide quotations or as material for didactic and moralising works for the edification of young gentlemen or to embellish political treatises.[30]

Horst Rüdiger is less specific in his criticism, mentioning only 'ein Publikum kunstbeflissener Standespersonen . . ., das in der antiquarischen Modewissenschaft dilettierte'.[31]

Tobias Smollett is typically more dismissive. The following observations stem from his own travels, beginning in 1763, and centre upon the

---

[28] See *Briefe*, i. 566 for a summary of the Winckelmann–Clérisseau relationship and correspondence.

[29] All references to the correspondence of Robert Adam are taken from John Fleming, *Robert Adam and his Circle in Edinburgh and Rome* (London, 1962). Subsequent references to this text will be incorporated into the body of the text in the form: (Fleming, page number). Cf. also Robert Adam (in fact his brother James), 'Journal of a Tour in Italy', *Library of the Fine Arts*, 2/9 (Oct. 1831), 165–78 and 2/10 (Nov. 1831), 235–45.

[30] Ludwig Curtius, 'Johann Joachim Winckelmann 1717–1768', in T. W. Gaehtgens (ed.), *Johann Joachim Winckelmann 1717–1768* (Hamburg, 1986), 5–19.

[31] Rüdiger, *Winckelmann und Italien*, 18.

English community abroad; they perhaps reveal as much about their author as about any actual state of affairs. He notes that

the moment they set foot in Italy, they are seized with the ambition of becoming connoisseurs in painting, musick, statuary, and architecture; and the adventurers of this country do not fail to flatter this weakness for their own advantage. I have seen in different parts of Italy, a number of raw boys, whom Britain seemed to have poured forth on purpose to bring her national character into contempt: ignorant, petulant, rash and profligate, without any knowledge or experience of their own, without any director to improve their understanding or superintend their conduct. One engages in play with an infamous gamester, and is stripped in the very first partie: another is poxed and pillaged by an antiquated cantatrice: a third is bubbled by a knavish antiquarian; and a fourth is laid under contribution by a dealer in pictures. Some turn fiddlers, and pretend to compose: but all of them talk familiarly of the arts, and return finished connoisseurs and coxcombs, to their own country. The most remarkable phaenomenon of this kind, which I have seen, is a boy of seventy-two, now actually travelling through Italy, for improvement, under the auspices of another boy of twenty-two. When you arrive at Rome, you receive cards from all your country-folks in that city: they expect to have the visit returned next day, when they give orders not to be at home; and you never speak to one another in the sequel.

He then moves on to complain at the lack of social distractions and meeting-places, besides the coffee-houses, although, in any case 'no Englishman above the degree of painter or cicerone frequents any coffee-house at Rome'. This social barrier had considerable implications for the prospects of aesthetic education.

According to these descriptions there are three main areas of interest for the traveller. The first impulse is *social*. Each of the commentators emphasizes the homogeneity of the travelling classes. Curtius refers to the 'cultured upper classes', and Rüdiger to 'Standespersonen'. They belonged to a world of 'operas, processions and garden parties', where the acknowledgement of other members of the social group was of prime importance—although it may not always have been answered. Likely alternative company such as that offered by the ciceroni or painters was excluded on social grounds; this may have damaged the prospects for aesthetic education since the ciceroni and artists were closer to art than the other temporary residents in Rome. We also remember that Winckelmann himself lived in artist households in both Dresden and Rome, and that his understanding of art owed a great deal to Oeser and Mengs, the heads of those households; Winckelmann also operated as a cicerone, albeit to an exclusive group of travellers, and he was able to enhance travellers' enjoyment of art through his work. Smollett suggests that because of the tendency to stick together people were not changed by travel to the degree that one might expect; they were inclined to maintain the negative personal qualities which they had brought from home (he isolates petulance, rashness, and profligacy). There is an indication in an earlier passage in the *Travels* that the traveller's wealth was what made him immune to change.[32] But the certain thing was that travel brought no liberation from the social mores prevailing at home. There are striking parallels here with the fears of the 'educationalist' Bishop Hurd, writing on the same theme. In a fictional dialogue concerning the value of foreign travel he has Locke describe the travellers' tendency 'to flock together into little knots and clubs of their own countrymen, or of such others as are most resembling in taste and manners to themselves'.[33] Noack describes a similar phenomenon amongst Germans, who met for generations in the same Roman cafés, forming a similarly exclusive band.[34]

A degree of *sexual* liberation was also associated with travel, although, if we are to take Smollett's interpretation literally, it scarcely appears to be a positive change. To be 'poxed and pillaged by an aged cantatrice' can scarcely have been the traveller's ambition, but there is no doubt that the inexperienced 'boys' who undertook the Grand Tour saw escape from home as a chance to indulge in sexual adventures. In the light of this fact R. S. Lambert's mournful elegy on the passing of the Grand Tour in the late nineteenth century seems particularly naïve. Some people then were still trying to maintain the tradition of the tour 'though railways killed its glory, and bourgeois manners debased its refinement'.[35] The actual business of travelling was uncomfortable and not at all glorious, even during the era of the steam train, and the abandonment of 'manners' a feature of the private life of the traveller. Indeed it could almost be described as an aim for some travellers who knew that their behaviour was not being watched so closely whilst they were away from home.

The time allocated to the *arts* was, according to our cynical referees, limited. Given the function of the arts as, in Curtius' terms, a 'decorative

[32] The three references to Smollett thus far were taken from a modern edition, namely Tobias Smollett, *Travels through France and Italy*, ed. Frank Felsenstein, The World's Classics (paperback series) (Oxford, 1981), letter xxix, p. 241.
[33] R. Hurd, *Dialogues on the Uses of Foreign Travel: Considered as Part of an English Gentleman's Education between Lord Shaftesbury and Mr. Locke* (London, 1764), 103.
[34] Noack, *Deutsches Leben* is entirely concerned with the German community in Rome over a long period.
[35] R. S. Lambert, *Grand Tour: A Journey in the Tracks of the Aristocracy* (London, 1935), 11.

background' to social activity, there can be little suprise that few people took them seriously. Rüdiger points out a double degree of superficiality. Not only were the travellers dilettanti, but they were interested in art merely as a 'Modewissenschaft'. Smollett is more destructive in his assessment. According to him, boys on their travels aimed only at the appearance of knowledge of the arts. He reports that 'all talk familiarly of the arts' and emerge as 'finished connoisseurs and coxcombs', but leaves us in no doubt as to which pursuits had taken most of their attention. The very idea of 'finishing' a study of the arts indicates the superficial level of the achievements at which they were aiming. He had clearly suffered the same experience as Lassels, who reported that the travellers were prone to cry out 'ô che Bela Cosa' (*sic*) indiscriminately, without any attempt to account for the merits of the work in question.[36] Many simply bought works of art to show off at home and this was part of the spirit of cultural consumerism mentioned earlier. In this connection Edward Wright reported that the British were so keen to exploit their buying power that the Italians feared for even the largest works of art, since 'were our Amphitheatre portable, the ENGLISH would carry it off'.[37]

It is important to note also the stress which Smollett lays upon direction and experience. Applying these notions to the teaching of the arts specifically (Smollett is talking of life in general) they could be seen as a call for preparatory study and for the employment of a tutor, both of which suggestions were disregarded by many travellers. In fact, neither of these things could be relied upon at all. Bishop Hurd was one of many contemporary writers who doubted the motivation and capacity of travellers and the ability of tutors to change them significantly. In his fictional dialogue he has Locke point out the absence of ideal pupils and tutors for 'the question at present is of no such rarities; but of raw ungovernable boys, on the one hand, and of shallow servile, and uninterested governors, on the other'.[38]

Even the selection of tutors at home to accompany the young traveller seemed to be aimed at containment, rather than enlightenment. Knox suggested that 'he should be a grave, respectable man, of a mature age'.[39] These comments suggest that there was more than a grain of truth in

---

[36] Richard Lassels, *The Voyage of Italy* (London, 1670), 151.
[37] Edward Wright, *Some Observations made in Travelling through France, Italy etc in the Years 1720, 1721 and 1722*, 2 vols. (London, 1730), i. p. vii.
[38] Hurd, *Dialogues*, 25.
[39] Vicesimus Knox, *Liberal Education: Or a Practical Treatise on the Methods of Acquiring Useful and Polite Learning* (London, 1781), 338.

Smollett's observations and indicate that fears for the well-being of students were justified.

Each of the three interpretations of travellers' wishes and actions given above is harsh. They are useful in undermining any vision of the eighteenth-century traveller as an earnest man in pursuit of self-improvement, broader knowledge of life, and, particularly, understanding of the arts. For many, a tour was the last opportunity to experience a degree of freedom before returning to responsibilities at home. Indeed, the impulse to travel often had a very conservative basis; if nothing else it prepared the traveller for his return home. Lassels describes a state of mind in the 'completed' traveller which does not indicate any inner transformation of the kind Winckelmann envisaged. In his view the traveller 'will be ready to come home at twenty, or one and twenty, a man most compleat both in body, and mind; and fit to fill the place of his calling'.[40]

Lassels sees the attainment of social graces, military and political awareness, and physical endurance as the main benefits of the Grand Tour. There is no question of challenging the fate ('calling') which awaits the traveller on his return. The tour is an exercise in containment, or a means to file down the rough edges of a character so that he fits his place in society more neatly. Knox is quite explicit in his support for such an exercise.[41] Lassels makes the containment process more explicit, noting approvingly that 'traveling takes my young nobleman four notches lower in his self-conceit and pride'.[42] There is no question of development of character, expansion of interests, or deepening of insight.

Such travellers might also learn to apply a gloss of culture to their conversation, which would mark their arrival in an adult world. Knox refers specifically to the 'lustre' of antiquarian knowledge and Hurd in his fictional dialogue has Locke refer to the 'shewy appendages of education' gained abroad, which presumably helped travellers to shine socially at home.[43] This gain in artistic knowledge was sometimes only attained incidentally; the arts were often a secondary pursuit.

Such sceptical descriptions of travel also serve as a standard against which to measure the serious purpose of those travellers who visited Italy intent upon an aesthetic education. Robert Adam provides the perfect example of this serious purpose but even he found himself distracted from it occasionally. The perspective from which he wrote—I

[40] Lassels, *The Voyage of Italy*, Preface.   [41] Cf. Knox, *Liberal Education*, 189.
[42] Lassels, *The Voyage of Italy*, Preface.
[43] Knox, *Liberal Education*, 189 and Hurd, *Dialogues*, 70.

mentioned that his family were not aristocrats but it is also important that he lived in Scotland, away from the cultural mainstream—is particularly revealing. His is a very useful case-study of a serious traveller. His attitude to travel will be measured according to the three categories suggested above: social, sexual, and artistic.

Many of Robert Adam's letters home were addressed to his sisters, who were apparently jealous of his social advancement and at the same time keen to hear more about it. It is therefore not suprising that he should, in his letters, have focused upon the social whirl in which he took part. The novelty of moving in aristocratic and cosmopolitan circles was reflected in an arrogant tone of voice in the correspondence, adopted as he tried to underline his sense of belonging to or sometimes even leading the social scene. His singing talents proved a convenient way of drawing attention to himself in company, and his obvious wealth eased his access into the foremost circles. Fleming indicates that his bank balance of £5,000 would have enabled him to travel in 'princely style' (Fleming, 106). The fact that he accompanied the nobleman Charles Hope for the early part of the trip was also useful. By the time he reached Paris he was a long way towards achieving his youthful ambition to 'make himself considerable' (Fleming, 100). On 12 December 1754 he wrote home from Paris, declaring his intention to 'lay in stock of good acquaintance that may be of use to me hereafter' (Fleming, 112). By Aix-en-Provence, the novelty of this striving was wearing off. The aristocrats of his acquaintance seemed to be preoccupied with gambling, an echo of Smollett's fears (Fleming, 118). Given Adam's business sense, such reservations towards the company he was keeping were significant. Any alienation from the upper classes—the building classes—was likely to hinder his plans to become a major architect. The need for introductions to society therefore remained important. In February 1755 he revealed his dependance upon Hope, since 'if I am not introduced at first by Hope to Cardinal Albani and the other great people to whom he has letters, I can never again have that opportunity'. However, he became increasingly aware that he would have to make a choice between social entryism and the desire for aesthetic education. After the adoption of Clérisseau as a tutor, and in the wake of his appeals for application to study, Adam was faced with a difficult choice: 'shall I lose Hope and my introduction to the great, or shall I lose Clérisseau and my taste for the grand?' (Fleming, 140–1)

This conflict of interests was not uncommon during the period. Nugent suggests that travel was 'the only means of improving the understanding, and of acquiring a high degree of reputation'.[44] Winckelmann himself complained of the requirements of courtly duty and their intrusion upon his own work. In Paris Adam had been able to reconcile work and play:

> We breakfast by eight, go out by nine in our machine and travel from one church to another with our books in our hands, making such remarks as we think proper of buildings, pictures and statues until half an hour past two when we come home for dinner, you may be sure well-disposed and wholesome. After dinner we dress, which is scarce completed till our coachman tells us 'tis time to go for the Opera or the French or Italian Comedy, one of which we never miss, Sunday or Saturday. (Fleming, 115).

The combination of still more to see, and an assiduous supervisor in Clérisseau, led to his routine becoming yet more cluttered as he headed further south; faced with a choice between art and high society Adam appears to have opted for the former.

The evidence suggests that his sexual adventures were limited, although he was writing home and therefore unlikely to reveal much. However, there is little doubt that he was occasionally distracted by society ladies. Writing from Florence in 1755, as he recovers from the carnival period, he talks of his fresh application to artistic studies, in terms which suggest the direction of his previous efforts:

> Now these days being over I am again returned to my studies—to feast on marble ladies, to dance attendance in the chamber of Venus and to trip a minuet with old Otho, old Cicero and those other Roman worthies whose very busts seem to grin contempt at my legerity. (Fleming, 133)

The implication is surely that Adam had been spending his time dancing with real ladies rather than bothering himself with the marble ones. Fortunately for his artistic future Adam had come into contact with some people who gave him a much clearer idea of the priorities for the serious traveller, and especially the visitor to Rome. Their advice was as follows:

> Wilton, Clérisseau and in short all my friends tell me that in order to do anything a-purpose in Rome I must apply to drawing, I must walk much about and sketch after the antiques. I must resolutely resolve to lay aside the fike-faks of company. I am sufficiently sensible of the reasonableness of this advice. I am conscious that hitherto, while I have dedicated my time to Gay Life I have done nothing else. (Fleming, 140).

---

[44] Thomas Nugent, *The Grand Tour*, 3rd edn., 4 vols. (London, 1778), i, Preface, p. i.

A specific set of expectations caused him to abandon prospects of social advancement and business contracts, at least in the short term. He believed in the possibility of a complete transformation of his artistic taste, through the sort of work envisaged in the above quotation:

> I hope to have my ideas greatly enlarged and my taste formed upon the solid foundation of genuine antiquity. I already feel a passion for sculpture and painting which I was before ignorant of, and I am convinced that my whole conception of architecture will become much more noble than I could ever have obtained by staying in Britain. (Fleming, 139–40)

This attitude contrasts with the superficial attitude of the travellers described by Curtius, Smollett, and Rüdiger. Adam looked forward to an inner conversion ('ideas', 'taste') with practical consequences (the new 'conception' of architecture gained could presumably change the shape of his buildings). The remnants of classical antiquity, and Renaissance art produced in the spirit of classical antiquity, were the agents of this change, and the relationship with the 'enlightened' Clérisseau the means to a fresh understanding of them. Again we are made to acknowledge the role of the individual tutor, something which will be of major importance in our later discussions of aesthetic education. The pupil–teacher relationship appears to have been of particular importance at this time. Justi noted that many contemporary scholars readily passed on their knowledge to visitors:

> der wissenschaftliche Verkehr [hatte] noch das unmittelbar-persönliche, lebendige jener Zeiten..., wo Philosophen und Naturforscher ihre Erfindungen jungen Fremden mündlich überlieferten, und der Zugang zu diesen Schätzen durch Reisen und persönlichen Kultus erlangt werden mußte.[45]

It was particularly convenient that some high-grade teachers were available in Rome at that time. As mentioned earlier, a frequent complaint was that the various people who worked as ciceroni did not have the qualities appropriate to their task. Whilst the general picture may have been gloomy there were still people available who were very good teachers. Adam's aesthetic education is particularly striking because it took place at the hands of Clérisseau, rather than Piranesi or Winckelmann. Adam did know Piranesi, who included his name on an engraving, so acknowledging Adam's potential as an architect.[46] Adam also knew Mengs and

---

[45] Justi, *Winckelmann*, ii. 138.
[46] Cf. Fleming, 170. There is a suggestion that the print featuring his name may have cost him a major subscription to the work in which it was contained.

Albani, and in Clérisseau he had a teacher closely acquainted with Winckelmann's teaching and indeed with Winckelmann personally.[47] But this makes it clear that there was more than a single level of effective teachers. Clérisseau would have to be regarded as a second generation teacher (in contemporary terms), not because of his age, but rather because of his obvious debt, in aesthetic matters, to Piranesi, and most particularly to Winckelmann. On the evidence of the lives of men such as Adam, one can point to a Roman scene, an atmosphere, or a pattern of expectations which would be conducive to serious supervised study of the arts. There was clearly a group of people whose interests and actions contrasted with those of the travellers observed by Smollett.

There was a certain uniformity of purpose amongst travellers with artistic interests and also a number of theories about the way in which one should best organize time in Italy. Certain recommendations made by Robert Adam have a very familiar ring to the reader of Winckelmann. (We will deal fully with what Winckelmann required of his pupils in Chapter 2.) To give one obvious example: Winckelmann believed that it was important to have early contact with works of art and aesthetic theories.[48] Robert Adam came to a very similar conclusion on the basis of his experience. When he wrote to his younger brother James in an attempt to encourage him to depart early for Italy he remarked that 'you are just now of the right age and every day's delay is losing time and of dangerous consequence as you suck in prejudice which with pain you will quit' (Fleming, 183).

These sentiments are very close to Winckelmann's, in his own statements on education. Characteristic of both writers, Winckelmann and Adam, is not only the insistence upon youth, but also the sense of urgency, conveyed by Adam in the phrase 'dangerous consequence'. This is far removed from the dilettantish engagement with the arts described by Rüdiger. Adam's suggestions for the ideal period of residence, and the manner in which time is to be spent abroad are also familiar from Winckelmann: 'To stay a couple of twelvemonths in Rome without a proper conductor who can point out the proper method of studying and, in a manner, by seeing his progress and works can inspire one with a taste

---

[47] Cf. Fleming, 162–4 for general circle of friends. Also Fleming, 227, where Robert Adam refers to Albani as 'my good friend'. Later James Adam met Winckelmann, albeit infrequently, even offering him the opportunity to look over a draft of his joint publication with Robert of *The Ruins of the Palace of the Emperor Diocletian at Spalatro in Dalmatia* (London, 1764) to which Clérisseau also contributed. Cf. Fleming, 307 and *Briefe*, ii. 237–8, 241, 243, 248, 503; iii. 220, 223, 831.

[48] Cf. KS 212–33 (*Von der Fähigkeit der Empfindung des Schönen*) and Ch. 2 below.

and love for the Grand, you will spend much time in Rome to little purpose' (Fleming, 182). The character of the conductor, the definition of proper method, the means of assessment and most importantly inspiration, the nature of grandeur: these are difficult notions. But the purpose was perfectly clear. Whoever the individual teacher, and whatever the detail of his method, the aim was to produce a pupil who could be described in terms like those used by Adam of Clérisseau. He talked of his companion as a man who had fully absorbed the antique/Roman atmosphere. He was a man 'whose Soul, Body and Guts are tinctured with it' (Fleming, 191).

The positive atmosphere of Rome in the 1750s and 1760s was produced by a happy confluence of factors. As was suggested in the introductory passages, some were broadly historical; others were specific to the publishing industry; perhaps more important are personal psychological factors, the arrival of individuals with the 'Fähigkeit zur Empfindung des Schönen', at a time when a number of inspirational teachers were operating. We will deal with individual beneficiaries of the situation in Rome in the later chapters. But it is clear already that in a limited number of specific cases we can assume an atmosphere in Rome contrary to that suggested by Curtius/Smollett/Rüdiger. We can find cases of travellers for whom artistic/aesthetic issues outweighed social/sexual concerns—or could be reconciled with them. In some instances they had a serious intention to undergo an aesthetic education.

1. THE PREPARATION FOR TRAVEL: HISTORIES AND THEORIES OF ART

Earlier I noted that there was a considerable expansion in travel literature and in literature dealing with the theory and history of art in the eighteenth century. This literature often determined the traveller's response to art. It was often of a didactic nature, and many of the authors claimed unique insights into art. Many of the attitudes towards art revealed in these books were, however, broadly similar in their assumptions. I will give a brief survey of some of the central ideas, many of which are also common to Winckelmann, so that the later discussion of his more original qualities will stand in a bolder relief. I will not give an account of the genesis of individual ideas, since this would inevitably involve an investigation of generations of writers, stretching back to antiquity, and often futile attempts to decide on the derivation of individual formulations. All I wish to indicate is that certain mainstream ideas were familiar to many serious travellers.

Many of the writers in the field of art theory described their task in similar terms to those of Daniel Webb: 'The persons for whom I write, are our young travellers, who set out with much eagerness, and little preparation; and who, for want of some governing objects to determine their course, must continually wander, misled by ignorant guides, or bewildered by a multiplicity of directions.'[49] To extend Webb's metaphor, it was the writer's function to signpost the route to an understanding of the arts, by the selection of worthy objects. But some 'governing objects' were replaced by *rules* for the interpretation of art. Du Fresnoy was one of the many writers who felt that he had a perfect understanding of art, modestly claiming that 'I shall satisfy my self with telling you, that this little *Treatise* will furnish you with infallible Rules of judging truly'.[50]

The various theories of art which were available to the public often offered similar guarantees of success in understanding art. The theories can be divided into six convenient categories, as follows:

(*a*) The production of art.
(*b*) The history of art.
(*c*) The moral content of art.
(*d*) The intellectual content of art.
(*e*) The formation of beautiful images: composite beauty.
(*f*) The formal analysis of beauty.

(a) The production of art

In the mid-eighteenth century it was a commonplace idea that art production depended upon external circumstance. The quality of art was seen to be determined by both the physical and socio-political climate of the period in question. Thus the excellence of Greek and Roman art could be explained by reference to the world in which it was created. I cite Edward Young as representative of this view:

An Evocation of vegetable fruits depends on rain, air, and sun; and Evocation of the Fruits of Genius no less depends on Externals. What a marvellous crop bore it in *Greece*, and *Rome*? And what a marvellous sunshine did it there enjoy?

---

[49] Daniel Webb, *An Enquiry into the Beauties of Painting; and into the Merits of the most Celebrated Painters, Ancient and Modern* (London, 1760), Preface, p. vi.

[50] C. A. du Fresnoy, *The Art of Painting*, trans. John Dryden (London, 1695), Preface, p. lviii.

What encouragement from the nature of their governments, and the spirit of their people?[51]

There are two points here. First we are alerted to the impact of the physical environment on art and, secondly, to the influence of socio-political factors. The direct equation drawn between the physical environment and the art which it produces may now seem a little naïve, and how sunshine inspired artistic production may similarly appear a little obscure, but these were acceptable theoretical premises in the eighteenth century. The obvious differences between the motivation of complex human 'Genius' and the nourishment of simple plant life seem not to have been at issue. The use of organic imagery to illustrate the necessity of the connection between the environment and its products is a common feature of writings on this theme at this period, not least in Winckelmann's writings.[52]

The bearing of socio-political factors upon art production was clearly also central. The 'spirit of the people' described above may prove difficult to define. However, the coincidence of 'liberal' (by contemporary standards) government and development of the arts is given as a significant historical fact. Like Winckelmann, many theorists saw the proof of this theory in Periclean Athens, where the arts flourished under an enlightened ruler.[53] Indeed at stages in Greek history it seemed as if society was organized specifically to offer perfect conditions for the working artists. De Piles's view was very like Winckelmann's. He cites Rubens approvingly in a discussion of the role of the academies with their gymnasia as perfect haunts for the working artist in ancient Greece. The human body, which was at this time assumed to be the most noble subject of art, was simply in better shape in Greece. Indeed it was a matter of honour to maintain the body well.[54] Furthermore the status of the artist was high. Public and private commissions were plentiful, and implicit in any praise for the high level of employment amongst ancient artists was an appeal for renewed patronage for contemporary artists. Daniel Webb, for example, made the general observation that 'the

---

[51] Edward Young, *Conjectures on Original Composition in a Letter to the Author of Sir Charles Grandison* (London, 1759), 46–7.

[52] See, for example *Werke*, iii. 61. The first pages of the first chapter of the *Geschichte der Kunst* establish the dominant organic images, which appear in particular concentration in Eiselein's composite edition. They recur *passim* in all Winckelmann publications.

[53] His preference for Periclean Athens is stated most clearly at *Werke*, v. 348–9 (GK 308–9).

[54] Roger de Piles, *The Principles of Painting*, English edn. (London, 1743), 90.

liberal, like the mechanick arts, depend wholly on the encouragement they meet with'. In his terms, the degree of encouragement given by a particular society to the arts could be seen as a measure of that society's quality, as 'proof of their politeness', or as a 'test of their humanity'.[55] In order to present the case for the encouragement of art more forcibly, some critics suggested that art offered concrete rewards. The moral fibre of the nation could be strengthened through art. Henry Home (Lord Kames) suggests that 'riches so employ'd [in the sponsorship of the arts], instead of encouraging vice, will excite both public and private virtue'.[56] This issue is dealt with at greater length in Section (c). At the very least if the prevailing social and political situation was positive, in the manner described above, then an increase in the quality and quantity of art was a necessary consequence. A familiar pattern of imagery is used to capture the situation. In Shaftesbury's terms, the ideal socio-political situation 'as from a proper soil, produced the generous plants'. He, along with many others, hoped to re-establish the 'natural growth' of the arts, which had been seen before, most noticeably in Greece.[57]

This is the central contradiction in much of the art-theoretical writing of the period. Whilst most writers appear to have been aware of the factors which determined artistic production in a given environment, many did not wish to abandon their idealistic attitude towards Greek art in particular. They asserted, for example, the supremacy of Greek formal criteria in art and indeed gave them absolute value. This position is untenable if, simultaneously, you assert that even these formal rules spring from specific historical conditions, i.e. are a response to specific stimuli. The theorists of this period could be said to be stranded between idealism and historicism.[58]

This theoretical difficulty becomes more apparent when we move on to discuss some of the contemporary art-historical notions. These were a logical development of the theories of art production mentioned above. The equation between environment and artistic production was seen to apply absolutely. Shaftesbury, for example, saw a pattern of 'the

[55] Webb, *An Enquiry*, 35–6.
[56] Henry Home, *Elements of Criticism*, 3 vols. (Edinburgh, 1762), i. v.
[57] I use the modern edition: Anthony A. Cooper (Earl of Shaftesbury), *Characteristics of Men, Manners, Opinions, Times, etc*, ed. John M. Robertson, 2 vols. (London, 1900), i. 155 and ii. 243.
[58] Cf. Hinrich C. Seeba, 'Zur Wirkungsgeschichte eines "unhistorischen" Historikers zwischen Ästhetik und Geschichte', *Deutsche Vierteljahresschrift*, 56 (Special Issue) (1982), 168–9; Walther Bosshard, *Winckelmann: Aesthetik der Mitte* (Zürich, 1960); Jürgen Jacobs, 'Der "Winckelmannische Faden": Zeitlosigkeit und Historizität in der Kunstanschauung des italienischen Goethe', *Wirkendes Wort*, 6 (1987), 363–73.

flourishing and the decay of Liberty and Letters', the one following the other meticulously.[59] This assumption enabled contemporary art historians to establish firm historical categories of art.

(b) The history of art

Besides the theory of production, a second stimulus for the investigation of the history of art seems to have been frustration at modern failure, when compared with the ancient achievement in art. Whilst the production theory might have enabled them to account for this disparity it did not remove a powerful sense of frustration. De Piles was bitter at the 'degenerate' state of contemporary art.[60] Given the dominant production theory this meant that the contemporary socio-political order (and indeed the 'spirit of the people' mentioned above) would also have to be seen as, in some sense, degenerate. Shaftesbury seems to be suggesting precisely this: 'Compare moderns with ancients. Consider the latter, their care and culture of bodies themselves by exercises, the Greek discipline.'[61]

The idealization of the Greek world and its art is one of the most strikingly ahistorical aspects of the theoretical work of the period. It was sustained alongside a clear awareness of the parallel cyclical patterns of rise and fall in political and art history. Winckelmann's art-historical work represents the most systematic application of these contradictory ideas; in this respect he was representative of mainstream historical thinking, but he applied the central notions more vigorously than his competitors. For example, his historical work echoes, in principle, the theory of Henry Home: 'A gradual progress from simplicity to complex forms and profuse ornament, seems to be the fate of all the fine arts; resembling behaviour, which from original candor and simplicity has degenerated into artificial refinements.'[62] Of course, not everyone adopted this sort of historical outlook. It would have been difficult to accommodate a full account of it in, say, a travel book, or work of aesthetic theory, and indeed such a digression might have undermined the writer's central purpose. Furthermore most writers lacked the continued access to the artworks and historical sources which Winckelmann enjoyed in Rome

---

[59] Cooper (Shaftesbury), *Characteristics*, i. 144.
[60] De Piles, *The Principles of Painting*, 89.
[61] From the modern edition: Cooper (Shaftesbury), *Second Characters, or The Language of Forms*, ed. B. Rand (Cambridge, 1914), 116.
[62] Home, *Elements*, i. 255.

and which enabled him to find a wide range of proofs for his historical method. The core of historical thinking was, however, common to many contemporary writers in this field. Winckelmann's art history could perhaps be most aptly described as the crystallization of contemporary thinking. It would not be too harsh to describe his contribution to art history as a quantitative rather than qualitative one. Even the detail of his categories of art, down to his typical descriptive epithets can be found in other writings. An example of the confused genesis of such art-historical categories, and the development of an appropriate terminology to describe them, can be found in Daniel Webb. Writing in 1760, he separates Egyptian and Greek art in a manner closely resembling Winckelmann's. Whereas before Daedalus all art was 'stiff and motionless'; later Greek art developed in 'grace' and 'motion', culminating in the Apollo Belvedere which represented 'the sublime of the art'. This development is due to 'the superior Genius of the Greeks', which is in turn due to the 'climate' and the 'chaste religion' and 'propriety' to be found there. Whilst this and much else in his work *An Enquiry into the Beauties of Painting* (especially the notion of imitation, and some specific prejudices against artists) is reminiscent of Winckelmann, his declared source at this point is Pliny.[63] Almost any parallel search for the source of the ideas of a particular writer is likely to lead in a different direction. It is more productive to evaluate the effectiveness of the given author in presenting those ideas afresh.

For most critics of the period art was more than a historical phenomenon. It was an instrument of moral or intellectual improvement.

(c) The moral content of art

Art has always been associated with educational purposes, of various kinds. In the eighteenth century, its major purpose appears to have been the moral improvement of the audience. To follow de Piles, art could simultaneously *'entertain'* and *'instruct'*.[64] Many critics did not wish the functions of art to be balanced in this way. For many the instruction was the most important element. Shaftesbury was perhaps the most influential supporter of this point of view, though he thought the separation of the pleasurable and educational functions of art was misleading, since pleasure could only be derived from feelings of moral elevation. The arts and the virtues shared, in his world view, a common—and essentially

---

[63] Webb, *An Enquiry*, 39–49.
[64] De Piles, *The Principles of Painting*, 4.

moral—source, and 'thus are the Arts and Virtues mutually friends; and thus the science of virtuosi and that of virtue itself become, in a manner, one and the same'.[65] Statements of this sort affected the travellers' expectations of art radically. It was not enough to explain art in, say, historical terms, or point to literary parallels. An understanding of art came to imply a high moral character in the viewer; the study of art became in effect a study of one's own notions of virtue. This degree of engagement with the work is very different from that of the objective historian, whose insight (as described in the two sections above) must improve with distance from the art examined. The discovery of the moral basis of art clearly put more pressure upon the viewer to exhibit taste, since a lack of taste implied a lack of moral understanding. It was assumed that 'a taste in the fine arts goes hand in hand with the moral sense, to which indeed it is nearly allied'.[66] Every traveller will have wanted to identify himself with 'moral sense', even when its precise characteristics were not clear. The writers of the period used the identification of their standpoint with moral truth as a powerful rhetorical weapon. This technique is clearly present in Winckelmann's writings and is used by him, and many others, to persuade the reader towards a particular standard of taste.[67] Who could resist Young's invitation (he is writing about the value of literature, in fact) to take from his theory the 'key', which will allow the reader access 'into a delicious Garden of Moral and Intellectual fruits and flowers'?[68] He there expresses an attitude which was prevalent amongst contemporary travellers. Armed with the key to the understanding of the arts by their reading at home, many appear to have felt that they needed to do no more than consume the fruit which Italy offered.[69] Rather than seek to understand or look at seriously the works of art on offer, many merely sought confirmation of the ideals and opinions which they had brought with them from home. Ironically, Winckelmann's publications may have operated on their audience in such a way, since they inculcated a specific set of expectations of art. Riedesel certainly showed signs of inhibition in dealing with art when he was aware that Winckelmann was looking over his shoulder.[70]

During the period art was then inextricably bound up with notions of moral utility. It was seen as leading to a greater awareness of virtue in the

[65] Cooper (Shaftesbury), *Characteristics*, i. 217.   [66] Home, *Elements*, i. 7.
[67] We need look no further than his *Gedanken* for confirmation of this technique. In it he conveniently identifies his position with that of all true connoisseurs (KS 27–59).
[68] Young, *Conjectures*, 5.
[69] This is surely a brand of the 'consumerism' mentioned earlier.
[70] See Ch. 3 for a detailed analysis of the problem.

individual spectator; this, in turn, should lead to a more virtuous society. It was seen as the means to achieve a moral education. But such an educational plan was radically different from that envisaged by Winckelmann, because it devalued the aesthetic element of the experience of art. The act of seeing, which I regard as the the core of Winckelmann's work (and which is the subject of Chapter 2), is devalued and replaced by what is essentially an intellectual decoding exercise, which enables the student to understand moral messages hidden invitingly just beneath the surface of the work of art. For Winckelmann the important thing was the manner of seeing; it was the process of learning to see which contained the potential for moral improvement. For thinkers such as Shaftesbury moral improvement came from simple pattern recognition; certain instructive symbols and images alerted the viewer to moral truths which the student was then to apply to his own life. There was no room for the imaginative engagement which we see in Winckelmann. His striving to allow his pupils to improve themselves from within through the refinement of their insight into art would be alien to many contemporary thinkers. For them the moral impetus came from the work of art rather than from its viewer; art was a codification of moral truths which the viewer could learn to identify with a little practice. This devalues the work itself, since it can then only be seen as a vehicle; its real beauty is in the ideas which it expresses. Winckelmann also saw art as a means of understanding the 'truth', in some very general sense, but without the immediate benefits which Shaftesbury, for example, suggests. This may be an extreme formulation, since it forms part of one of Shaftesbury's moral dialogues, but it is not untypical: art is seen as a vehicle for moral messages and 'thus beauty and truth are plainly joined with the notion of utility and convenience, even in the apprehension of every ingenious artist, the architect, the statuary or the painter'.[71] But the close relationship between beauty and truth was clearly one that could be abused. Bishop Hurd showed a fictional Shaftesbury fearing for the moral equilibrium of the traveller, since 'such is the unhappy condition of human nature, that in striving to cultivate it's powers, you furnish the opportunities, at least, of its corruption'.[72] Art had a profound moral effect, but presumably it did not need to be positive; art could potentially corrupt as much as the alien manners of the people whom the traveller was likely to meet. If morality was accepted as operating in this way then it was not suprising that people were conservative in their attitude to travel, which

[71] Cooper (Shaftesbury), *Characteristics*, ii, 267.
[72] Hurd, *Dialogues*, 70, 21.

ITALIAN TRAVEL IN THE EIGHTEENTH CENTURY   27

I suggested earlier was the case. Their fears for the traveller had a moral as well as a social basis.

Shaftesbury's moral outlook was shaped by his religion. The expectation that art should be a source of moral instruction above all else led him largely to ignore its formal or compositional elements. In this standpoint he was more extreme than most of his contemporaries; though, on a more general level, his identification of beauty with truth was common to generations of theorists. The idea may have been Platonic in source, but was readily adapted to fit Christian expectations of art. Some theorists, such as Winckelmann, left it unclear whether truth and beauty were, for them, derived from an idea, in the Platonic sense, or were echoes of the word of God. Others made it quite plain how they understood the workings of artistic inspiration. Du Fresnoy is here discussing the inspiration of the ancient poet and painter.

> For both of them, that they might contribute all within their power to the sacred Honours of Religion, have rais'd themselves to Heaven, and having found a free admission into the Palace of *Jove* himself, have enjoy'd the sight and conversation of the Gods; whose Majesty they observe, and contemplate the wonders of their Discourse; in order to relate them to Mankind; whom at the same time they inspire with those Coelestial flames, which shine so gloriously in their Works.[73]

More usually the precise mechanism of this inspiration was left unexplained. We are rarely told how a physical object can appeal to us on a spiritual, or moral plane. De Piles states that human figures can, in art, be used to represent the 'Divine, Spiritual *and* Inanimate' as if the process were self-explanatory.[74] He also offered a number of technical prescriptions for painting but did not explain how one can move from the perception of beauty to the understanding of truth. It was a contemporary assumption that the two ideas belonged together; and it led to a number of theoretically difficult suppositions. It became a commonplace to believe that people blessed with moral insight must by definition be physically attractive, since beauty and truth belong together. This is implicit in de Piles's statement on Leonardo da Vinci, indicating that 'his Morals were good, and his Body and Mind Beautiful'.[75] A similar idea was at the forefront of Winckelmann's mind in the search for the ideal pupil, although a degree of homosexual self-interest was also present.[76] The idea is patently absurd, since it would be just as easy to prove its

---

[73] Du Fresnoy, *Art of Painting*, 3.
[74] R. de Piles, *The Art of Painting and the Lives of the Painters*, English trans. of French original (London, 1706), 40.
[75] Ibid. 116.   [76] See KS 212, 215–16.

opposite as the thesis itself. Within Winckelmann's circle of acquaintances the example of the ugly Clérisseau would have served to prove the absence of a link between physical appearance and insight into art.[77] Socrates' appearance might also have provided powerful evidence. Nevertheless it was a commonplace idea that physical appearance and moral standing corresponded closely. Moral insights were also often expressed in physical terms. Daniel Webb, for example, followed a conventional line on the relationship between represented objects and their moral impact. He suggested that 'every argument of sorrow, every object of distress, renews the same soft vibrations, and quickens us to acts of humanity and benevolence'.[78] The use of the term 'vibration' suggests that the work is having a physical impact upon the receiver. It provides a stimulus to which one responds directly ('quickens us'). Whilst this may give us a useful impression of the way in which art affects its spectators, it is misleading as an explanation. Physical and aesthetic responses are not identical. Francis Hutcheson found himself in a similar theoretical impasse. He described virtue as 'a lovely Form', and suggested that there was such a thing as a 'moral sense of Beauty'. The terminology appropriate to the description of physical appearances is being deliberately combined with the language of moral philosophy in order to suggest the mixed effects of art. He is struggling to find a terminology appropriate to the full range of aesthetic effects, from the physical to the moral. He even suggests that there is a distinct third sense, 'An INTERNAL SENSE', which enables us to process such mixed stimuli.[79]

Hutcheson was not alone in suggesting a separate third faculty. Mark Akenside, for example, was of a similar opinion. He called it, simply, the imagination, and it held the 'middle place between the organs of bodily sense and the faculties of moral perception'.[80] This ambivalent position constitutes the central difficulty in a system of theoretical aesthetics. It was not one that Winckelmann was able to resolve. He did, however, show us aesthetic response in action. Whilst he shared many of the theoretical premises described above, he was uniquely able to give expression to the effects of art upon the individual observer. He was able to demonstrate a way of seeing, ranging from sensitivity to physical impressions to awareness of the moral implications of art. Understanding

---

[77] There is a caricature of Clérisseau at Fleming, 136. Riedesel was also a less than perfect physical specimen. See the biographical section of Ch. 3.
[78] Webb, *An Enquiry*, 34.
[79] Francis Hutcheson, *An Inquiry into the Original of our Ideas of Beauty and Virtue* (London, 1725), Preface, pp. vi–vii.
[80] Mark Akenside, *The Pleasures of Imagination* (London, 1744), 5.

art was, for him, more than a question of 'realizing conceptions'. It involved the engagement of the whole man. Like Webb he felt that works of art had failed if 'they satisfy the understanding, but they do not touch the heart'.[81] The moral decoding exercise, described above as typical of one brand of art criticism, did no justice to the total experience of art. Winckelmann had scant regard for those who saw art merely as an intellectual puzzle-solving exercise.

(d) The intellectual content of art

Not all contemporary theories of art saw the pursuit of moral truths as art's main purpose. The study of art could be seen as a purely intellectual pastime. It offered the observer an opportunity to apply his learning from other fields like history or literature and also to establish some criteria for judging the intrinsic merit of works of art. In order to understand painting de Piles suggested that the observer needed 'a Penetration and Fineness of Wit, with the Principles of Painting'. These involved an understanding of 'costume' (i.e. manners), 'Poesy' and 'Allegories'.[82] Wit therefore involves an awareness of history, literary history, and the conventional stock of symbols in literature and visual art. In effect de Piles seems to be calling for a classically educated scholar who could understand the grammar of the arts.[83] In de Piles's opinion 'Penetration and Fineness of Wit', wholly derived from education and unaccompanied by natural insight, do not guarantee an understanding of art. But to accept such a view was to undermine the status of the writers of aesthetic theory who were keen to present themselves as having more than a partial insight into art. In asserting that art was wholly subject to reasonable explanation, they were able to reassert their authority. The self-confidence of the enlightened theorist is reflected in statements such as the following by Henry Home. It was, in his opinion, the function of criticism 'to show that the fine arts are a subject of reasoning as well as of taste'. He felt more at ease in the pursuit of 'wise and good purposes' in art, than in tracing vague criteria for taste.[84] Whilst these quotations, taken in isolation, do Home something of a disservice, they are not unrepresentative of the period. A large number of critics seem to have

---

[81] Webb, *An Enquiry*, 124 and 169. [82] De Piles, *The Art of Painting*, 67.
[83] Winckelmann doubted the value of having 'ein Grammaticalisches Gehirn'. People who analyse art in this way would 'schwerlich eine Empfindung des Ganzen [des ganzen Kunstwerks] und eine Entzückung in sich erwecken' (KS 219).
[84] Home, *Elements*, i. 241, 249.

sought, along with de Piles, 'the Approbation of Men of Sense'.[85] This is a very persuasive formulation, since who would wish to deny that they had some such sense? De Piles's work was highly influential; his approach was intellectual. In his description of Raphael's *School of Athens* he treats the painting first and foremost as an allegorical/historical puzzle.[86] He talks elsewhere of enthusiasm in response to the sublime, but shows little trace of it in his writing.[87] Another influential figure with a similar approach is du Fresnoy. In *The Art of Painting* he provides a bibliography to help with the raw materials of interpretation, and provides a list of conventional allegories.[88] This approach is an naïve as that shown by Winckelmann in his work on allegory; the *Versuch einer Allegorie* marks a very crude departure from his approach in other writings, where the allegorical unravelling of the themes of works of art was seen either as a starting-point for a deeper aesthetic engagement with the work in question or as a means of pinpointing the historical position of that work.[89] Certainly he did not see this sort of puzzle-solving as an end in itself, unlike some of the authors mentioned above.

Sections (c) and (d) were concerned with the content of art and some representative ways of explaining it. The following sections deal with aspects of contemporary formal analysis.

(e) The formation of beautiful images

Many critics were of the opinion that the artist worked by selecting the best parts of nature and bringing them together in his work. There was a widespread rejection of the naturalistic portrayal of the physical world, in favour of the idealistic presentation of its best parts in combination. As Shaftesbury puts it: ''tis from the many objects of nature, and not from a particular one, that those geniuses form the idea of their work'.[90] The selection was, according to de Piles, to be made 'by judicious Enquiries into the Effects of Nature, and attributing to her, not so much her

---

[85] De Piles, *Art of Painting*, 117. [86] De Piles, *The Principles of Painting*, 46 f.
[87] Ibid. 70. [88] Du Fresnoy, *The Art of Painting*, 107–8.
[89] Winckelmann's theory of allegory does not fit neatly with many of his other comments on art. It seems pedantic and superficial in a manner to which he objected elsewhere (KS 215). Fischer sees it as part as grander undertaking to overcome a 'Schwundstufe des bildhaften Denkens' with 'eine Anstrengung zur Rettung der idealen Gegenständlichkeit und damit zur Rettung der idealen Würde der Kunst', which is expressed most powerfully in the description of the Belvedere Torso. See Bernhard Fischer, 'Kunstautonomie und Ende der Ikonographie: Zur historischen Problematik von "Allegorie" und "Symbol" in Winckelmanns, Moritz' und Goethes Kunsttheorie', *Deutsche Vierteljahresschrift*, 64 (1990), 247–77 (247–56). [90] Cooper (Shaftesbury), *Characteristics*, i. 96.

common Productions, as the Perfections of which she is capable'.[91] But it was a more difficult process to arrive at the *'general idea'* than the *'particular idea'* of nature.[92] Daniel Webb made it sound simple:

> The artist, therefore, observing, that nature was sparing of her perfections, and that her efforts were limited to parts, availed himself of her inequality, and drawing these scattered beauties into a more happy and compleat union, rose from an imperfect imitative, to a perfect ideal beauty.[93]

The process is very similar to that described by Winckelmann.[94] And many critics, like him, felt that the art of discriminating between degrees of beauty had been lost to the modern artist. In response he formulated his theory of imitation. According to this if we imitate ancient art we are faced immediately with ideal beauty and so do not have to search for its less concentrated expression in nature. The path to understanding of beauty through nature is a longer one. The notion of imitation, like that of composite beauty described above, was by no means original. Both were common to a number of contemporary theorists, and both have a distinct history in older theoretical literature. Again precise sources are difficult to identify. Daniel Webb cites Cicero on the separation of mechanic (naturalistic) and ideal art and it is clear that he is only one of many ancient writers who discussed this topic.[95] De Piles refers to Scaliger's very similar and much later theory.[96] The neo-Latin writers were probably a very fertile source of theories of imitation, since they themselves were interested in the imitation of ancient literary forms. The example of the working methods of the great Renaissance artists could also be used as proof of the success of the method of imitation. De Piles describes how Michelangelo discovered his 'ideas': 'His studying after the *Antique*, and the Elevation of his *Genius* inspir'd him with them.'[97]

(f) The formal analysis of beauty

It was a logical extension of the theory of composite beauty to investigate the formal properties of the parts which went to form the beautiful whole. The most important formal feature for Winckelmann was the

---

[91] De Piles, *The Art of Painting*, 118. [92] De Piles, *The Principles of Art*, 2.
[93] Webb, *An Enquiry*, 40–1.
[94] Most famously in his explanation of the creation of 'eine blos im Verstande entworfene geistige Natur' (KS 34). Cf. also KS 37–8. [95] Webb, *An Enquiry*, 4–5.
[96] De Piles, *The Principles of Painting*, 86.
[97] De Piles, *The Art of Painting*, 159.

outline or silhouette. He was fascinated by the impact of serpentine lines, which he saw as the best expression of beauty. He also believed that these serpentine lines were the most important stylistic component of representations of the human body. The study of lines is more logically associated with the arts of drawing and painting. Hogarth, who worked in these fields, provides the most extensive formulation of a 'line theory'. Winckelmann's theory is very closely related to Hogarth's.[98] It was typical of the age that in order to explain a particular artistic phenomenon, in Winckelmann's case the beauty of sculpture, the theorist should reach out into related fields of study. The terminology of moral philosophy was, for example, consistently applied to aesthetics. The interchange within the arts—literary and visual—was still more wide-ranging.[99]

There is one major difference between the approaches of Hogarth and Winckelmann. The latter did not think the analysis of the formal properties of art incompatible with the investigation of its content. Indeed he regarded the two as mutually dependent. But Hogarth regarded any move in the direction of moral interpretation as a failure to recognize essentials. People who do not understand the formal structure of art find themselves 'obliged so suddenly to turn into the broad, and more beaten path of moral beauty; in order to extricate themselves out of the difficulties they seem to have met with'. He had little time for those who were 'continually discoursing of effects instead of developing causes'.[100] On the other hand he shared Winckelmann's opinion on the basic shape of the serpentine line, agreed that the distribution of fat and muscle in the represented body could be used to emphasize the effect of the line, and that clothing or drapery could be used to accentuate the effect still further. A number of other influential theorists talked in very similar terms.[101]

There was then a pattern of common expectations of art in the mid-eighteenth century. The examples given above were deliberately taken from a wide range of treatises, dealing with the individual arts and art in general, as well as philosophical and psychological questions, in order to

[98] See Justi, *Winckelmann*, iii. 189–96. He here suggests that Winckelmann must have known Hogarth's work but also that there were alternative sources for the idea of the serpentine line.

[99] Cf. Webb, *An Enquiry*, 197; Du Fresnoy, *Art of Painting*, p. xx (Translator's Preface) and p. 3.: J. B. Dubos, *Réflexions critiques sur la poésie et sur la peinture*, 2 vols. (Paris, 1719), 384.

[100] William Hogarth, *The Analysis of Beauty*, Facsimile of first edn. of 1753 (Menton, 1971), p. iv.

[101] Cf. Webb, *An Enquiry*, p. 66; du Fresnoy, *Art of Painting*, p. 16; de Piles, *The Principles of Painting*, 95; KS 39—'der griechische Contour'.

give some impression of the important themes in contemporary aesthetics. They reflect some of the major currents of thinking on the arts, many of which interacted in a manner which confused their sources. Those that I have isolated are, in many respects, central, but they were chosen in the first instance because they are some of those in which Winckelmann was most passionately interested. His aesthetics did not differ in principle from many contemporary theories. However, to arrive at this conclusion is not to dismiss his contribution to aesthetics. Indeed, it will only serve to emphasize the extent of his contribution over and above the teaching of these general principles.

In the following chapter I shall argue that certain aspects of Winckelmann's characteristic manner of seeing represent genuine aesthetic engagement. His approach, as manifested in the set-piece descriptions of statues, marked a radical development of the approaches to art mentioned above. The range and depth of his engagement with art differed qualitatively from that of contemporary critics. It was this engagement which formed the basis of his appeal to visitors to Rome and of his teaching method. This study of Winckelmann and his pupils is not, however, important merely because it illustrates aspects of the contemporary theory and practice of travel and the study of art. It gains significance because Winckelmann's ideas constitute the effective starting-point of an elaborate debate in Germany—lasting in a recognizable form for over a century—as to the nature and value of beauty in the visual arts and by extension literature. This debate, which centred on differing interpretations of the Laocoön statue, was addressed by the most important literary figures and philosophers of the period after Winckelmann and indeed any attempt to establish standards of good taste, however different these standards might have been from Winckelmann's own, necessarily involved some discussion of the Winckelmannian inheritance. The genesis of this debate has been very ably discussed by a number of modern critics, perhaps most compactly by Nisbet.[102] Here, however, it is my intention to focus more closely on Winckelmann's specific manner of seeing than on his broader conclusions about art.

[102] H. B. Nisbet, 'Laocoön in Germany: The Reception of the Group since Winckelmann', *Oxford German Studies*, 10 (1979), 22–63.

2
Johann Joachim Winckelmann and Roman Ingarden on the Reception of Works of Art

IN the previous chapter I discussed the expectations of different categories of travellers in Italy during the eighteenth century. I must now limit myself to one specific category of traveller, namely that represented by Winckelmann and his chosen pupils. Winckelmann's presence in Rome was a significant attractor for many visitors. He went beyond being merely a participant in Italian travel and art circles and became himself part of the reason why people headed for Rome. It is important to explain how and why this man acted as a focal point for Italian travellers who were interested in art. Historical and biographical coincidence undoubtedly played their part—he was certainly the right man in the right place at the right time—but to focus exclusively on these aspects of his rise to fame and consistent popularity could prove misleading. The 'Leben und Wunder Johann Winckelmanns' must be acknowledged but they should not be allowed to distract from the core of his aesthetic.[1] The evidence of Winckelmann's rise from humble beginnings in Germany to a prestigious position in Italy which gave him access to the highest circles in the Vatican, the most powerful social groups and, correspondingly, the great art collections, would have had an immediate appeal for potential travellers. The eminence of his patrons will also have caused his name to circulate widely and effectively. But Winckelmann had more than a superficial appeal to travellers. His *curriculum vitae* and contemporary position may have proved attractive to a general audience of travellers, but it was his expression of aesthetic experience that enabled him to develop a hold on his élite circle of students. We must establish some criteria for measuring Winckelmann's recorded

---

[1] Cf. Ernst Bergmann, 'Das Leben und die Wunder Johann Winckelmanns', in *Festschrift für Johannes Volkelt (zum 70. Geburtstag dargebracht)* (Munich, 1918), 229–64. The phrase 'das Leben und die Wunder Johann Winckelmanns' comes from Winckelmann himself and was subsequently used by his contemporaries. Cf. *Briefe*, ii. 276, 476. Biographical accounts of Winckelmann's achievements constitute the bulk of secondary material on him (see Bibliography).

responses to art and, by extension, those of his pupils. These responses explain why he was able to capture such attention and inspire devotion to art in visitors during his time in Rome; they would perhaps also account for his ability to attract patronage. In this context it is important to define the term aesthetic and distinguish it from rival terminology for the experience of art. We must also consider the extent to which an aesthetic attitude can be learnt or reproduced through exposure to a 'qualified' teacher. The attempt to determine the key components of Winckelmann's responses to art will be a reductive process and it will involve the elimination of many parts of Winckelmann's total vision of art in the search for its aesthetic core.

In order to arrive at a working definition of the term aesthetic I will use material from two radically different sources. First, there are the statements of Winckelmann himself and, secondly, the works of the modern Polish philosopher Roman Ingarden. The parallel use of such apparently unrelated source material clearly requires some justification.

Both Winckelmann and Ingarden had as their central concern the reception of works of art. In both an awareness of the processes of reception awoke the desire to sharpen the responses to art in others. They were interested in the mechanisms of aesthetic education. However, their critical apparatuses do appear incompatible at first glance, and their fundamental differences in approach might seem more significant than any common ground. A brief survey of their respective methodologies makes clear the extent of the problem. Ingarden largely restricted himself to the theoretical exposition of the issues of art reception, whereas Winckelmann presented, via his practical criticism, an insight into his personal responses to art. The strength of Ingarden's arguments in favour of his particular paradigm of reception came from his philosophical analysis, rooted in the system of phenomenological philosophy of his teacher Husserl.[2] Winckelmann's moments of insight did not enable him to establish a comprehensive system to account for aesthetic experience, but he could win over his audience with persuasive descriptions of the experience itself; when he wrote art history his approach was more systematic but his aims more limited. In their methodologies Ingarden and Winckelmann could not then have been further apart. However, their conclusions on the nature and effects of aesthetic experience seem to coincide remarkably, given their different starting-points. At times

---

[2] Edmund Husserl (1859–1938) was Ingarden's teacher in Göttingen and Freiburg. I am not concerned to discuss the total system of phenomenological philosophy but make use of specific conclusions in a manner which does not require exposition of the whole.

they used similar terminology in their appraisals of aesthetic experience and even demonstrated similar limitations and blind-spots.

Both Winckelmann and Ingarden were convinced that aesthetic experience depended upon the interaction of the observer and the work of art. Both believed some receivers of art were better qualified than others and so more likely to respond appropriately to a given work. They were convinced of the educational value of art and believed that at its best it could enable metaphysical insights. This effect was more likely in connection with harmonious, or unified works of art, terms which indicate their adherence to a conservative, 'classical' ideal.[3] Both found the question of value in art problematic, with Ingarden struggling to identify firm criteria for value and Winckelmann so convinced of his values that they sometimes appear to be prejudices.

These broad parallels between the two authors seem to show potential areas of weakness in their respective theories. Particularly problematic is the question of the ideal reception of the ideal and harmonious work of art. The framework within which the two men were operating was evidently quite narrow and many works of art and many students were excluded by them as inappropriate. However, my point is not that either Ingarden's or Winckelmann's conclusions about aesthetic experience have any objective merit but rather that they are similar in their content. If that is so then Ingarden's statements provide us with a convenient measure of some of Winckelmann's observations. At the very least the philosopher Ingarden's aesthetic theory is internally consistent and this consistency is reflected in his meticulous use of his chosen terminology. The same could not be said of Winckelmann, who often provided changing metaphorical statements of his views; his works rely upon our ability to follow his inferences, which are conveyed in a style described as 'barock', or 'wunderlich' to the point of obscurity.[4] From now on I shall consistently transpose Winckelmann's statements into Ingarden's terminology in order to make the implications of his aesthetic explicit and to enable myself to identify its essential components more clearly. On this basis I will be able more easily to differentiate Winckelmann's expression of aesthetic experience from that of his pupils.

In order to transform the general statements and assumptions about

[3] The term 'classical' is more obviously appropriate to Winckelmann. But much modern literature, with less emphasis on formal integrity and the lucid expression of ideas, would be difficult to accommodate in Ingarden's scheme.

[4] *Winckelmann von Goethe*, ed. E. Howald (Erlenbach, 1943), 108. The text contains Goethe's contributions to the publication Johann Wolfgang Goethe (ed.), *Winckelmann und sein Jahrhundert, in Briefen und Aufsätzen* (Tübingen, 1805).

THE RECEPTION OF WORKS OF ART

the Winckelmann–Ingarden relationship given above into a practical critical tool we need more concrete examples of the parallels between the two authors. I have divided the whole complex of aesthetic experience, as presented by them, into four sections:
1. The pupil/receiver: preconditions for aesthetic experience.
2. The first phase of aesthetic interest.
3. Aesthetic engagement.
4. The consequences of aesthetic engagement.

1. THE PUPIL/RECEIVER: PRECONDITIONS FOR AESTHETIC EXPERIENCE

Winckelmann saw aesthetic education as something which was restricted to a narrow circle of potential students. There were a number of qualifications which enhanced a student's prospects of responding positively to art. Some of the qualifications were more specific than others and, viewed from a twentieth-century perspective, certain of them seem élitist. However, on closer examination they merely reflect aspects of the eighteenth-century social structure, combined with some of Winckelmann's personal preferences. For example, Winckelmann saw the business of art appreciation as something which was very demanding of an individual's time and energies. In the eighteenth century this meant that it was largely the preserve of the upper classes, since they had the freedom to satisfy such demands. Winckelmann acknowledged this basic fact very clearly in his brief but programmatic work on aesthetic education, the *Abhandlung von der Fähigkeit der Empfindung des Schönen* (KS 211–13).[5] This work was, tellingly, dedicated to an aristocrat, Friedrich Rudolph von Berg, and in it Winckelmann made it clear that aristocrats were likely to prove the best receivers of art; indeed in Berg Winckelmann felt that he had proof of the strength of this argument about the exclusive audience for art.[6] When he mentions those 'welche, nebst der Fähigkeit, Mittel, Gelegenheit und Muße haben' he must have been thinking predominantly of aristocrats or those, like himself, who were guaranteed their patronage. As a member of the Albani household

[5] All references in this section are taken from the same Winckelmann text. No more specific references are given since this would lead to needless repetition of page numbers, so short is the essay.

[6] Berg was ultimately something of a disappointment. Cf. Leppmann, *Winckelmann: Eine Biographie*, 238–9 for an account of the failed relationship and the parallels with Winckelmann's love for Lamprecht.

Winckelmann's personal 'Muße' was assured, and so he was, in general, free to move amongst those 'die nicht den ganzen Tag ein schweres und unfruchtbares Feld zu bauen verdammet sind' and so could focus their attention on art.

This was particularly important to Winckelmann because of the drudgery which he had experienced in his life before leaving for Rome. Even as a schoolboy he had been forced to supplement the family income through singing. Then, despite his success at school, he was forced to study theology because no fees were demanded in that faculty. When he became a teacher, after university, things scarcely improved, and he could only find time for his private studies by foregoing sleep and working through the night. The appointment in Bünau's library which followed his brief teaching career promised a greater freedom to study, but the reality involved researching and writing by proxy for his new employer. The freedom which he was given in Rome no doubt seemed particularly great in the light of what had gone before, even if his employment did involve some inconvenient guiding and time-consuming work in the Vatican.[7] But not all people who were in the appropriate financial and social position had aesthetic sensibility. In the *Abhandlung* Winckelmann gives the example of a travelling British nobleman who, despite his superficial credentials, showed little response to works of art.[8] Although the man was blessed with the necessary 'Muße' he showed no signs of the 'Fähigkeit zur Empfindung des Schönen'. Winckelmann notes in desperation that 'bey einigen befindet sich diese Fähigkeit in so geringem Grade, daß sie in Austheilung derselben von der Natur übergangen zu seyn scheinen könnten; und von dieser Art war ein junger Britte vom ersten Range, welcher im Wagen nicht einmal ein Zeichen des Lebens und seines Daseyns gab, da ich ihm eine Rede hielt über die Schönheit des Apollo und anderer Statuen der ersten Classe'.[9] Within the exclusive

---

[7] See Ch. 3 for a discussion of Winckelmann's attitude to his employment in Rome. The biographies by Justi and Leppmann survey his unhappy early working life.

[8] Most famously he attacked Frederick Calvert (Lord Baltimore). See *Briefe*, ii. 479 for a survey of the letters on the subject. Winckelmann was not alone in disliking this 'grosser spleeniger Sonderling'. Cf. John Morris, 'The Lords Baltimore', *Maryland Historical Fund Publications*, 8 (1874), 52–61. Ironically, Winckelmann's friend, Volkmann, translated his major publication into German (Leipzig, 1768). The text concerned was: Frederick Calvert (Lord Baltimore), *A Tour to the East in the Years 1763 and 1764 with Remarks on Constantinople and the Turks: Select Pieces of Oriental Wit, Poetry and Wisdom* (London, 1767).

[9] The statues mentioned here are, from Winckelmann's perspective, the most important ones. They provided him with the definitive aesthetic experiences discussed in Section 3(*b*) of this chapter.

social group from which Winckelmann chose his pupils there was then a separate meritocracy, based upon ability to respond to art.

Fortunately, Winckelmann believed that he had found a number of means to enhance the prospects of developing an aesthetic sensibility in his pupils, even against the odds. Considerable natural qualifications were required nevertheless, one of which was quite indispensable. Alongside a measure of good breeding the most important qualification for a potential pupil was membership of the male sex. Only very rarely did he make any reference to women in the context of the fine arts; in his letters he occasionally discussed the social function of women in Rome but only one—Mengs's wife—appears to have fascinated him in her own right as a woman.[10] Like class, this particular restriction could also be regarded as a reflection of the eighteenth-century social order which placed severe limitations upon women. But Winckelmann's exclusive choice of male students can also be explained by his homosexuality. Not only would his approach to pupil selection have been likely to offer him the chance to teach young men whom he would find physically attractive, but it would also have offered him the chance of finding some whose whole disposition could match his own. These he would have been in a particularly strong position to teach. In such a case the close relationship between teacher and pupil, on which he insisted, would have been encouraged through a powerful natural empathy.[11]

The *Abhandlung von der Fähigkeit der Empfindung des Schönen* provides the most concentrated statement of Winckelmann's other requirements of his pupils. The dedication to Berg is significant. The work was not dedicated to this minor aristocrat for the same reason as Winckelmann had for his other dedications. He was neither seeking patronage nor expressing gratitude for support in his work.[12] Winckelmann intended this small pamphlet as an expression of his love for Berg, but in a form which would make it publishable. To achieve this Winckelmann was apparently forced to change his original plans for the text, in particular he omitted the quotation from Pindar with which he intended to open the work. The quotation would have suggested quite clearly the place which Berg occupied in his heart; but eventually, and at Berg's suggestion, it was replaced by quotations which refer only implicitly to

---

[10] Cf. Leppmann, *Winckelmann: Eine Biographie*, 240–1.
[11] This ideal pupil–teacher relationship is clearly not of Winckelmann's own invention and was most famously anticipated by the Platonic Socrates. Cf. K. J. Dover, *Greek Homosexuality* (London, 1978), 153–70 (164).
[12] Most of Winckelmann's dedications were tactical in nature. Cf. KS 27–8, 234, 247. Such tactics were a necessity in a world where patronage was so important.

the fact that Berg was 'schön von Gestalt, und von der Gratie übergossen'.[13]

Winckelmann did not, however, arrive at his choice of von Berg as an ideal pupil simply on the basis of a sexual attraction. Indeed he claimed that their friendship was 'rein . . . von allen ersinnlichen Absichten'. It was certainly convenient that Berg was an attractive man since Winckelmann saw a pleasant exterior as a good sign of a healthy mind, claiming that 'wir insgemein denken wie wir gemacht sind'.[14] Winckelmann believed that body and mind were in harmony in Berg's case since he found 'in einem schönen Körper eine zur Tugend geschaffene Seele, die mit der Empfindung des Schönen begabt ist'. Berg apparently exhibited all of the key signs of an aesthetic sensibility, to the extent that in writing the *Abhandlung* Winckelmann admitted that 'der Inhalt ist von Ihnen [von Berg] selbst hergenommen'. This naturally made the time spent with Berg pleasant for Winckelmann, especially as in him he saw a reflection of his own best qualities. Given that Winckelmann had indicated that Berg would be the perfect example of an aesthetic sensibility it seems slightly narcissistic when he suggests that 'die Uebereinstimmung der Geister [Winckelmann/Berg] meldete sich bey mir, da ich Sie das erstemal erblickte'. The 'Geist' presumably contained the aesthetic faculties, which Winckelmann regarded as of central importance, so that being the perfect pupil was rather like being Winckelmann. Unfortunately, when he talked about the factors which might indicate the presence of the 'Fähigkeit' in Berg's case Winckelmann was not very specific; Berg's qualities went without saying, but he did deal at some length with those which might appear in other potentially sensitive pupils.

The potential pupil might, we hear in the *Abhandlung*, reveal an early sensitivity to literature, or perhaps show a precocious interest in drawing, even when he has not been encouraged in this direction. Inborn talents, such as those which are connected with our aesthetic sensibility, tended to come to the surface, even in those who had experienced a 'vernachläßigte Erziehung'. They could, however, be hindered by certain aspects of the process of growing up. Winckelmann observes, in connection with the aesthetic sensibility, that 'bey angehender Jugend ist diese Fähigkeit, wie eine jede Neigung, in dunkele und verworrene Rührungen eingehüllet, und meldet sich wie ein fliegendes Jucken in der Haut, dessen eigentlichen Ort man im Kratzen nicht treffen kann'. Winckelmann is thinking here of the problems associated with awakening male

---

[13] Cf. Rehm's discussion of the matter at KS 431.   [14] Cf. Ch. 1.

sexuality. This awakening could distract the pupil from the proper objects of aesthetic contemplation. Winckelmann hoped for someone who would be able to overcome the 'verworrene Rührungen' of youth and sublimate his distracting natural urges into, for example 'ein natürlicher Trieb zum Zeichnen'.[15] Which is not to say that Winckelmann felt that the whole 'fire' of youth had to be suppressed in order to allow the flourishing of our aesthetic capacities. Indeed, the mind of the pupil was to be 'erhitzt' by exposure to works of art; he did his best to exploit youthful imaginations whilst they were still 'feurig'; but it was important to beware of those who had 'sehr feurige, flüchtige Köpfe'. Such people would be unable to respond in a manner which was 'zart', or showing sensitivity and subtlety, and instead tended to be 'heftig' in their treatment of art. Winckelmann seems to be hinting at an ideal pupil who could combine enthusiasm with delicacy of response and youthful eagerness with an unusual degree of mature insight. That these were to be found in the young Berg was a happy coincidence.[16] However, Winckelmann felt that there were steps that could be taken to improve the chances of developing an aesthetic sensibility in people who already possessed some of the basic qualifications.

As we have already seen, Winckelmann believed that responsiveness to literature was a firm indication of an aesthetic sensibility. In addition he was convinced that literature could be used to accelerate the sensitization of the pupil to the arts, suggesting that 'zuerst sollte dessen Herz und Empfindung, durch Erklärung der schönsten Stellen alter und neuer Scribenten, sonderlich der Dichter, rührend erwecket, und zu eigener Betrachtung des Schönen in aller Art zubereitet werden, weil dieser Weg zur Vollkommenheit führet'. In parallel with these efforts the pupil should be exposed to some works of visual art, in a controlled manner. Winckelmann felt the need to prescribe the appropriate works, because few other authors, in his opinion, had had anything worthwhile to say about art since Plato, thus leaving students of art to operate in a vacuum. This explains why much of the *Abhandlung* is little more than a list of great works of art; Winckelmann felt that this sort of groundwork still remained to be done and it was, significantly, also a feature of his various *Sendschreiben* to other travellers heading for Rome.[17] Whilst the

[15] The word 'Trieb' more usually has sensual connotations. In Winckelmann these sensual 'Triebe' must be sublimated into a drive towards aesthetic fulfilment.
[16] It is important that Winckelmann could believe this even if the evidence was to the contrary. Conviction fired his enthusiasm to teach. Sichtermann points out that Justi is wrong to suggest that Winckelmann should have seen reason and found more appropriate pupils (KS, p. xxi (Introduction)). [17] See KS 190–3, 203–9.

Abhandlung was dedicated specifically to Berg it contained a good deal of advice for other Northern Europeans who had spent much of their early life in the country, remote from the big cities which were more conducive to an aesthetic education. These cities had the advantage of better art collections as well as a number of teachers with whom the pupil could have personal contact, a vital ingredient for successful education in Winckelmann's programme. None the less, Winckelmann did provide a number of compromise suggestions which would enable a pupil like Berg to begin his aesthetic education even if stranded in the countryside. He suggested, for example, the study of bas-reliefs and paintings in the form of engraved reproductions, or the study of coin copies. These would enable the pupil to begin to make art-historical distinctions between works and to begin to differentiate the technical and stylistic requirements of the various art-forms. Ultimately this could only be done with the help of the 'Urbilder', the originals of the high-grade works of art which, in a sense, defined the limitations or possibilities of different art-forms. In line with his own firm prejudices Winckelmann had very clear benchmarks of quality, provided by ancient statuary, the paintings of Raphael, and the architecture of St Peter's in Rome (to use the examples given in the *Abhandlung*). Naturally the list of appropriate works outside Rome, or Italy in general, reflects these prejudices, particularly with regard to Raphael and the great collections of ancient statuary. But the very paucity of the list of works to be found outside Rome serves to confirm that the real place for the serious student of art was in Rome, where there was a much greater concentration of art. Any other place was, by comparison, 'nothdürftig' in what it offered. Something could be done to hone the 'seltene Gabe des Himmels' given to those with an aesthetic sensibility, even outside Rome, but anyone wishing to follow Winckelmann's order to 'gehe hin und sieh' could really only do it there.

Ingarden was less specific than Winckelmann in his requirements for the ideal receiver of art.[18] He did not, for example, intend all potential students of art to come from a narrow social band. Neither did he attempt to prescribe the exact works which were worthy of attention, or the towns which would reward a visit in this connection. However, there is little doubt that Ingarden felt that the business of art appreciation, at the highest level, was restricted to a very small group of people. Whilst it may have differed in its social composition from that preferred by Winckelmann it nevertheless had many similar features.

---

[18] He was describing general properties rather than personal experience.

Ingarden's ideal subject was someone, 'der künstlerische Kultur und Erfassungsfähigkeiten besitzt' (OK 244). The first required quality of a likely student, cultural exposure, clearly depended to a large extent upon social or educational advantages. Whilst these were, by the 1930s, no longer the preserve of the aristocracy, they were still not necessarily offered to the man on the street. Therefore, despite the two centuries which divide Winckelmann and Ingarden, both could be seen as referring to similar types of social, and so cultural advantage, given to some people interested in art. Unlike Winckelmann, Ingarden did not think that personal appearance, or even sex, might affect responsiveness to art; such ideas had largely run their course by the twentieth century. The second quality, the power of comprehension, was intuitive, although it might only become apparent in a sympathetic cultural environment. The fact that Ingarden referred to the two qualities separately (rather than, perhaps, seeing the 'Erfassungsfähigkeit' as an integral part, or product of, 'künstlerische Kultur') suggests that he felt, like Winckelmann, that only a small number of those with privileged access to culture revealed the necessary aesthetic sensibility. Ingarden only rarely mentions the specific qualities which are important for the observer of art. In general he refers simply to some types of observer/reader as 'kompetent' and others as showing 'unkoordinierte Tätigkeit' without making clear the exact nature of their responses and, more particularly, why they should have been so (EKW 181, 195).[19] He notes that acute responses to art often depend on an 'ästhetisches Taktgefühl' (EKW 22). The use of the term 'Gefühl' is misleading. It suggests a purely intuitive or even emotional response. In fact in his scheme the 'Taktgefühl' enables us to balance our knowledge of 'künstlerische Kultur', our store of cultural knowledge, with our personal 'Erfassungsfähigkeit'. The point is made clearly elsewhere when he refers to the misleading interpretations produced 'bei naiven, keine künstlerische Kultur besitzenden, aber empfindlichen Betrachtern von Kunstwerken' (EKW 160–1). In such a case the personal response is so strong that it causes the receiver to overlook logical restraints imposed by 'künstlerische Kultur'. The overall response therefore lacks balance. Ideally, any receiver would be able to combine his knowledge of art/culture and his personal responsiveness to art in a productive manner. Ingarden often portrays this process as a combination of intuitive and conscious intellectual processes:

Das Wesentliche ist dabei, daß der Betrachter entsprechende Fähigkeiten besitzt, die entsprechenden, zu dem vom Kunstwerk herrührenden Qualitäten

[19] He refers to matters of competence *passim*.

komplementären ästhetisch wertvollen Qualitäten zu erraten und zu erschauen und sie zu aktualisieren, und zwar unter einer solchen Auswahl und Anordnung, daß sich daraus die positiven, sinnvoll zueinander gehörenden ästhetischen Wertqualitäten des Ganzen ergeben. (EKW 16–17)

The two verbs 'erraten' and 'erschauen' give the impression that the viewer is responding to something mysterious or grand whose mechanisms are not clear. The verb 'erraten' indeed suggests that they may be concealed. On the other hand the viewer tries to respond to a work in a manner which is 'sinnvoll'. He must try to impose some order upon his responses ('Auswahl', 'Anordnung') to aesthetic features of the work. The putative existence of an individual with the ideal combination of qualities was central to the theses of both Winckelmann and Ingarden. As Ingarden notes:

Dieser Punkt ist für die Entscheidung bezüglich der Existenz und der Objectivität der Werte von einer besonderen Wichtigkeit, weil gerade die höchsten Werte—sowohl auf dem Gebiet des Ästhetischen als auch dem des Sittlichen—meistens nur für besonders hoch qualifizierte Menschensubjekte zugänglich sind. (EKW 87–8)

These qualified people do not fall into conventional categories. According to this view, neither the intellectual bias of the critic, nor the intuitive powers of the artist are individually adequate to the task of art appreciation. Ingarden describes the failings of both critics and artists in explaining works of art in a manner reminiscent of Winckelmann:

So wie es bis jetzt zu sein scheint, verfügen die Künstler über zahlreiche und verschiedenartige Erfahrungen, besitzen aber keine Fähigkeit, sie anderen zu übermitteln; die Theoretiker dagegen besitzen eine gewisse formal-sprachliche Ausbildung und auch gewisse Einsichten in die bereits geschaffenen Bilder, aber ihre unmittelbare Erfahrung und die Einsicht in den Weg, der von der ersten Kompositionsahnung zum konkreten Bild führt, ist noch immer viel zu wenig befriedigend, um eine wirklich erfolgreiche Zusammenarbeit zu ermöglichen. (EKW 74)

We are reminded here of Winckelmann's role as the popularizer of many notions, apparently taken from Oeser and Mengs, who offered him the opportunity to observe directly the creative processes. On the other hand he also maintained contact with and pre-eminence among critics, whilst remaining quite dismissive in his attitude towards most of them. These facts suggest that Winckelmann felt himself to occupy the sort of middle ground described above by Ingarden.[20] The above passage also suggests

---

[20] Winckelmann was notoriously dismissive of scholars. Lessing was a famous victim, described as 'ein Universitätswitz aus der Uckermark, welcher mit Paradoxen sich

that Ingarden, like Winckelmann, laid great stress upon the 'unmittelbare Erfahrung' of works of art.

In the light of such ideas of the ideal pupil/observer it seems natural that both authors should insist that there is such a thing as a good response to art, 'soll es zu einer leistungsfähigen ästhetischen Erfahrung kommen' (EKW 20). Again, in dealing with the mechanisms of reception on the basis of a philosophical system, and in insisting upon our taking each case on its objective merits, Ingarden often disguises his fundamental idealism. However, it does occasionally surface. Some works of art, interpreted by good critics, lead in his view, 'zur Erscheinung synthetischer positiver ästhetischer Werte *hoher Ordnung*' (my emphasis) (EKW 7). There is an implicit order of responses to art, and correspondingly some aesthetic experiences represent an ideal achievement. This attitude is confirmed when he locates a parallel between the scheme of 'Werte' which he establishes and Platonic 'Ideen' (EKW 117). At another point he cites Hegel on the theme of unity in a work of art. If this was achieved then we could be aware of an 'in der Erscheinung durchleuchtende Idee' (EKW 196). There are some striking similarities here with Winckelmann's idealism, which has a Platonic core. Ingarden's aesthetic does not, however, contain any identification of the ideal with the divinity, as Winckelmann's does.

Even this superficial comparison of the preconditions for and conclusions of, aesthetic experience, indicates considerable common ground. In the next section we shall deal with the substance of the descriptions of aesthetic experience in Winckelmann and Ingarden.

2. THE FIRST PHASE OF AESTHETIC INTEREST

In the above discussion it was suggested that aesthetic experience was more than a sensual/emotional response to a work of art. However, the immediacy associated with the senses and emotions is, according to Ingarden, not absent from genuine aesthetic activity:

Das ästhetische Erlebnis fängt an, wenn auf dem Hintergrund eines wahrgenommenen oder phantasiemäßig vorgestellten realen Gegenstandes eine besondere Qualität (gewöhnlich eine Gestaltqualität) zur Erscheinung gelangt, die den Erlebenden nicht 'kalt läßt', sondern ihn in einen eigentümlichen

hervorthun will' (*Briefe*, iii. 220). He was positive about his work in general but feared that he had simply not *experienced* enough art (*Briefe*, iii. 199, 204). Ironically, Rehm shows how Winckelmann uses some of Lessing's ideas (*Briefe*, iii. 498).

Erregungszustand versetzt. Die durch sie hervorgerufene Erregung nennen wir die 'ästhetische Ursprungsemotion'. Sie hat mit dem sogenannten 'Gefallen' nichts zu tun. (EKW 3)

This excitation, or arousal, on first contact with the work was expressed more directly by Winckelmann. In the *Abhandlung*, he talks of the capacity, characteristic of the ideal pupil, to respond quickly to aesthetic stimulation. The 'äußerer Sinn' deals with the visual stimuli in the following manner:

Fertig und schnell muß derselbe sein, weil die ersten Eindrücke die stärksten sind und vor der Ueberlegung vorhergehen: was wir durch diese empfinden, ist schwächer. Dieses ist die allgemeine Rührung, welche uns auf das Schöne ziehet, und kann dunkel und ohne Gründe seyn, wie mit allen ersten und schnellen Eindrücken zu geschehen pfleget, bis die Untersuchung der Stücke die Ueberlegung zuläßt, annimmt und erfordert. Wer hier von Theilen auf das Ganze gehen wollte, würde ein Grammaticalisches Gehirn zeigen, und schwerlich eine Empfindung des Ganzen und eine Entzückung in sich erwecken. (KS 219)

The 'Entzückung', or 'Rührung', identified by Winckelmann, appears to have a similar source to the 'Erregung' identified by Ingarden. These responses immediately follow exposure to the work, and constitute an intuitive, non-intellectual response to its general properties ('das Ganze' (W)—'eine Gestaltqualität' (I) of some sort). The precise source is obscure ('dunkel' (W)—'eine besondere Qualität' (I)). They do not represent an end in themselves, but rather provide the stimulation for further critical involvement. A vague sense of 'Gefallen' is not an appropriate stopping-point.[21] Ingarden talks in terms of an 'Ursprungsemotion', and makes it clear at the start of the above passage that he is only describing the early stages of the aesthetic process ('fängt an'). Winckelmann refers to the subsequent phase of aesthetic experience as a period of 'Ueberlegung'. We have to look elsewhere in Ingarden's work for references to the equivalent critical engagement which succeeds initial arousal. The observer, according to Ingarden, next begins to search for 'das rein Qualitative', i.e. the aesthetically active properties of the work (EKW 4). More emotively, he describes a 'Verlangen nach anschaulichem Haben und Besitzen der erregenden Qualität' (EKW 3). Broadly speaking, both Winckelmann and Ingarden identify the receiver's urge to explore the way in which a work of art operates on him.

The last, and most important stage described above is the subject of Section 3, which deals with the anatomy of their criticism of art. But the

---

[21] In Winckelmann's work 'Gefallen' is a response to grace in art for 'die Grazie ist das vernünftig gefällige' (KS 152). Cf. '*Von der Grazie in Werken der Kunst*' (KS 157–62).

receiver cannot, according to either Winckelmann or Ingarden, automatically move on to pin down the qualities of the work of art which have initially attracted him, and express his responses to them. One stumbling-block is the language used to express aesthetic experience. Winckelmann and Ingarden use very different registers of language—and both styles and argumentative methods are regarded individually as extreme examples of their kind—but in their different ways both men were trying to wring meaning out of their own experiences of art.[22] Both also invented new terminologies in the attempt to arrive at more accurate interpretations. Ingarden, as well as offering practical evidence of the difficulties of doing justice to aesthetic experience, discusses the problem on the theoretical level:

> Es entsteht nämlich die Frage, ob bei dem Übergang von der unmittelbaren Bewertung zur sprachlich-begrifflichen Fassung des bewerteten Gegenstandes keine Fehlleistung geschieht. Die Hauptschwierigkeit, mit der wir alle zu kämpfen haben, liegt darin, ob es uns gelingt, in den Gebilden der vorhandenen Sprache Begriffe zu finden, welche das unmittelbar Gegebene, rein Qualitative und oft Irrationale adäquat wiedergeben. Und es handelt sich nicht bloß darum, daß die faktisch vorliegenden Sprachen in dieser Hinsicht sehr unvollkommen sind. Es kommt hier auf das eventuelle durchaus prinzipielle Versagen der Sprache an, die ursprünglichen Gegebenheiten der ästhetischen Erfahrung wiederzugeben. (EKW 17)

According to this view, the positive qualities of a work of art may form an intricate web, or 'synthetisches Gebilde', which is 'eigenartig', or even 'einzigartig', and so resists expression. There is one possible response to this difficulty, namely repeated viewing, since 'die Rückkehr zur unmittelbaren Erfassung und Bewertung ist hier unentbehrlich, um überhaupt auch nur den angenährten Sinn des gefällten Werturteils zu verstehen' (EKW 18).

This principle was also important to Winckelmann, who always felt it was essential to look at the 'Urbilder'. But even then the immediacy of aesthetic experience could not always be captured in words. Rationalizations of the problem of adequate expression, similar to those offered by Ingarden, can be seen at various points in Winckelmann's work but they did not help to remove his sense of frustration at failing to express himself completely. This is particularly evident during his attempts to

---

[22] We have already had some indication of Winckelmann's style. A stylistic analysis of one of his descriptions forms the substance of this chapter. Wellek believes that the 'technicality' of Ingarden's language may have affected his reception as a critic. See René Wellek, *Four Critics: Croce, Valéry, Lukács, and Ingarden* (Seattle, 1981).

provide descriptions of the famous statues of the Vatican collection. We need only look at the different versions of the Apollo Belvedere and Belvedere Torso descriptions to see a man struggling to do justice to great works of art (KS 267–85). In the version of the Apollo description which was finally adopted for the *Geschichte der Kunst* Winckelmann appeals for help from the Muses, or, more precisely, from art itself, in completing his tribute:

Die Kunst selbst müßte mir rathen, und die Hand leiten, die ersten Züge, welche ich hier entworfen, künftig auszuführen. Ich lege den Begriff, welchen ich von diesem Bilde gegeben habe, zu dessen Füßen, wie die Kränze derjenigen, die das Haupt der Gottheiten, welche sie krönen wollten, nicht erreichen konnten. (KS 268)

Winckelmann's letters at this period in his life are full of references to the impossibility of his chosen task.[23] The following parallel example of this frustration at the job in hand is taken from the end of the *Abhandlung*. The presence of such a passage in this text is significant because it was intended to establish the possibility of aesthetic education; simultaneously Winckelmann seems to be highlighting a considerable difficulty in the programme because 'die höchste Deutlichkeit kann Dingen, die auf der Empfindung bestehen, nicht gegeben werden, und hier läßt sich schriftlich nicht alles lehren, wie unter andern die Kennzeichen beweisen, welche Argenville in seinen Leben der Maler von den Zeichnungen derselben zu geben vermeynet. Hier heißt es: gehe hin und sieh' (KS 233).

The fact that aesthetic experience is based upon an 'Empfindung' makes it difficult to explain and eventually leads the student back to look at the work again, in the hope of greater insight. 'Unmittelbare Erfassung', or in Winckelmann's terms repeated 'seeing', was the only way to overcome difficulties of expression. The effect of art upon the individual was not concrete or easily measured like the biographical details in which Argenville traded. Winckelmann saw a partial solution to this problem in the refining of his language. He strove for concision and clarity, as well as range and depth of expression, and was perfectly aware that in attempting to gain the maximum return from the German language

---

[23] A fine example of this difficulty is to be found in a letter to Francke, describing his efforts to capture the essence of the Apollo Belvedere. This description 'erfordert den höchsten Stil, eine Erhebung über alles was menschlich ist'. The effect of the work was 'unbeschreiblich' and the description something which he would not have undertaken if he had not been pushed by Mengs (*Briefe*, i. 212).

THE RECEPTION OF WORKS OF ART

he was establishing new standards for its future use.[24] However, the process of description never became any easier because his depth of insight was constantly increasing. He once saw the head of a beautiful Pallas figure which was 'ja so schön, daß ich mich glücklich preise, durch dieses Werk meinen Begriff noch erhöhen zu können' (*Briefe*, iii. 49). The problem which went with this was the capturing of such 'Begriffe' in verbal form. Metaphor and simile proved to be the most valuable tools at his disposal for creating a 'Bild' of a given work of art. Discussing a book by Mengs in a letter to Geßner he notes the value of such images:

> der Verfaßer hat vermutlich die Schwierigkeit eines handgreiflich klaren Begriffs [of beauty], den niemand hat geben können, eingesehen, und deswegen hat er denselben in ein erhabenes Bild gefaßet, welches ich niemahls ohne Rührung habe lesen können, und ich preise Gott, der solche Kraft zu denken im Menschen geleget hat. (*Briefe*, ii. 161)

The value of imagery resided in the fact that it provided, for the reader, an experience analogous to that generated by the original work of art. The term 'Rührung' was also used to describe the 'ästhetische Ursprungsemotion' (see above), a firm indication that Winckelmann was referring to an analogous, similarly stimulating literary/aesthetic experience. This could be regarded as an alternative to criticism, a form of translation of aesthetic experience.

Winckelmann experienced the difficulty of adequate expression more acutely than Ingarden, perhaps because Ingarden (at least in the field of the visual arts) restricted himself to theoretical issues. And, besides, the two men worked under very different circumstances. Winckelmann worked on a writing style 'in welcher ich die höchsten Kräfte von Nachdenken und Ausdrücken zu zeigen gesuchet habe; und die dennoch von der heiligen Inquisition könnte gelesen werden' (*Briefe*, ii. 158). These difficulties were made more extreme by the need to translate some works into French, or to write them in French or Italian. Lack of familiarity with the written languages clearly made successful expression less likely.[25] His work as a guide to foreigners as well as Germans will only have

---

[24] Winckelmann repeatedly suggests that his writing in German is a patriotic undertaking. This is in part true but Koch points out that his style in fact depends upon his exposure to and use of stylistic components taken from the three live and three dead languages which he knew besides German. See Hanna Koch, 'Johann Joachim Winckelmann: Sprache und Kunstwerk', *Jahresgabe der Winckelmann-Gesellschaft*, 1956–7 (Berlin, 1957), 18. His ideas are similarly heterogeneous.

[25] Cf. Johann Winckelmann, *Description des pierres gravées du feu-baron de Stosch* (Florence, 1760) and *Monumenti antichi inediti spiegati ed illustrati* (Rome, 1767).

served to make the problem more immediate; the audience was present and expected instant illumination. Even when he could write or speak in German there was not an appropriate established register for the expression of aesthetic experience. The fact that Winckelmann was always keen to provide illustrations of the works of art in question in his books, to stand alongside his descriptions, may indicate a degree of uncertainty at the success of his work. These illustrations would provide the opportunity to regenerate the 'Ursprungsemotion', if the description should fail to reproduce or sustain it. Sadly the quality of these illustrations was very poor and would have been unlikely to call forth any real response in the reader. At best they would only have offered an approximate idea of the appearance of the works being described.[26]

3. AESTHETIC ENGAGEMENT

(a) Ingarden's paradigm of reception

Ingarden's paradigm of reception was from a system of phenomenological philosophy; it was directed at the study of literature and most particularly at the investigation of the ontological status of the literary work of art. However, he believed it to hold true, in its basic tenets, for all art-forms and it could be readily adapted to the visual arts by making allowances for the different sign systems involved. It is therefore reasonable to cite his books on literary theory, where general issues are at stake. Nevertheless, I have avoided this where possible by limiting reference to two more general studies, the *Untersuchungen zur Ontologie der Kunst* and *Erlebnis, Kunstwerk und Wert*.

Ingarden's aesthetic has three central elements: the work of art; the aesthetic object; the observer/receiver. The most striking aspect of his thesis is the emphasis placed upon the latter two elements. The work of art is not necessarily of central interest and when Ingarden shows formalist inclinations these are normally inspired by the desire to explain how the work operates upon the reader/viewer, i.e. how formal features help to generate certain aesthetic objects. The term 'aesthetic object' requires definition. In the context of Ingarden's aesthetic it signifies the product

[26] The illustrations in the *Monumenti* are not of a quality commensurate with Winckelmann's efforts in this department. The quality and cost of illustrations is a constant theme in Winckelmann's letters. Cf. also Ernst Osterkamp, 'Zierde und Beweis: Über die Illustrations-prinzipien von J. J. Winckelmanns *Geschichte der Kunst des Altertums*', *Germanisch-Romanische Monatsschrift*, 70 (ns 39) (1989), 301–25.

of the interaction of the observer with the work of art. Faced with a particular work the observer selects the aesthetically relevant material. To use Ingarden's terms, he begins to distinguish those properties of a work of art which are 'axiologisch neutral' from those which are 'axiologisch valent' (EKW 165). When we look at a particular 'Gemälde'—in his terms simply a frame containing paint-covered canvas, not a work of art in the more general sense—we do not respond to every feature on it. Instead, in processing its various properties we form in our minds a 'Bild', derived from the aesthetically active qualities of the painting (OK 208). Ingarden would have described the 'Gemälde' as a 'künstlerisch' phenomenon, the 'Bild', on the other hand as 'ästhetisch'—the aesthetic object (EKW 25). The connection between the two realms is direct, but not always unambiguous. To extend the example above, it may prove difficult to identify the positive features of a 'Gemälde' which make us describe the 'Bild' it generates as, say, 'noble'. Because he makes aesthetic experience depend upon the receiver in his paradigm, Ingarden has been seen as preparing the way for purely subjective judgements of art. He defended himself vigorously against this charge, asserting that though an individual view of art may be partial, it need not lack objective value; our responses are rooted in an object, namely the work of art itself. This issue is dealt with more fully later.

Ingarden describes the process of reception, and, in particular, the generation of the aesthetic object, in a variety of terms. To follow Ingarden: aesthetic activity involves the filtering out of material which is 'wertneutral', in favour of that which is 'ästhetisch relevant', and ideally contains 'positive Wertqualitäten' (EKW 143). Features which fall into either of the last two categories can be described as aesthetic. They are the true concern of the enlightened observer. Ingarden also describes the process in various terms which help it to seem more concrete. The work of art, for example, is described as a structure containing 'Unbestimmtheitsstellen', which are filled by the receiver (the verbs used include 'ausfüllen' and 'ergänzen'). The act of filling is called a 'Konkretisation' of the work.[27] In essence he is describing the suggestiveness of works of art, and the responsiveness of observers, and insisting that the one should match the other. Much of the dynamism of the process is lost in Ingarden's analyses because of the rigour of his argument, although the implicit energy is sometimes made explicit. In the following passage he traces the aesthetic process from the stage of initial arousal described in

[27] Cf. E. H. Falk, *The Poetics of Roman Ingarden* (Chapel Hill, NC, 1981) for a good introduction to the central ideas in Ingarden's aesthetic.

Section 2, to the moment when the aesthetic object is fully formed. The description assumes a work which can provide an aesthetic object that is 'ergänzungsbedürftig', or revealing the 'Unbestimmtheitsstellen' mentioned above:

> so nimmt das ästhetische Erlebnis im weiteren Verlauf die Gestalt eines unruhevollen, anstrengenden Suchens nach den ergänzungsfähigen Qualitäten an. Die Erschauung der ursprünglich erregenden Qualität stillt sogleich das Drängen nach ihr und verwebt sich mit dem ästhetischen Genießen dieser Qualität. Gewöhnlich ruft dieses Genießen ein neues Begehren nach anschaulichem Haben ästhetisch erregender Qualitäten hervor, die von dem ästhetisch Erlebenden entweder an dem dargebotenen Kunstwerk gesucht oder in einem Phantasie-Schauen entworfen werden, und, dem Gegebenen aufgepropft, mit demselben verschmelzen. (EKW 5)

Personal imagination clearly has a major role in interpretation, though Ingarden here insists that any analysis should have some basis in the object, even if it is only 'aufgepropft' on it. The verb 'verschmelzen' indicates that the constituent phases of reception may become difficult to distinguish. The tension between clarity of critical thought and aesthetic engagement is a recurring feature of Ingarden's aesthetic. At one point above he talks of the need to 'abstrahieren' during full reception of a work. Elsewhere, on the other hand, he insists that any criticism be 'fundiert', or 'verankert' in the aesthetic object, and, ultimately in the work of art (OK 216 'abstrahieren'; OK 212 'fundieren', 'verankern'). Such difficulty is perhaps inevitable in dealing with the 'quasi-reale Welt' of aesthetic objects (EKW 7). The aesthetic object is, after all, produced by creative forces in the observer. The 'sichtbares Prinzip' which leads to the creation of the aesthetic object may not be clear to anyone but the individual observer (OK 281). The moment of interaction, described above, is not in this scheme the final phase of aesthetic experience but its creative phase, since 'die Konstituierung des struktuierten, selbstgenügsamen, qualitativen Ganzen bildet das letzte Ziel der schöpferischen Phasen des ästhetischen Erlebnisses' (EKW 6).

This is followed by a more passive stage in which the assessment of the work of art takes place, on the basis of the qualities identified in the aesthetic object. Ingarden describes the stages undergone already as: '1. die emotionalen (die ästhetische Erregung, das Genießen), 2. die aktivschöpferischen (das Bilden des ästhetischen Gegenstandes, als eines qualitativen struktuierten Ganzen)'. The third phase contains different elements, namely 'die passiven, hinnehmenden (anschauliche Erfassung der schon konstituierten qualitativen Gebilde)'. The 'charakteristische

Dynamik und Unruhe des Suchens und Findens' of phases one and two, is followed by 'Beruhigung' (EKW 6). In this state of calm the observer is able to attach a 'Wertantwort', or value-judgement, to the 'Wertqualität' (or '-qualitäten') found in the aesthetic object.

If we return to the 'Gemälde/Bild' example, we may see the value of dividing aesthetic activity into phases. The sense of beauty which we feel in response to a particular painting does not mean that beauty is a primary quality of that work. To use Ingarden's terms, 'die "Schönheit" oder die "Vollkommenheit" ist aber nicht etwas, was sich im Gegenstand sozusagen direkt konstituieren ließe' (EKW 205). It is a secondary property, and so derives from the 'Bild', rather than the 'Gemälde'. The omission of the intermediate stage in aesthetic experience devalues any value-judgement that may be made. If the aesthetic object is not formed then there is no basis for assessment, besides emotional response, or prejudice. Such appraisals of a work Ingarden dismisses as 'bloßes Urteilen' (EKW 9). He repeatedly emphasizes the appropriate moment for value-judgements:

Die Bewertung ist sozusagen die Konklusion und die eigentümliche Reaktion des Erfahrenden auf dasjenige, was sich im ästhetischen Erlebnis gestaltet und uns enthüllt hat. Sie kann von diesem Grunde nicht abgelöst werden, soll sie sich im ursprünglichen Ernst vollziehen. (EKW 9)

He also asserts that the most common departure from the proper procedure involved the attachment of value-judgements directly to the work of art. This idea gives us a useful means of measuring the approaches of many of Winckelmann's followers. If, as will be suggested later, Winckelmann's reception conforms, to a large extent, to Ingarden's paradigm, then any departure on the part of a pupil will indicate some flaw in the process of aesthetic reception and so by extension in their aesthetic education. Winckelmann appears to have created some pupils who were not 'critical enough', which is how Ingarden dismisses those with a superficial approach:

Die Wertantwort ist durch die Ausgestaltung des ästhetischen Gegenstandes und durch die Verhaltensweise des Erlebenden bedingt. Vermöge der angedeuteten Beziehung zwischen dem Kunstwerk und dem ästhetischen Gegenstand schreibt sie die am ästhetischen Gegenstand haftenden Werte oft dem Kunstwerk selbst zu, besonders, wenn der Erlebende auf die Erlangung der Erkenntnis des Kunstwerks eingestellt ist, ohne dabei aber kritisch genug zu sein. (EKW 21)

The enthusiastic desire to understand, described in the penultimate line above, was clearly a characteristic of each of Winckelmann's pupils, indeed it was a prerequisite for his full attention to them as students. It is therefore interesting to consider whether they too fell into the trap of attaching value-judgements prematurely before engaging themselves fully with the work of art. And we must also consider the extent to which Winckelmann contributed to their hastiness by providing them with a fixed set of values for art evaluation.

As a result of a critical approach to a given work of art the receiver attaches a value-judgement. But what objective merit can such a judgement have, dependent as it is upon the sensibility of an individual observer, even if he is, in the last stages of his assessment, calm in his approach? Ingarden rejects the Horatian premiss that 'de gustibus non est disputandum', and insists that beauty, for example, is an objective product of aesthetic experience (EKW 10). According to him, different individuals do not locate different sorts of beauty, but rather different aspects of the complex 'beauty'. Any view of a work of art can only be partial since 'jede Erfassung eines Kunstwerks—sei es ein Werk der Plastik, der Musik oder der Literatur—ist immer partiell. Sie zeigt es bloß in einer Auswahl seiner Eigenschaften' (EKW 11). The presence of such a 'Variabilitätsgrenze' in aesthetic judgements does not undermine their basic value (EKW 22). Each receiver can select 'verschiedene Assortimente der ästhetisch relevanten Qualitäten', but as long as these can be proven to derive from the particular work, they are of value. The only danger comes when criticism is not faithful to the 'Grundart' of the work (EKW 150). The best guarantee of reliability is to cover every possible aspect of the work. In literature he suggests territory from sound to meaning which has to be covered, with the relationship of the parts to the whole and to one another to be illuminated (EKW 47). If the observer stresses any aspect of the work unduly, and therefore produces a distorted aesthetic object (with relation to its constituent parts) he is overstepping his mark as a critic. Although it has been suggested above that criticism is a creative process, that creativity, according to Ingarden, has necessary limits. If the observer creates an aesthetic object only loosely connected to the work, or produces a 'Bild' in his mind unlike any plausible 'Bild', his work ceases to be critical, because in this case 'der Betrachter ist dann ein größerer Künstler als der Schöpfer des Bildes selbst' (OK 242). This is clearly not a positive condition, since creative energy is being misdirected. It is interesting to measure Winckelmann's art criticism in the light of such reservations; how did the 'Bild' in his mind's eye relate to the artefact which he was describing? Ingarden clearly mistrusts any attempt at normative criticism. Where the observer is overintrusive, and tries to shift attention to private concerns, he is to be ignored. Some critics have particular formal or thematic obsessions, which can lead them to false judgements. Thematic prejudices are most disruptive in this respect, since they force the critic to look too far beyond the work. Ingarden is particularly distrustful of those who only see a work as valid if it confirms particular political, social, or religious ideals (EKW 134–6). There is room for such interests only if they do not mean that, in the course of the interpretation, the critic fails to do justice to the overall structural/thematic composition of the work in question.

A unified structure can be found in works of many different schools, such is the complexity and relativism of Ingarden's aesthetic value-scheme. This is another aspect of his anti-normative approach. After all 'in jeder künstlerischen Richtung gibt es gute und schlechte Kunstwerke. Man sollte also nur die einzelnen Werke bewerten' (EKW 51). Notions such as beauty are clearly more elusive than any normative approach could allow since 'streng gesprochen ist die Schönheit eines jeden echten und großen Kunstwerkes in voller Völle und synthetischer Einheit etwas ganz Spezifisches, das nur unmittelbar erfaßt, nicht aber rein begrifflich streng bestimmt werden kann' (OK 168). We are here returning to the linguistic problems mentioned in Section 2.

Winckelmann's attitude towards the whole problem of value in art is clearly rather different from Ingarden's. Whilst acknowledging the difficulty of adequately expressing beauty, he none the less claims his poetic vision of it as a norm. Ingarden would have insisted that it could, at best, be a partial view, at worst a prejudice. Perhaps Winckelmann falls into the trap described below by Ingarden. He is discussing the dangers of all prejudgements of works of art:

> Es werden dann dem Kunstwerk Eigenschaften und Werte zuerkannt, die ihm selbst gar nicht zukommen. Mannigfache vom Kunstwerk bloß zugelassene oder auch vorgeschriebene Konkretisierungsmöglichkeiten werden gänzlich übersehen oder sogar bewußt ausgeschlossen. Die aktualisierte Möglichkeit wird als eigene Bestimmung des Kunstwerks gedeutet, so daß die bloße Potentialität mancher in ihm vorbestimmten Momente übersehen wird. Das spezifische Wesen des Kunstwerks wird dadurch falsch aufgefaßt. (EKW 21–2)

Given the difficulty of even approaching an adequate definition of the factors which cause beauty, Ingarden tries to avoid any further difficulty due to personal bias, by justifying partial views of works of art. His view of the evaluative phase of aesthetic experience is clearly radically different from Winckelmann's. Nevertheless the two men's evaluations of the process of aesthetic engagement are strikingly similar.

(b) Winckelmann's paradigm of reception

Die Fähigkeit das Schöne in der Kunst zu empfinden, ist ein Begriff, welcher zugleich die Person und Sache, das Enthaltende und das Enthaltene in sich fasset, welches ich aber in eins schließe... (KS 212)

As the above quotation suggests, Winckelmann was aware of the reciprocity between the work of art and its receiver. Evidence of their interaction is best taken from his practical criticism, since he rarely deals with the issue on a theoretical level. In the same essay he provides a description of the ideal reception, deriving from a highly tuned sense of beauty:

Das wahre Gefühl des Schönen gleicht einem flüßigen Gipse, welcher über den Kopf des Apollo gegossen wird, und denselben in allen Theilen berühret und umgiebt. Der Vorwurf dieses Gefühls ist nicht, was Trieb, Freundschaft und Gefälligkeit anpreißen, sondern was der innere feinere Sinn, welcher von allen Absichten geläutert seyn soll, um des Schönen willen selbst, empfindet. (KS 217)

Understanding art is, according to this view, based on close, disinterested, and sensitive study. The image of the cast suggests that as a result of this the work and receiver become as one. The 'Person und Sache' of the earlier quotation are inseparable in high aesthetic activity. The parallels with Ingarden's theory are already quite apparent. The examination of Winckelmann's method in action confirms this idea of the reception of art, and shows the process of interaction, leading to appraisal, to be more vigorous than Ingarden suggested in his more measured way. This vigour is to be found in the verbal activity of the descriptions.

In this section we shall focus on the *Beschreibung des Torso im Belvedere zu Rom* (KS 169–73). This description is in many respects typical of Winckelmann's writing, and is suited to our purposes particularly because of the extensive 'Unbestimmtheitsstellen' which the torso offers as a work of art. The statue is 'verstümmelt', and therefore makes considerable demands upon the receiver's imagination. There is, of course, the danger that the link between the work and the aesthetic object derived from it may become overstretched since the work does not offer much visual information as the basis of judgement. A further danger resides in the fact that the description has a very clear educational purpose, despite Winckelmann's modest claims for it. The description is, at best, a 'Probe', but one of a significant kind:

Man sehe sie an, als eine Probe von dem, was über ein so vollkommenes Werk der Kunst zu denken und zu sagen wäre, und als eine Anzeige von Untersuchung in der Kunst. Denn es ist nicht genug zu sagen, daß etwas schön ist: man soll auch wissen, in welchem Grade, und warum es schön sey.

This he clearly attempts in this description, and it is perhaps with a certain false modesty that he longs for an improvement upon his own work:

> Es wäre zu wünschen, daß sich jemand fände, dem die Umstände günstig sind, welcher eine Beschreibung der besten Statuen, wie sie zum Unterricht junger Künstler und reisender Liebhaber unentbehrlich wäre, unternehmen und nach Würdigkeit ausführen könnte.

It is typical of Winckelmann, and in keeping with his polemical/educational purpose that his conclusions often precede his argument. In the first quotation above we have already been told that the torso is perfect. We are led to the work with our conclusions as to the value of the work already formed. The torso we already know by reputation to be one of the great works of classical art, and Winckelmann certainly does not allow that point to escape our attention. This is not to say that the analysis, when it arrives, is insubstantial. It is simply the case that Winckelmann assumes for himself a superior vantage-point, and chooses to lead the reader to 'appropriate' conclusions by the most direct or persuasive method. The notion of leadership is particularly important in this essay. After his introduction Winckelmann notes:

> Ich führe dich itzo zu dem so viel gerühmten, und niemals genug gepriesenen Torso eines Herkules; / zu einem Werke, welches das schönste in seiner Art, und unter die höchste Hervorbringung der Kunst zu zählen ist, von denen, welche auf unsere Zeiten gekommen sind.

We are reminded of Winckelmann's work as a guide and of his attempts to educate a generation of travellers. However, the verb 'führen', in this context, has some inappropriate associations. It suggests command/control on Winckelmann's part, whereas it later becomes clear that the work of art itself had a considerable role in shaping his reactions. In a telling verbal echo we later see the work 'leading' Winckelmann. Whilst he contributes a good deal to the process of aesthetic appreciation, there is an equal contribution from within the work. Although he never describes this contribution as an energy the patterns of verbal activity suggest a transfer of energy and so underline the reciprocity between receiver and work of art. This relationship is only discovered under close scrutiny of the torso. He points out that 'der erste Anblick wird dir vielleicht nichts, als einen ungeformten Stein sehen lassen'. This superficial impression can only be overcome by closer examination. It is, however, misleading when he says in the same passage that this must take place 'mit einem ruhigen Auge'. On the contrary there appears to be a good deal of activity in the aesthetic process. The eye is only still in the way that a cinema screen is still whilst hundreds of images move across it. The only moment of genuine calm is that when conclusions are formed as a result of aesthetic engagement.

We shall focus upon the moment of interaction with the work as the most striking aspect of Winckelmann's vision. In the preamble to the description of the torso, we see a typical, if as yet hypothetical, pattern of interaction. He discusses the prospects of 'in die Geheimnisse der Kunst einzudringen', if the viewer responds actively. If this penetration is achieved 'alsdenn *wird* dir Herkules . . . erscheinen, und der Held und der Gott *werden* . . . sichtbar werden' (my emphasis). The verb-forms give the impression that the work is moving towards the observer, whilst the receiver is essentially passive. Their appearance is a reward for the effort, suggested by the verb 'eindringen'. The meeting-point would be on an aesthetic plane, similar to that suggested by Ingarden. There are repeated instances of this mutual interaction in the course of the torso description.

In the opening paragraph of the description proper Winckelmann deals with the subject-matter of the statue—the divine Hercules, as opposed to the more common representations, in literature, of the heroic man—and isolates two physical properties which underpin it. The torso exhibits 'Stärke und Leichtigkeit'. These qualities, as the next paragraph makes clear, are suggested by the 'mächtige Umrisse dieses Leibes'. The interest in line is typical of Winckelmann, indeed it is an obsession of his.[28] But the equation between the physical properties of the work and Winckelmann's interpretation of them is complex. Drawing on his stock of literary and historical knowledge he can actively enhance his image of an artefact, in this case the statue of Hercules. Acknowledging the input as his, he notes:

Ich sehe . . . die unüberwundene Kraft des Besiegers der gewaltigen Riesen, die sich wider die Götter empöreten und in den phlegräischen Feldern von ihm erleget wurden. (My emphasis.)

This stage corresponds to the penetration ('eindringen') described above. Simultaneously the work is portrayed as responding with further suggestions, offering a deeper insight:

und *zu gleicher Zeit stellen mir* die sanften Züge dieser Umrisse, die das Gebäude des Leibes leicht und gelenksam machen, die geschwinden Wendungen desselben in dem Kampfe mit dem Achelous *vor*, der mit allen vielförmigen Verwandlungen seinen Händen nicht entgehen konnte. (My emphasis.)

[28] Line theories were common at the time as I make clear in Ch. I.

THE RECEPTION OF WORKS OF ART 59

Quite how such impressions derive from outline is left obscure. The metaphorical term 'Gebäude', which Winckelmann made his own, perhaps makes the issue more complex, since it is not certain which properties it may involve. It is clear, however, that Winckelmann does not regard himself as imposing the interpretation upon the work. His cultural awareness may make initial access to the works possible, but the work actively stimulates his search for a more profound understanding. The battle described in the above quotation is not present in the torso and yet certain of the physical properties of the statue seem to allude to it, allusions which can be picked up by the qualified receiver. To return to terms used earlier, the 'Bild' generated on the aesthetic level is not identical with the work which helped to create it, but is directly related to it. The link in this case seems to involve serpentine lines present in the statue and emphasized in the imagined body in movement during battle.

This pattern repeats itself in the following paragraph, which reads:

In jedem Theile dieses Körpers *offenbaret sich*, wie in einem Gemählde der ganze Held in einer besonderen That, und *man siehet*, so wie die richtigen Absichten in dem vernünftigen Baue eines Pallastes, hier den Gebrauch, zu welcher That ein jedes Theil gedienet hat. (My emphasis.)

The opposition of the verbs 'sich offenbaren' and 'sehen' suggests alternating activity and passivity on the part of the receiver, according to a familiar pattern. The difficulty of locating the precise mechanism of the interaction is implicit in the double use of simile. The very presence of imagery is testimony to the creative engagement of Winckelmann and it is interesting that the simile is taken from other art-forms. Presumably Winckelmann imagines the 'grammar' of these arts to be simpler than that of statuary. This is certainly the case in architecture, which depends for its effects, according to Winckelmann, almost wholly upon geometry.[29] In this respect the parallels are rather misleading since his interpretation of the torso does not rely upon the unravelling of simple mathematical principles. Indeed, earlier in this description he had mentioned the 'Geheimnis' at the core of art. This attempt to make the process of interpretation seem more direct/simple than is obviously the

---

[29] Winckelmann's publications on architecture are to a large extent concerned with mathematical questions and matters of proportion etc. Cf. KS 174–85 (*Anmerkungen über die Baukunst der Tempel zu Girgenti*). On the basis of other people's measurements Winckelmann tried to establish principles of construction, 'Regeln' (KS 185). See also J. Dummer, 'J. J. Winckelmann und der griechische Tempel: Versuch eines Plädoyers', in id. (ed.), 'Griechische Tempel: Wesen und Wirkung', *Beiträge der Winckelmann-Gesellschaft*, 8 (Stendal, 1977), 103–111.

case perhaps derives from his sense of the necessity of the connection between the work and his interpretation.

The sense of necessity is immediately reconfirmed. He says that 'Ich kann ... [die Schulter] nicht betrachten, ohne mich ... [der Stärke] ... zu erinnern' (my emphasis). Talking of the chest he compares it to his literary/historical image of Hercules: 'Eine solche Brust *muß* sich so prächtig und erhöht gezeigt haben' (my emphasis). The integrity of his image of Hercules is such that he does not simply provide illuminating parallels from literature of Hercules in action, but shows some internal life in the statue itself: 'Mit was für einer Großheit *wächst die Brust an*, und wie prächtig ist die *anhebende* Rundung ihres Gewölbes!' (my emphasis.) The architectural term 'Gewölbe' is misleading in suggesting a fixed state, though the noun does have a clear verbal root. For Winckelmann the work of art is always in motion. Earlier the verbal activity suggested that the work was responding to the input of the observer. Here the verbs suggest a more definite movement, and the use of the prefix 'an' in both verbs is significant because it gives an imaginative impression of movement towards the observer. The present tense/present participle and the exclamation mark add immediacy to the impression. We are reminded of Lessing's idea of the pregnant moment in the visual arts, the choice of which can add an epic element to our vision.[30] In Winckelmann's version the work has an internal energy, which allows the story to be acted out before our mind's eye.

The description of the side of the torso provides further evidence of activity in the generation of the aesthetic object. The muscles are initially not described by shape but rather by their 'Wirkung und Gegenwirkung', or the balance 'von abwechselnder Regung und schneller Kraft'. The metaphor employed in the description adds to the sense of movement. The side is compared to a sea whose waves 'anwachsen'. Like waves which are 'verschlungen' and then 'hervorgewälzt' by surrounding water and in a state of constant flux ('schwebend'), the muscles of the torso 'flow' into one another, emphasizing the sense of 'Bewegung'. These impressions draw the receiver towards the work; Winckelmann again makes the interaction during the aesthetic phase seem very concrete. Echoing his description of the waves, he notes that 'unser Blick wird gleichsam mit verschlungen'. The observer has become part of an organic process, with his response echoing the activity imagined. A similar process is shown later in the description, where a landscape comes

---

[30] Cf. Gotthold Ephraim Lessing, *Werke und Briefe in zwölf Bänden*, ed. Wilfried Barner (Frankfurt am Main, 1990), vol. v/2, 31–4.

alive. The observer does not judge the work of art from afar, but is drawn towards it by his awareness of the aesthetically significant qualities. These qualities have an almost physical attraction; the aesthetic object is alive in these descriptions. The difference between the work and the aesthetic object seems great in Winckelmann's description. Indeed, it would be difficult to reconstruct the work of art from his description. In this particular case any attempted reconstruction would provide a more complete picture than the torso itself. This passage from Winckelmann may be a rather crude example of a reaction to 'Unbestimmtheitsstellen', but for that reason makes the processes involved clearer.

The description continues with further evidence of the difficulty of maintaining a critical distance as an observer. He notes: 'Hier möchte ich stille stehen', in order to absorb his impressions. The verb 'mögen' suggests his powerlessness in this state of aesthetic rapture; the adverb 'stille' confirms that there has been a good deal of activity thus far. The beauty of the work is still operating upon him. He describes a state of 'unzertrennliche Mitteilung', which suggests an intimate relationship between work and receiver. Winckelmann does not feel that he is imposing his interpretation upon the work, and who would need to when 'ein Begriff erwächst zugleich hierher aus den Hüften'? But he does not totally devalue his role, or suggest that he is passive in the operation. The 'Begriff' is contained in 'Andeutungen', which he is sensitive enough to understand.

A reciprocity between the work and its receiver, which results in the formation of a subtle impression of the aesthetic object, is a constant feature of this description. In the following paragraph a number of constructions occur which show the work operating upon Winckelmann:

> durchfährt meinen Geist
> und ich werde . . . geführet
> da mein Geist zurück gerufen wird
> Ich wurde entzücket

He is led into ever greater acquaintance with the object, something which he compares to entering a building 'so wie ein Mensch, welcher nach Bewunderung des prächtigen Portals an einem Tempel, auf die Höhe desselben geführet würde, wo ihn das Gewölbe desselben, welches er nicht übersehen kann, von neuem in Erstaunen setzt'. This religious image is appropriate given the metaphysical aspirations in Winckelmann's aesthetic. The associated notion of being led and, moreover, of being led upwards is also significant in Winckelmann's descriptions, as has been suggested above. Variations upon the verbs 'führen', 'rufen', 'wachsen', and 'sich erheben' indicate mystical elevation. Indeed, Winckelmann formulates the experience of art as a process of 'Offenbarung'. Earlier we heard that the key properties of the work 'sich offenbaren'. Later we hear that 'in der Ruhe und Stille des Körpers offenbaret sich der gesetzte große Geist'. The observer appears to be locating the spiritual energy generated by the artist. It is the artist's gift 'die Materie geistig zu machen'. The physical object provides only a means of access to the spiritual realm:

> Diese vorzügliche und edle Form einer so vollkommenen Natur ist gleichsam in die Unsterblichkeit eingehüllet, und die Gestalt ist bloß wie ein Gefäß derselben; ein höherer Geist scheinet den Raum der sterblichen Theile eingenommen, und sich an die Stelle derselben ausgebreitet zu haben.

These are the major components of the 'Geheimnis' of art and there is little mistaking the source of much of the terminology used to capture it. Winckelmann imagines the process of induction into and revelation of the mysteries of aesthetic insight as comparable to the learning process of an acolyte. The rewards, in terms of spiritual well-being, he also saw as equivalent to those offered by more conventional faiths and famously referred to himself as reborn in Rome.[31] And this was achieved by responding to visual stimuli in art. When you do this 'es sammelt sich ein Ausfluß aus dem Gegenwärtigen und wirket gleichsam eine plötzliche Ergänzung'. The 'gegenwärtig' element is the observer's life/art experience, which, in conjunction with the work of art, leads to a fulfilling concretization ('Ergänzung'). This terminology could almost be Ingarden's and illustrates the common ground in their treatment of the reception of works of art.

4. THE CONSEQUENCES OF AESTHETIC ENGAGEMENT

Ingarden was primarily concerned with theoretical questions connected with the ontology of works of art, and whereas he did manage to extend this undertaking to incorporate some practical criticism, he rarely addressed the important question of what we stand to gain from the study of art. For Winckelmann, on the other hand, this question was of great importance. As we have seen, he cast himself (and was confirmed by others) in the role of educator. As well as observing the changes which

---

[31] See below for references to Winckelmann's rebirth.

took place in his pupils, he was acutely aware of the transformation which the study of art brought about in himself. It would be no exaggeration to suggest that his life seemed to him only to have gained significance through the study of literature and, eventually, of art. The study of these different art-forms was not for him ancillary to the business of living but was essential to it. Art gave his life shape; his inner life was given substance by art. These images, of shaping or substantiation, are critical. I have consciously chosen terms which reflect the central terminology of Ingarden's and Winckelmann's related theories of art reception because it is clear that whilst works of art are completed by exposure to an observer (through the creation of an aesthetic object) there is also a sense in which the observer is made more complete by exposure to art, or fulfilled by it. (It would perhaps be taking things too far to suggest that a person could be 'concretized' by exposure to art.) This was certainly the case for Winckelmann; and the way in which he described his fulfilment highlights the reciprocity between a work of art and its observer, as suggested above. Goethe will provide an even better example because he uses a terminology still more reminiscent of reception theory.[32]

Winckelmann constantly reflected upon the ways in which he was being affected by art. Its impact could be measured in a number of ways. Perhaps most striking was his claim to have been physically affected by a work of art. His description of the Apollo Belvedere provides striking evidence of his empathy for statuary. In the final version of the description, in the *Geschichte der Kunst*, Winckelmann still talks of struggling to capture the beauty of the statue in words, and indeed refers to his own inadequacy for the task. This could easily be seen as a rhetorical trick to engage his audience, but it gains in credibility from the fact that he eventually finds himself describing the effect of the work on himself (i.e. the generation of the aesthetic object) rather than the work of art itself (the artefact), in a pattern similar to that in the torso description. The effect of the work on him is described in the following terms:

Ich vergesse alles andere über dem Anblicke dieses Wunderwerks der Kunst und ich nehme selbst einen erhabenen Stand an, um mit Würdigkeit anzuschauen. Mit Verehrung scheint sich meine Brust zu erweitern und zu erheben, wie diejenige, die ich wie vom Geiste der Weißagung aufgeschwellet sehe, und ich fühle mich weggerückt nach Delos und in die Lycischen Hayne, Orte, welche Apollo mit seiner Gegenwart beehrte: denn mein Bild scheint Leben und Bewegung zu bekommen, wie des Pygmalions Schönheit. (KS 268)

[32] See Ch. 5.

Winckelmann imagines himself looking like Apollo. His physique is, in his mind's eye at least, becoming statuesque, radiating 'Würdigkeit' in the same manner as the statue of the god. As well as a shift in posture Winckelmann goes on here to imagine a sudden coming to life on his own part, inspired by the work of art. The comparison with the awakening of Pygmalion is particularly apposite and provides very firm evidence of the reciprocity between the observer and work of art. To expand: we have already seen, in the torso description, how Winckelmann could bring alive works of art imaginatively. The driving force behind this engagement was love of art, as well as deep admiration, or even love, for the figures represented in the great works of (supposedly) Greek art. The parallels with the Pygmalion myth are clear in this case. But in the passage above Winckelmann imagines himself brought alive, or at least given fresh energy by art. The work of art as well as the observer has life-giving powers; the relationship between the work of art and the observer is reciprocally gratifying. It is also fundamental, since the work and the observer apparently depend upon one another for life. This is a powerful metaphor but it is not without its difficulties. We can understand the life which a viewer brings to a work of art, but how does a work of art bring a person to life? Certainly, we may feel better for our exposure to art, but any improvement is likely to be to our spiritual rather than our physical lives. Winckelmann allows for this by making clear the fact that the imagined physical changes in himself, described in the above passage, reflect a spiritual change. His expanded chest is a mark of an altered state of mind which features a new degree of 'Würdigkeit' and 'nobility' appropriate to contemplation of Apollo; in the same way the outward appearance of the statue is the sculptor's means to articulate a spiritual or moral state. Through contemplation of objects which themselves display, say, nobility (and any good one must reveal 'eine edle Einfalt und stille Grösse') one can become more noble. This causal link is problematic—evil in art would generate evil in life—and perhaps as a result of this Winckelmann had little time for works which were not beautiful, or at least graceful, or for observers who were not competent to identify subversive art.[33] But in any case there appears to be an osmotic process at work by which the moral or spiritual content of a work of art can be transferred to its observer. The particular moral qualities

[33] Ugliness was, of course, an extreme deviation from the norm of 'edle Einfalt'. Even the lack of a degree of 'Grazie', or subtlety in the work of a great artist such as Michelangelo opened him to criticism (KS 161–2). Those viewers who were attracted by crude artistic effects (such as those offered by Bernini) or 'das Schöne und das Mittelmäßige' in the same measure did not have a true aesthetic sensibility (KS 213).

embodied in a statue, in its themes and physical appearance, become significant for the observer and can enter his particular moral scheme; here they operate as models for the observer's judgements, and perhaps, ultimately, for his future behaviour. The clearest indication that this was happening in Winckelmann's case was the common perception of him as a Greek; this implied that he had inherited the range of (albeit idealized) moral and even political values of his favourite historical state largely through its art. Goethe was evidently of this opinion, and Winckelmann was also commonly portrayed as a Greek in statues and paintings, although that was not particularly unusual at the time.[34] However, the question of what we gain, or learn, through art goes further than this. Clearly beauty in art was the vehicle which inspired Winckelmann to the sort of moral insight suggested above. However, beauty could, in his view, do rather more. More than alluding to moral or spiritual states which were historically (or mythologically) specific, beauty was a medium for direct communication with God, and so with the source of all definitive morality. According to Winckelmann the highest source of beauty was in God. He said unequivocally that 'die höchste Schönheit ist in Gott!' (*Werke*, iv. 60) However, God was a rather loose term for Winckelmann; God represented an Essence or an Idea of the greatest purity, untainted by materiality, but one which defied definition. We are not confronted with a Christian God, much less the specific one offered by the Protestant or the Catholic denominations. The divinity embodied for Winckelmann some aspects of Christianity (much of his terminology and imagery is derived from Pietism and has specific associations), but also accommodated the ancient gods and even Platonic Ideas.[35] There was a realm of pure spirituality; there were essential Truths, alluded to in each code (Christian, or otherwise), which could be summed up by the term God. The problem for mankind, given the nature of the

---

[34] For representations of Winckelmann in art cf. Arthur Schulz (ed.), 'Die Bildnisse Johann Joachim Winckelmanns', *Jahresgabe der Winckelmann-Gesellschaft, 1953* (Berlin, 1953); Hans Zeller and Ulrich Steinmann, 'Zur Entstehung der Winckelmann-Büsten von Friedrich Wilhelm Doell', *Jahresgabe der Winckelmann-Gesellschaft* (1954–1955), 18–46; Andreas Flittner, 'Das Basler Winckelmann-Portrait', *Deutsche Vierteljahresschrift*, 45 (1933), 757; R. Lullies, 'Ein Bildnis J. J. Winckelmanns von Anton Graf', *Jahrbuch der Hamburger Kunstsammlungen*, 11 (1966), 53–60; Carol Heitz, 'Un nouveau portrait de Winckelmann, *Études germaniques*, 16 (Jan.–Mar. 1961), 26–30.

[35] The question of religion in Winckelmann is a complex one. Perhaps the most concise treatment is to be found in Koch, 'Sprache und Kunstwerk', 60–3 (especially language of religion). See also Adolf Düppengießer, 'Der "gründlich geborne Heide": Religion, Theologie und Kirche bei Winckelmann' (inaugural dissertation, University of Passau (Passau, 1981)).

existence of God, was to make the divinity and the corresponding morality comprehensible. The artist was particularly qualified to achieve this; he could give form to ideas, but a form which did not reveal its material basis. Statues could be created which overcame their essential nature as pieces of rock and instead signified Ideas, or ideals. This was certainly the case where ancient artists depicted their gods; although they were conventionally represented in human form they remained somehow ethereal and superhuman. For Winckelmann the most important example of the effort to capture the divine spirit was the Apollo Belvedere:

Die Statue des Apollo ist das höchste Ideal der Kunst unter allen Werken des Alterthums, welche der Zerstörung derselben entgangen sind. Der Künstler derselben hat dieses Werk gänzlich auf das Ideal gebauet, und er hat nur eben so viel von der Materie dazu genommen, als nöthig war, seine Absicht auszuführen und sichtbar zu machen ... Ueber die Menschheit erhaben ist sein Gewächs, und sein Stand zeuget von der ihn erfüllenden Größe ... Gehe mit deinem Geiste in das Reich unkörperlicher Schönheiten, und versuche ein Schöpfer einer Himmlischen Natur zu werden, um den Geist mit Schönheiten, die sich über die Natur erheben, zu erfüllen: denn hier ist nichts Sterbliches, noch was die Menschliche Dürftigkeit erfordert. (KS 267)

The work of art is in this conception merely a pathway between the crude materiality of the world which we inhabit and the ideal world. (The essential purpose of a pathway is to allow movement to and fro; we have already identified the nature of this movement in the section on aesthetic engagement (3 above).) The Apollo has a human form, but one which is refined to remove evidence of earthly provenance. The effect of the statue is to prevent us from reflecting upon our 'menschliche Dürftigkeit' and to draw us into 'das Reich unkörperlicher Ideen', because in order to do justice to the work we have to become 'Schöpfer' and operate on an ideal level. The fact that the observer must become a creator, and so operate with ideals, in order to appreciate art, is a firm indication of its educational function; we have to improve ourselves in order to approach an understanding of art. Whilst it is essentially material it alludes to that which is ideal and so immaterial. In this respect it performs a vital function because it allows us to operate through our senses (which we mere humans must) and yet still establish some contact with the supersensual realm of ideas, or God. Winckelmann makes clear this function, in theoretical terms, in a letter to Bianconi:

La perfezione essendo incompatibile coll'umanità e solo in Dio e dall'uomo non potendo essere realmente concepito che quello che cade sotto i sensi, perciò il Creatore sapientissimo ha inprontato nell'uomo una Idea visibile della perfezzione e questa è quello che chiamiamo Bellezza. (*Briefe*, i. 377)

This was not a novel idea but it was none the less of critical importance to Winckelmann who found in it both an explanation of the excellence of many works of art and a proof that aesthetic interests could be life-improving, something which he experienced himself.[36] When we have had contact with the True or Essential, albeit at one stage removed through the medium of art, it must inevitably affect our thinking. For Winckelmann it meant perhaps that he knew what it was to be noble. In the realm of ideas there was perhaps a paradigm of Nobility; in the concrete form of a statue, like the Laocoön, he could see something deriving from that essential Nobility, a pattern of represented behaviour in a form which did it justice. He felt perhaps that through the work of art he had caught a glimpse of an eternal Truth.

Such moments of insight transformed Winckelmann. He confirmed the effect that art had upon him when he referred to himself as reborn in Italy. To a large extent this feeling could be related to the general change for the better in his life which came with the move to Rome, but I feel that it reflects most concretely a new-found freedom to study art and learn from it. His happiness was measured according to unusual criteria because 'ich bin nicht glücklich nach dem gemeinen Begriff der Menschen zu reden, aber in mir selbst bin ich es, und höchst zufrieden, welchen Zustand ich mit keinem Menschen vertauschen wollte' (*Briefe*, ii. 121). Material comfort was clearly important to Winckelmann, as is evident from his constant references to it, but he certainly felt that there was something else to his happiness in Italy. The pleasures associated with art were far superior to those to be found in any other part of his life. Remarking on the discovery of a Faun's head in 1763 he says that 'ein solches Vergnügen gilt mehr als ein Monat Frölichkeit bey Hofe' (*Briefe*, ii. 210). But, more seriously, he elsewhere described himself as 'un enfant nouvellement né' when he reflected on the freedom which he enjoyed in Italy by comparison with the period working for Count Bünau in Germany (*Briefe*, ii. 99). He also noted in 1762: 'Ich würde sagen: ich habe bis in das achte Jahr gelebet; dieses ist die Zeit meines Aufenthalts in Rom und in anderen Städten von Italien' (*Briefe*, ii. 275). Here he is really counting the years when he was able to work unhindered and focus

---

[36] This was a favourite notion of Winckelmann's. Rehm collects the references to it at *Briefe*, ii. 432. He also points out a potential source of the idea in Plotinus and its use by Mengs and Goethe.

his attention upon art; there is, I think, little doubt that art made the major contribution to his rebirth. The fact that the idea of rebirth is very specifically associated with a spiritual or religious awakening is perfectly appropriate. We spoke earlier of the role of art in providing access to the Truth, the Ideal, or Perfection. This is also the case with Christianity, which offers examples of such Revelation as the stimulus for people to be reborn, and dedicate their lives to the Lord.[37] Winckelmann's theology and aesthetics allowed this rebirth to take place through the medium of art rather than Scripture. It is scarcely suprising when Winckelmann describes a likely trip to Greece, the source of ideal art, as a 'Wallfahrth' (*Briefe*, iii. 302).

[37] One could similarly talk in terms of Orphic or Eleusian induction, such is the heterogeneity of Winckelmann's aesthetic.

3
Johann Hermann von Riedesel

JOHANN HERMANN VON RIEDESEL, Freiherr zu Eisenbach, occupies an interesting position in literary history. His life and work are interpreted largely in terms of his connection with more famous contemporaries. His friendship with Winckelmann and the work which he produced whilst, broadly speaking, under Winckelmann's supervision, is the starting-point for most discussion (although discussion of Riedesel's work is, in any case, rare). Otherwise we hear about Goethe's reading of Riedesel. In the latter context we are reminded that Goethe carried Riedesel's book on Sicily by his side as a 'Talisman', or 'Brevier' during his own Italian Journey.[1] Neither of these connections is damaging to Riedesel's reputation; but we may begin to suspect that any work which seems to gain significance only by reference to other parallel works has no great intrinsic merit. It would be easy to cheapen Riedesel's achievements by describing his work as merely derivative of Winckelmann, or as a feeble prototype for Goethe's description of Sicily. However, the fact that Winckelmann and Goethe were both very positive in their judgement of Riedesel is a good indication that he is worth taking seriously in his own right.

Riedesel's aesthetic insights are different in character from those of Winckelmann or Goethe. Winckelmann's influence on Riedesel's first publication was direct and measurable. But Riedesel should not be seen as an extension of Winckelmann. His work was useful to Winckelmann, is generally instructive, and would have been attractive to contemporaries because of the novelty of the material.[2] On the debit side it lacks the depth of insight and particularly the passionate engagement with art which we know from Winckelmann and from Goethe; indeed 'it is *not* Winckelmann, to be sure: we miss his passion and perception'.[3] This is

---

[1] These comments made in Girgenti, Sicily. Cf. i. 31, 164–5 (IR 258) for his fullest statement on Riedesel.
[2] See Osterkamp's account of the 'discovery' of Sicily for the German public: E. Osterkamp (ed.), *Sizilien: Reisebilder aus drei Jahrhunderten* (Munich, 1986), 361–88. In his view Winckelmann may have precipitated interest in Sicily. Noticeably, Riedesel's account of Sicily is the first in the collection.
[3] Constantine, *Early Greek Travellers*, 131.

something which is sometimes overlooked. The secondary literature on Riedesel contains numerous references to the parallels in the views of the two men and to Riedesel operating as a second Winckelmann on his travels. Rehm refers to Riedesel working 'in seinem [Winckelmanns] Geist' (*Briefe*, i. 605). Edschmid talks about the 'entscheidende Anregungen' given to Riedesel by Winckelmann and this view is supported by Rehm, who felt that 'ohne Winckelmann hätte Riedesel kaum so gesehen, wie er gesehen hat'.[4] Such moderate claims are typical and not unreasonable. But they are taken further. Justi suggests that Riedesel and Winckelmann had an 'ähnliche Empfindungsweise' but then suggests that he '*dasselbe* suchte, liebte und empfand' (my emphasis) as Winckelmann.[5] Edschmid (as Becker) takes a similar view of the Winckelmann/Riedesel relationship, seeing Winckelmann as Riedesel's 'geistiger Vater'; he even claims that Riedesel saw things 'mit den Augen des genialen Freundes' and worked '*ganz* in seinem Geist' (my emphasis), although this could be seen as faint praise (*Levante* (Introduction), 24, 20, and 17). Views such as Becker's are difficult to substantiate. It is hard to believe that Riedesel saw in exactly the same way as his teacher and that genius is readily transferable between individuals. Contrary to Becker's assumption a capacity to appreciate art is not transmitted from teacher to pupil naturally, as from father to son. Evidently information can be transferred between individuals, albeit with varying degrees of success. Thus Winckelmann was able to pass on a good deal of his knowledge to others, not least to Riedesel. However, qualities of mind are more difficult to transfer. Hence it would be unreasonable to expect Riedesel to see in the same way as Winckelmann. The irony is that Becker's view loyally follows Winckelmann's. The latter thought that in Riedesel he had found the perfect pupil, one who might be able to reproduce his level of insight into art. We must examine in detail Riedesel's qualifications as a pupil for Winckelmann and the type of training which he underwent. Winckelmann's own prescriptions for the ideal pupil will serve as a benchmark here. It then remains to see whether Riedesel's published work and other statements on art indicate the complete realization of Winckelmann's plans for an aesthetic education. It will be interesting to discover whether writing on art proves to be a reliable guide to the transmission of aesthetic sensibility. It certainly provides the only substantial

---

[4] *Sizilien*, 7; W. Rehm, 'Johann Hermann von Riedesel: Freund Winckelmanns, Mentor Goethes, Diplomat Friedrich des Großen', in id., *Götterstille und Göttertrauer: Aufsätze zur Deutsch-Antiken Begegnung* (Berne, 1951), 215.
[5] Justi, *Winckelmann*, iii. 338.

body of evidence, but is it to be trusted? We have some idea of how aesthetic sensibility—Winckelmann's aesthetic sensibility—did manifest itself in his writing but must we expect that it will always express itself similarly in others? What proof can we ever look for that aesthetic education has taken place?

1. THE PREPARATION FOR THE VISIT TO ROME

In Chapter 2 I dealt at some length with those interrelated factors which, according to Winckelmann, could positively affect the prospects of aesthetic education, namely wealth, location, youth, and sensibility.[6] I will now take each of these factors in turn and measure the advantages which Riedesel enjoyed against the standards suggested by Winckelmann. All of the biographical material is taken from three sources. Two of the sources are closely related. The biographical information in Rehm's essay *Johann Hermann von Riedesel, Freund Winckelmanns, Mentor Goethes, Diplomat Friedrich des Großen* and the introduction to the translation of Riedesel's second work, the *Randbemerkungen über eine Reise nach der Levante* by Eduard Edwin Becker are based upon very similar sources (family and political archives); the third source, used by the authors mentioned above, but reassessed here, is Winckelmann's side of the correspondence with Riedesel. I will generally summarize or condense the material offered by Rehm and Becker, rather than cite them at length.

(a) Wealth

According to Winckelmann wealth was not important for its own sake but because it enabled a greater degree of freedom for those who enjoyed it. Art could only truly be enjoyed by those whose minds were not distracted by more mundane things or, to borrow one of Winckelmann's colourful images, who were not condemned to plough barren fields.[7] Despite his status as a 'Freiherr' Riedesel seems at points to have feared that ploughing fields could become a reality for him, although a degree of exaggeration is clearly present in this assessment of his plight. He certainly did not look forward to the prospect of returning to the family estates, after his years of travelling, to live the life of a small country squire, fearing that 'bientôt mon langage ne sera que celui d'un solitaire

---

[6] See Ch. 2, Section 1.   [7] See Ch. 2.

campagnard de récolte, d'améliorations, de chiens, de chevaux; je sens bien combien cela peut être ennuyant et insipide!' (*Levante*, 41) This certainly would have provided a stark contrast with his previous life-style but, luckily for him, he was never forced to face it because he had soon embarked on a political/diplomatic career (detailed by Becker) which kept him far from the family estates. In any case this worrying period for Riedesel post-dates his time with Winckelmann; certainly during the 1760s he was free to contemplate ever more extensive travels without any obvious compulsion to settle down. Ironically, the writing produced in consequence of these travels reveals an interest in the rural economy; he was happy to observe it but less willing to participate in it. On the whole his family made few demands on him.

The Riedesel family was well established and well connected with strong traditions of military and civil service; some members of the family had also been content to run the estates. Given Johann Hermann's apparent dislike of life in the country, there remained only two obvious alternative types of employment. Johann Hermann was unable to become a soldier because of his small stature and hunched back and so his final decision to work as a diplomat was predictable. Riedesel had, whether by design or not we do not know, an early life and education which would suit him for this task. Money was available to provide him with tutors and with financial support while at university; more importantly, he could finance the extensive travels which were vital preparation for a future diplomat. Despite occasional debts, the family finances were sufficiently stable to provide Riedesel with the traditional education of an aristocrat.

Interestingly, a lack of ready cash did at one point encroach upon Riedesel's relationship with Winckelmann. There is a suggestion that the delay in his leaving Lausanne for Rome, and so Winckelmann, in 1765–6 came down to want of money. The evidence is to be found in Winckelmann's letters to him of the period. Winckelmann tried hard to persuade him that he could live as cheaply in Rome as in Lausanne, and gave some tips as to how that could best be done with 'Sparsamkeit' (*Briefe*, iii. 97, 157, 163). At one point Winckelmann even wished that he were in a position to lend money to Riedesel (*Briefe*, iii. 158). This seems slightly ironic since at other points Riedesel offered to sponsor Winckelmann for a Greek trip which would clearly have required a major investment.[8] It also seems strange to hear Winckelmann offering this

---

[8] See Rehm's account of the recurring plan for a Greek trip at *Briefe*, iii. 534. The planning/dreaming was particularly intense during 1767.

type of assistance when we consider that he spent much of his time trying to secure his own financial future rather than provide for others.[9] We must suspect that Riedesel's temporary embarrassment will only have served to endear him to Winckelmann, since only rarely, and indeed only in Rome, was he in a position to help people out with money.

Riedesel's financial problems were perhaps more in the nature of cash-flow difficulties, which could cause occasional embarrassment. On the whole Riedesel enjoyed a very high degree of financial independence. The freedom which this brought him, along with his elevated social position, meant that, in Winckelmann's terms, the first prerequisites for an aesthetic education were satisfied. However, such basic qualifications were by no means a guarantee of success. Some of Winckelmann's bitterest attacks were reserved for noblemen who remained philistines despite their advantages of birth and wealth.[10] However, in Riedesel's case social and financial advantage was to prove productive. His formative years were used effectively in preparation for the central experience of a visit to Italy and study with Winckelmann, although they were perhaps planned with rather different ends in mind.

Documentary evidence of Riedesel's early education is sparse. Becker was able to identify the French 'Erzieherin' who looked after Johann Hermann and subsequent generations of the family; reasonably enough Riedesel's preference for the French language is traced to her, but it was more or less a social requirement at the time.[11] Other attempts to identify important formative influences on Riedesel, particularly with reference to his later love for classical antiquity, are speculative. There is little evidence that any of his tutors affected him positively in this direction, with a couple of exceptions. Becker suggests that the family priest, Adam Gerhard Dieffenbach, may have awakened his interest in classical antiquity. The most concrete evidence of Dieffenbach's interests was in his publication entitled: *Ob ein Prediger von den Büchern, so man* auctores classici *nennet, ein Liebhaber seyn dürfe?*, a question which he answered in the affirmative. Dieffenbach had previously been the 'Hofmeister' to Riedesel's friend and relative Wilhelm Christoph Diede and had accompanied him to various universities; his academic credentials were confirmed by his election to the 'Königliche Deutsche Gesellschaft' in

---

[9] References to his impecunity abound in Winckelmann's correspondence, particularly during the Seven Years War, when he was cut off from his Saxon patron.
[10] See Ch. 2, and n. 8.
[11] R. E. Keller, *The German Language* (London, 1978), 485–92 gives a survey of the contemporary linguistic situation.

Göttingen. It seems very likely then that Diede would have inherited some of his interests over the years and also likely that Riedesel may have been exposed to them either directly, or indirectly through Diede with whom he maintained a long correspondence. Both Riedesel and Diede were diplomats and so had a shared interest in the political issues of the day, but their friendship may have been further encouraged by a common interest in the ancient world, inspired by Dieffenbach.[12] But this is little more than speculation. The same is true of Becker's assessment of Riedesel's school and university days because the evidence is so incomplete.

At the Academy at Idstein which Riedesel perhaps attended later he would, Becker suggests, have been influenced by a Swiss language master who had travelled as far as India and was also a good classical linguist. His name was Heinrich Fröhlich, but again it would be impossible to be more precise about his role in shaping Riedesel's interests. We might expect to find more positive indications of the likely pattern of Riedesel's development in the records of his university, Erlangen. Sadly, we find little help. Becker locates some information about lecturers etc. which might, on closer examination, help to explain aspects of Riedesel's work as a diplomat, but from our perspective there is little of interest. Erlangen did not even possess a tutor in Greek. There is, however, evidence even at this stage that Riedesel was developing a taste for the antique. His sketch-books of the period are full of drawings after the antique.[13] The source of this interest must nevertheless remain obscure. The pattern of education which emerges is typical of contemporary aristocrats and even the degree of classical interest identified by Becker could scarcely be regarded as exceptional. His extensive use of classical quotation in his texts is by no means unusual.[14]

---

[12] See bibliographical note at *Levante*, 62. I have been unable to see this material, although Becker suggests that it is dominated by political discussion and so not directly relevant to this book.

[13] Becker refers to the sketchbook and indeed uses samples from it (*Levante*, 15, 23, 35, 51). See also the bibliographical note at *Levante*, 62. I was unable to examine these sources.

[14] Cf. Pierre Augustin Guys, *Voyage littéraire de la Grèce ou lettres sur les Grecs anciens et modernes, avec un parallèle de leurs mœurs*, 2 vols. (Paris, 1771) provides the best example of the use of quotation in contemporary travel literature, albeit in connection with a different country. Constantine, *Early Greek Travellers*, 147–67 (156) shows the method of comparison between ancient and modern used by Guys. Winckelmann uses quotation in a radically different way in his descriptions. Cf. Koch, 'Sprache und Kunstwerk' and, in particular Hans Zeller, *Winckelmanns Beschreibung des Apollo im Belvedere*, Zürcher Beiträge zur deutschen Literatur- und Geistesgeschichte, 8 (Zürich, 1955).

(b) Location

In the better-documented part of Riedesel's life we rarely see him in the same place for very long, until he finally settles in Vienna. His travel had a clear educational function which related both to his future life as a diplomat and to the development of his understanding of art. If, as was suggested above, the substance of Riedesel's schooling was not exceptional, then the amount of travelling which he subsequently undertook to round off his education would, by contrast, certainly have been exceptional. The connection with his future career as a statesman is clear. Travel would have provided exposure to different places and politics and would also have offered the possibility of establishing contacts that could be exploited later. This was particularly true of his visit to Britain. His knowledge of the political community and the number of contacts he established there made him a very likely candidate for a diplomatic job in England. His Italian journeys would also have been useful in this respect. Given the number of important Europeans travelling in Italy he must have also made contacts there which would be useful to him later. The fact that he was a friend of Hamilton, the English Ambassador in Naples, would, for example, have made introductions to the highest circles inevitable (*Briefe*, iii. 354 and 553).

Riedesel's travels began in German-speaking states in 1761–2. The places visited included Regensburg, the location of the Reichstag, and later Vienna and the Kaiser's court. It seems clear that Riedesel was primarily concerned to establish himself in the political world at the time. Key evidence of this, provided by Becker, is the fact that he seems to have become a 'Herzoglich Württembergischer Kammerherr' (if we accept Becker's interpretation of certain expenses 'zum Etablissement' incurred during 1761 in Stuttgart—the title was not used of him until 1763). There appears to be no evidence that Riedesel was particularly concerned with the arts but this is hardly surprising, given the almost total lack of detailed information about this stage of his life.

We know that in 1762 Riedesel undertook a more extensive journey, although again we lack detailed information. Becker traces his withdrawals of money and was able to show that he travelled through Strasbourg, Paris (for an extended period, with withdrawals from early March to late May), Lyons, and Marseilles. This interest in France would perhaps not have been to Winckelmann's taste, but it is consistent with Riedesel's Francophile upbringing. Furthermore, French political institutions would have been a necessary object of study for a potential statesman. These travels were, despite the apparent political focus, consistent with some of Winckelmann's principles for the early stages of an aesthetic education. As we know, Winckelmann believed that pupils could most easily be sensitized to art in a big city where they would have access to collections and people with knowledge of the arts. This was certainly a possibility for Riedesel, even if we sense that at this stage the arts were only an incidental interest for him. He seems to have made a point of escaping his highly provincial home in order to visit major centres. While he was clearly not interested exclusively in the arts he would scarcely have been able (or inclined, if we are to believe his Erlangen sketch-books) to ignore them. A degree of cultural exposure, at the very least, belonged to the role of statesman and, inevitably, the major political centres which drew his attention will also have been the dominant cultural centres. Rulers often underlined their power with the accumulation of works of art. This may (and we can only speculate) have had a convenient side-effect for Riedesel, in the form of early exposure to substantial collections of art. Certainly each of the major courts had a relatively high concentration of art. Riedesel's tour then took him to Italy. Money was collected in Genoa, Turin, Milan, Rome, Naples, Rome (again), Florence, and Venice. The important records of this trip, and the central experience of meeting and studying with Winckelmann, will be discussed in due course as will the detail of his second Italian journey, which began in 1765 and was extended to incorporate further travel (to Sicily and the East, Portugal, Spain, and eventually England, Scotland, and Ireland) with his return home delayed until spring 1771. Predictably his political interests did not wane during this period. However, there is, particularly during his time in Italy and Sicily, a strong emphasis upon the arts. This interest seems to have been developed as a result of his exposure to Winckelmann.

(c) Youth and sensibility

Youth was important to Winckelmann because it offered the opportunity to start aesthetic education early. In young men a particular sensitivity to art could be identified and developed under close supervision. Winckelmann was not able to exercise such influence at an early stage in Riedesel's life; Winckelmann dreamt of an ideal situation in which a tutor would regulate the pupil's diet of literature and art, especially during the awkward stage of adolescence when he might become distracted from them (see Chapter 2). But Riedesel was only 21 years old when he arrived in Rome in 1762 and still impressionable enough at this stage for Winckelmann to assert that he was a friend 'den ich mir gleichsam hier erzogen' (*Briefe*, iii. 314). He was exposed to Winckelmann over a long period and the latter would clearly have kept close control of his exposure to art and taken care to form his opinions of it. To this extent their period of friendship and shared study in Rome may have compensated for the less sharply focused earlier period of his education. The situation which they enjoyed was perhaps as close to the Socratic ideal as Winckelmann might reasonably have hoped to achieve. But his homosexual self-interest, reinforced by the theory that a beautiful mind rightfully belonged in a beautiful body, was not satisfied by Riedesel. The portrait of Riedesel reproduced in the Becker edition of the *Levante* (probably by Anton Raphael Mengs) is not at all flattering, but to that extent it is consistent with the other testimonies that we have of his appearance. Becker cites two sources. First Graf Lehndorff described him as 'ein kleiner buckliger Mann, der aber Geist besitzt und große Welterfahrung hat'. Secondly Prince Eugen von Württemberg suggested in a letter to Rousseau that 'ce jeune homme est d'autant plus intéressant, que la nature semble avoir donné autant de laideur à sa petite figure que de beauté à son caractère' (*Levante*, 11). The slight tone of surprise in both of the comments ('der aber', 'intéressant', 'd'autant plus que') suggests that these authors along with Winckelmann believed in the coincidence of beauty of mind and beauty of body and saw Riedesel as an exception to this rule. But Winckelmann was willing to overlook flaws in his pupil's outward appearance in favour of other qualities.

There is very little evidence concerning Riedesel's natural (pre-Winckelmann) responsiveness to art and literature. By the time he wrote his books his aesthetic education was presumably complete, or as near to that state as it was to come. Otherwise his correspondence with Winckelmann is the most prolific source of information about his natural attitude towards art. Conveniently, since only Winckelmann's side of the correspondence survives, we have an assessment of Riedesel which is made according to precisely those criteria which interest us. However, even here it is often difficult to distinguish whether Winckelmann was praising the natural abilities of Riedesel, or congratulating him on talents developed during his visits to Rome—under Winckelmann's supervision, of course. There is a further difficulty in dealing with the testimony given in the letters. Winckelmann's assessment is not necessarily reliable: for two separate reasons. First, the correspondence with and passing references to Riedesel clearly date from a period when

Riedesel was heavily under his influence; it is reasonable to assume that from the very beginning Winckelmann felt that he was educating Riedesel and was shaping him according to his own wishes. Any praise of the particular qualities of Riedesel's insight could therefore be seen as a subtle form of self-congratulation. Secondly, Winckelmann was very manipulative in his correspondence. He attempted to maximize the benefit which would accrue to him—in terms of help with publications, establishing contacts, or even guaranteeing income—by manœuvring his correspondents. This manipulative tendency is by no means absent in the letters to Riedesel.[15]

Despite these difficulties we have the clear impression that Winckelmann felt he was building on solid foundations in working with Riedesel, 'da Sie [Riedesel] unter vielen Tausenden der einzige sind, der das Schöne gleichsam von Natur kennet' (*Briefe*, iii. 348). This is a firm indication that Winckelmann believed Riedesel to possess the elusive ability to appreciate beauty which he sought in his pupils. On the other hand in the opening paragraph of the draft of the *Sendschreiben von der Reise eines Liebhabers der Künste nach Rom an Herrn Baron von Riedesel* Winckelmann is rather cooler in his assessment of Riedesel (KS 203–9). He apparently exhibited 'vorläufige Einsicht' in his preparations for the visit to Rome and drew 'großen Nutzen' from the experience, but these phrases suggest industry and application rather than sparkling natural insight (KS 203). There is a very strong parallel here with Goethe's assessment of Riedesel's Sicilian report, in which he seems to praise assiduity rather than flair.[16] Winckelmann fluctuates between these two degrees of positive assessment—of his insight and/or his industry—throughout his letters to Riedesel and in other letters which mention him. At the top end of the scale of comments we hear, for instance, that he has 'das Auge eines Kenners' (albeit in connection with the merits of a young man admired by Winckelmann) (*Briefe*, ii. 311). At another stage Winckelmann even describes him as a replacement for the departing Mengs, with whom Winckelmann clearly shared many insights into art and to whom he owed, at the very least, some of his knowledge

---

[15] Winckelmann's correspondence with his publisher Walther provides a good example of his tendency to manipulate. In that connection cf. H. A. Stoll, 'Winckelmann, seine Verleger und Drucker', *Jahresgabe der Winckelmann-Gesellschaft, 1960* (Berlin, 1960).

[16] Goethe praised Riedesel for his 'ruhiger Vorsatz, Sicherheit des Zwecks, reinliche schickliche Mittel, Vorbereitung und Kenntniß' and not for his poetry. He was a 'stiller aber nicht stummer Freund' (i. 31, 164–5; IR 258). It is difficult to judge the quality of such praise; it seems a little faint.

of the practical side of the visual arts (*Briefe*, iii. 61).[17] Perhaps most clearly Winckelmann remarks in a letter from 11 January 1764 that Riedesel is to be pitied for his absence from Italy because he is so far from the works of art 'welche Sie, mehr als andere, schmecken und empfinden können' (*Briefe*, iii. 6). There could hardly be a firmer indication that in Winckelmann's opinion he had fine taste and a high degree of sensitivity to art—even if you allow for a degree of flattery. His opinion of Riedesel was still very high in 1767 when he noted that his observations on Girgenti were important because 'Sie [Riedesel] mehr und gründlicher als andere gesehen haben' (*Briefe*, iii. 267). Here again it was Riedesel's thoroughness which was being praised. This may seem, in isolation, rather half-hearted praise but when we combine it with the statements on the clarity of Riedesel's vision and his status as a connoisseur, we have a picture of a man whose insights into art were qualitatively as well as quantitatively superior to those of most of his contemporaries.

It is interesting, however, that when Winckelmann mentions Riedesel in his correspondence with third parties he does not mention his appreciation of art but rather his more general qualities as a friend and potential patron. He was honourable and worthy, as one might expect, and also a patriot (*Briefe*, iii. 314, 359). These were, for Winckelmann, not empty formulas. In naming him a patriot he was placing Riedesel alongside himself, since Winckelmann regarded himself as a true patriot.[18] Given Winckelmann's high self-opinion this was very high praise indeed.

The tone of reference to Riedesel in Winckelmann's letters is consistently positive, whether with regard to the arts or other matters. For a number of reasons mentioned above it may be difficult to establish the extent to which he thought Riedesel had great natural talent in advance of his arrival in Rome. However, the letters do provide strong evidence of the development of their friendship which was based upon shared interest in the visual arts and the classical world. The very existence of this friendship is the strongest proof that Winckelmann felt Riedesel to be a particularly sensitive soul. At one point Winckelmann referred to Riedesel as one of only three true friends (*Briefe*, iii. 157). Given the very tough conditions which he imposed for friendship and the fact that it

---

[17] Cf. Leppmann, *Winckelmann: Eine Biographie*, 145–6, 159 f. for a brief treatment of the relationship between the two men and their work. Also Justi, *Winckelmann*, ii. 31–8 and *Winckelmann von Goethe*, ed. Howald, 113–18. Even a superficial reading of Mengs's published work indicates its similarity to Winckelmann's theory. Cf. A. R. Mengs, *Opere*, 2 vols. (Venice, 1783).   [18] See Ch. 2 n. 24.

provided the basis of his pedagogical method, the importance of this statement must not be underrated.

2. FRIENDSHIP

(a) The private letters: Introduction

As I remarked earlier, the evidence of the Winckelmann–Riedesel relationship is not plentiful. Apart from Riedesel's published works we have only one side of their personal correspondence upon which to draw.[19] While this correspondence is significant it is no more substantial than many other correspondences which Winckelmann maintained. Others match it in quantity of letters and in the range of subjects covered, for example those with C. Füßli, S. Geßner, Wille, Wiedewelt, Mengs, Muzel-Stosch, Berg, and Schlabbrendorf. Similarly, for Riedesel the correspondence with Winckelmann does not seem to have been of unique importance. His letters to his cousin Diede (the only other substantial private correspondence of which we have any real evidence) are more numerous than those that we can calculate he sent to Winckelmann, although they have very different subject-matter. The exchanges between the two men would perhaps have been more extensive if they had not spent so much time together during Riedesel's visits to Italy in 1762–3 and 1765–67 where their proximity precluded the need for letters. But it is interesting that many of the most striking letters date from 1766–7 when both men were in Italy but living apart, with Winckelmann prevented from joining Riedesel by his work (see below). Their separation at this point seems to have been a very painful fact for both of them.

In dealing with the private letters we must be aware of an important hindrance to a clear understanding of them which compounds the difficulty of interpretation mentioned earlier. The early editor of the Winckelmann letters, Carl Wilhelm Dassdorf, was responsible for the loss of the original letters to Riedesel, as well as many others. If this were not problematic enough for more modern editors and readers of the letters, we also have to contend with the fact that, by his own admission, he altered parts of the letters. Walther Rehm is very harsh in his judgement of Dassdorf. He notes Dassdorf's acknowledgement that the *Briefe an seine Freunde* were openly and 'wohlbedächtig gekürzt' to

---

[19] *Sizilien* is also in the form of letters ('Sendschreiben') but is different in character from the private letters.

protect correspondents who were still alive. It was perhaps a political necessity but, as Rehm points out, this editorial intervention, plus the loss of many papers, means that it is now impossible to reconstruct many of the original letters.[20] None the less the letters to Riedesel as they stand appear very freely written and are at times controversial in subject matter, and so if there was indeed some interference with them by Dassdorf it appears not to have been too extreme.

(b) Forms of address

It can be difficult for the modern reader to come to terms with the effusive nature of much eighteenth-century correspondence. The degree of praise and flattery which was conventional in letters of this period, and the grand formulas through which these sentiments are expressed can make it very problematic to assess the underlying tone of a correspondence.

These difficulties are clearly present in Winckelmann's letters to Riedesel. The tone of Winckelmann's letters is also affected by a tendency, mentioned earlier, to exaggerate the intimacy of relationships. Because of his humble background Winckelmann was (especially during his first years in Rome) a victim of a system which demanded individual patronage of those scholars who had no independent means. Riedesel's status as a nobleman and potential patron—as well as friend—meant that he too received letters which were rather overpoweringly friendly.

If we look simply at the forms of address and the manner of their signings off we would have an impression of a very warm friendship. In an early letter Riedesel is referred to simply as 'theurster Freund!', but very shortly afterwards he had been promoted to the status of a 'sehr werthgeschätzter theurer Freund!' (*Briefe*, ii. 296, 311). A little later Winckelmann declares that 'ich bin lebenslang mit der größten Achtung und Freundschaft ... Dero (W.)' (*Briefe*, ii. 313). Friendship, as one might expect, was a consistent theme with Winckelmann, but in the case of his relationship with Riedesel this friendship was heightened to love. He refers to his friend 'mit ewiger Liebe und Freundschaft' (*Briefe*, ii. 320). Elsewhere he is his 'theurster und geliebter Freund!' This love is further confirmed in the same letter when he signs off: 'Ich küsse Sie herzlich als Ihr wahrer Freund und Diener' (*Briefe*, iii. 22). Over and above the idea of physical expression of love in a kiss, this statement introduces a

---

[20] *Briefe*, i. 463. Daßdorf's editorial policy is discussed by Rehm at *Briefe*, i. 459–67. Cf. *Winckelmanns Briefe an seine Freunde*, ed. K. W. Daßdorf, 2 vols. (Dresden, 1777–80).

new aspect of their relationship. The description of Winckelmann as a servant does, of course, reflect the relative social status of the two men, but more than this it would seem a fine testimony of the strength of their friendship. Winckelmann was not inclined to see himself as in any way inferior to his contemporaries, no matter what their social status. The idea of his, in some sense, belonging to Riedesel is further reinforced by his reference to himself as 'ihr ewiger und eigner', a parallel phrase also being used in later letters (*Briefe*, iii. 67 and, for example, *Briefe*, iii. 84, 286).

However interesting these forms of address may seem, and no matter how revealing of their relationship they may appear to be, it is important not to lose sight of the fact that they are largely formulaic; they appear in similar forms in other letters too numerous to mention, and were not even personal to Winckelmann, being closely related to those used by many others at this time. It would be easy to overstate the quality or meaning of the phrases used by Winckelmann of his friend. Whilst we have little reason to doubt Winckelmann's sincerity in using such formulas we similarly have no reason to assume that they may have particular significance when they are used of Riedesel. In fact in assessing the formulas that he uses we are safest if we measure them quantitively. The number of positive references to their friendship is high, indeed it is the most consistent feature of their correspondence. The words used similarly fall into a consistent pattern, echoing those mentioned above. Amongst other references to his relationship are the following:

Briefe, iii. 6	Friendship
iii. 28	Kisses, friendship, love
iii. 61	'in dem Schooße der Freundschaft'
iii. 84	Love, friendship
iii. 124	Friendship, love, kisses
iii. 125	'Süßigkeit', kisses
iii. 233	Winckelmann as 'Verliebter', love, kisses
iii. 285	'Dulcissime Amicorum!'

The reference to Winckelmann as a lover would seem to be an extension of the conventional pattern of reference to co-correspondents; the sense of their love has, as it were, been made more active. However, it is very difficult to gauge the value of this addition since the elaboration of standard formulas seems to be a key letter-writing technique for Winckelmann. It is a technique which begins with simple alteration of the formulaic 'Ihr ewiger und eigner' into 'Ihr ewiger, ganz eigner Freund' and culminates in some of the more lyrical statements (e.g. *Briefe*, iii. 286). But the cumulative effect of the greetings and signings-off is to make us believe with Constantine that 'even allowing for the tone of the age they are often effusively affectionate'.[21]

It is impossible for us to judge whether the affection was reciprocated given the missing letters. It would be unfair to compare the tone of the forms of address in Riedesel's published 'Sendschreiben' where Winckelmann is described as his friend, or even his 'werthester Freund', since we would expect the tone of the publications to be cooler (*Sizilien*, 140–1, 19). In order to gain a clear idea of the quality and reciprocity of their friendship we must look at the substance of the letters.

(c) The real evidence of friendship

Many readers of Winckelmann's letters to Riedesel notice something special in their general tone which distinguishes them from many of his other communications. In Justi's view the letters have 'einen eigenen warmen, getragenen Ton; diesmal hat sich die Empfindung nicht im Gegenstand vergriffen'.[22] The implied error is Winckelmann's affection for Berg. Walther Rehm places the letters to Riedesel in a category of letters exchanged with newer friends, in particular those made in Rome when he was already a scholar of high repute:

> Da [in the letters mentioned above] war es nicht nötig, sich ins beste Licht zu setzen, da konnte der Briefschreiber mitunter auch aus freien Stücken den Vorhang vor der deutschen Lebenszeit fortziehen und im Gefühl des Bestandenhabens, im Blick auf das Erreichte, von der Not einer harten Jugend erzählen. Und so erwirbt ihm, nach Goethes Worten, 'diese schöne Gesinnung der Freundschaft das Herz manches Trefflichen, und er hat das Glück, mit den Besten seines Zeitalters und Kreises in dem schönsten Verhältnisse zu stehen'.
>
> Aber die freiesten, eigentümlichsten Briefe sind doch die, die Winckelmann den 'würdigen Jünglingen' widmete, all denen, die ihn in Rom aufsuchten und seinen Umgang erfahren hatten: die Briefe an Berg, Riedesel und den Grafen Schlabbrendorf, an Leonhard und Paul Usteri, an Heinrich Füssli und Christian von Mechel. Hier gibt Winckelmann sein Persönlichstes, hier spürt man die Macht der Freundschaft, die ihn erleuchtet, die Kraft des Schauens, den freudigen Willen zur Aufmunterung und zum 'Unterricht', das Vermögen eines wirklich pädagogischen Humanismus und auch das Charisma des geborenen Bildners, der aus innerstem Beruf die junge Generation zur 'edlen Muße' und zum Urquell des Schönen führen möchte. Und meist fand er dankbare Herzen. (*Briefe*, i. 31–2)

---

[21] Constantine, *Early Greek Travellers*, 128. [22] Justi, *Winckelmann*, iii. 410.

The following section of this chapter is designed to illustrate the extent to which Rehm's general observations on a block of Winckelmann correspondence are confirmed in the particular case of his letters to Riedesel. The key idea here is that of friendship; and friendship is important because it encourages a sense of freedom. To cite Rehm, it enabled Winckelmann to speak 'aus freien Stücken' and to reveal 'sein Persönlichstes'. We must investigate the things which he felt able to say when he was given this freedom. We must also look at the 'Unterricht' that was on offer and how Winckelmann revealed his manner of seeing art. Certainly Winckelmann's letters to Riedesel in part constitute an attempt to prolong his pupil's education despite his absences from Rome.

Like Rehm I find the clearest statement of the value of friendship (and by extension teaching) to Winckelmann in Goethe, although in a different passage. Goethe suggested that 'er [Winckelmann] empfand sein eigenes Selbst nur unter der Form der Freundschaft, er erkannte sich nur unter dem Bilde des durch einen Dritten zu vollendenden Ganzen'.[23] Here we see an image which is very closely related to those mentioned in Chapter 2. There the discussion was of the manner in which an observer of a work of art in some sense completes it through his participation. Similarly I discussed the manner in which the viewer himself is made more complete by exposure to art, how he is fulfilled by his aesthetic education and perhaps made a better human being. Now we hear, in Goethe's version, how these acts of completion are preceded by another, namely the coming together of master and pupil, under the sign of friendship, to form a more perfect whole. Aesthetic education is apparently based upon multiple acts of synthesis, one of which—the establishment of friendship—pre-dates shared observation of art. But before we can observe this complete partnership in action, viewing art, we have to establish how it developed and how the sense of freedom between the two manifested itself. Apart from the references to the love and friendship that existed between them, what concrete evidence do we have of the nature of their relationship?

We know that the two men spent a good deal of time together during Riedesel's visits to Italy. However, unlike many of the noblemen who passed through Winckelmann's hands in Rome, Riedesel was incorporated into the group of scholars and artists who formed what we might call the Winckelmann circle. In his letters to Riedesel Winckelmann mentions Reiffenstein, Berg and Mann in a manner which suggests

[23] *Winckelmann von Goethe*, ed. Howald, 99.

Riedesel's familiarity with them (*Briefe*, ii. 297). Elsewhere we hear that Riedesel travelled with Reiffenstein. Interestingly, Reiffenstein was not only a close friend of Winckelmann but also met Goethe in Rome where (along with Tischbein, Oeser, Volkmann, and Riedesel) he represented one of Goethe's indirect contacts with Winckelmann (*Briefe*, ii. 306). Riedesel also travelled with Winckelmann, not least during their famous ascent of Vesuvius in 1767, where they were also in the company of d'Hancarville, another member of Winckelmann's inner circle (*Briefe*, iii. 316–18). Furthermore Riedesel was in contact with the Füsslis in Zürich and Hamilton in Naples, indicating that even outside Rome he and Winckelmann shared many friends (*Briefe*, iii. 92–3, 534, 354). Riedesel was, however, not a vague appendage to this group. Winckelmann refers at points to his key friendships and his friendship with Riedesel is consistently placed among them (*Briefe*, ii. 96; iii. 157, 489).

As with the forms of address it would be easy to dismiss these statements of friendship alone as rather empty formulas, or as strategic praise, were their content not supported by a great deal of corroborating evidence.

On 17 March 1764, on his return from a trip to Naples, Winckelmann wrote to Riedesel that he had seen a great deal, 'und mehr würde ich es geschmeckt haben, wenn ich das Vergnügen mit Ihnen hätte theilen können' (*Briefe*, iii. 28). This quotation seems to confirm the value of the friendship in a manner which relates closely to that described by Goethe in the passage cited earlier. As Goethe suspected, the value of friendship resided in the fact that through it you could expect more complete experiences. The whole, comprising friends working together, is greater than its component parts. That Winckelmann was aware of the value of having a partner with whom to share aesthetic experiences is confirmed by other statements of a similar kind.

In July 1764 Winckelmann offered Riedesel the prospect of another visit to Rome. He would be picking up where he left off on his previous visit:

Sie könnten sich sehr genau einrichten, und dennoch Rom angenehmer noch, als das erstemal genießen: denn zum wahren Genusse gehört nur Zeit und ein Freund; das erste beruhet auf Ihnen; den Freund finden Sie in mir. Sie haben unsere schönste Natur nicht einmal gesehen, ja die schönste Natur, glaube ich, die unter der Sonnen ist, und diese finden Sie zu Castello. Hier müssen Sie mit mir mehr als einen Tag seyn, und mit aller Bequemlichkeit auf des Herrn Cardinals Villa wohnen, Sie müssen das schönste Gestade an dem ganzen Mittelländischen Meere, welches zu Nettuno ist, mit mir genießen. Sie haben nur einen Bedienten nöthig, welcher kochen kann, und dieses wissen die mehresten Welschen Bedienten. Mein Herz würde noch einmal so weit werden, als es ist: denn ich habe mit niemandem mit so ungebundner Freyheit, als mit Ihnen gesprochen, und ich würde an allem Ihren Vergnügen Theil nehmen, und es auf alle Weise zu befördern suchen. (*Briefe*, iii. 49–50)

This passage is interesting for a number of reasons. The treatment of nature as an aesthetic phenomenon is unusual in Winckelmann, whereas the plea for time and leisure is more familiar.[24] But the most important point is the revelation that aesthetic pleasure is enhanced ('angenehmer ... genießen', 'wahrer Genuß') by the presence of a friend. This enhanced pleasure is then shared ('Theil nehmen', 'mit mir') to give a more complete experience to both participants. Of course, we are also given the impression that the partnership is not evenly balanced. Winckelmann (through his patron) provides his pupil with the setting and, more importantly, the encouragement ('befördern') which will enhance his pleasure. This encouragement we can take to include a degree of instruction in the appreciation of beauty. The repetition of the verb 'müssen' would also indicate that Winckelmann has a firm idea of those things to which he wishes to expose Riedesel on this trip, a sort of microsyllabus to underpin the broader programme of training which Riedesel also underwent. These arrangements do not, however, preclude pleasure on Winckelmann's part. Through his relationship with Riedesel he experiences a sense of pleasure so intense that he expresses it in physical terms, imagining his heart expanding. This metaphor provides an obvious indication of his love for Riedesel (and one that is not merely formulaic), but more importantly it reminds us of another passage, this time in one of his published works, where Winckelmann imagines himself physically transformed by what is essentially a spiritual experience.[25] The parallel images help to confirm just how important the friendship with Riedesel must have been to Winckelmann. In order to do justice to it he draws upon the same source of language as that used to express his experience of art, which was clearly the central experience of his life. Naturally, Riedesel will have made a less concrete contribution

---

[24] Nature was largely uninteresting to Winckelmann as an aesthetic phenomenon, although, ironically, it provides him with many of his key metaphors. Cf. Koch, 'Sprache und Kunstwerk', pp. 91–95 ('Die Natur'), which emphasizes the importance of man rather than nature in Winckelmann. Koch sees Winckelmann's writing as the antithesis of Klopstock's, since the latter is concerned with man giving himself up to nature. The only striking response to nature comes as he crosses the Alps on his journey home. The sight of them apparently contributed to his deepening depression because it served to underline his remoteness from the more refined environment of Rome.   [25] See Ch. 2.

to Winckelmann's understanding of art than Mengs or Oeser. Each of these working artists contributed technical knowledge of art which enhanced Winckelmann's understanding of it—again crucial acts of synthesis which made Winckelmann's aesthetic more complete. In his relationship with Riedesel Winckelmann undoubtedly cast himself in the role of teacher. None the less, Riedesel's presence enhanced the experience of art for Winckelmann and whilst he may not have enabled him to understand more completely the technique and history of art he increased his teacher's pleasure in them. He could also perform some useful services for Winckelmann.

I have already mentioned the ways in which Winckelmann tried to help Riedesel to finance a trip to Rome. This attempt at assistance, despite its failure, gives us an indication of the sincerity of Winckelmann's interest in Riedesel. Riedesel for his part seems to have done a great deal to encourage Winckelmann. Most obviously Riedesel's efforts were central in the many attempts to persuade Winckelmann to travel beyond Italy. He offered himself as a sponsor of further travel with Greece (including at various points Magna Graecia, in particular Sicily) as his initial target.[26] This attempt was not unique but was particularly warmly received by Winckelmann and mentioned in his correspondence to others. In a letter to Francke of 9 September 1767 Winckelmann suggests that Riedesel was very insistent on the trip to the extent that '[er] lässet mir weder Ruhe noch Rast, und er bestehet auf dieser Reise' (*Briefe*, iii. 314). Winckelmann turned him down at this stage because of work on the third volume of the *Monumenti Inediti* which, ironically, he had not completed by his death. The trip to Greece had a projected duration of two years and so would have caused a major interruption in Winckelmann's packed publication schedule. Riedesel's ability to finance such undertakings (despite the fact that it was never exploited) was one of the most obvious ways in which the differences in social, and so financial, status between the men manifested itself.[27] The emphasis was, however, never upon the differences between the men. Riedesel's advantages were in fact used to bring the men together, and the projected trip was perhaps meant to be the most complete act of union, since it would take them briefly out of society and so bring them together in a way which they

---

[26] See n. 8 above.
[27] Becker deals at great length with the Riedesel finances (*Levante*, 12 f.). There could not be a starker contrast with the real financial difficulties which Winckelmann experienced.

found difficult, even when they were both living in Italy (see below). Joint travels were planned particularly during 1767, when the two men found it frustratingly difficult to co-ordinate their movements in Italy. Indeed the plan became more elaborate, even expanding to include the possibility of a visit to Egypt (*Briefe*, iii. 267, 274, 300 (Egypt)).

None of these projects was ever realized, but in the course of their friendship Riedesel managed to render a number of other important services to Winckelmann. To this extent Riedesel's practical actions echo Winckelmann's willingness to be the 'servant' of his aristocratic friend. At the very least he was reciprocating the help which he had received in understanding art.

Winckelmann did make use of Riedesel in other contexts which do not pertain directly to his aesthetic education but reveal the solidity of their relationship. In 1763 Winckelmann mentioned Riedesel in a letter to his publisher Walther. It is clear from this letter that Riedesel was being used as a mediator/postman between the two men (*Briefe*, ii. 330). Similarly in 1764 he was used as an intermediary in dealings with a professor from Göttingen who wanted details of Winckelmann's biography. These he apparently enclosed in a letter to Riedesel, a fact for which he apologizes (*Briefe*, iii. 44). This was a role which Winckelmann often imposed upon his friends since they could often save him postage or provide him with safe addresses to which to send his material. Riedesel was particularly useful to him in the period between his two visits to Rome, which corresponded to the most concentrated period of publication for Winckelmann, but this use of a friend to sort out practical problems continued later. For example, in 1767 Winckelmann talked of his enthusiasm for a visit to Sicily. He hoped that Riedesel would be able to arrange permission for drawings to be taken of some of his new friend the Prince Biscari's vase collection (*Sizilien*, 65–73).

Less concretely Riedesel was responsible for the dissemination of Winckelmannian views in other important social circles. His reports of life in Italy and tutelage under Winckelmann to the enlightened Württemberg court must have encouraged debate.[28] He seems to have mentioned Winckelmann often and Winckelmann acknowledged this, thanking Riedesel 'für die Erinnerung an meine Wenigkeit in einer frölichen Gesellschaft' (*Briefe*, ii. 349). It is difficult to establish quite which company is meant here, but we can imagine the pattern which Riedesel's reminiscences must have taken. Similarly we can imagine the

[28] Cf. Constantine, *Early Greek Travellers*, 132 and Rehm, 'Riedesel', 207.

positive impact which they must have made, particularly upon those who had not managed to travel. His little reminders of Italy at least had the potential to spread Winckelmann's doctrines amongst a small but influential group of people.

Riedesel also helped Winckelmann in a more personal way. As a friend and correspondent he provided Winckelmann with an audience not only for his views on art (which are discussed later) but also for his opinions on a number of other subjects. Winckelmann felt no need to be guarded in his comments when he was writing to Riedesel and their relationship seemed to be untouched by the need for reserve or political compromise. This seems to have been an extension of their pattern of conversation when they were together, of which Winckelmann said: 'ich habe mit niemanden mit so ungebundner Freyheit, als mit Ihnen gesprochen' (*Briefe*, iii. 50). But what form did this freedom take? To extend the image used by Winckelmann above, it is clear that Winckelmann was at times bound to maintain a discreet silence about the more negative aspects of life in Rome because of his dependence upon the favour of others. His private correspondence provided him with an outlet for his negative feelings, although this did contain an element of risk. It resided in the fact that his letters were often passed on amongst his friends or at least read out to others. This risk was also present when he spoke openly to Riedesel, since he too passed on the content of the letters. However, his trust in his friend's discretion was clearly very considerable because in his letters he felt able to raise a number of delicate topics.

He discussed, for example, scandalous episodes that were taking place in Italy as well as the shifts in his circle of friends. He particularly enjoyed his associations with adventurers such as Wilkes, whose movements are traced in his letters to Riedesel (*Briefe*, iii. 83, 97, 289). He also felt free to air his very strong views on other people's publications and his prejudices against individuals and nations. These attacks are not unique to his correspondence with Riedesel, but they are perhaps a more substantial feature here than elsewhere.[29] He could also safely complain about his employment. The amount of time demanded by his various occupations in the Vatican and more generally as a guide were also a constant theme. In November 1763 he noted that 'itzo gehet meine Plage in der *Vaticana* an; daher ich sehr wenig Zeit übrig habe' (*Briefe*, ii. 353). Parts of his hectic life-style were, of course, enjoyable but

---

[29] There are numerous examples of the fluctuations in Winckelmann's friendships and of his attacks on individuals and nations. Cf. *Briefe*, ii. 296 (Lami); ii. 311, 353 (Britain); ii. 350 (Duke of Gordon); iii. 7 (Watelet); iii. 50 (Duke of York); iii. 92, 316 (Füsslis).

increasingly he saw his numerous commitments as a burden. In early 1764 he was managing to balance his library work with the pleasurable task of guiding interested compatriots through Rome (*Briefe*, iii. 6). By the end of 1765 he seemed pleased to escape the 'Plackerey' of the library to accompany the Prince of Mecklenburg-Strelitz (*Briefe*, iii. 142). However, we hear in 1766 how his role as guide to this Prince meant that he was unable to guide the Prince of Anhalt-Dessau (*Briefe*, iii. 157). Anhalt-Dessau was robbed of his attention in much the same way as Riedesel was years before. Winckelmann at one point admitted: 'Ich habe mich weniger um Sie [Riedesel] verdient gemacht, als um andere auch nach Ihrer Zeit' (*Briefe*, iii. 82). We are also presented with the problem that the presence of Mecklenburg-Strelitz might prevent Winckelmann from seeing Riedesel on his second trip to Italy (*Briefe*, iii. 142). The delicate balancing act between his various jobs was, of course, difficult to maintain, and every new commitment meant less time for his research and for his friends. On occasions he could say no to new commissions as a guide, but for the most part he was obliged to succumb to pressure from his patrons.[30] He was dependent upon the sponsorship of his patrons, the 'nothdürftig Brod auf Lebenszeit' provided by the Vatican and the supplementary income provided by guiding (*Briefe*, ii. 305). Certainly this meant that his work progressed more slowly than he would have liked, but it had the advantage of providing him with a degree of financial independence. Furthermore the high standing which his various jobs brought with them, plus the increasing access to the highest social circles, helped to support his considerable ego. This pleasure is most evident in his letters to friends in Germany who had no access to this world, but it also features in his letters to Riedesel. In these letters he reveals his pride in his new-found status. In March 1763 he reported his promotion to the position of 'Ober-Aufseher der Alterthümer' after Venuti, along with details of his earnings. He also mentions the possibility of gaining a *scrittorato alla Vaticana*. Significantly he writes about his publication plans and projected period of residence in Rome in the same letter. Clearly both his research and his residence depended upon his ability to guarantee a stable income (*Briefe*, ii. 306). In a letter of May 1763 he signs himself off with the title 'Président des Antiquités de Rome', so revealing his pride in this new appointment (*Briefe*, ii. 321). In October of the same year he mentions the possibility of another promotion but this time one which would require a move to the Prussian court

---

[30] He did manage 'ein rundes Nein' to a German count (*Briefe*, iii. 84).

(*Briefe*, ii. 348). These constant reminders of his 'arrival' as a scholar, including his guiding of dignitaries (even when he dismisses them as pupils) reveal his openess with Riedesel. He seems to have taken great pleasure in the attainment of high status, a fact which is confirmed by his constant reference to new achievements in his letters. He was meticulous in reporting his election to academic societies, the positive reception of his works and even pirate editions of his work whose very existence offered testimony of his standing.

Of course, a price had to be paid for achieving this high degree of success. I mentioned above the hindrance to research and the threat of missing the visits of friends such as Riedesel because of work. The delays to Winckelmann's publication schedule can easily be imagined but the price paid in terms of friendship was also very high. The presence of Mecklenburg-Strelitz was not the only threat to meetings between Winckelmann and Riedesel. Given the very warm declarations of friendship between the two men it is striking how little they saw of each other during Riedesel's second visit. Winckelmann was clearly fully committed at this stage and did not have the freedom to visit friends at will. This kept them apart and one cannot miss the irony in the fact that two men who were brought together through Winckelmann's work as a guide were later kept apart by that same job. This situation also reflects a paradox in Winckelmann's life. The very job which offered him the prospect of freedom also at times robbed him of freedom. There are various references to the fact that Riedesel and Winckelmann were frustrated in their attempts to meet. Even after Mecklenburg-Strelitz's departure the situation was not eased. In February 1767 Winckelmann mourned the impossibility of meeting in Naples:

Ich muß billig mein Schicksal beklagen, daß ich den süßesten meiner Freunde nicht habe genießen können, da er mir nahe war, und daß sich derselbe von mir entfernet, da ich zum Genusse desselben gelangen konnte. Ich kann weder im Sommer, noch verstohlner Weise nach Neapel kommen, und es würde einer Thorheit ähnlich sehen, als ein Verbrecher, unter fremden Schutze dahin zu gehen, wohin mich weder Pflicht noch Nothwendigkeit rufen. (*Briefe*, iii. 237)

The reasons for their failure to get together at this stage did not stem from Winckelmann alone; Riedesel's reluctance to leave Naples is also difficult to explain. As Becker points out they did overcome this difficulty (with Riedesel apparently helping to settle the 'Verstimmungen' of the Neapolitan court with regard to Winckelmann) and they later spent two months together in Naples. This period was one of intensive study and Becker suggests that they visited Portici some twenty times and Pompeii three times, as well as visiting other nearby locations (*Levante*, 26). However, after Winckelmann's departure in mid-November there is no evidence of another meeting. Becker mentions the possibility of a meeting during the carnival of 1768 but there is little evidence to suggest that it took place, apart from Winckelmann's expressed hope that Riedesel would travel up to Rome with Hamilton (*Briefe*, iii. 335, 350, 354). This meant, of course, that the two men did not meet again before Winckelmann's death.

But despite their occasional failures to meet they maintained a high degree of intimacy in their correspondence. They even discuss sex.

Naturally enough the surviving letters from Winckelmann to Riedesel post-date the latter's first visit to Rome. During this visit Riedesel would presumably have become aware of Winckelmann's sexual preferences, and so in their subsequent correspondence there was little reason for Winckelmann to make a secret of them. In the first of the letters he mentions Niccolo Castellani, who was also to feature in subsequent letters (*Briefe*, ii. 296). The boy was in fact first mentioned in a letter to Stosch in 1759. In it Winckelmann asked Stosch to find out the boy's name, although he simultaneously admitted that his interest in the boy was a 'Narrheit'. Winckelmann planned at this stage to dedicate a work to the boy as soon as his work on the Stosch catalogue was complete (*Briefe*, ii. 67). In the letter to Riedesel, which was written just over three years later, his interest in the boy appears not to have waned, and by then he knew his name and something of his history. He was 'aus einem der besten Häuser. Zu meiner Zeit war er etwa 16 Jahr, aber ein vollkommenes Gewächs. Stosch sagte mir in vergangnem Jahre, daß er viel von seiner Schönheit verloren habe' (*Briefe*, ii. 296). Riedesel could now look out for the boy because he was at this time in his home town, Florence. Riedesel's reply to Winckelmann apparently contained confirmation of Castellani's fading beauty since Winckelmann later comments that 'man gehet also gewisser und mit beständigern Ideen in marmornen Schönheiten' (*Briefe*, ii. 312). He was referring directly to the antique head of a faun which still retained its beauty and so could be compared favourably with Castellani.

In this letter we are given some idea of Winckelmann's preferred physical type, namely young men who have not gone beyond 'die Gränzen der Jünglingschaft', or 'des Frühlings unseres Lebens' (*Briefe*, ii. 312). However, these were not merely passive interests. He was also prepared to pursue them in a manner which might cause scandal.³¹ Discussing the same boy in a letter to L. Usteri in September 1763, he declared the innocence of his intentions towards Castellani. In his version 'keine Neigung war so rein als diese' (*Briefe*, ii. 344–5). None the less Usteri appears to have warned him that his interest in the boy could be compromising, causing Winckelmann in turn to reject this danger, or at least dismiss the importance of public criticism since 'im übrigen liegt mir wenig an das was man in Deutschland über diesen Punct von mir denken möchte. In der Geschichte kann ich den strengen Moralisten weit mehr Gelegenheit dazu gegeben haben' (*Briefe*, ii. 345). The point was presumably Winckelmann's declared intention to dedicate a work to Castellani, whom he scarcely knew. Such a dedication would clearly make Winckelmann's interest in the boy public, and the public treatment of Winckelmann's sexuality was likely to be a matter of some delicacy. Despite the fact that it was also essential to his aesthetic, as the reference to the *Geschichte der Kunst* confirms, it remained a matter which had to be dealt with discreetly.

The fact that he was prepared to raise such matters with Riedesel was a sign of the trust that he had in him. Perhaps he felt that Riedesel would be in a better position to understand his pedagogical intentions, since he first got to know Winckelmann as a teacher. Certainly young men feature a good deal in their correspondence. In a letter of October 1763 Winckelmann mentioned the *Abhandlung* dedicated to Berg. He admits in the letter that it was 'etwas frey geschrieben' and also mentions the hope that it will not be seen by any important (potential) patrons (*Briefe*, ii. 349). Given that theoretical aesthetics was not a notoriously controversial field, it is clear that Winckelmann saw the disadvantage even of the implied expression of his sexual interests in a work dealing primarily with aesthetic education. These sexual interests are apparent in the text, although interwoven with the parallel aesthetic concerns. In fact there is a remarkable coalescence of aesthetic and sexual interests in this work as elsewhere in Winckelmann. His aesthetic doctrine demanded that the ideal pupil of art should be captured 'bey angehender Jugend', and determined that sensitivity to art was more likely 'in wohlgebildeten Knaben' than in others. The ideal pupil should also be more sensitive to male than to female beauty (KS 215–16). In the same letter to Riedesel he also mentions his intention 'einen wohlgebildeten Knaben . . . zu mir zu

---

³¹ Cf. *Briefe*, iv. 55 and, in particular, iv. 444 for a draft of a love letter, conceivably by Winckelmann. If his it would suggest that he had not ruled out a direct approach to the boy.

nehmen und zu erziehen, um mir in demselben eine Gesellschaft zu bilden' (*Briefe*, ii. 349).[32]

Much later, in January 1767, Winckelmann wrote to Riedesel in Naples suggesting that he should write to him 'ob Sie Schönheiten unter dem weiblichen Geschlechte entdecken. In unserm Geschlechte habe ich dieselben gefunden' (*Briefe*, ii. 234). Again his interest in young men corresponds with his academic interests, in this case the attempt to discover remnants of Greek beauty in contemporary Italy. Rehm indicates the ways in which this sort of observation is incorporated into his publications and mentioned in his correspondence (*Briefe*, iii. 494). But it was not just an academic task; it was a pleasure.

All of the young men mentioned were subject to time in the same manner as Castellani. Given Winckelmann's preference for more juvenile beauty this meant that he was constantly losing interest in these boys as they grew older. One way of preventing the onset of adolescence was castration. Winckelmann does not seem to have suggested surgical intervention in specific cases, but in a letter to Riedesel of May 1763 he mentions the general theme and doing so uses a familiar metaphor, namely that of the passing spring. The image was used of Niccolo Castellani only one month earlier (*Briefe*, ii. 312–13):

Die Flüchtigkeit des Frühlings unserer Jahre hat mir, wie Ihnen, manche betrübte Betrachtung verursachet, sonderlich da mir keine billige Proportion unter den verschiedenen Altern des Lebens zu seyn scheinet; die schöne Jugend ist mehrentheils, wie der heurige Frühling, kaum zu merken. Hierzu fanden die Morgenländer in unserm Geschlechte durch die Verschneidung ein Mittel, und vielleicht hatte die Verschneidung der jungen Mädgen bey ihnen eben die Wirkung. (*Briefe*, ii. 320)

Castration seems a radical answer to the problem of transient youth. But it does reflect some of Winckelmann's preferences. This interest in the shape of pre-pubescent boys might suggest that Winckelmann's sexual inclination is paedophile rather than simply homosexual. His interest in more mature males such as Berg would tend to contradict this, but the idea receives some confirmation in other letters in which he expresses his admiration for a child ballerina; and his praise of hermaphrodite forms in his published works would also indicate that his preferences were not sexually specific.[33] Of course, these interests could also be explained in

---

[32] Another productive synthesis is suggested by the phrase 'eine Gesellschaft bilden'.
[33] Cf. *Werke*, ii. 102; iv. 334; vi. 94; vii. 214; and especially iv. 76–8. The ballerina is mentioned at *Briefe*, i. 440.

art-theoretical rather than sexual terms. As was mentioned earlier, Winckelmann's notion of beauty was based to a large extent on theories of silhouette, closely related to Hogarth's work on the serpentine line. In the pre-pubescent child the lines of the body are gently serpentine and to this extent they are to be preferred to the more muscular lines of the adult male or the more curvaceous figure of the mature female.

The references to the young boys and to castration, however brief, assume an understanding of the underlying issues on the part of the correspondent. Indeed Winckelmann indicates that the two men share one opinion on the passing of youth. He says that it affects 'mir, wie Ihnen [Riedesel]' and causes them both to reflect. Winckelmann's confidence in expressing such views in his letters suggests that he also expected his friend to understand the subtext to his statements, namely the way in which sexual preference can inform aesthetic judgements.

It was not unknown for Winckelmann to offer very different views of his friendships, depending on his audience. Often people with whom he dealt respectfully face to face were dismissed behind their backs. This occurred only once with regard to Riedesel. Riedesel at one point found himself caught up in the delivery of some free copies of the *Sendschreiben von den herculanischen Entdeckungen*. In a letter to Walther of July 1763 Winckelmann noted sarcastically that 'ich habe nichts besonders zu schreiben, als Ihnen zu melden, daß das Paket der Sendschreiben glücklich verlohren gegangen ist; Herr Wagner macht sich loß, weil ich es dem Hrn. von Riedesel zu übermachen aufgetragen, und dieser, an welchen ich mit nachdrücklicher Feder geschrieben, schämet zu antworten' (*Briefe*, ii. 330). Otherwise his references to Riedesel are uniformly positive. Riedesel was, in Winckelmann's view, a 'liebenswürdige und tugendhafte Person', or a 'Patriot', whose work was 'lehrreich' (*Briefe*, iii. 271, 277). Some of these epithets are then recombined in a letter to Francke in which Riedesel is portrayed as 'ein würdiger Patriot, mit einer großen tugendhaften Seele begabet, und von Vermögen und Stand' (*Briefe*, iii. 314). In a letter to Heyne in January 1768, Winckelmann seems almost to suggest that he and Riedesel share a mission:

Der Deutsche, dessen Namen Sie zu wissen verlangen, will nicht genannt seyn. Er ist ein freyer Reichsstand, und hält sich nun zum zweytenmal in Italien auf. Er ist mein Freund, und mein Herz wallt ihm entgegen, so oft ich an ihn gedenke; denn er ist einige Monate zu Neapel. Er ist ein Patriot, nicht weniger als ich, ob er gleich von Franzosen erzogen, und zu Paris geraume Zeit gewesen ist. Er hat sich von mir erbitten lassen, eine ausführliche Beschreibung seiner Reise durch

Sicilien und Großgriechenland, und zwar in Deutscher Sprache, mir von jedem Orte seines dortigen Aufenthalts zuzuschicken, welches ihm besser im Französischen gelungen wäre. Ich werde dieselbe in der Schweiz, wie sie ist, drucken lassen, und Sie werden daraus ersehen, was annoch vorhanden ist. Ich erwarte denselben in weniger Zeit zu Rom, um mit ihm von seiner Reise nach Constantinopel vorher zu sprechen. Der Reise wird sein Name nicht vorgesetzt. (*Briefe*, iii. 359)

This statement reinforces our view of their friendship. The phrase 'mein Herz wallt ihm entgegen' is certainly more powerful than many of the formulaic expressions of friendship mentioned earlier. The physicality of the image relates it more closely to that of the expanding heart as a symbol of friendship. It also gives us some idea of their working relationship, which was built upon the foundation of friendship and depended upon mutual trust. The passage also makes it clear that Winckelmann used Riedesel as a source of information. He was not as free to travel as Riedesel and so he used Riedesel as an observer. In Sicily Riedesel did Winckelmann the favour (suggested by the phrase 'sich erbitten lassen') of describing the ancient sites. His confidence in Riedesel is reflected in the apparently bland claim that in his work the reader will find 'was annoch vorhanden ist'. Winckelmann is confident that Riedesel will record accurately. The fact that Riedesel was such a loyal pupil of Winckelmann that he failed to notice a great deal, particularly from the Middle Ages, is naturally overlooked.[34] Winckelmann was not just confident in his ability to record information. He also thought that Riedesel expressed himself well enough for the book to be published 'wie sie ist'.[35] Given Winckelmann's interest in language and the expression of ideas this suggests a very high regard for Riedesel's work.

However, their working relationship was clearly not based only on the one-way movement of information, from Riedesel to Winckelmann. There are very strong indications in this passage of the power which Winckelmann had over Riedesel as a teacher. He was apparently not automatically qualified to make the high-grade observations which he made in Sicily. When he mentions Riedesel's planned trip to Greece he also mentions his expectation of seeing him 'um mit ihm von seiner

---

[34] This matter is considered at length in my treatment of *Sizilien*. Of course, from Winckelmann's perspective such oversights constituted good taste.

[35] The extent of Winckelmann's editorial intervention is unknown. He planned an introduction to the work (*Briefe*, iii. 267, 274). He also suggested that he would edit the text where necessary (*Briefe*, iii. 286). We know that the introduction was not provided; we cannot know how much Winckelmann added, although we know that he did not have time to edit the whole (*Briefe*, iii. 373–4).

Reise nach Constantinopel vorher zu sprechen'. There can be little doubt as to the likely nature of this projected conversation which, as far as we know, never took place. Winckelmann would have prepared him for what he was about to see by restating his methods of assessing art, both historically and aesthetically. He would have provided Riedesel with a methodology for his studies. The fact that they did not meet and that after Winckelmann's death Riedesel was forced to work more independently was to have striking consequences for his writing. The planned preparations for the Greek trip were nothing new. Before the Sicilian journey Riedesel had undergone a period of training, an aesthetic education, with Winckelmann dutifully providing a bibliography on Sicily. Their letters, as we shall see, contain very strong indications that Riedesel was familiar with many of Winckelmann's theories, and so that his education was progressing. But before we deal in detail with Riedesel's treatment of art we must cite the final, most powerful evidence of the friendship which enabled them to work together.

'Geh hin und sieh!'—this demand was, as we have seen, central to Winckelmann's approach to art (KS 233). The critic had to learn to look with his own eyes. It was therefore a mark of the greatest respect when Winckelmann entrusted the business of seeing Sicily to Riedesel. Together they were able to achieve more than either of them could individually. Without Riedesel Winckelmann would never have 'seen' Sicily. To borrow an image used earlier the two men together form a more complete whole.[36] However, their interaction was meant to go further than helping one another with their work. We gather from the letters that they were in fact planning to work on the same publication. Riedesel intended at one stage to provide a French translation of the *Geschichte der Kunst*. Given Winckelmann's fussy attitude towards translation and his desire to preserve the quality of his language, this shows remarkable confidence in Riedesel.[37] The possibility of the translation was discussed during 1765 when Winckelmann's reputation was at its peak and so his work most likely to be pirated. The prospect of using the French-educated Riedesel to counteract this tendency constitutes a fine tribute to their friendship and also to Riedesel's understanding of Winckelmann's work.

---

[36] Rehm deals with Winckelmann's use of material provided by Riedesel at *Briefe*, iii. 534–5.
[37] There are thirty-seven references to translations of the *Geschichte der Kunst* in the third volume of Winckelmann's letters alone. See *Briefe*, iii. 605.

The visual arts and related topics

The five main sources of information on Riedesel's approach to art are clearly the *Briefe*, *Sendschreiben eines Liebhabers*, *Sizilien*, *Levante*, and the Scottish letters. The texts will be examined in this order in Sections 3–7 and each discussion will be divided into the following subsections:

(*a*) General thematic correspondences. Matters perhaps not directly related to the visual arts but with some bearing upon their understanding.
(*b*) Theories of art production.
(*c*) Historical stylistics.
(*d*) Enthusiasms: the moments of high aesthetic engagement.

3. THE LETTERS

(*a*) The remarkable feature of the letters is the small amount of space given to discussion of the arts. Winckelmann's side of the correspondence is primarily concerned with his career, practical arrangements of various kinds, and casual discussion of the latest society scandals; only occasionally does he mention the arts. We remember that in discussing Castellani Winckelmann regretted how age ruined beauty and by contrast then praised the permanence of the arts, but this reference could scarcely be described as more than incidental. Many of the other shared interests that emerge are unilluminating commonplaces. There are, however, some striking omissions. We miss any discussion of general geographical/political/religious issues which feature in Riedesel's own work and were fundamental to Winckelmann's understanding of art history. Such issues were not only interesting in their own right but also helped to explain the nature of the artistic superstructure. The only mentions of politics in the letters are directly tied to comments on the associated artistic culture in a way that confirms this theory (see Section (*b*)).

(*b*) There is some limited evidence to suggest that discussions of cultural history in the letters were determined by the production theory which we know from Winckelmann's work.[38] Winckelmann, like many of his contemporaries, saw a connection between artistic production in a given society and that society's geographical location and economic and political structures. In the letters to Riedesel he does not refer to art

---

[38] We know this theory to be common to the period. See Ch. 1.

production but does discuss, on a similar basis, the connection between environment and responsiveness to art. He doubts whether the Swiss are likely to respond well to art (*Briefe*, iii. 92). The Saxons have more cultural advantages indeed 'in Sachsen würden Sie [Riedesel] mehr Geschmack antreffen, auch bey Leuten, welche Italien nicht gesehen haben; aber Sie würden itzo der Meister derselben seyn können' (*Briefe*, ii. 348–9). The reasons for the relative failure of these places are not made explicit but one major component is their distance from the 'Mitte' of Greece, or the world cultural centre Rome. The physical climates of Northern Germany and Switzerland could not be further from the ideal envisaged by Winckelmann.[39] The political organization of the countries may also have been unsuited to the arts, although again we can only infer this. Neither could provide the most important aspect of environment, namely the stock of ancient art upon which the aesthete depended for his training. But to reach Italy was not enough. In dealing with the current poor state of scholarship and the arts in Florence Winckelmann comes close to identifying the political requirements for cultural bloom, noting that 'itzo da kein Hof mehr daselbst ist, sind die Künste gänzlich gefallen mit sammt der Gelehrsamkeit' (*Briefe*, ii. 296). The assertion of the role of the court in encouraging the arts is closely related to his instruction that the student should head for cultural and political centres, and preferably for Rome, discussed above (Section 1(*b*)). He tells Riedesel that 'es ist alles im Ueberfluß hieselbst'. This plenitude was, in his view, a prime characteristic of the great cultural centres which were also economically successful (*Briefe*, iii. 49). More concretely, he feared that any distance from Rome also marked distance from the best source of beautiful objects (*Briefe*, iii. 6).

In a very abbreviated form these few comments reflect one of Winckelmann's central theories. The fact that he was able to talk in these terms to Riedesel suggests some familiarity with the material on the latter's part. This suggestion is given some weight by the fact that Winckelmann also referred to attempts to identify different types of beauty in human beings in a joint undertaking with Riedesel.[40] The distinctions made between different types of beauty were also based upon a climate theory, according to which an Egyptian woman exposed to excessive heat will be less beautiful than a Greek raised in a more moderate climate. Beautiful

---

[39] The notion of the 'Mitte' is particularly associated with Walther Bosshard and his book *Winckelmann: Aesthetik der Mitte* (Zürich, 1960).

[40] See Section 2(*b*) above. Also the attempt to identify 'die Erycinische Schönheiten' (*Briefe*, iii. 268).

models were also one of the important prerequisites for artistic production. But this evidence of Riedesel's exposure to the production theory is superficial and would not alone provide any proof of a far-reaching aesthetic education. The discussion and employment of the theory does not advance beyond many contemporaries.

(c) Most of the treatment of the arts in this correspondence takes the form of reports on new discoveries. This is a logical consequence of Winckelmann's position at the source of great art, writing to people who were less fortunate. But his remarks lack detail. Even when a beautiful mosaic was unearthed in his presence he simply referred to a likely future publication on the subject (*Briefe*, iii. 28). The fact that such a challenging aesthetic experience was left almost without commentary suggests two things. First, that he was reluctant to express his judgement imperfectly and secondly that these letters were really little more than notes intended to whet the appetite of his correspondent. Therefore he rarely did more than allude to the historical and stylistic qualities of works of art. Some of the praise was very unspecific; he merely suggested various degrees of beauty, the highest of which was achieved by a cameo which was 'der schönste Stein vielleicht auf der Welt' (*Briefe*, iii. 22). Of course, a work of art could, in Winckelmann's terms, only be beautiful if it complied with certain very specific criteria. To that extent Winckelmann could benefit from a form of shorthand; he could suggest stylistic or historical features by the use of simple epithets. According to this scheme things became less beautiful the less they conformed to certain ideals derived from Greek art. He would occasionally indicate the nature of any move away from the Greek ideal with a little additional information. The Pallast Pitti was spoiled by the 'Toscanische Begriffe' in its architecture; these undermined the noble simplicity to be expected of the best art in whichever form. Similarly Florentine paintings were described as 'ängstlich', a term which stands in direct contrast to the calm which Winckelmann required of art (*Briefe*, ii. 296). More specifically Riedesel was expected to understand what it meant for something to be 'im ältesten Griechischen Stil' according to Winckelmann's own historical categories (*Briefe*, ii. 349). The fact that the subtext of such comments was, we must assume, clear to Riedesel indicates that he had very considerable knowledge of Winckelmann's art value-scheme.

On occasions Winckelmann clearly felt the need to reinforce his judgements on the quality of works with significant comparisons. At one point he praised a Faun's head 'welcher alle hohe Schönheiten, die ich bisher betrachten können, übertrifft' (*Briefe*, ii. 312). We are naturally tempted to think of the Apollo Belvedere, the Laocoön, or the Belvedere Torso in this connection, since in his descriptions of them Winckelmann was attempting precisely to describe 'hohe Schönheiten'. In this case the connection to the other statues was not made explicit but later he did use their example. He saw a statue of a prisoner 'welcher nicht weit unter den Laocoön zu setzen ist' (*Briefe*, ii. 312). By this time Winckelmann's description of the statue had long been published and so the qualities— the stoicism, the calm in the face of adversity—of the prisoner statue could easily be projected through the comparison with Laocoön. He used this method again later. The head of a statue of Antinous was of the highest quality since 'nach dem Apollo und dem Laocoon ist dieser Kopf gewiß das schönste unter der Sonne' (*Briefe*, iii. 125). We are meant to think immediately of Winckelmann's views of these statues rather than of their general properties.

He could also characterize the style of a work by reference to an artist whose work he had already examined in publications. He described a Venus figure 'die alle übrige Venus, ja die Florentinische bey weitem übertrifft, und welche des Praxiteles würdig ist' (*Briefe*, ii. 44). These characterizations of works were, however, by no means exhaustive and Winckelmann appears to have been perfectly aware of this because he referred Riedesel to his publications for fuller treatments of some subjects (*Briefe*, iii. 68, 126). These letters were often hastily composed and, in any case, brief, many of them intended to inspire Riedesel's second visit. There can scarcely have been a more efficient way to encourage someone with Riedesel's antiquarian interests than to offer him inviting glimpses of the latest discoveries. This treatment of the arts also left room for the main concerns of the letters which were rather different.

(*d*) There is clear evidence that Riedesel was not merely a good listener to Winckelmann. On numerous occasions Winckelmann appears to be answering questions from Riedesel, although for the most part these are technical in nature (*Briefe*, ii. 312, 313, 323, 353; iii. 44, 282, 289). These questions hint at an active mind but the only evidence of any enthusiasm or engagement we have is secondhand, through Winckelmann, who implied that Riedesel had an 'Empfindung' which was absent in his Swiss friends (*Briefe*, iii. 92). From what we know of the nature of this correspondence there seemed to be little opportunity to express aesthetic engagement. It seems almost wholly absent on Winckelmann's side, although we hear at one point that 'es ist vor wenig Tagen ein Kopf einer Pallas zum Vorschein gekommen, welcher alles an Schönheit übertrifft, was das menschliche Auge sehen können, und was in eines Menschen

Herz und Gedanken gekommen. Ich blieb wie von Stein, da ich ihn sahe' (*Briefe*, iii. 50). This looks very much like the preparatory stage for aesthetic engagement, associated with feelings of impotence in dealing with the work, which we saw in the torso description. He describes his initial response to the same statue elsewhere in even more striking terms, noting that 'ich blieb stumm, taub und wie sinnenlos, da ich denselben erblickte' (*Briefe*, iii. 55 (to Francke)). It contains the promise of an attempt to see more than we expect from 'das menschliche Auge' and to explore the metaphysical allusions in art. The letter cannot accommodate such an investigation, but at least provides some indication of the intensity of Winckelmann's responses to art. We must look elsewhere for any parallel enthusiasm on Riedesel's part.

4. THE SENDSCHREIBEN VON DER REISE EINES LIEBHABERS DER KÜNSTE NACH ROM AN HERRN BARON VON RIEDESEL

This text presents the same difficulties as the letters. We do not have Riedesel's own comments but remarks aimed at him, this time with the additional difficulty that he never received them. This document remained a fragment and was related to an unfulfilled project involving *Römische Briefe* to be addressed to Winckelmann's friends.[41] Winckelmann admitted that this basic introduction to Rome was not appropriate for Riedesel who already knew the city well (KS 203). The important thing was apparently to be the dedication to Riedesel as a sign of friendship, rather than the content of the work. He did point out, however, that he covered ground in the *Sendschreiben* that he and Riedesel had discussed (KS 204). To this extent it can give us some idea of the preparation Winckelmann provided for Riedesel.

Because of the specific nature of the material covered in this document there is no discussion here of more general topics (*a*). Furthermore the work contains no references to the production theory. It does contain a basic and incomplete guide to Roman geography and history but no connection is made between these environmental conditions and the art that they produced (*b*). It does, however, contain some indication of the way to approach works of art.

(*c*) This fragment only provides guidelines to the treatment of architecture. Conveniently this reflects Riedesel's major interest in Greece

[41] See Rehm's notes at KS 449; *Briefe*, iv. 431. Also KS 186–95.

and Magna Graecia. Winckelmann recommends that 'in der Baukunst sind die Form und Ordnung der Bauart, die Zier<lichkeit>rathen und die Materien zu betrachten, und hier könte ich in Absicht der Alten auf meine Anmerkungen über die Baukunst verweisen, man kan aber in wenig Anzeigen die Beobachtungen des Liebhabers leiten' (KS 207). He was here picking up where he had to leave off in the *Abhandlung*, which could not accommodate detailed treatment of individual art-forms. He was providing a practical schedule for describing a building and it was clearly like the one used by Riedesel, whose works contain much detail of the features mentioned above. There is also an indication that a fuller methodology is to be found in Winckelmann's systematic publications. The extent to which Riedesel took this bibliographical hint, with his knowledge supplemented by exposure to the author himself, will be clear from my treatment of his books. In this *Sendschreiben* Winckelmann offers examples of some architectural styles along with clues for making more subtle stylistic/qualitative distinctions between buildings. One of the features to be checked in looking at Roman buildings was the amount of decoration since '<die Zierlichkeit oder> die Zierrathen und deren Überfluß an Basen der Säulen und an dem Gebälke zeugen von der Zeit der Kayser, und je verschwenderischer dieselben sind, desto später ist die Zeit derselben' (KS 208). This was not only a historical judgement but also a qualitative one. Such 'late' works clearly deviated from the ideal architectural simplicity described in the *Anmerkungen über die Baukunst der Alten* (*Werke*, ii. 440–71). The praise of the grand and simple over the fussily detailed influenced Riedesel very profoundly.

Naturally this text lacks any indication of Riedesel's engagement with art (*d*). It was not even intended for people whose aesthetic education was at a stage which would allow informed response to art. The only comments on Riedesel's particular sensibility do not sound too encouraging. As we have heard before, he exhibited 'vorläufige Einsicht' in Rome and took 'großen Nutzen' from the experience. This is hardly the terminology of revelation.

5. SIZILIEN

(*a*) Riedesel does not focus exclusively upon the arts in his guide to Sicily. The novelty of the undertaking meant that he reported everything of interest, or at least everything of interest to him. Many of the things reported are largely incidental and fall into no obvious pattern. Other topics are raised with some regularity and so can be assumed to be of importance to Riedesel. Correspondences with Winckelmann could be suggested almost anywhere, from Riedesel's obvious liking for a tipple, to his occasional dismissal of the French, but the most substantial links outside the arts were in two areas, religion and politics.

Riedesel's attitude towards organized religion was sceptical in the manner of an eighteenth-century rationalist. There are numerous references in the text to his doubts about the misuse of religious faith. He was particularly hard on the church as a manager of funds and property donated by believers. He saw the church misusing alms and mismanaging estates (*Sizilien*, 118). The main priority of churchmen was apparently to guarantee their own comfort; the successful ones were no more than 'reiche Müßiggänger', exploiting 'der Aberglaube und der Fanatismus' of their supporters (*Sizilien*, 102). Many of the faithful were impressed by miracles. Riedesel had very little time for these and could not look at the Madonna de Finibus, 'da ich mir nicht Andacht genug zutraute' (*Sizilien*, 117). When he did take miraculous claims more seriously he was disappointed. The corpse of St Nicholas of Bari apparently still perspired profusely but Riedesel could not accept this, saying: 'ich steckte meinen Kopf auch hinein, und hörte das Geräusche einer kleinen Röhre von Wasser, wodurch ich alsobald von dem Wunder überzeuget ward' (*Sizilien*, 127). He shows no more respect on other occasions (e.g. *Sizilien*, 52, 63). His antipathy to superstition is clear in his brief account of the titles of two Kings of Sicily:- 'Wilhelm der Gute ist so benennet, weil er abergläubisch und den Pfaffen ergeben; der andere hat den Zunamen des Bösen bekommen, weil er weiser, vernünftiger und von Vorurtheilen befreyet war. Dieses Exempel bestärket mich in der Nachläßigkeit des allgemeinen Rufes, und der Verachtung desselben' (*Sizilien*, 22). His creed seems to have been a brand of liberal humanism based upon the hope of reasonable organization of life in this world. This meant that he was sceptical about those who did things in the hope of reward in the next world and preferred those who could administer the present. These views make him very much a man of his age and do not reveal a specific debt to Winckelmann. This is not to say that these views were not shared by Winckelmann. The casting off of inhibitions connected with conventional religion was a necessary prerequisite for aesthetic insight in the Winckelmannian manner, which demanded a less doctrinaire understanding of patterns of spiritual enlightenment than those provided by the contemporary clergy. Riedesel was happy to question the prevailing doctrine but his objections were primarily practical and critical. Winckelmann's attitude was more constructive. He hoped for harmonized physical and spiritual development in mankind, after the model of the ancient Greeks. Strangely, he still said that the highest beauty was in God. As we saw earlier, he did not define his God in a way that would reveal him as a Catholic or a Protestant; in fact God seems to be used as a convenient metaphor for an absolute, ideal principle, closely related to the Platonic 'idea'. The most accurate expression of the 'idea' was to be found in the representation of Greek divinities in statues—again scarcely the doctrinaire Christian view. This flexible attitude to the nature of the Absolute was reflected in a flexible attitude towards narrower issues of religious doctrine. To that extent the fact he was publicly a Catholic was of little importance to him. His famous statement to the effect that he still sang Protestant hymns in Rome would confirm this opinion.[42] Winckelmann's exploitation of the wealth and power of churchmen to his own ends could similarly be seen as a reflection of a cynical attitude to the Church like that shown by Riedesel. But Winckelmann's cynicism was born of a positive impulse, namely the desire to supplant conventional spirituality with a new brand of aestheticism. We must doubt whether Riedesel's motivation had the same source.

Riedesel's background would make us expect many of his interests to be political. This expectation is confirmed in the text itself; Riedesel deals not only with aspects of the political systems in Magna Graecia but also with the economic and social consequences of those systems. These interests did not, however, mark a point of divergence between Riedesel and Winckelmann. In his role as editor, or prospective editor of the book Winckelmann made no mention of a need to alter or remove the political component of the *Sendschreiben* or the observations on economics. In part this is because in Winckelmann's view of art history politics had a very important role to play (see section (*b*) below). However, where politics is mentioned in more general terms, and not related directly to developments in the arts we might expect a degree of divergence in interest between the two men. On closer inspection this seems not to be the case.

Riedesel makes it clear from a very early stage in his guide to Sicily that he will not focus exclusively on the arts. He will report 'auch andere Gegenstände betreffendes' (*Sizilien*, 19). He is in part referring to his observation of natural curiosities, customs, attire, etc. But a large part of his time was taken up with observation of the political and economic status quo. The fact that the political organization of Sicily and Southern

---

[42] See *Briefe*, iii. 566; iv. 249.

Italy was so fragmentary (despite the presence of an overall ruler) meant that he was offered a large number of different situations for comparative study. The starting-point was always direct observation of the agricultural and so, by extension, economic health of the particular province. The most consistent feature of this text, alongside the search for remnants of Greek culture, is the reporting of production figures and trade balances. Indeed the two main interests stand side by side throughout the text in a manner that suggests that the author felt that he was recording things of comparable historical interest. Typical of this approach is his discussion of the worthwhile things to see in the vicinity of Messina. In fact there were very few, but Riedesel reveals his interests even when expressing his dissatisfaction. He reports that 'von Altherthümern ist gar nichts auf dieser Küste erhalten, und die Cultur des Landes ist auch vernachläßiget; weshalben ich in Meßina meiner [*sic*] Wanderschaft um diese Insel... fortgesetzet habe' (*Sizilien*, 93–4). The two sides of his approach to the sights of Sicily could not, however, always be kept in balance. Inevitably different places were interesting for different reasons, and where antiquities were absent Riedesel did not hesitate to report predominantly or exclusively on political/economic questions (e.g. *Sizilien*, 107). But for the most part the two matters were reported side by side. The treatment of the city of Palermo as the first major site provides us with an indication of the pattern that will follow. The core of the description is, of course, the survey of the important archaeological material and art. This is surrounded by reports on the economic health of the region (*Sizilien*, 20–3). Here the economic report is only brief, showing total income, details of the distribution of that income, and population figures which are meant as an indication of economic success. On other occasions the treatment is more profound, particularly in respect of the sources of income in agriculture and trade. Riedesel was particularly meticulous in reporting local specialities; he tells us about shellfish that produce valuable fibres, and about giant chestnut trees, amongst many other things (*Sizilien*, 113–14, 82).

These are not, however, neutral reports or attempts to provide a little general knowledge. Riedesel's observations served to confirm his political beliefs and these often made him critical of the prevailing situation. The general picture that we are offered of the economic climate in Magna Graecia is by no means positive. Riedesel saw a high degree of unrealized potential in local agriculture and trade. For the most part the climatic conditions were right and the trade potential evident. Similarly there was often evidence of an historical precedent for economic success; the archaeological remains, in particular, suggested that larger populations once inhabited the area (*Sizilien*, 45, 54, 89). The general picture is one of decay when compared with earlier achievements.

Riedesel went to some lengths to identify the precise reasons for instances of economic underachievement. These were usually traced back to parallel instances of political failure, namely maladministration of the economy. The administrative duties at this time fell to the local aristocrats/landowners, although they had to work within a financial framework imposed by the king. Despite the allegiance of class, Riedesel openly criticized the contributions of the local aristocracy and the general financial mismanagement by the crown. Agriculture could easily have been developed if conditions had been provided to encourage production, but this rarely happened.

It was not the case in the vicinity of Lecce, for here 'die Produckte und die Fruchtbarkeit des Landes, nebst der Emsigkeit und Geschicklichkeit der Einwohner, könnte diese Provinz zu der reichsten des Königreichs und einer der besten in der Welt machen, wenn solches nicht durch die schlechteingerichtete Finanzordnung verhindert würde' (*Sizilien*, 121). The draining effect of the various taxation and quota schemes upon the local economies and the allied disincentive to produce are treated critically by Riedesel. In Lecce the problem affected most acutely the cultivation and processing of a type of tobacco. He reports that 'jeder Besitzer von Lande oder Erdreich kann nur eine gewisse Anzahl Pflanzen ziehen, welche er stückweise an den König veraccisiren muß; die übrigen sind Contrebande, und werden vernichtet, wenn die Pachter des Tabacks visitiren lassen. Dieser Taback, Flachs, Hanf, Baumwolle, und das Oel, welches sehr häufig wächst, könnten die vortheilhafteste Ausfuhr in diesem Lande verursachen, wenn nicht widrige Auflagen dieses verhinderten' (*Sizilien*, 121). Here the criticism is aimed at the King and in Malta, in a parallel case, he points out the injustice caused by unfair taxation on the part of the 'Großmeister', whose incomes amount to 'ohngefähr 18,000 französische Louis d'Or; diese erhält er von einigen Domänen in der Insel, von denen Annaten der Commanderien, und von dem ungerechten Wucher des Getraides, wovon er das Monopolium hat, und das er so theuer verkauffet als er will; weshalben, unerachtet das Volk keine Taxen und Auflagen entrichtet, dasselbe doch in der Theure des Brodtes dem Großmeister eine grosse Abgabe zahlt' (*Sizilien*, 49–50). The exploitation of local workers is a common theme in the text. In his account of Agrigento he includes a full paragraph on the squalid conditions experienced by farm-workers whose lives could easily be changed for the better if more land was made available for them to work.

> Der Feldbauer oder Landmann besonders ist genöthigt, elend zu leben, weil die Reichen die Felder allein besitzen, und die Mönsche besonders lieber die Erde unbebauet lassen, als viel dafür ausgeben; der Taglöhner im Felde gewinnet nur 15 Neapol. Grani des Tages mit saurem Schweisse. Wenn eine gute Regierung die Ordnung, Gerechtigkeit und Gleichheit hier herstellte, würde dieses der glücklichste Winkel der Erde seyn. (*Sizilien*, 43)

The underlying principle which informs Riedesel's views appears to be the desire to maximize any potential, whether of the land or the man working it; and the contemporary government and taxation systems did little to encourage this. Interesting here is the inclusion of another brand of offender against a sensible socio-economic order, namely the Church. Church and aristocracy made their mistakes in tandem and abused their power in similar ways. This theme emerges most powerfully when Riedesel looks down at Sicily from Mount Etna upon a scene of neglect:

> Hier hatte ich Ursache, über den elenden Zustand des jetzigen Siciliens, in Vergleichung des alten, zu seufzen; so viele Städte, so viele verschiedene Völker, so viele Reichthümer sind vernichtet; kaum die ganze Insel hat so viele Einwohner als Siracusa allein vor Zeiten hatte, 1,200,000. Menschen; so viele herrliche Gegenden, welche Frucht brachten, sind wüste aus Mangel der Arbeiter; so viele geraume Seehafen ohne Schiffe, aus Mangel des Handels; so viele Menschen mangeln Brod, weil die Edelleute und Mönsche alle Güter besitzen! (*Sizilien*, 77)

The scene is one of systematic neglect of the land, collapse of the employment market, and failure to exercise sensible political leadership. A further measure of his general dissatisfaction can be seen in the second *Sendschreiben*. Riedesel travelled through the very fertile land between Avellino and Naples and saw happy people and productive fields, in very stark contrast to the spectacle from Mount Etna. However, rather than celebrate this state of affairs, he points out that it is freak result of favourable conditions and exists despite the prevailing political situation because 'die Bevölkerung, der schöne Feldbau, der Ueberfluß an Lebensmitteln, der Anblick glücklicher Menschen, alles zeuget von dem Wohlbefinden dieses Landes: Wie noch viel seliger könnten die Einwohner desselben leben, wenn eine weise Regierung dazu beytragen wollte!' (*Sizilien*, 139) Even agricultural success was not enough for Riedesel; alone it meant nothing. The aim was to maximize the freedom of the population, and economic success was apparently only part of the prescription for achieving this; it had to be accompanied by the 'Ordnung, Gerechtigkeit und Gleichheit', mentioned above, which the contemporary administration failed to provide (*Sizilien*, 43). Quite what measures he envisaged it is difficult to say. Certainly his approach to the improvement of conditions sounds very modern and politically very liberal; but to that extent they are typical also of many of his enlightened contemporaries who sought a more reasonable and equitable exploitation of natural resources and human labour. However, whilst the most obvious source for these sceptical assessments of the status quo in Magna Graecia is to be found in the thinking of the Enlightenment another major impulse comes from the presence, at the back of his mind, of an idealized vision of Greece whose great achievements provide a benchmark against which to measure those of subsequent eras. This ideal image was not incompatible with enlightened thinking; arguably it represents a crystallization of contemporary theory, projected back into the Greek world. But Riedesel's reliance upon this benchmark is unusually strong and betrays the influence of his tutor Winckelmann, who took the principle further than the contemporaries described in Chapter 1.

The constant comparison of modern cities with their idealized ancient equivalents provides a more negative view of the contemporary situation than would simple observation, without the benefit of a convenient historical yardstick. At points Riedesel reveals his direct sources of information about the previous state of Magna Graecia, but on the whole he mixes information from the limited ancient and modern literature on Sicily with his own observations of archaeological remains, which often amend accepted views.[43] But the exact details of the source material were not as important to him as the basic fact that the history of this area was a Greek history. After all the inspiration for the trip was the search for the Greek past in the archaeology and art of the region and as it manifested itself in the appearance, customs, and costumes of the contemporary population, an undertaking directly inspired by Winckelmann.

If Riedesel accepted Winckelmann's view of Greek history then his approach, like Winckelmann's, will have been dominated by an idealized view of Periclean Athens. This period represented for Winckelmann the culmination of Greek artistic culture. And this culture reflected the prevailing economy and the political system which were assumed to be at their best during this period. Such assumptions about Athens could

---

[43] Sources mentioned include Virgil, Diodorus, Strabo, Cicero, Vitruvius, Pancrazi, d'Orville, Fazellus, Cluvers, and Gruter. He also used the spoken testimony of, for example, Biscari.

themselves easily be challenged, but Winckelmann's view of Greek history becomes still more problematic when he projects the imagined qualities of a fraction of Greek culture onto Greek culture as a whole. This sort of historical delusion *vis-à-vis* the Greeks, which allows only a broad positive assessment of their achievements, is also a feature of Riedesel's writing. Indeed this whole area of Winckelmann's theory was clearly very familiar to Riedesel as we shall see particularly in Section (*b*), where we deal with Riedesel's treatment of art production. However, parts of it were also taken over into his treatment of topics, like the Sicilian economy, which were not in the first instance examined in their connection with the arts. Here his generalized view of the Greeks—for the most part known as 'die Alten' or identified by the adjective 'alt'—which was not tied to any specific historical period, but based on an interpretation (Winckelmann's) of Periclean Athens, allowed him to form a composite picture of past successes, compared to which any modern achievements would pale into insignificance.

This approach clearly affects Riedesel's analysis of the contemporary situation in Magna Graecia. In the text he maps the decline of the Sicilian agrarian economy and trading system. Represented graphically, with a verticle scale measuring economic performance and a horizontal scale measuring time, his view of Sicilian economic history would show a line descending from top left to bottom right. The position suggested by the points at the bottom right-hand end of the graph could be illustrated by reference to Riedesel's texts, which show many of the realities of the eighteenth-century economy. If, however, we were to attempt to trace such a graph backwards in time we would find it increasingly difficult to justify the plotting of the points. Indeed the early historical development would perhaps best be indicated by a broken line to indicate uncertainty and lack of evidence. Much of the material that was available to Riedesel was not reliable (as his own corrections of assumed facts show) and even modern researchers find it difficult to form a clear impression of ancient Sicily. Davies even reports that many regions are epigraphic deserts.[44] But to Riedesel's mind's eye the line could not have been more distinct, nor the fact that it led back to a high-point in the fifth century BC which reflected the perfect condition of the model contemporary Greek state of Athens.

The problems caused by this sort of approach are easily illustrated from Riedesel's text. Travelling in Calabria he noticed that the towns

---

[44] Cf. J. K. Davies, *Democracy and Classical Greece* (London, 1978), 18.

were perched on the hilltops, and that any ancient ruins were to be found at the foot of the hills. The reason: 'weil alle Städte in dieser Provinz, der bösen Luft wegen, die den ganzen Sommer durch in derselben herrschet, auf Hügel und Berge gebauet sind; welches bey den Alten nicht so gemein war, da die grosse Bevölkerung dieser Gegenden die böse Luft verhinderte und unbekannt machte' (*Sizilien*, 103). This conclusion needs to be checked. It seems very likely that the basic observation—that at some point the population was larger and the land cultivated more successfully—is true. However, any evidence will presumably relate to specific periods rather than to the ancient world in general; the phrase 'the ancients' is simply too flexible and can encompass, according to taste, almost any historical period before the Middle Ages, or, as Riedesel and Winckelmann show, an idealized composite of various periods and places. The parameters of such a phrase are determined by the given author; and Riedesel, following Winckelmann, defines his terms very loosely. In a passage cited earlier he looked at modern Sicily 'in Vergleichung des alten', which existed 'vor Zeiten' (*Sizilien*, 77). On the same page he refers to the loss of 'die Griechische göldene Freyheit' which was recorded 'vor Zeiten'. These passages beg many questions. For example: which particular brand of Greek? What period of Greek history? What freedoms? The answers to these three questions are found in Winckelmann. This sweeping historical method certainly led Riedesel into some interesting contradictions.

For example, his uncritical view of the Greek past does not allow for the fact that the breakdown in politics, economics, and culture generally in the modern period may have been stimulated by decisions taken much earlier, perhaps early enough for them to have been taken by 'ancients'. By extension, it does not allow for the fact that the 'ancient' and so 'ideal' socio-economic system may have sown the seeds of its own downfall or that the modern situation may have grown organically out of an earlier one. As a result, in Riedesel's view of economics in Magna Graecia ancient and modern stand in opposition; this contrasts with his observations on customs and physiognomy which reveal a high degree of continuity between the ancient and modern worlds. The same brand of thinking leads to similar contradictions in Winckelmann's work and their main cause can likewise be found in a highly idealized vision of Greek society. The vision was so powerfully presented that it allows little possibility for compromise on questions of the greatness of the ancient world. Riedesel seems to have been able to accept a sanitized version of Ancient History and the supposed achievements of 'die Alten' uncritically. The same dichotomy can, of course, be observed in Winckelmann, who united minute, scientific analysis of artefacts with sweeping historical generalization in the same art-historical scheme. He like Riedesel managed to reconcile an idealized and ahistorical view of Greece with genuine historical insights. This reproduction of the weaknesses of the teacher's approach in the views of the pupil is, of course, not a positive feature, although it does perhaps testify to the teacher's persuasiveness. It can and does lead to false assumptions. It is ironic that in the latter part of the fifth century Sicily came under Athenian influence and so was liable to pay tributes to the state in much the same way that it did later to the King of Naples. This was perhaps preferable to the autocratic rule that they had experienced until then, but it was scarcely the ideal that Riedesel imagined.[45] In fact the picture that emerges of Sicily during this 'golden age' is of an unstable and then of a satellite culture. The direction that was taken by the culture of 'die Alten' was not always predictable or uniformly good even during its supposed best periods, and this basic fact contrasts with Riedesel's uniform positive vision of their activities.

(b) Ingrid Kreuzer, among others, suggested that the climate/production theory should logically have resulted in historical relativism and historicism but in Winckelmann's case did not.[46] But Winckelmann could not accept the relative merits of different cultures in the manner of Herder.[47] He measured all art, like all economies and societies, against the achievements of Periclean Athens, where, it was assumed, everything conspired to create the perfect workplace for the artist.

In the section of the *Geschichte der Kunst* entitled 'Von dem Ursprunge der Kunst und den Ursachen ihrer Verschiedenheit unter den

[45] If we compare Davies's findings on classical democracy and, in particular, his comments on Sicily (ibid. 28, 154–61) with Riedesel's assertions on those matters, we become fully aware of the extent of the latter's idealization of Greek culture.

[46] See Ch. 1 n. 25.

[47] Herder admired the Greeks but could not accept that their culture should be adopted as a model for other radically different cultures. The different interests of the two men are discussed widely: E. Aron, *Die deutsche Erweckung des Griechentums durch Winckelmann und Herder* (Heidelberg, 1929); A. E. Berger, 'Der junge Herder und Winckelmann', in *Studien zur deutschen Philologie: Festschrift der germanischen Abteilung der 47. Versammlung deutscher Philologen und Schulmänner in Halle* (Halle, 1903), 83–168; C. Ephraim, *Wandel des Griechenbildes im achtzehnten Jahrhundert: Winckelmann, Lessing, Herder*, Sprache und Dichtung: Forschungen zur Sprach- und Literaturwissenschaft, 61 (Berne, 1936); H. C. Hatfield, *Winckelmann and his German Critics 1755–1781: A Prelude to the Classical Age*, Columbia University German Studies, 15 (New York, 1943); Herder's most direct response to Winckelmann is to be found in his essay on him. Cf. A. Schulz (ed.), 'Die Kasseler Lobschriften auf Winckelmann', *Jahresgabe der Winckelmann-Gesellschaft Stendal, 1963* (Berlin, 1963), 31–62.

Völkern', Winckelmann makes clear how the physical climate affects people and their disposition to create art in the conventional manner (see Chapter 1), noting that 'durch den Einfluß des Himmels bedeuten wir die Wirkung der verschiedenen Lage der Länder, der besonderen Witterung und Nahrung in denselben, in die Bildung der Einwohner, wie nicht weniger in ihre Denkungsart. Das Klima, sagt Polybius, bildet die Sitten der Völker, ihre Gestalt und Farbe' (GK 35). He imagined the effects of climate to be very direct. For example the vocal cords would tighten in cold weather causing more abrupt speech patterns. This accounted in his view for the harsher sound of northern languages, and even of Northern Italian dialects. Most strikingly it also accounted for the absence of some letters/sounds in cold climates (GK 36; also see *Sizilien*, 114). The effect of climate on physical appearance also meant that in some locations there were likely to be fewer people who would be beautiful in the specific way that would make them great models for artists (GK 39). The best physical environment was, of course, to be found in Greece, and the best of Greek conditions in Ionia (GK 40). The ideal was a balanced moderate climate, since excessive cold and heat would have a negative effect on the population (GK 40–1). The effects were not merely physical. The above quotation suggests that the 'Denkungsart' of a given society would also be affected, and this, of course, would in turn be reflected in its culture:

Die Art, zu denken, sowohl der Morgenländer und mittägigen Völker als der Griechen, offenbart sich in den Werken der Kunst. Bei jenen sind die figürlichen Ausdrücke so warm und feurig als das Klima, welches sie bewohnen, und der Flug ihrer Gedanken übersteigt vielmals die Grenzen der Möglichkeit. (GK 41).

This theory seems fragile. The connection made between the literal heat in the East and the metaphorical heat of the art produced there is certainly problematic for the modern reader. But Winckelmann's work was in keeping with the latest climate theories and was internally consistent.

He extended the discussion beyond the physical climate to include the other key aspects of the environment. He was always keen to establish the extent to which 'die äußern Umstände, sonderlich die Erziehung, Verfassung und Regierung eines Volkes mitwirken' (GK 41). We have already seen how in Periclean Athens there was assumed to be a happy coalescence of environmental and particularly political factors which encouraged art production. The same method was used to account for the art production of less fortunate nations and parts of Greece during various periods.

In the *Geschichte der Kunst* Winckelmann explains the inferiority of Egyptian art. If we leave aside the stylistic criteria we are left with a harsh 'environmental' explanation:

Die Ägypter haben sich nicht weit von ihrem ältesten Stil in der Kunst entfernt, und dieselbe konnte ihnen nicht leicht zu der Höhe steigen, zu welcher sie unter den Griechen gelangt ist; wovon die Ursache teils in der Bildung ihrer Körper, teils in ihrer Art zu denken, und nicht weniger in ihren sonderlich gottesdienstlichen Gebräuchen und Gesetzen, auch in der Achtung und in der Wissenschaft der Künstler kann gesucht werden. (GK 41)

This explanation includes, or implies, all of the main environmental factors and includes one small but important addition. Active encouragement of the arts was a crucial by-product of a good working environment and again it was at its peak among the Greeks (GK 135–7). There was a distinct overall fall in the quality of art in Greece after the period of Athenian ascendancy, which naturally reflected changes in the environment. Since the geographical conditions in Greece were reasonably consistent the main focus was upon political changes; after the great Athenian period these offered less and less hope for the arts. With admirable exceptions the best features of Greek art declined in tandem with the loss of 'freedom' caused by changes in the political situation. Ultimately they were absorbed, in a diluted form, into Roman art; this absorption reflected the parallel loss of political independence. Such ideas were familiar to Riedesel, even in their detail.

When Riedesel examined the environment of Sicily he was very meticulous. We saw in Section (*a*) how he recorded the political, economic, and social aspects of the environment. The treatment of economics centred on agriculture and so brought with it extensive discussion of the physical environment. He links these factors to the arts in a very familiar manner. In the brief summary of Winckelmann's method given above, I pointed out the connection made between the physical climate in which people live and their appearance and disposition. Riedesel makes this connection equally strongly. On the Monte di Trapani he finds particularly beautiful women, indeed 'sie sind so weiß, als eine Deutsche oder Engelländerin seyn kann, haben aber die schönsten schwarzen Augen, voller Leben und Feuer, und die regelmäßigsten Griechischen Profile; die reine, heitere und feine Luft ist die natürliche Ursache hievon' (*Sizilien*, 26). Certain aspects of this account seem very familiar. The black eyes are a Greek characteristic particularly admired by Winckelmann.[48] We also

[48] Cf. KS 32.

see again the balance of Greek beauty. The women have Northern European traits (the skin tone) and southern/eastern traits (the eyes are lively, full of fire) in the ideal combination. This, of course, befits a nation which occupies the ideal 'Mitte'. The contrast with the population of Malta is very stark. He believes 'daß niemals hohe und idealische Schönheiten auf diesem ungemäßigt heissen und in Africa gelegenen Felsen gebohren worden' (*Sizilien*, 51). This judgement echoes Winckelmann's assessment of African beauty (GK 46–51).

The basic connection between climate and appearance is made many times in the tour of Magna Graecia. Since he was talking about a climate very similar to that in Greece the judgements on the appearance of the people were generally positive in tone.[49] He believed in this connection very firmly, even though at times it made his assessment of human beings seem rather harsh. In the area around Agrigento the climate was excellent, as evidenced by the fine crops grown there. It was also the place where the best horses were reared. A logical extension of the fertility of the area was the fact that the town was renowned for the beauty of its women (*Sizilien*, 43). Climate did not affect human beings alone, as Winckelmann had already made clear in the *Geschichte der Kunst*, where he pointed out that 'die Tiere sind in ihren Arten, nach Beschaffenheit der Länder, nicht verschiedener, als es die Menschen sind, und es haben einige bemerken wollen, daß die Tiere die Eigenschaft der Einwohner ihrer Länder haben' (GK 35; also 39–40). In the light of this statement it is not surprising that Riedesel should have found animals and human beings of the same high quality in the same place.

In Winckelmann's scheme beautiful people were important, in the first instance, because they could give artists some idea of the nature of ideal beauty. This issue was not discussed by Riedesel, presumably because of the depressed state of the arts in Sicily, which required few models. Physical beauty could, however, be useful in other ways, particularly as it was the surest indicator of the 'Denkungsart' of a people; fragments of Greek beauty could also accompany fragments of Greek character. In Agrigento the men were very jealous and kept the women out of sight; Riedesel saw this as a very Greek characteristic, but one which was out of control in Sicily (*Sizilien*, 94, 96). Other clues to their underlying 'Denkungsart' were also present. For example, in his view 'Witz und Verstand herrschet noch unter den Einwohnern der Stadt, vor andern Städten Siciliens, und vornehmlich die alte Gastfreyheit und Urbanität

---

[49] There is occasional criticism of the Greek climate, e.g. *Sizilien*, 94–5. Rehm, 'Riedesel', 236 discusses his tendency to idealize the local climate.

gegen Fremde' (*Sizilien*, 43). There can be little doubt where the adjective 'alt' is leading us, namely back to an idealized Ancient Greece. During that period the natural qualities of the local inhabitants would not have been distorted by later behavioural patterns, imported after the period of greatest Greek influence. However, enough of the qualities associated with 'die Alten' shine through to keep Riedesel's spirits up.[50]

Between Catania and Taormina Riedesel found again the combination of beautiful climate, reflected in the fertility of the land, and beauty:

> Die Einwohner sind ungemein leutselig und höflich ... Die Weiber sind weiß, und haben die schönsten griechischen Profile; sind munter und leutselig; und man siehet, daß die Männer durch die Eifersucht solche hier nicht furchtsam und scheue machen: Sie sind arbeitsam, und ich fand sie alle beschäftigt, besonders mit Leinwandweben. (*Sizilien*, 83)[51]

The physical appearance of the women is familiar from the passage cited earlier, but it is not just their appearance that catches Riedesel's attention. Aspects of their character are also important. The beauty of appearance was matched by 'beauty' of character; they were 'munter und leutselig' also. The jealousy of the men was more moderate than he saw elsewhere. This pleasant character then manifests itself in hard work. Riedesel saw a direct connection between employment and happiness and was upset by the lack of work being done in contemporary Magna Graecia. Again his thinking not only reflects contemporary views on the rural economy but is in line with Winckelmann's non-economic insights. Winckelmann also praised 'Beschäftigung'. He makes his view clear when comparing Ancient Egyptians with their modern counterparts. The former were 'mäßig und arbeitsam', whereas the latter are 'in der Faulheit eingeschläfert und suchen nur zu leben, nicht zu arbeiten' (GK 39). The Greeks were, of course, always viewed more positively than the Egyptians and so there can be little doubt about their industry.[52]

Riedesel found this combination of perceived Greek qualities in the population at a number of locations, some of them unexpected. He expected to find the people living near Mount Etna wild, in keeping with their local landscape. However, quite the opposite proved to be true. Although they did not live in the perfect physical environment these

---

[50] A similar search for Greek character can be found in the work of Pierre Augustin Guys, discussed by Constantine, *Early Greek Travellers*, 151–5.

[51] The location, near Mount Etna, would perhaps not have corresponded to Winckelmann's ideal.

[52] There is a certain irony in this praise of industry. We remember that Winckelmann insisted upon leisure time for his pupils who were, by definition, spared any hard labour.

people had had the advantage of isolation. This meant that many remnants of their 'Originalcharakter', which was in Riedesel's eyes distinctly Greek, remained intact (*Sizilien*, 48). They had not been exposed to changing cultural patterns in the same way as many other people in Magna Graecia and especially Malta had been (*Sizilien*, 49, 97). We hear:

Ich habe hier, wie aller Orten wo wenig Fremde hinkommen, die Menschen nicht durch die Menschen verdorben sind, wohl natürliche Menschen wohnen, gute, willfährige und wahrhafte Leute gefunden; sie sind wohl gebildet, und die reine und heitere Luft des Berges macht sie munter, lustig und frölichen Herzens; die Weiber sind schön, von weisser Haut und lebhaften Augen, die Männer von der Sonne verbrannt, aber groß, gesund und leutseliger Art; sie sind aufrichtig, dienstfertig, und man findet sich unter ganz guten Leuten in diesen Dörfern, welche wohl bevölkert sind. (*Sizilien*, 80)

This description presents in miniature many of the things that Riedesel and Winckelmann associated with the best Greeks. They include physical appearance, character, industry—and if these qualities, present because of the influence of the local geography, manifested themselves throughout Magna Graecia you would expect that many of the preconditions for art production had been met. It would require only that the broader political/social/economic environment be positive for this to be almost certain. However, that was exactly where things had gone wrong. The people on Etna also give us a false picture because they lived essentially outside the social order. But even then it did intrude upon them. Riedesel mentioned that the local wine had some of the roughness that you might associate with local terrain. He did not trace the flavour back to this aspect of the environment because he clearly believed that in this respect the positive aspects of the Sicilian climate outweighed the bad; on the contrary he was critical of 'der schlechten Bauart in einem sonst so glücklichen Clima' (*Sizilien*, 80). The tactical decisions about agricultural methods were, of course, the preserve of the local landowners, who in turn worked according to financial rules imposed by the king; it was in this area that modern Magna Graecia failed to match up to expectations. The physical climate had naturally not changed since better days and isolated members of the population still showed their Greek selves, but the area as a whole had lost the sure foundations of an integrated environment, in the Winckelmannian sense. Therefore the prospects for artistic production were very remote. The theory was confirmed in practice since Riedesel finds little to admire in the local modern art. A distinct note of melancholy enters his text:

Kurz zu sagen: Das Clima, der Boden des Landes, und die Früchte desselben sind noch so vollkommen als sie jemals gewesen; die Greichische göldene Freyheit aber, die Bevölkerung, die Macht, die Pracht und der gute Geschmack sind nicht mehr in derselben, so wie vor Zeiten, zu finden; die jetzigen Einwohner müssen sagen: *Fuimus Troes*. Jedoch ist auch wahr was Solinus sagt: *Quicquid Sicilla gignit, sive soli foecunditatem, sive hominum ingenia spectes, proximum est iis, quae optima dicuntur*. (*Sizilien*, 98)

He has seen (as he summarizes at *Sizilien*, 94–8) only 'Überbleibsel der Griechen' and most of those in the appearance and character of the people who still retained something of their nature; the broader scene offered less hope. These Greek characteristics have become more rare 'durch die vielen Veränderungen von Einwohnern, Regenten und der Regierungsform'; and Riedesel's analysis of the economic health of the island certainly provides damning evidence of the incompetence of the contemporary regime (*Sizilien*, 95). The overall outcome was a removal of the freedoms necessary to encourage art, not least because of the lack of money caused by economic failure. A corollary of the lack of political and economic dynamism was the lack of cultural centres which would have helped focus attention upon the arts.

In Syracuse Riedesel was rather laconic about the lack of any real cultural and intellectual impetus since 'unerachtet in neuern Zeiten kein Theocrit und Archimedes in dem jetzigen Siracusa gebohren worden, so ist doch den jetzigen Einwohnern dieser Stadt Witz und Verstand nicht abzusprechen' (*Sizilien*, 63). Elsewhere he takes the problem more seriously, notably in Lecce:

Von merkwürdigen Sachen oder Menschen in Lecce kann ich weiter nichts sagen; denn ich muß gestehen, daß ich in keiner Stadt des ganzen Königreichs Neapel so wenig Leute von Kenntniß oder nur natürlicher Fähigkeit angetroffen habe, welches wohl die Menge des müssigen, stolzen und armen Adels verursachen mag. (*Sizilien*, 121–2)

He later provided a partial explanation for this situation by referring to the poor quality of the air, when compared to more lively towns such as Bari; but he remained convinced that the real problem with Sicily lay in the political/economic aspects of the environment. The only answer for the artist was to escape it. This is implicit in Riedesel's comments on the painter Testoni, who has 'ein großes Talent; er würde ein grosser Mahler geworden seyn, wenn er in Rom studiert hätte' (*Sizilien*, 31). The very existence in modern times of a painter with talent was a matter of surprise. The general change in the Sicilian character, for example, would almost seem to exclude that possibility. Increasingly the balanced approach to art characteristic of the Greeks has been replaced by an attitude more typical of more Eastern peoples because 'bey einem erstaunlichen Feuer haben sie [the Sicilians] kein Phlegma, das zu der Ausführung in den Künsten nöthig ist' (*Sizilien*, 94). This criticism is, of course, very closely related to the criticism of Eastern art provided by Winckelmann. The basis for that criticism, as for Riedesel's was the dominant vision of Ancient Athens, whose artists combined imaginative fire with the calm necessary to realize their imaginative plans.

In Magna Graecia the chain of causes which lead from geography to a work of art was broken in several places, according to Riedesel's analysis. Many of his 'Vorurtheile' about Sicily therefore had to be amended; but he amended them using the same method which will have caused him to expect so much in the first place, namely Winckelmann's particularly prejudiced version of the environment/production theory (*Sizilien*, 140). He retained some hope for future positive developments in the area but looked to America as the most likely prospect for a future cultural bloom. This use of the production theory to look into the future marks a departure from Winckelmann. It also reveals a difference in emphasis between Riedesel and Winckelmann with regard to the importance of the various aspects of environment. Riedesel, in looking to a future in America, does not mention the physical environment as a positive factor. America will simply offer political advantages which in turn will encourage the arts. However, whilst this historical observation was clearly based on a certain logic, Riedesel could not pursue the argument to its logical conclusion. He could not prevent himself from looking back over his shoulder to the achievements of Ancient Greece and hoping that a culture of that quality would flower again in Magna Graecia. Sadly, the only evidence that spoke for this prospect was the geography of the region and according to his method that would only ever provide part of the requirements for artistic production. The fact that his treatment of Sicily none the less ends with a nostalgic look backwards (in a quotation from Horace) is a fine testimony to the influence of his teacher. This is also confirmed in the intimate tone in which he referred to his teacher; they shared a secret—the belief in the possibility of a reborn Greek culture:

Ich beschliesse hier meine wenigen Anmerkungen über die verschiedenen Provinzen des Königreichs Neapel, welche in ältern Zeiten selbst Königreich und mächtige Republiken waren. Kein Schatten dieser alten Grösse ist mehr übrig. Die Macht, der Handel, die Kriegs- und Seewissenschaft, die Verbesserung des menschlichen Verstandes, alles scheinet sich immer mehr nach Norden zu ziehen. Mit der Zeit werden die Europäer in Amerika Schutz, Erziehung, Sitten und Cultur des Verstandes suchen müssen. Die mächtige Natur behält jedoch beständig ihr Recht, und die Wirkungen des Clima sind noch immer dieselben in den jetzigen Einwohnern dieser Länder. Obgleich die übrigen Umstände sie ersticken, so sind sie doch meinem Auge nicht entwischet; ich habe dieses bey verschiedenen Gelegenheiten in diesen Sendschreiben bemerkt; und ob solches gleich nicht gegen jedermann behaupten mögte, so wage ich doch, Ihnen mein Freund es zu sagen, weil ich weiß, daß Sie mir gleichförmig in diesem Stücke denken. *Naturam expellas furca, tamen usque recurret*. (*Horat*) (*Sizilien*, 140)

Riedesel's method for explaining the production of great art mirrored that of many contemporaries; in its subject-matter and detail it owes a more specific debt to Winckelmann. For the most part he applied this method systematically to account for changes in Sicilian culture and by extension changes in the pattern of art production. The pattern which emerges is of decline from a high point in the ancient world to the point of virtual non-production of art in contemporary Sicily. If this decline were plotted graphically it would mimic the graph of economic (and by implication political) performance imagined in Section (*a*). The political aspects of environment seem more important than the physical aspects because the basic geography remained constant.[53] The logical outcome of this approach is an attempt to identify a political situation which would be more favourable to the arts. This Riedesel does and suggests that America and the North are likely to replace the Greek world as cultural centres—a view with which Winckelmann could scarcely agree. But this logical conclusion was undermined by an idealistic reluctance to abandon the belief that Greece would re-emerge as a cultural force. Again we see in Riedesel the combination of clear-sighted argument and idealization of history which was typical of his teacher and more extreme than in the work of most contemporaries. Again there is a suggestion that faith in a teacher can sometimes affect the pupil's ability to reason clearly. Riedesel's vision lacks perspective, depth. If details of Greek history could be left out because their quality was obvious (to the initiated) then the details of medieval art and society could be left out because of their 'obvious' lack of quality, again according to very strict Winckelmannian criteria. The production theory could be used to account for the characteristics of society and culture in the apparently 'barren' medieval period. But according to the Winckelmannian scheme

[53] But cf., for example, *Sizilien*, 94. The physical environment was clearly not always what it had been.

these matters simply cannot be of interest and so, in following his teacher, Riedesel systematically overlooks them.

This particular blindspot of Riedesel's is dealt with at length by Edschmid/Becker. He sees Riedesel as 'ein bedeutender Meister im Übersehen' (*Sizilien*, 10). He details many of the omissions, particular those which reveal a lack of sensitivity to the Germanic past.[54] These very omissions are the perfect proof of Winckelmann's influence. But if the pupil 'overlooks' then we must doubt the quality of his aesthetic education.

(*c*) Riedesel took over the finer points of stylistic/historical analysis from Winckelmann. I have divided the evidence of this debt into two further subsections. The first deals with the broad principles of periodization, on a stylistic rather than a production basis, that Riedesel inherited from Winckelmann. The second section deals with more specific stylistic details where the main issue is not dating but the quality of the given object.

Because of the paucity of art production in contemporary Sicily, Riedesel found that most of his attention was taken up with antiquities. This corresponded in any case with one of the major aims of the journey. The antiquities were mainly architectural remnants and could be placed broadly in the following historical periods: Greek, Roman, medieval. Because previous writers on Sicily had made many mistakes Riedesel's observations are often in the form of corrections. He corrected on the basis of Winckelmann's stylistic guidelines.

The emphasis on architecture in *Sizilien* conveniently reflects Winckelmann's interests when he and Riedesel first met. Winckelmann published the *Anmerkungen über die Baukunst der Alten* in 1762, the same year that Riedesel arrived in Rome for the first time. This work had been planned in 1759 and expanded until its delayed publication three years later.[55] During that same period he also produced the *Anmerkungen über die Baukunst der alten Tempel zu Girgenti in Sicilien* (1759) which, as we shall see, was important for *Sizilien*, in which Riedesel describes the same temples (KS 174–85). The interest in architecture was not exclusive and Winckelmann during this period also produced work

---

[54] See also *Sizilien*, 15; *Levante*, 24; K. Edschmid, 'Riedesel in Apulien', *Goethe-Kalender* (1941), 179, 181–2, 187–8, 191–2. The focus upon the the German past in these publications is perhaps best explained by the wartime publication dates.

[55] See Rehm's notes at KS 442. Also the *Fragment einer neuen Bearbeitung der Anmerkungen über die Baukunst der Alten* (1762–8) (*Werke*, ii. 475–506).

on theoretical aesthetics and two works on the Stosch collections.[56] But architecture perhaps played a more central role than at any other point during Winckelmann's career. It therefore seems likely that Riedesel will have discussed architecture with Winckelmann. Of course, Riedesel's journey did not come until some five years later and so it would be difficult to prove continuity of interest. Also by the very nature of his undertaking, Riedesel could not cover the same amount of ground in architecture as Winckelmann, but he did have the benefit of first-hand exposure to works which Winckelmann had not seen; this allowed him to try out their shared theories.

The broad outlines of Riedesel's method are revealed in his briefer examinations of individual works. These contain a shorthand which would only have been accessible to people who, like him, thought along similar lines to Winckelmann. The production theory connected the quality of a work with the period of its production. For brevity he could, by indicating the period of a work, give a shorthand idea of its quality. If stylistic features indicated Greek workmanship then the implication was high quality. He did not need to be more expansive because the implications of the word 'Greek' were clearly as positive as those of the word 'Gothic' were negative. With Greek examples he was in fact often more expansive, as we shall see. However, in dealing with Roman and later architecture he often did not proceed beyond listing the features which justified his dating of the work. Sometimes even these were absent. This omission was not merely a practical necessity. The letters were addressed in the first place to Winckelmann; it was therefore enough for Riedesel to indicate briefly the period of the work for the reader to have a good idea of the building in question. The method was economical but not necessarily vague. It was particularly effective with buildings because ancient architecture was based upon very strict rules. Winckelmann pointed out that buildings were 'nach der Notwendigkeit auf allgemeine Regeln und Gesetze der Verhältnisse gegründet' (GK 137). Riedesel's purpose was to examine the degree of adherence to these rules and report any small deviations of historical interest. Greek and Roman architecture shared common basic principles and thus Winckelmann was able to say that during the Roman period 'blühte die Baukunst in gewissem Maße, und es wurden in Rom Werke aufgeführt, dergleichen an Größe und Pracht Griechenland in seinen besten Zeiten nicht gesehen' (GK 388). This, of

---

[56] On the one hand the *Erinnerung über die Betrachtung der Werke der Kunst* or *Von der Grazie in Werken der Kunst*; on the other *Nachrichten von dem berühmten Stoßischen Museo in Florenz* in the period before Riedesel's arrival (KS 149–68).

course, stood in opposition to the general scheme of his history of art which saw Roman art as decadent; as a result architecture was scarcely mentioned, even by Winckelmann, because its history would have spoiled the general scheme. The explanation of the continued success of architecture lay in the mathematical nature of the subject and Winckelmann knew 'daß die Baukunst, welche vornehmlich mit Maß und Regel zu tun hat, und in welcher alles nach denselben bestimmt werden kann, eine angewiesenere Vorschrift, als die Kunst der Zeichnung insbesondere, hat, uns also nicht so leicht abweichen noch verfallen konnte' (GK 389).

Riedesel's allusive method of dealing with the history of architecture was based upon very similar thinking. Within the overall framework of architectural principles applying to Greek and Roman art, Riedesel points out a number of key stylistic variants. The distinctions made were not unique to him but fall into a general pattern provided in the last instance by Winckelmann, whose theory was itself a composite of various others, advanced by his own systematic approach. Winckelmann was the most immediate and dependable source of information, even if not the most original. When stylistic distinctions could be made easily, Riedesel had no need to refer the case to Winckelmann; he could simply record that things were 'mehr römischer als griechischer Bauart' (of some tombs near Girgenti) with an indication of the chief criteria in the judgement (in this case the use of building material) (*Sizilien*, 41). However, decisions about the dating of buildings were not always so easy to reach. Riedesel discovered this when trying to date theatres. Here shape was the primary issue. A perfect semi-circle indicated Roman work rather than Greek; the stonework and the architectural orders were also likely to be different. Such features combined gave many clues towards the date of construction of buildings, but the evidence was not always unequivocal. In Taormina the shape of the theatre was easy to distinguish as a semicircle but 'mithin weiß ich nicht, ob man dieses Theater für griechisch ausgeben könne?' (*Sizilien*, 88). The shape would indicate Roman origins or at least a later Roman development of a Greek original. There was also other evidence to support this supposition in the brickwork and use of architectural orders. But the interesting point in the description is uncertainty in Riedesel's voice. The question is presumably directed at Winckelmann who, on the basis of his superior knowledge, could be expected to provide answers. That is made more likely when we look at a passage earlier in the description of the same building. After an extensive examination of the stage area he remained uncertain about the reasoning behind some parts of the plan. Riedesel does not attempt to provide any clarity himself but says: 'das will ich Ihrer Entscheidung überlassen'. This deference is taken a stage further later in the same paragraph for 'hier zu entscheiden, würde von mir apocryphischen Antiquario eine grosse Verwegenheit seyn; welches ich also dem Patriarchen der Alterthümer überlassen will' (*Sizilien*, 86). Riedesel clearly knew and cited other authors—indeed in the description of Taormina he admitted that he looked for answers elsewhere—but it was to Winckelmann that he turned in cases of difficulty (*Sizilien*, 86).

He also did field-work for Winckelmann; and this was not just a matter of working generally on the same project—the temples at Agrigento—but of checking specific data for his teacher's records. Riedesel's examination of these temples follows quite clearly the guidelines contained in Winckelmann's *Anmerkungen über die Baukunst der alten Tempel zu Girgenti in Sizilien*. Winckelmann formed his theories about the temples on the basis of ancient and modern descriptions and relevant architectural theory, citing Vitruvius, Diodorus, Pliny, Pancrazi, and Robert Mylne. Riedesel mentions Pancrazi and Vitruvius and cites Diodorus in his description, and it is clear that he was familiar with them, but his description was in the first instance a direct answer to questions raised by Winckelmann, on the basis of his study of these authors (*Sizilien*, 35–40). Winckelmann's account begins with a description of the Temple of Concordia. Riedesel begins with the nearby Temple of Juno Lacinia, which has identical proportions. Riedesel points out the thirty-four columns that surround it; this corresponds with the count in the other temple (*Sizilien*, 35 = KS 175–6). Riedesel's report also confirms the order, shape, and decoration (though not size) of the columns of these two temples, also described by Winckelmann (*Sizilien*, 35 = KS 177). These correspondences are hardly suprising. They also come to the same conclusions about windows in the walls of the Temple of Concordia. As Riedesel notes, 'man sieht deutlich, daß die jetzigen Oefnungen in die Mauer in neuern Zeiten gebrochen worden' (*Sizilien*, 35). This observation was predicted by Winckelmann, who even suggests that they were created by the Saracens (KS 178). These correspondences alone would not be enough to prove a debt to Winckelmann, but stronger parallels in their treatments of the buildings emerge. The general stylistic impression of the temples is very similar in both accounts. Riedesel 'kann . . . deutlich die Schönheit der edlen Einfalt und wenigen Zierrathen in der Baukunst beurtheilen; nichts kann diesem, in Vergleichung anderer kleiner Tempel, an Schönheit verglichen werden, und das Auge wird durch die Uebereinstimmung der wenigen aber edeln und harmonischen

Theile zu dem ganzen Gebäude entzücket' (*Sizilien*, 35). This combination of criteria is very familiar to the reader of Winckelmann in whose opinion noble simplicity was a valid aim in all art-forms. Naturally, he makes the point for simple architecture in his account of the temples at Girgenti, although without the enthusiasm which comes from first-hand exposure. According to him 'die Verzierungen an dem Tempel zu Girgenti... sind, wie überhaupt in den ältesten Zeiten, groß und einfältig. Die Alten sucheten das Große, worinn die wahre Pracht bestehet... Die Einfalt bestehet unter andern in der wenigen Ausschweifung... alles geht nach fast geraden Linien' (KS 179). Both men process information in very similar ways.

Riedesel did not stop when he had confirmed Winckelmann's expectations. In describing the nearby Temple of Jupiter he offered both confirmation and also expansion of Winckelmann's material. The core of his report was confirmative. Winckelmann was in part dependent upon Diodorus's report on the temple for information on the general dimensions and details of the columns, although he pointed out a miscalculation (KS 179–81). Riedesel checked these dimensions, with reference to Diodorus, and confirmed the mistake reported by Winckelmann (*Sizilien*, 38). Riedesel also confirmed Diodorus's theory (reported by Winckelmann) that a man could stand in the flutes of the columns (*Sizilien*, 38 = KS 181). In addition, Riedesel found that Winckelmann's assertion about the presence and position of pilasters was correct (*Sizilien*, 38 = KS, 180–1). He was, however, also able to supplement Winckelmann's knowledge. Winckelmann speculated that 'die Cornische, von welcher sich nichts erhalten hat, würde etwa 8 Fuß in der Höhe gehabt haben' (KS 182). It can hardly have been coincidental that Riedesel spent so much time trying to find this missing link in the architecture and measuring it. He 'suchte den ganzen Tag ein Stück von der Cornische, allein vergebens; bis [er] endlich den folgenden Tag glücklicher war, und ein sehr beschädigtes Stück antraf, das 4 Palme in die Höhe hatte, welche Proportion ziemlich mit denen übrigen Theilen, der dorischen Ordnung gemäß, übereinstimmet' (*Sizilien*, 38).[57] Despite the difference in the expected result there can be little doubt that Riedesel's observations were a response to questions implicit in Winckelmann's account or posed verbally on the same basis. He filled in gaps wherever these were present—and here I am deliberately echoing the

---

[57] In fact the calculations of the two men differ. Winckelmann suggests a proportion cornice/triglyph of 8/10 units, Riedesel of 4/12 units. This would upset Winckelmann's calculations at KS 182–3.

terminology of previous chapters: we are confronted with another act of synthesis. Winckelmann did not mention the design of the capitals but Riedesel reported that they were 'di Forma oder Maniera rustica', which he (and so Winckelmann) clearly did not expect; this sort of additional information would have allowed Winckelmann to elaborate his perception of the rules of architecture. Although shared source material would in part account for similarities in their approaches it seems clear that Riedesel's investigations were at times directly stimulated by Winckelmann himself. Riedesel's research was an attempt to answer questions set, perhaps not for the first time, but most immediately by Winckelmann. The other secondary literature was seen through a filter; the filter was Winckelmann's reception of that work and his qualified acceptance of it.

Apart from separating Greek from Roman style Riedesel also distinguished between ancient and modern. He confidently identifies a gateway on the Monte di Trapani as Norman, in a manner which suggests that the explanation is self-explanatory—'mir kommen aber solche zweifelsohne für Ueberbleibsel der Normänner vor' (*Sizilien*, 26). On occasions he provides greater justification for his judgement but on the whole the criteria by which he judged are assumed to be understood by the reader.

The smaller art-forms were somewhat more problematic because the stylistic criteria were more subtle. Riedesel, however, shows remarkable confidence in dealing with these works, particularly when it comes to the general matter of periodization. He was particularly brief where works conformed to stylistic/historical norms:

Coins. Near Martanna there are many 'die aber meistens von der Römer Zeiten sind' (*Sizilien*, 120).

Urns etc. There were four urns in Palermo cathedral and 'der Porphyr ist von der schönsten Art; die Formen derselben sind nicht ganz in dem Griechischen Stil, aber zu schön für die Zeit der Könige welche darinnen begraben liegen' (*Sizilien*, 21). In Mazzara there were urns in the cathedral but 'es ist römische und mittelmäßige Arbeit' (*Sizilien*, 28). Similarly some urns in Agrigento are simply 'römisch' (*Sizilien*, 35). Some 'Schaalen' in the collection of Bishop Lucchesi are 'in egyptischem Style gearbeitet' (*Sizilien*, 42).

Statuary. In Palermo he comes across a group of figures, noting that 'das ganze Werk aber ist zweifelsohne neu, und schlecht gearbeitet' (*Sizilien*, 22). In Barletta he was more specific for 'auf dem Marktplatze von Barletta ist eine Statue von Erzt, colossalischer Grösse, aber von schlechter Arbeit, und Römischer Manier wie es scheint' (*Sizilien*, 129).

Mosaics. In Monreale cathedral he dismisses the mosaic because of 'die Gothische Musiaco-Arbeit, wovon die Sicilianer so viel Geschrey machen' (*Sizilien*, 22).

The shorthand assessments were apparently based on a very clear sense of the stylistic features of the works which would identify their period and provenance. The most likely source for these is Winckelmann, but it would be difficult to prove a direct connection in most cases because of the very small amount of detail which is given. It is only when he refers directly to Winckelmann, in the manner seen above, that we can be absolutely sure of his influence in determination of historical style in art. But we have many clues that it may have been the case in Riedesel's treatment of more specific stylistic details in art.

'Soll ich mich in Beschreibung aller besonder Kirchen und Palläste einlassen? Ich überlasse dieses andern, welche mehr Gedult zu schreiben und lesen, als wir beyde haben'—this comment reveals the extent to which Winckelmann and Riedesel's shared view of art was historically exclusive, favouring the ancient world (*Sizilien*, 21).

In architecture the criteria for high quality were clear and derived from Greek models. The simplicity and grandeur observed at Agrigento were the qualities to which all architecture should aspire. Any deviation from this norm meant failure and so dismissal. The crassest deviations came in the modern period. In Lecce Riedesel found little to praise for there was 'der elendste Geschmack und höchste Gothicismus in der Baukunst, und die unendlich kleinen und vervielfältigten Verzierungen daran sind unerträglich' (*Sizilien*, 120). The local artists clearly conspired to achieve the opposite of the ideal by opting for effect through detail rather than through monumental grandeur. Two churches were excepted from this blanket criticism because 'die Facaden der Jesuiter- und Theatiner-Kirchen sind die besten und am wenigstgezierten' (*Sizilien*, 121). The Carthusian monastery at Stilo was built to the same scale as ancient monuments but was let down by its decor, 'denn das Gebäude des Klosters und die Kirche sind zwar sehr groß und weitläufig aber in dem schlechtesten Gothischen Geschmack gebauet' (*Sizilien*, 102). Again it was fussy detail, in his terms, that detracted from the overall effect of the church. This criticism was not levelled exclusively at Gothic buildings. For example 'unter allen andern Kirchen in Messina ist die von St. Gregorio noch in dem weniger schlechten, jedoch Neapolitanischen

Geschmack, mit vieler Vergoldung und Arbeit in Marmor von allen möglichen Farben zu sehen' (*Sizilien*, 90). On the other hand any attempt to apply the building principles of the ancients were welcomed. Biscari was planning to build new properties 'welche ohne Zierrathen, rein, und dem alten guten Geschmack gemäß erbauet werden müssen' (*Sizilien*, 65). Similarly the cathedral in Catania 'ist die gröste und schönste Kirche in der Insel. Sie ist nicht mit einer Menge Zierrathen, wie der dortige üble Geschmack eingeführt hat, überhäufet, aber mit einer schönen Kuppole versehen, und stellet ein majestätisches Gebäude vor. Die Kirche und das Kloster der Jesuiten sind sehr reich und kostbar gezieret, aber nicht in so gutem Geschmack' (*Sizilien*, 64).

A building could only be beautiful if it conformed to these narrow expectations and this naturally occurred most in ancient buildings. The temples in the old town of Selinus were 'gänzlich niedergerissen, man kann aber noch die Bauart, die Grösse, und die Verhältnisse aus den ungeheuren Massen erkennen' (*Sizilien*, 28). The aesthetic impact achieved by simple means could not be reproduced in buildings which depended upon distracting detail for their effect. 'Ungeheuer' is a characteristic adjective in Riedesel's descriptions of ancient architecture (*Sizilien*, 30). It hints at a degree of critical impotence when faced with such grandeur. The effects are so powerful as to force him into a passive attitude as an observer. We can look again at his description of the Temple of Concordia at Agrigento. The key weapons of his critical armoury are removed in dealing with such a work and its aesthetic effects for 'nichts kann diesem, in Vergeichung anderer kleiner Tempel, an Schönheit verglichen werden, und das Auge wird durch die Uebereinstimmung der wenigen aber edeln und harmonischen Theile zu dem ganzen Gebäude entzücket' (*Sizilien*, 35). In dealing with modern works he could always compare them with past masterpieces and arrive at a relative judgement. In dealing with an original he could not use any handy benchmark; as he said, nothing can be compared to them. His attempts to account for the works through mathematics and explanation of the rules of architecture do little justice to the aesthetic impact of the buildings. His eye 'wird . . . entzücket'; this is not the Riedesel who actively dismissed works of inferior quality. In this respect he reproduced the initial passivity of a Winckelmann in dealing with a work of art. But we must later investigate whether he was able to activate his critical intelligence in coping with these great works, in the way which we have seen in Winckelmann. Certainly Winckelmann anticipated that the viewer would learn to cope with them. In a passage concerned with the importance of stylistic simplicity, he discusses the expansion of spirit necessary to accommodate great art. The terminology resembles that of the description of the Apollo Belvedere:

> Die Formen eines solchen Bildes sind einfach und ununterbrochen und in dieser Einheit mannigfaltig, und dadurch sind sie harmonisch; ebenso wie ein süßer und angenehmer Ton durch Körper hervorgebracht wird, deren Teile gleichförmig sind. Durch die Einheit und Einfalt wird alle Schönheit erhaben, so wie es durch dieselbe alles wird, was wir wirken und reden: denn was in sich groß ist, wird mit Einfalt ausgeführt und vorgebracht, erhaben. Es wird nicht enger eingeschränkt oder verliert von seiner Größe, wenn es unser Geist wie mit einem Blicke übersehen und messen und in einem einzigen Begriffe einschließen und fassen kann, sondern eben durch diese Begreiflichkeit stellt es sich in seiner völligen Größe vor, und unser Geist wird durch die Fassung derselben erweitert und zugleich mit erhaben. Denn alles, was wir geteilt betrachten müssen oder durch die Menge der zusammengesetzten Teile nicht mit einmal übersehen können, verliert dadurch von seiner Größe, so wie uns ein langer Weg kurz wird durch mancherlei Vorwürfe, welche sich uns auf denselben darbieten, oder durch viele Herbergen, in welchen wir anhalten können. Diejenige Harmonie, welche unsern Geist entzückt, besteht nicht in unendlich gebrochenen, geketteten und geschleiften Tönen, sondern in einfachen lang anhaltenden Zügen. Aus diesem Grunde erscheint ein großer Palast klein, wenn derselbe mit Zierrathen überladen ist, und ein Haus groß, wenn es schön und einfältig aufgeführt worden.

(GK 149–50)

The terminological parallels to Riedesel's work are apparent but there is some question as to whether Riedesel felt himself 'erweitert' and correspondingly 'erhaben' in the manner which Winckelmann describes. It could just be that he would not say so. Although there is a passive stage in Winckelmann's perception of great works (he too 'wird . . . entzückt') he imagines a stage when he can 'begreifen', 'fassen' 'einschließen', or 'übersehen', all verbs which suggest successful, active intellectual and imaginative engagement.

Riedesel writes less about art-forms other than architecture. Correspondingly we are unable to pinpoint direct correspondences with Winckelmann's views. For the most part his views largely correspond to the broad contemporary scheme suggested in Chapter 1. The notion of ideal beauty (composite beauty), as opposed to natural beauty was important to Winckelmann, since he saw this as the way in which the artist could suggest his divine inspiration. It was, however, not an uncommon interest and so Riedesel's introduction of it need not have been inspired by Winckelmann, even if the language seems familiar. In his description of the properties of the hero of a bas-relief in Girgenti cathedral Riedesel suggests that he had in mind an ideal of the kind envisaged by his teacher:

> alles, was das Alterthum von schönen Formen und Ideen bis zu unsern Zeiten erhalten, ist an ihr [der Hauptfigur] zu finden; man siehet einen der schönsten Menschen, aber nicht einen gemeinen, sondern von der Natur zu besondern Unternehmungen bestimmten Sterblichen; er ist über die andern Figuren erhaben, grösser als dieselben, schöner, vollkommener, kurz ein Meisterstück der Natur, und ihrer Nachahmerin, die Kunst. Die übrigen Figuren, welche seine Gefehrten vorstellen, sind ebenfalls Meisterstücke von Richtigkeit in denen Proportionen und schönen Formen; aber weniger schön als die Hauptfigur.
> (*Sizilien*, 32)

The same distinction between nature and idealized nature is implicit in Riedesel's comments on a fragment of a statue of Bacchus in the Biscari collection. The work was, according to Riedesel, 'so schön, als ich jemals etwas gesehen habe'. It was also 'in dem besten griechischen, ausgearbeiteten und zierlichen Style', taken so far that it made the work 'ein Wunder der Kunst und Muster der schönen Natur' (*Sizilien*, 69). This was the basis of Greek art, in Winckelmann's opinion. The combination of a theory of ideal beauty of this type plus specific stylistic characterizations might suggest that Winckelmann had provided some stimulation here.

There were many less equivocal parallels with Winckelmann's opinions on artistic quality. For example, Riedesel criticized some statues by Gaghini in Palermo cathedral in the following terms: 'seine Manier ist nicht übel; allein alle seine Statuen sind kurz, und die Stellungen übertrieben' (*Sizilien*, 21). This sounds very like Winckelmann's criticism of Bernini and other artists with baroque tendencies.[58]

He did not only inherit opinions about statuary. An earthenware vase in Girgenti was 'von der schönsten elliptischen Form' (*Sizilien*, 34). This concern for line could reasonably be attributed to Winckelmann, although his interest in line stemmed from an interest in human contour.[59] Other vases in Catania reveal qualities which we know were of fundamental interest to Winckelmann for 'jene [die Formen] sind bis ins Unendliche verschieden; der gute Geschmack und die edle Einfalt und Zierlichkeit der alten Griechen zeigt sich in denselben durchgängig' (*Sizilien*, 68). But not only the forms of the best vases conformed to Winckelmann's expectations but also the subject-matter of their illustrations, since 'die Sujets der Figuren schienen alle aus der griechischen

---

[58] Winckelmann attacks Bernini *passim*.   [59] See Ch. 1.

Historie und Mythologie zu seyn' (*Sizilien*, 70). Like Winckelmann he thought Greek subject-matter to be of primary interest.[60]

Clear (Winckelmannian) criteria for the qualitative assessment of works of art are, however, the exception in this publication. Riedesel's judgements generally only allude to the properties of the works rather than clearly enumerating them in the way shown above. Even the examples of positive qualities given above, although they could be traced back to Winckelmann, need not necessarily depend on him. In the case of the Girgenti vase the interest in shape can plausibly be attributed to Winckelmann, although the phrase 'die schönste elliptische Form' is not very specific. The other statements on the quality of the vase seem even more vague. The figures represented on it are 'von der schönsten Zeichnung in den Profilen und den richtigen Proportionen in den Contours' (*Sizilien*, 34). This suggests that Riedesel had a scale against which to measure beauty; if objects can be the 'most beautiful' and proportions be 'correct' then that must be the case. We are tempted to look for the ideals of human form in Winckelmann and take these qualitative judgements as references back to his aesthetic. The assessment of one vase continues with a number of other judgements which seem to depend upon an external value-scheme. The vase represents 'den besten griechischen Styl aus den guten Zeiten'; clearly two definitions are missing here, of the words 'best' and 'gut'. Furthermore it belonged to a period 'als die Kunst am höchsten bey dieser Nation blühte'. Again we need to know the scale against which these achievements are being measured. Similarly we need to know how this vase can stand as proof 'von dem Geschmack und der Kunst der Nation'. Clearly it can only represent a particular brand of taste in a particular historical/geographical segment of the nation, something which is in fact suggested by Riedesel's subsequent analysis of the style of Sicilian pots in general (*Sizilien*, 34). The statements seem unhelpful in isolation; they depend upon an external referent for any clarity. The judgements make sense in the light of Winckelmann's value-scheme, which provides neat and narrow definitions of taste and quality. This value-scheme was naturally understood as the basis of any discussion of art between the two men and is implicit in Riedesel's text. In this case Riedesel gives us a very firm indication of where we are to look for the key to his analysis. Riedesel doubted Pancrazi's interpretation of the story illustrated on the vase. The final

---

[60] Cf. N. Himmelmann, 'Winckelmanns Hermeneutik' (doctoral thesis, University of Mainz (Mainz, 1971)) and M. Käfer, *Winckelmanns hermeneutische Prinzipien*, Heidelberger Forschungen, 27 (Heidelberg, 1986).

decision was left to Winckelmann—'überlasse ich Ihrer Entscheidung'. Similarly the paragraph ends with a question aimed at Winckelmann about the general nature of Sicilian pottery. These questions make it clear that when confronted with fresh difficulties Riedesel turned to his more experienced senior. They also add weight to the theory that Riedesel was dependent upon Winckelmann for many of his historical/ aesthetic judgements. Without an implied value-scheme Riedesel's treatment of art in Magna Graecia would seem highly impressionistic. When we realize that the observations were in the first instance intended for Winckelmann and in any case based on his theories then they make more sense.

It is, however, interesting that Riedesel's text cannot sensibly be read in isolation from Winckelmann's work. Education is conventionally seen as liberating the student to operate independently; aesthetic education we might therefore expect to liberate the pupil to deal with art independently. This definition certainly applies to Winckelmann's own aesthetic education; he was self-taught but achieved a high degree of personal enlightenment. But the effect that Winckelmann's teaching had in the case of Riedesel was constricting; this is true not only in terms of the art covered but also in terms of the effect on the pupil. The vast amount of information and the critical method which Riedesel inherited from Winckelmann helped him to project an impression of mastery in dealing with art; on closer examination this mastery seems barely to disguise total dependence upon the teacher. Riedesel does not appear to have gone in for such self-analysis and so he can innocently suggest that 'in meinen Muthmassungen und Schlüssen aber habe ich bloß meinen ersten Gedanken ohne Nachlesung anderer Schriftsteller, als welche ich auf einer so beschwerlichen Reise nicht mitführen konnte, und ohne weiteres Nachdenken, wozu ich auf der Reise keine Muße hatte, gefolgt' (*Sizilien*, 99). His use of the secondary literature in connection with mainland Italy may have been limited—although in Sicily it seemed, on his own admission, quite extensive—but that was not really the point. Even where secondary literature was available much of it was redundant because Winckelmann's theories provided alternative views. Riedesel's 'erste Gedanken' were for the most part already second-hand because they had been determined by Winckelmann. In fact the same passage contains a reference to Winckelmann correcting any false impressions. Riedesel was always looking back over his shoulder, risking nothing. This leads to the common impression that Riedesel's work lacked something (see Section (*d*)). That something was original input, since even when he dealt with new material he dealt with it in an established manner, the Winckelmann manner. This has important implications for his aesthetic education.

In the introduction to the *Geschichte der Kunst* Winckelmann separated himself from run-of-the-mill art historians. They could be relied upon to tell us that things were beautiful; Winckelmann wanted to tell us why they were beautiful (GK 10–11). This was the reason for his historical and stylistic analysis of art. But what was the effect of his discoveries upon his pupils? They inspired people like Riedesel, but they also had an unfortunate side-effect. For example, they removed the need for others to check 'worinnen die Schönheit einer Statue besteht' (GK 10). At best Winckelmann's pupils would be called upon to provide fresh corroborating evidence to support the theories, which had the status of truths— even when they, particularly the production theory, seemed open to doubt. Thus Winckelmann's achievements in part removed the necessity—or the preconditions—for aesthetic engagement on the part of pupils. Because of this his pupils were not necessarily any better than the art historians whom Winckelmann had criticized in the *Geschichte der Kunst*. Those men failed because they called things beautiful without justification. Riedesel also accounts for works of art in a shorthand which indicates that he took his justification from somewhere else, namely Winckelmann. 'Beauty', 'greatness': Riedesel used the terms as if they were self-explanatory. He could call things beautiful but did not react to the beauty. This lack of engagement with art meant that Riedesel was unlikely to feel as moved by it as Winckelmann clearly was. His contact with art was mediated by Winckelmann and so it could not have the sort of direct spiritual impact that was recorded in Winckelmann's great descriptions. Aesthetic education as spiritual enlightenment through active engagement with art seems unlikely in Riedesel's case. He accumulates and evaluates information about art, which is a very different thing.

(*d*) Earlier in this chapter I listed some of the claims made by critics suggesting that Riedesel perfectly reproduced Winckelmann's manner of seeing. The general view matched that of Luigi Correra, who says that Riedesel looked at art 'con l'anima del suo grande maestro ed amico Winckelmann'.[61] I believe this to be only partly true, or even untrue when it was matter of reproducing feeling for art rather than information about it.

---

[61] *Un viaggiatore tedesco in Puglia nella seconda metà del sec. XVIII: Lettere di I. H. Riedesel a J. J. Winckelmann*, ed. and trans. Luigi Correra (Bari, 1913), 11.

The descriptions of Riedesel's enthusiasm for art in the secondary literature do not stand up to much scrutiny. Rehm described the desire for 'unmittelbares sinnliches Sehen' characteristic of the period and of Riedesel; we also hear about his 'offenes Ohr' und 'helles Auge'.[62] The evidence of Sections (a)–(c) above—and Rehm's own analysis of Riedesel's Winckelmann reception—would be enough to suggest that what we have in Riedesel's case is in fact 'mittelbares Sehen', through Winckelmann; this meant that his eyes were not quite as open as they might have seemed. Most of the descriptions of art (the exceptions are described below) offer no real sense of the immediacy of response to art that we might expect on the basis of Rehm's comments. Indeed Rehm himself points out that Riedesel had a 'nüchterne Art' and that he did not provide the 'begeisterte Schilderung' we know from Winckelmann.[63]

Edschmid/Becker comes to similar rather contradictory conclusions. In an article on *Riedesel in Apulien* Edschmid talks about 'die Kühle, die seine Begeisterung auszeichnete'.[64] It is a very special brand of enthusiasm that leaves the participants cold.

In the introduction to the *Levante* Becker builds up a powerful picture of Riedesel's enthusiasm. On occasions 'weit ging ihm das Herz auf' (*Levante*, 21). This corresponds to the state in which we find Winckelmann at his most euphoric, and Becker must have been aware of the most obvious precedent for the experience in the *Apollo* description. Similarly temples 'versetzten ihn in Begeisterung', with this enthusiasm encouraged by the friend Winckelmann for whom he had a 'schwärmerische Liebe'. He could achieve all of these heightened states because 'er ging mit offenen Augen durch das Land'; he was 'der begeisterte Besucher' (*Levante*, 22, 23, and 30). The claim that he kept his eyes open corresponds to Rehm's claim that we can see his 'unmittelbares Sehen' reflected in the texts. Becker, however, undermines his own claims for the enthusiastic Riedesel when he admits that he saw 'mit den Augen des genialen Freunds'; these eyes were not open to all new impressions. As we have seen they were focused upon very specific objects and were unresponsive to many others. Riedesel does not, in any case, reproduce many aspects of Winckelmann's vision.

Kasimir Edschmid finds himself drawn into other almost contradictory statements on Riedesel's ability to enthuse. The following passage is simply very difficult to understand:

[62] Rehm, 'Riedesel', 227, 223.   [63] Ibid. 238.
[64] Edschmid, 'Riedesel in Apulien', 176.

Er [Riedesel] hatte sehr bestimmt Vorstellungen darüber, an welcher Stelle er sich hinreißen lassen dürfe und wo nicht. Sah er zum Beispiel einen alten Tempel, so geriet er in Enthusiasmus. Sein ganzes Wesen fing an zu fiebern. Aber er gab sich sogleich Mühe, diese Erregung nur als die eines Fachmanns darzustellen. (*Sizilien*, 9)

The sense of constraint conveyed by the verb phrase 'sich hinreißen lassen dürfen' is underlined by the rather cool expression 'in Enthusiasmus geraten'. The verb 'dürfen' also contains an implicit reference to Winckelmann, who determined what should be seen. Neither of the phrases seems to allow the possibility that the same man will 'fiebern' at the next opportunity. We are tempted to ask how unenthusiastic someone has to be for Edschmid not to see them as boundlessly dynamic. Edschmid actually admits that there is no evidence of fever in Riedesel's response when he says that it is disguised under businesslike language. How then does he know that the situation ever existed? The literary evidence is non-existent since Riedesel is consistently 'fachmännisch' in his language; Edschmid even said that 'Riedesel's Sprache ist nicht sehr klangvoll', and that he wrote 'kein sehr deutungsreiches Deutsch'.[65] The only way that Riedesel's psychological state could be expressed for later generations was through his language and that lacks almost any expression. In that case all of Edschmid/Becker's conclusions are merely suppositions. The same is true of such statements as the following:

Vom Geiste aus gesehen, war die antike Welt der Raum, in dem er wirklich atmete, in dem er sich frei und klar bewegte und in dem er auch tatsächlich Ewiges zu genießen verstand. (*Sizilien*, 11)

This strikes me as the perfect summary of the aesthetic response of Johann Joachim Winckelmann rather than of Johann Hermann von Riedesel. The general statement about enthusiasm for antiquity is clearly appropriate to both Riedesel and Winckelmann. But whom do we remember breathing deeply when faced with antique statuary of exceptional quality? Whom do we remember transported onto the Elysian fields and moving freely amongst the ancients? Who saw beauty as giving access to eternal ideas and perhaps ultimately to God? Clearly Winckelmann— and if such ideas are present in Riedesel they are at a subliminal level which could not justify Edschmid's categorical belief in their existence. It seems that Edschmid projected qualities known to be present in Winckelmann onto Riedesel, in the assumption that Winckelmann had

---

[65] *Sizilien*, 14, and K. Edschmid, *Italien* (Stuttgart, 1969), 879.

been able not only to teach a historical method but also to transfer his personal genius to his pupil. Such assumptions undermine Edschmid's account and make it seem too impressionistic. His uncritical approach also manifests itself in his views on Winckelmann's posthumous influence on Riedesel. He asserts that Winckelmann 'gab diesem [Riedesel] die Richtung für sein ganzes Leben'.⁶⁶ The evidence is, on the contrary, that Winckelmann's influence was already fading during the trip to the Levant; the later letters from Britain show fresh aesthetic impetus from a another completely different source.

The idea that Riedesel was a second Winckelmann colours numerous accounts. Each is thus as unsatisfactory as the next because although they claim 'una squisita sensibilità artistica' for Riedesel they can only bring evidence that he was 'interessato a scoprire, a sapere, a raccogliere dati e notizie che possano servire al suo corrispondente'.⁶⁷ In fact the imagined artistic sensibility was Winckelmann's and it was not transferred to Riedesel.

Few critics point out the lack of aesthetic engagement in Riedesel. The point is implicit in Osterkamp's comparison of Riedesel's and Goethe's respective responses to Greek architecture in Sicily since 'für Riedesel waren die Tempel eine altertumskundliche Entdeckung, für Goethe eine ästhetische Herausforderung'.⁶⁸ Here the collection of information and the aesthetics of response to art are clearly in opposition. Riedesel's limitations are made more obvious in Tuzet's account. She was of the view that 'ces comptes-rendus méticuleux nous semblent parfois fastidieux; d'autant plus que le style de l'honnête Riedesel est assez plat. Il ne rend aucunement la grandeur et la poésie de ces ruines. Ce n'est point, semble-t-il, froideur naturelle, mais défaut d'expression.'⁶⁹ Both critics notice that Riedesel stops short of dealing with the most difficult poetic/ aesthetic aspects of the experience of art; he does not rise to that challenge in the way that his teacher had done. This corresponds to the view of Riedesel offered by Winckelmann, who, as we saw earlier, above all praised his thoroughness.

If we take the moments of greatest enthusiasm in the *Sendschreiben* and compare them with those in Winckelmann's work very clear differences emerge which suggest that the Osterkamp/Tuzet view of Riedesel's

⁶⁶ Edschmid, *Italien*, 880.
⁶⁷ T. Pedio, *Johann Hermann von Riedesel: nella Puglia del'700 (lettera a J. J. Winckelmann)*, Itinerari Meridionali, 3 (Lecce, 1979), 27.
⁶⁸ Osterkamp, *Sizilien*, 373–4.
⁶⁹ H. Tuzet, *La Sicile au XVIIIᵉ siècle vue par les voyageurs étrangers* (Strasbourg, 1955), 29.

responsiveness is the most accurate. Winckelmann's pattern of response to great work had various clear characteristics:

> Linguistic and stylistic dynamism reflecting personal engagement with art. Verb-forms reflecting relationship with the object.
>
> Imaginative reconstruction of damaged works and imaginative experience of the context of the work's creation or themes through feeling of transportation into the Ancient world.
>
> Feelings of improvement. His 'completion' of the work rewarded by the feeling that he was more complete himself as a result of his experience.

We have already heard the general assessments of Riedesel's style as flat. The most obvious explanation of this is naturally the fact that he was not writing in his first language, French, but using German in order to conform with Winckelmann's patriotic intentions for art history. Ironically at the time of their first meeting Winckelmann had just written the Stosch catalogue in French. We also remember that Winckelmann and Riedesel intended to collaborate on the French translation of the *Geschichte der Kunst*. But it is difficult to know how much weight to give to the view that Riedesel sacrificed expressive possibilities in adopting German. There is some evidence that his French style is more fluent, but as the later Section 5 (*d*) makes clear, the expression of his enthusiasm in *Levante* was as limited as that revealed in *Sizilien*.

The stylistic features which reflected Winckelmann's relationship with an individual work of art most powerfully were the verb-forms; they helped to reveal the dynamic of his reception. The pattern in the aesthetic descriptions was one of alternating activity and passivity reflecting the exchange between the viewer and the object. The work of art was in Winckelmann's perception not merely an artefact but revealed an aesthetic life of its own. It rewarded the viewer's interest with insight into other more subtle aspects of its existence.

There is little evidence that Riedesel saw works of art in this way. For Riedesel most objects were in a fixed state. They did not exist in the problematic way identified by Winckelmann and explored philosophically by later reception theorists. Riedesel had no difficulties with the ontological status of the work of art. This was, by contrast, of central importance to Winckelmann since it was only through an exploration of the peculiar expressive qualities of art that one could hope to come into contact with the highest beauty in God; this highest beauty was not concretely present in the work of art but through contact with the approximations to it available in art the viewer could begin to imagine the nature of absolute beauty. Art inspired philosophical speculation. Edschmid seems to have been unaware of the importance of this enthusiasm and dynamism for Winckelmann's aesthetic. He acknowledged at one point that 'Johann Joachim Winckelmann hatte gerade der staunenden Welt gezeigt, wie man, an große Gedanken angelehnt, Kunstgeschichte schreiben und Kunstanschauung vermitteln könne'.[70] However, the phrase 'an große Gedanken angelehnt' suggests a rather superficial relationship with the great ideas of beauty and divinity. Indeed Edschmid seems to have been sceptical about aesthetic, imaginative, philosophical involvement with art. This was carried over into his assessment of Riedesel's responses to art which he described positively because 'Riedesel war kein Ästhet und kein geistiger Snob, er war kein Phantast, der Ruinen anbetete und kein Schönling, der kritiklos erlesene Dinge verehrte, sondern ein Jüngling von präzisem Verstand, der sich durch die Bewunderung antiker Monumente nicht davon abbringen ließ, die harten Gesetze des Lebens anzuerkennen und mit zielbewußtem Instinkt über die schlüpfrige Erde zu wandeln.'[71] This seems to be a tacit acknowledgement of the fact that Riedesel was not an aesthete in the Winckelmann mould. Winckelmann could almost literally 'anbeten', he was an aesthete and a fantasist—but all of these things in a positive, enlightening manner. He was also a snob and that is more difficult to see positively. Edschmid's use of the words aesthete, fantasist, snob, 'Schönling' imply a complete failure to understand the type of aesthetic education that Winckelmann was trying to provide; in fact it is difficult not to take all of this passage as an attack on the unworldly Winckelmann and praise of the earthbound Riedesel. However, if we look at Riedesel's contribution from Winckelmann's point of view we are made to reflect upon the limitations of a method of dealing with art based only upon precision and knowledge of the rules. His method may, as Edschmid suggested, have been appropriate for the analysis of politics and economics; his critical mind would also have been useful for writing art history. However, aesthetic engagement required properties more likely in the 'aesthete'. Riedesel's mind by contrast focused upon the properties present in the artefact and assessed them in a very worldly, non-aesthetic manner. As we have seen most of Riedesel's judgements about art took the basic form: 'the work is/is not beautiful and is/is not Greek'. The judgements were often correct but could only be used to understand the

---

[70] Edschmid, *Italien*, 877.   [71] Ibid. 877.

historical status of the work. Beauty was not a philosophical invitation for Riedesel but rather the sum of a number of concrete stylistic criteria. In Riedesel's version the historical and aesthetic status of the work of art were one and the same. Its aesthetic status offered no mystery and so was not investigated. As a result the verb pattern in his descriptions does not suggest any sort of reciprocal relationship with the work of art. If anything the pattern suggests passivity on Riedesel's part. The characteristic phrases for the description of aesthetic effects follow the pattern: 'es fällt gut ins Auge' (*Sizilien*, 35, 36, 37, 39, 40 etc.). This passive position is also present in Winckelmann's aesthetic descriptions but only as a precursor to more active engagement with the work of art. In Riedesel it leads only to a listing of the qualities which lead to the particular assessment.

As Koch proved, a large part of the dynamism of Winckelmann's language came from the fact that it was rich in metaphor and rhetorical variety. She showed that the particular power of his language came not just from the presence of metaphor but from the particular combinations of metaphor. Characteristic for Winckelmann was the use of images derived from antique literature in combination with images of, say, agriculture, most likely traceable to his time in Germany. The register of the language also shifted from the heights of classical rhetoric to earthy German expressions. These combinations of register were necessary because Winckelmann was attempting to provide a means to express aesthetic experience in German. This was no easy task and its difficulty is reflected in the numerous revisions which the most important descriptions of art underwent before they did justice to his personal experience.

This honing of language was inconceivable for the busy Riedesel. The *Sendschreiben* were intended as brief reports and any editing work was to be done either by Winckelmann or the publishers. It is striking, however, how little Winckelmann's attempts to express enthusiasm for art influenced Riedesel.

Even in his most famous passages Winckelmann used a lot of submerged quotation in the attempt to provide powerful expression of aesthetic experience. To that extent Zeller's analysis of the use of quotation in the descriptions underlines Koch's thesis that Winckelmann was attempting to provide a language for aesthetics using all available means. He was using a complex composite language in order to provide the best definition of beauty. The important thing about Winckelmann's use of quotation was the fact that it was integrated into his key descriptions, reworked, and so personalized. He did not allow others to speak for him.

The contrast with Riedesel's method is quite clear. When he was confronted with something of particular interest or beauty he allowed others to speak directly. As a result any aesthetic experience remained that of the original author and Riedesel's participation was confined to sympathy with that author. Unlike Winckelmann he did not find a voice of his own through exposure to others. We can see this in his reaction to the temples at Agrigento. They offered a massive aesthetic challenge and Riedesel began his description on an enthusiastic note:

Hier rief ich aus:
>   ——Hic vivere vellem,
>   Oblitusque meorum, obliviscendus & illis,
>   Neptunum procul e terra spectare furentem. (*Sizilien*, 32)

This moment of apparent excitement is followed by a report on his tiredness and not by any explanation of his enthusiasm. In order to explain the aesthetic impact of the temple of Olympian Jupiter he cites at length Cluver's translation of Diodorus (*Sizilien*, 37–8). He does later introduce his own comparison with St Peter's to give a better idea of the impact (this is dealt with in the section on imaginative reconstruction) but his extensive dependence on Diodorus brought no new, personal assessment of the aesthetic properties of the work to his reader, Winckelmann, who had himself already used Diodorus' account. Riedesel also used quotation in three other ways: to summarize the political position and future prospects of Magna Graecia; to locate and characterize ancient sites; on one occasion to indicate the 'aesthetic' impact of landscape.[72] Like many earlier travellers Riedesel seems to have great pleasure in confirming the extent of his classical education, a somewhat 'conservative' undertaking.

In this use of quotation there are clear parallels with their use in the *Voyage littéraire* rather than Winckelmann's poetic descriptions. Here the purpose was essentially to check literary evidence against the evidence of one's own eyes and not to make active, creative use of quotation. Essentially the *Voyage littéraire* served to prove the erudition of the author and to confirm/enhance that of the reader. To that extent *Sizilien* conforms to expectations of the genre.[73] Of course, all of these other uses of quotation were also present in Winckelmann's texts; indeed he

---

[72] For politics cf. *Sizilien*, 43, 98, 139, 140. For location: *Sizilien*, 30, 36, 43, 45, 55, 57, 106. For 'horridus montes': *Sizilien*, 119.

[73] Cf. Constantine, *Early Greek Travellers*, 128–67. Riedesel and Guys were clearly involved in related enterprises.

specialized in updating and improving the references in other peoples' work. But the key moments of aesthetic response were characterized by a more active use of quotation.

Given these basic dissimilarities in the treatment of art it is surprising that we should at other points find parallels in their methods. One of the most important aspects of Winckelmann's description of the Belvedere Torso was his reconstruction of the total form of the statue on the basis of the available fragment. In Sicily Riedesel was faced with lots of fragments, but largely of buildings. In Catania the ruins did not give a very firm idea of the original disposition of the buildings but 'man sieht einige kleine Kennzeichen der alten Stadtmauer, des Circus und einer Naumachie, in dieser Gegend. Es sind aber mehr idealische Muthmassungen als wirkliche Denkmale des alten Catania' (*Sizilien*, 67). We might expect the 'unimaginative' Riedesel to have difficulty in dealing with such fragmentary evidence. In fact he does on occasions imaginatively reconstruct works on the basis of ruins. The description of Agrigento with which Riedesel provided Winckelmann was intended to record the measurements that would help Winckelmann to build up a picture of the original buildings. This was little more than an archaeological undertaking. He did not, however, always leave the reconstruction to Winckelmann. His own description of the Temple of Olympian Jupiter contains a view of the building going beyond archaeology to provide an indication of its aesthetic properties. He ends his list of measurements with the following passage:

Dieses ist, was ich mit Gewißheit von den Ueberbleibseln dieses Tempels habe messen können. Mir hat es genug gethan, weil ich mir daraus einen Begriff von der Grösse desselben machen konnte. Ich wünschte, die Grösse von St. Peter in Rom und die Verhältnisse mit diesem Tempel vergleichen zu können: Daß der letztere prächtiger und schöner in das Auge gefallen, glaube ich ganz gewiß, und nichts kann majestätischer als dieses Gebäude erdacht werden. Stellen Sie sich, mein Freund, die Grösse der Säulen, die zierliche Form des Tempels, welche weit schöner als ein Creutz, dem St. Peter gleichet, ist; die Ansicht des ganzen Gebäudes, die Festigkeit in den Pilastern, die schöne Bildhauerarbeit, wovon Diodorus redet, und welche jezo völlig zerstört ist, kurz alles zusammen genommen vor, so glaube ich, daß ein viel edlers Gebäude als St. Peter in Rom in ihrer Einbildung entstehen wird. (*Sizilien*, 39–40)

This praise of an ancient temple over St Peter's is a direct answer to Winckelmann's praise of St Peter's over ancient temples (he names the Temple to Olympian Jupiter) in the *Sendschreiben von der Reise eines*

Liebhabers dedicated to Riedesel (KS 205). Riedesel in fact uses Winckelmann's own method against him in asserting the superiority of one building over another. He combined what he had read (here Diodorus) with what he had seen and then added the vital element of imagination in order to reconstruct the building. He moved beyond the 'Gewißheit' provided by his usual empirical method to operate on the level of 'Begriffe'. He 'wished' and 'believed' and asked Winckelmann to 'imagine': nothing is certain in this description and even the pleasure that the building awakens is conditional upon our imaginative reconstruction of it. The crucial verb 'gefallen' is controlled by the implied conditional 'würde'. We are twice asked to accept Riedesel's belief in the quality of the building. There are clear hints here of enthusiastic engagement which goes beyond archaeology and art history. However, unlike Winckelmann, Riedesel does not find himself drawn into speculation as to the nature of beauty; this can in part be attributed to the fact that he was dealing with architecture. The 'ideal'—in this case 'mathematical'—nature attributed to architecture by Winckelmann meant that it could not embody the ideal/divine qualities identified in sculpture. Whilst the simplicity and harmony of the best architecture could be seen as a reflection of the simplicity and harmony associated with God it could not represent subtle gradations of divine qualities in the way that a statue could: the pride of Apollo and Laocoön or the heroism of Hercules could not be reduced to mathematical formulas. Winckelmann essentially saw architecture as a lower art-form, and it tellingly failed to produce the moments of high aesthetic pleasure for him which we know from his exposure to statuary. Correspondingly this sort of enthusiasm is rare in Riedesel. The fact that Riedesel only ever shows engagement with architecture is an indication of his limitations as an aesthete. His enthusiasm is borne upon mathematical near certainty in assessing buildings. Imagination is kept within the bounds of reason.

More common than an attempt to imagine the aesthetic qualities of reconstructed buildings is the attempt to imagine the practical archaeological features of the buildings. This is particularly apparent in his descriptions of theatres in which he tried to establish the exact pattern of usage (*Sizilien*, 59–61 and 85–6). This was the case in Syracuse, although he did here indicate an intention to go beyond practical investigation. The ruins themselves had an aesthetic impact through their 'Grösse' and 'Majestät'; in addition, the fact that he spent two days examining them might indicate that he was trying to imagine their original form. However, there is no record of this imaginative engagement (*Sizilien*,

59). He can only repeat his claim for the beauty of the place, namely that 'der Anblick dieses Theaters ist einer der besondersten und schönsten in Sicilien' (*Sizilien*, 60–1). The nature of its impact remains uninvestigated. Similarly, in his treatment of other temples he tends to restrict himself to the collection of data. Even the first temple he saw on the site of old Segestus failed to stimulate any enthusiasm (*Sizilien*, 25).

Given this essential coolness of response—however explicable by reference to the nature of architecture—it is hardly suprising that Riedesel did not find himself transported by art in the same way that we saw in Winckelmann. In part it was unnecessary because he was already in Greek territory. Rehm shows us how Riedesel's use of quotation from ancient authors was a celebration of the fact that he was following in their footsteps.[74] Whilst the opportunity to travel into Magna Graecia and even Greece itself did present itself to Winckelmann he never in fact travelled beyond Paestum. This meant that his experience of Greece could only ever be imaginative and because the picture of Greece was of his own imagining it was experienced more intensely. Certainly Riedesel's description of the realities of Greece seems flat by comparison.

The most important consequence of Winckelmann's engagement with art was the feeling of self-improvement that it engendered. This was the core of aesthetic experience and aesthetic education. Given that the engagement with art was lacking in Riedesel's case it is hardly surprising that he did not experience the transformative power of art. The Sicilian journey served largely to confirm a number of prejudices about art and related subjects; because of its confirmative nature it could not offer any sense of revelation. Without revelation—an experience which was central in Winckelmann's response to art—the observer could only hope for a refinement of his knowledge of art. This was the case for Riedesel, who does not mention any feeling of improvement through exposure to new art. He records his pleasure in art, but unlike Winckelmann (and indeed Ingarden), who took the existence of pleasure as a stimulus to closer examination of aesthetic experience, Riedesel apparently declares himself content with the feeling itself. Most telling of all is his failure to distinguish qualitatively between that pleasure and a number of others that were offered to him during his journey; the primacy of aesthetic experience as defined by Winckelmann was not maintained by

---

[74] Rehm, 'Riedesel', 217. Ironically, Riedesel only felt transported in as far as he felt cold enough to be in Siberia. I disagree with Rehm that Riedesel was 'ins antike Leben zurückversetzt' during his trip (p. 222). Again I suspect that this is someone writing about Riedesel whilst thinking about Winckelmann.

Riedesel. Indeed many of his most enthusiastic moments did not concern the arts at all.

Riedesel seems particularly sensitive to the beauty of nature. Rehm points out that at times we can almost hear the voice of Winckelmann when Riedesel describes nature.[75] He suggests that when Riedesel compares Etna with Vesuvius he sounds like his teacher. But the most persuasive evidence of a parallel voice comes when Riedesel looks down from Etna from where 'man glaubet über die Natur zu gebieten, und scheint über die Menschheit erhaben, wenn man sich über alles, was sterblich ist, so hoch empor siehet'.[76] This does indeed sound like Winckelmann, most particularly in his description of the Apollo Belvedere. However, the parallels are deceptive. The notion of being 'über die Menschheit erhaben' was naturally important to Winckelmann. Some of his heroes achieved this through superhuman action, subsequently represented in stone; through exposure to those works of art the viewer himself could feel more noble himself. Riedesel enjoys an illusion of this same power simply by climbing a volcano; he is physically above the rest of humanity and not spiritually elevated as was the case with the figures that Winckelmann described in these terms. The parallel which Rehm identifies is an empty one and it might even be possible to suggest on this basis that Riedesel may have misunderstood Winckelmann, whose vocabulary he seems to have been using.

His other moments of enthusiasm for nature are less problematic. The combination of moonlight, seascape, and the sound of nightingales leads him to say that 'so war dieses der rührendste Genuß für mich, der mir eine heimliche, aber süße Melancholie einflößte'. This description of a feeling for nature is actually more subtle than his analysis of his feelings for art. He seems more comfortable in dealing with the five elements of this complex response to nature—'Rührung', 'Genuß', 'Heimlichkeit', 'Süßigkeit', 'Melancholie'—in a manner which is not present in his (non-)treatment of aesthetic responses. He is much more expressive in his treatment of a number of subjects outside art. The transience of power and greatness and the decay of the economy are dealt with in an engaging rhetorical manner which contrasts with the customary dryness of his prose (*Sizilien*, 54 and 77). A similar tone is introduced to mourn the oppressive fortifications of Malta and the loss of freedom which they imply (*Sizilien*, 48). He is also engaging when he deals with agriculture and

---

[75] Rehm, 'Riedesel', 222–3. All rather ironic when we consider Winckelmann's indifference to nature (n. 24 above).

[76] Rehm, 'Riedesel', 223 cites *Sizilien*, 77.

some of the peculiar techniques and products that he saw on his travels (*Sizilien*, 46 and 82). What we must explain is how an aesthetic education which should have led him to feel comfortable in expressing his responses to art in fact seems to have led to a rather different situation.

On reflection a number of factors appear to have been involved. The fact that Riedesel was writing in his second language, I suggested, might have had an inhibiting effect. This argument seems superficially plausible, but as we have also seen Riedesel was capable of expressing his enthusiasm for nature and political freedom using conventional rhetorical methods in German. At one point there was even evidence of engagement with a work of art to the extent that he reconstructed it imaginatively, praising its aesthetic impact rather than coolly listing likely features as we might expect from a good archaeologist. The potential for the expression of aesthetic engagement was present even in his second language.

A second explanation of the absence of engagement is similarly fragile. It could be argued that the text, in the form of letters, could simply not accommodate an account of Riedesel's enthusiasm alongside all of the information that also had to be relayed. Riedesel's busy timetable would also have served to reduce the possibility of its expression; Riedesel after all had said that he was writing down his first thoughts. The argument holds water for as long as we expect to find a systematic treatise on aesthetics along with a detailed account of personal responses to art. But this is clearly an unreasonable expectation given the nature of the text and I was at no point searching for such evidence. The nature of response to art can be revealed incidentally—in the same way that responses to nature and politics are revealed in *Sizilien*—and does not rely upon the presence of a systematic investigation of the problem. Working within the sort of restrictions imposed by the *Sendschreiben* format means that there is less opportunity for a full treatment of aesthetic response; it does not, however, by its nature exclude the possibility of some treatment. Indeed the fact that the *Sendschreiben* were addressed to a known aesthete might have increased the possibility of some attempt being made to do justice to aesthetic experience, if there was any.

More problematic is the nature of the material covered in Magna Graecia. In as far as the text deals with art it deals mostly with architecture. As we have seen, the nature of architecture makes it less likely to draw aesthetic responses out of observers. Indeed Winckelmann himself did not achieve the same level of enthusiasm for architecture whose effects could be explained away more easily than those of statuary, which required more of the observer. It is therefore not suprising that most of Riedesel's observations on buildings were archaeological in nature. Other art-forms are discussed in the text but in no case does Riedesel move beyond an art-historical account of individual work, with most statements on their provenance and quality determined by Winckelmannian values. The opportunity for engagement existed; Riedesel indeed indicated that many works were of the highest quality but he never described their aesthetic impact. The question is whether there was a response, and if so why it was not expressed.

Still more difficult to assess is the effect that a visit to real Greek territory may have had on someone whose education made him believe that Greece must be the ideal country. The reality was disillusioning for Riedesel, at least as far as political and social realities were concerned. He still clung to an idealized view of ancient Greece but this ideal was certainly coloured by his exposure to the latest manifestations of that culture. It is impossible to say to what extent this disillusionment may have affected his ability to respond to the local art. There is a very stark contrast between the matter-of-fact manner with which Riedesel deals with the artefacts that he discovers and the more poetic treatment of the products of Greek culture which Winckelmann produced from afar in Rome. Of course, not all of Winckelmann's work is characterized by this particularly charged brand of enthusiasm. Indeed it represents only a tiny fraction of his work, the rest of which is often matter-of-fact in much the same way as Riedesel's. However, the effort which Winckelmann put into the great descriptions, plus his own statements suggesting a relatively low status for 'mere' scholarship when compared to the true experience of art, make it clear that they are the standard against which we should measure responses. For him, as subsequently for Goethe, the act of writing about art was the most powerful means to achieve insight into the individual work, to create aesthetic objects and through them to know oneself. There is no evidence of aesthetic engagement of a similar quality in Riedesel.

The tempting general conclusion is that Riedesel was a rather cold fish, who was able to collect data but not to enthuse. There would certainly be little evidence to contradict this view, but similarly little to prove it conclusively. Again the most charitable view might be that Riedesel did have a passion for ancient art but not the ability to express it. But the evidence presented above suggests that Riedesel did in fact have the ability to express his interest in other topics. The lack of expression when faced with art seems a strange result of a near-perfect training (in Winckelmann's terms), a training whose results can be seen in art-historical judgements but which apparently did not succeed in the vital task of sensitizing the pupil and enabling aesthetic response. In such a case the student is left with the more limited pleasure of applying another man's ideas.[77] Whilst these ideas may have been important to Riedesel, their adoption was not necessarily an entirely positive feature. Winckelmann's 'presence' as a teacher and so source of ideas may have inhibited pupils. I have already suggested that Riedesel inherited a number of doubtful prejudices about Ancient Greece from Winckelmann. I also suggested that the apparent exhaustiveness of Winckelmann's theories of art history, and the persuasiveness of their presentation, may have removed the necessity for his pupils to search for explanations of the nature of beauty themselves. This search was what, in Winckelmann's view, distinguished him from other art historians; ironically, his pupils did not have (or did not take) the opportunity to distinguish themselves in a similar way. We have seen how the shorthand used by Riedesel to account for art can only be understood properly by reference to Winckelmann, who provided him with most of his historical and qualitative criteria, even when they only differ in emphasis from contemporary standard views. Thus Riedesel experienced art through Winckelmann and did not have the proximity to it which enabled engagement in the manner which we know from Winckelmann. His few moments of lyricism come in discussions of politics and nature, areas in which his own expertise and interest were not similarly inhibited. Whenever Riedesel discussed art he appeared to be looking back over his shoulder at Winckelmann. He revealed a high degree of deference to Winckelmann, which can reasonably be explained by his elder's superior knowledge, but which perhaps also restricted his ability to make personal judgements; at moments of difficulty he could choose to have decisions made remotely through Winckelmann.[78] Winckelmann is consistently present in *Sizilien*, and not just as the implied source of many of the judgements; Riedesel refers to him directly on a number of occasions (e.g. *Sizilien*, 33, 34, 47, 70, 71,

---

[77] Of course, there is a pleasure in applying someone else's ideas and discovering the truth in them. However, it is not one that Winckelmann would have appreciated. We remember how unhappy he was working for Count Bünau. Cf. Leppmann, *Winckelmann: Eine Biographie*, 84–90. Also Martin Bollert, 'Johann Joachim Winckelmann als Bibiothekar des Grafen Bünau', in *Festschrift für G. Leidinger* (Munich, 1930), 19–24.

[78] Only A. Schulz in 'Johann Hermann von Riedesels Reise durch Sizilien und Großgriechenland', ed. A. Schulz, *Jahresgabe der Winckelmann-Gesellschaft*, 1964 (Berlin, 1965), 14 deals with Riedesel's deference to Winckelmann but even he does not see it as a problem, or source of inhibition.

84, 86, 104). Of course, the text was written for Winckelmann at his request (*Sizilien*, 19, 99, 140).

One could argue that rather than inhibiting Riedesel Winckelmann made the best of a bad job. This does not, however, correspond with Winckelmann's positive view of Riedesel, from which one could only infer slight reservations about his enthusiasm. But there is no evidence that Riedesel's aesthetic education was complete in Winckelmann's terms. Whilst he clearly collated information in a Winckelmannian manner, and so inevitably knew more by the end of his journey, there is no sense of revelation.

6. LEVANTE

Many of the problems in dealing with the *Levante* are the same as those that we encountered in *Sizilien*. The concision which we saw in the *Sendschreiben* to Winckelmann is reproduced in this work which does not, however, show Winckelmann's influence in the same concentrated manner. The book contained, by the author's admission, *remarques*, and so was not designed to be systematic or exhaustive.[79] Becker points out that, in contrast to *Sizilien*, it is even difficult to establish his exact route and the timing of the journey on the basis of the text (*Levante*, 27–8). A three-month stay in Athens is reduced to a few pages of notes (*Levante*, 30). In a reserved judgement Michaud points out that 'commes simples remarques, ses notes remplissent ce que promet le titre'.[80] But Dohm, in his introduction to the 1774 German translation, indicates that the appeal of this book is broadly the same as that of *Sizilien* and 'so muß es jedem, der sich von unserem Verfasser durch Sicilien und Neapel hat leiten lassen, sehr angenehm seyn, eben dem scharfsinnigen Beobachter der Natur und der Menschen, und dem feinen und gelehrten Kenner der Kunst und des Altherthums durch Griechenland und die Türkey zu folgen'.[81] As in *Sizilien* Riedesel managed to combine a wide variety of interests, and the order in which Dohm presents the various aspects of the text accurately reflects the importance of non-artistic

---

[79] All references to the German edition: Johann Hermann von Riedesel, *Randbemerkungen über eine Reise nach der Levante 1768*, trans. L. M. Schultheis, introd. E. E. Becker (Darmstadt, 1940).

[80] L. G. Michaud, *Biographie universelle*, New Edition, 42 vols. (Paris, 1842–65), xxvi. 3.

[81] *Johann Hermann von Riedesel: Bemerkungen auf einer Reise nach der Levante*, ed. and trans. C. W. Dohm (Leipzig, 1774), p. iii.

concerns. In fact the text reveals something of a shift in interest away from the arts when compared to *Sizilien*. Correspondingly there is a move away from dependence upon Winckelmann. This is not to say that ideas familiar to Winckelmann are absent from the text. However, they are present only in a more dilute form. The most obvious departures from Winckelmannian norms are the use of French and the virtual exclusion of the visual arts in the second part (Chapter VIII onwards) of the text. This movement away from Winckelmann is best explained by Winckelmann's death in 1768, which removed the pressure of likely 'censorship'. Becker argues that Riedesel may have heard of Winckelmann's death in Athens because after his stay there Riedesel effectively dropped the arts and concentrated on anthropology.[82] This argument is weakened by the fact that the text was written later than 1768 and so Riedesel would have had the chance to re-edit the first part to make a more even whole, if he had been so inclined (*Levante*, 27). None the less the basic point remains quite clear: Riedesel's interests were no longer as closely tied to Winckelmann's as they had been only a year earlier. His most direct debt in this text was to the publications of other travellers in the region, and it was so direct as to cause accusations of plagiarism. Stoll describes the information in the text 'unverfroren abgeschrieben', although his attitude towards plagiarism seems very modern.[83] Dohm is less critical—at worst gently sarcastic—with regard to the lack of original content in the text; it certainly did not affect his desire to publish the work and his foreword was presumably not written to put off readers. The text contained a blend of topics agreeable to the public and so to booksellers:

Und in der That findet man hier doch, besonders über das *Clima*, den *Character* u.s.w. der *Griechen* und *Türken*—wo nicht Nachrichten, doch *Reflexionen* und Urtheile—welche, wie mich dünkt, *neu* genannt zu werden verdienen. Und außerdem bleibt dem Herrn Verfasser noch das nicht kleine Verdienst, auch schon bekannte Sachen auf eine so interessante Art zu sagen, daß der gelehrte Leser beynahe vergißt, daß er sie schon wußte und derjenige—welcher nicht Zeit und Gelegenheit hatte, die voluminösen Werke der *Tournefort*, u.s.w. zu lesen—es dem Schriftsteller doppelt dankt, der so wichtige Materien auf eine so unterhaltende Art zu sagen, und in einem so engen Raum einzuschließen wußte.[84]

---

[82] There are no direct references to Winckelmann, although a mention of the Albani villa perhaps implies a connection with Winckelmann (*Sizilien*, 94).
[83] H. A. Stoll (with Gerhard Löwe) (eds.), *Entdeckungen in Hellas: Reisen deutscher Archäologen in Griechenland, Kleinasien und Sizilien* (Berlin, 1979), 22.
[84] *Johann Hermann von Riedesel: Bemerkungen auf einer Reise nach der Levante*, ed. and trans. Dohm, pp. iv–v.

Tournefort was only one of the sources used to put together this book. He used Spon and Wheler and referred to Stuart and Revett, Le Bruyn, and Du Loir.[85] These writers represent only one level of influence upon the text—and it is one whose existence Riedesel readily admitted. Perhaps more important was the influence of contemporary anthropology and political theory—including ideas used by Winckelmann—which shaped his whole manner of seeing Greece.

(*a*)–(*b*) Riedesel's account of the physical, political, economic, and religious environment in Greece is familiar in its basic tenets to the reader of *Sizilien*. He accounts for the full range of factors which would help to determine the quality of local art in a manner which would have been agreeable to Winckelmann and would have been familiar to most contemporary readers. But in this text he largely ignores the opportunity to make connections between environment and art and restricts himself to investigation of geographical/political/economic factors in their own right. Making systematic use of such investigations to provide a basis for art-historical study was one of Winckelmann's key contributions to contemporary thinking. In not following his teacher in this matter Riedesel consigns himself to the mainstream of contemporary thought.

This movement is particularly apparent in the second half of the text, which contains elaborate examination of some of the questions of environment. The chapter titles give a very firm indication of this: he investigated in turn questions of race, customs, law, religion, politics, physical climate, and trade, i.e. all of the important aspects of the Greek environment. But there is no question in *Levante* of Riedesel looking back over his shoulder at Winckelmann. Despite the similarity in material Riedesel's declared source is not Winckelmann. I noted earlier the books on Greece that were used by Riedesel. Whilst using these texts he was, however, operating within a theoretical framework apparently derived from more general theorists, particularly Montesquieu. The starting-point of the climate/production theory, the assertion that physical environment shapes physical appearance and character of the affected population, is traced back quite unequivocally to Montesquieu. In Chapter XI he cites his *Esprit des lois* to the effect that 'die Herrschaft des Klimas ist die stärkste aller Herrschaften' (*Levante*, 158). Clearly Riedesel believed in this maxim and his faith is reflected in the confusion caused by his observation of the unfavourable climate in Athens, whose

---

[85] Riedesel did not hide his sources: Spon and Wheler: *Levante*, 72, 77; Stuart and Revett: *Levante*, 106; Du Loir: *Levante*, 126; Le Bruyn: *Levante*, 129; see also *Levante* (introd.), 29 for Riedesel's testing of source material.

population had once been a model for others. He asks: 'Wie kann man jedoch den Einfluß des Klimas auf die Völker leugnen?' (*Levante*, 115). This theory had the status of a truth and it was one which he sought to confirm rather than doubt. Chapter XI is essentially a proof of the theory. He describes the central thesis of the chapter in the following terms: 'In den gemäßigten Zonen, sagt de Montesquieu, sind die Völker unbeständig in ihren Sitten, ihren Lastern und selbst in ihren Tugenden. Das Klima ist nicht entschieden genug, um ihnen in diesen Dingen Festigkeit zu geben. Es scheint fast, als ob dieser Schriftsteller Griechenland im Auge gehabt habe.' (*Levante*, 158).[86] The substance of the chapter is then taken up with confirmative evidence of the predicted Greek character. It seems clear that Riedesel is in this text looking back over his shoulder at Montesquieu rather than Winckelmann. Rehm even indicates that other more general aspects of Riedesel's approach could be attributed to Montesquieu.[87] Further aspects of Riedesel's thinking in this text are similarly traceable to Rousseau rather than Winckelmann. In his search for the ancient Greek character Riedesel applies a principle of his:

Vom Grundsatz ausgehend, daß alle Hauptstädte der Welt vom Ehrgeiz und von der Selbstsucht bevölkert werden, und daß die beiden Leidenschaften die Charaktere ihrer Einwohner bestimmen, folgte ich J. J. Rousseau's Rat, welcher sagt, daß man in die Touraine, nicht nach Paris gehen muß, um die Franzosen kennen zu lernen, und erforschte die Wesensart des Inselvolkes und der Athener, welche, fern vom Thron und von ehrgeizigem Streben dem Ackerbau und Kleinhandel hingegeben, ursprünglicher, wahrer und weniger durch den Islam verdorben sein müssen. (*Levante*, 133)

This principle was clearly applied not just in this text but also in *Sizilien* and it only helps to increase our impression that in fact all along Riedesel owed a greater debt to French theorists than to Winckelmann himself. We have already heard the assertions that Riedesel was a true pupil of Voltaire and now we can add unequivocal debt to Rousseau and particularly Montesquieu. By extension it is tempting to think that any similarity between Riedesel and Winckelmann's approaches comes from the fact that Winckelmann was similarly dependent upon French theorists. It is perfectly possible to prove this connection; his own notebooks show him to have read Voltaire and Montesquieu and much work has been done on his relationship with the French Enlightenment.[88] It would seem

---

[86] Cf. also *Levante*, 145, 153–4.   [87] Cf. Rehm, 'Riedesel', 241–2.
[88] Cf. A. Tibal, *Inventaire des manuscrits de Winckelmann déposés à la Bibliothèque nationale* (Paris, 1911), 128, 135. See also Ch. 1 n. 26 for the connections with mainstream enlightenment thinking.

that the debt to Winckelmann detailed earlier in this chapter could be something of an illusion, and one which could only be sustained by leaving aside all reference to these background sources, as indeed I did in Section 5. I did this with a very specific purpose, namely to show how Winckelmann made Riedesel use a brand of historical thinking (perhaps unoriginal) for special purposes in the exploration of art history. That was Winckelmann's original contribution: to take a historical method (perhaps a composite of many) designed to account for life in general and apply it specifically and systematically to the arts: this historical approach was then supplemented by an aesthetic investigation of the individual work of art which was still more original. In *Sizilien* Riedesel went some way to following him in this application of art-historical principles, although his work lacked the aesthetic core which we associate with Winckelmann. He did, however, show signs even in this text of drifting towards more general interests and so of returning to a mainstream brand of historical thinking, not focused strictly on the arts. This is not to devalue his observations but merely to point out that they are not always identical to Winckelmann's—which in turn indicates that the effects of aesthetic education were in Riedesel's case not as Winckelmann would have hoped, perhaps because his pupil's interests were wider. In *Levante* the focus is diffuse, and the arts could not be described as the centre of the work. The first consequence of the change, noted above, was the reassimilation of the production theory (Section (*b*)) into a more generalized historical scheme (Section (*a*)). Art is no more than one of many interesting products of history. This means that many of the plausible attributions of (art-) historical ideas to Winckelmann (as the most recent source of a historical method, if not an excusive one) which we saw in *Sizilien* no longer seem quite as convincing. In the case of that text the constant reference to Winckelmann, his editorial role, and the focus upon the arts makes it reasonable to assume that he was providing the most direct reminders of the historical method, even if it was not strictly his own. However, when direct control over the material by Winckelmann was removed Riedesel apparently drifted back towards a more general application of a historical method, clearly related to Winckelmann's, but not containing many of its key components—especially the focus on art. The naming of Montesquieu and Rousseau only serves to confirm the move back into the mainstream. The shift in interest does not entirely divorce Riedesel from Winckelmann: after all the climate/production theory retains many of its characteristics in the general application. The difference is that in this text, as in Montesquieu, the examination of physical environment, race, politics, and religion are interesting in their own right: the Greeks are interesting as Greeks and only incidentally as the people who produced great art. In Winckelmann's version the Greeks were really only interesting in as far as they produced great art: in order to reconstruct his opinions on politics (in Section 5(a)) I had to work back from his opinions on art. In *Levante* Riedesel makes more use of a general historical rather than an arthistorical scheme since his work has an anthropological rather than artistic core, particularly from Chapter VIII onwards. Even in the first chapters the treatment of art does not match that of *Sizilien*. Rather than using his own observations, as was necessarily the case in Sicily, he could for the most part refer to other people's work. Even if in Magna Graecia he was dependent on Winckelmann for much of his methodology at least he researched the sites himself. There is less evidence of such assiduity in Greece. In fact the prerequisites for aesthetic engagement are largely missing in his account, if it is a true record of his response to art. To that extent an aesthetic education has been replaced by a general education with an emphasis on politics.

(c) The relatively small amount of coverage given to qualitative assessment of art appears to follow the pattern established in *Sizilien*, even if it is based upon selective quotation from secondary sources. He provides some general surveys of the available material and some detail of individual works. As in *Sizilien* his judgements (and those of others which he chooses to employ) seem to be informed by absolute standards for art, themselves based on an idealized view of the best Greek art. The justification of the Greek ideal is, however, not as fully explained in *Levante*. In *Sizilien* he sometimes gave a very firm idea of the stylistic criteria which determined excellence, but in this text we have only a very compact shorthand.

The periodization of a work of art is again the surest shorthand method of indicating its quality. On Paros he saw 'zwei heldische Statuen in barbarischem, oder gothischen Stil' (*Levante*, 94). These could not be compared for quality with earlier statues carved in stone from the same island, a stone 'aus dem die alten Griechen uns jene unnachahmlichen Meisterwerke der Bildhauerkunst hinterlassen haben, die wir in Rom bewundern' (*Levante*, 95–6). Works are judged to be of high quality according to how far they conform with very narrow stylistic criteria. These are alluded to at points in the text. For example, it was not enough even to use genuine remnants of ancient buildings in the hope of reproducing their greatness. A destroyed castle on Paros was constructed out of 'die schönsten Marmortrümmern und antiken Säulen'. Riedesel none the less criticized the building because 'man siehet sofort, daß die Hand, die es schuf, ebenso barbarisch war, wie die Türkenhand, die es zerstörte; denn sie benutzte zum Bau dieses Hauses die schönsten Säulenreste und die herrlichsten Basreliefs wie gewöhnliche Steine'. The building from which the building blocks were taken would have surpassed the newer building since it will have had 'edle Proportionen' uniting the qualities of its individual features in a harmonious whole, rather than throwing together details (*Levante*, 94–5). He automatically praised any comfirmation of ancient artistic principles of this kind and noted any deviation from them.

Even within Greek styles of architecture there were limitations to what was permissible. The 'Tempel des Erechtheus' in Athens was 'im reizvollsten ionischen Stil' but at points too heavily decorated, since 'das Karnies, das sie [die Karyatiden] tragen, ist mehr ausgeschmückt, als es der jonische Stil gestattet' (*Levante*, 109). This sensitivity to excessive décor was particularly noticeable in *Sizilien* and marked a point of very close correspondence between him and Winckelmann. Like the latter he saw the ideal architectural form to be that of the great ancient temples. In Sicily the prime examples were at Agrigento; here he has the Parthenon. For him it was the most beautiful building in the world, dating from the best period and embodying 'die edle und wahre Schönheit der männlichen Einfachheit'. Although his account of the building is brief it also contains a further reinforcement of the stylistic ideal in architecture. He praised the Parthenon by comparison to later Roman work. The Romans, he asserts, introduced bases to columns (which they did not have in the Parthenon) to satisfy their desire for 'Prunk' and 'Luxus' over simple and noble beauty (*Levante*, 104). This was the beginning of the historical development away from Greek ideals and towards a concentration on detail rather than total effect in architecture, identified by Winckelmann. Of course, there were exceptions to the historical rules but they served only to prove them in the final analysis. The former 'Sophienkirche' in Constantinople was erected in the sixth century, the period 'des niedergehenden Reichs' (*Levante*, 126). However, the architects overcame the disadvantage of their environment to create a great work, comparable with St Peter's and St Paul's (*Levante*, 125). He explained their achievement in the following terms: 'Die Architekten dieses stolzen Tempels, des einzigen Denkmals, das dem sonst so düsteren und bewölkten sechsten Jahrhundert zur Ehre gereicht, sind Athemius und Isodorus, von denen man sagen möchte, daß sie durch ihren Geschmack und ihre Begabung sich in die schönsten Zeiten, da die Künste in Griechenland blühten, zurückversetzten' (*Levante*, 126). It was the art of 'die schönsten Zeiten' which provided the starting-point for all judgements. Within this sort of secure framework of standards in art Riedesel could be confident in his assessments of works. He felt no need to elaborate on his judgements. Athens cathedral was 'in sehr schlechtem Geschmack' (*Levante*, 114). Smaller works of art were assessed in a similar way as 'ein herrliches Werk', or as of 'mittelmäßige Arbeit', or containing 'mittelmäßige Figuren' (*Levante*, 101, 94, 78). Even apparently fuller descriptions contain the same shorthand. For example: 'Im Garten des venezianischen Konsuls fand ich den Torso eines Kriegers, sehr schön und von gutem Stil, auf dem Harnisch sah man zwei Darstellungen der Pallas, die Ägide in Händen haltend, von sehr guter Ausführung.' (*Levante*, 116) Taken in isolation none of the qualitative assessments are very useful: when we consider the system from which they are derived, or to which he relates them, namely Winckelmann's, we have at least some idea of the parameters of the terms good and beautiful. This shorthand is a very convenient way of conveying information, particularly when the text was only meant to contain 'Randbemerkungen'. Riedesel takes concision one step further in choosing to refer his readers to secondary literature rather than offer descriptions himself. At one point (in Athens) he even says: 'Ich überlasse den Kunsthistorikern die Erklärung dieser Skulpturen' (on the Lantern of Demosthenes) (*Levante*, 107).[89] There are parallels here with Riedesel's deference to the art historian Winckelmann in *Sizilien*; the more experienced man was invited to step in and solve difficult problems at a number of points. He did not regard himself as competing with these art historians and this is a clear indication of the relative superficiality of his interest in the arts which is more apparent in this text than in *Sizilien*. But that is not to say that the text is generally superficial. He did not, after all, leave the examination of the local political climate to political theorists: he tried to get to the bottom of those matters which interested him most.

(*d*) At points he described the reason for his trip in terms which suggest that it was inspired by a deep enthusiasm for Greece. For example he travelled to Samos 'um am Grabe von Leontychus und Rhadine zu seufzen und die Wohnstätte jenes glücklichen Sterblichen, Polykrates, und die Heimat des weisen Phythagoras zu bewundern' (*Levante*, 82).

[89] *Levante*, 106–7. His treatment of the Homeric scenes indicates that he is a good pupil of Winckelmann's.

The two verbs suggest the sort of involvement that we have been looking for and which inspired him in his search to rediscover the Ancient Greeks. He was 'so wie ein Forscher, der ein halbzerstörtes Basrelief deuten möchte, Arme und Beine hinzudenken muß, um den Gegenstand zu erraten' (*Levante*, 134). This simile is, of course, very inviting from my perspective; the process of reconstruction bears an uncanny resemblance to Winckelmann's imaginative reconstruction of the Belvedere Torso. However, Riedesel was not describing a work of art but the Greek people; similarly he was, in the preceding quotation, describing an enthusiasm for historical personalities. It was in these areas that his enthusiasm was most apparent and had the most significant impact on his style. If we take his decription of the greatest building in the world, the Parthenon, as indicative of his response to art in Greece, a clear picture emerges. He wrote about Periclean Athens as the greatest period and then the Parthenon as the greatest work. The building exhibited 'wahre Schönheit der männlichen Einfachheit' but this brand of beauty apparently meant that he never recovered from a state of 'Achtung und Bewunderung'. In his attempt to account for the aesthetic impact of the work he begins to measure and compare styles. The language of the description is flat: the temple *has* forty-four columns, each of them *has* a span of 6½ spans and *is* worked in a particular way. It *is* practically undamaged. You can *see* the decorative statues and some 'zeigen schöne Arbeit'. Furthermore 'der ganze Fries der Cella ist mit den denkbar schönsten Basreliefs geschmückt, die die Geschichte der Geburt und andere auf Minerva bezügliche Begebenheiten darstellen; einige sind abgeschlagen und fortgeschafft worden'. Neither the beautiful basreliefs nor the removal or destruction of works of art receive any comment. This is cool cataloguing of artefacts and is all the more suprising since his declared secondary sources contain all of this basic material. You might imagine that his extended stay in Athens might have led to a more mature aesthetic judgement of the building, or perhaps of his response to its noble simplicity. This was clearly not the case and in the concluding passage of the chapter on Athens we see some of the reasons why not. He notes that:

> man verläßt ungern die Athener und ihre Ruinen. Die Erinnerung an die alten Zeiten verknüpft sich mit der gegenwärtigen, ebenso wie der Reisende, nachdem er alle Schönheiten des heutigen Roms gesehen hat, stets wieder mit Erstaunen und Bewunderung zum Pantheon und Kolosseum zurückkehrt. Ich muß noch die merkwürdige Geschicklichkeit der athenischen Albaner in chirurgischen Operationen erwähnen. (*Levante*, 118)

The order of the first sentence is important. He was interested in the people first and the art second. A second duality of interest exists between the present and the past. Whereas in Winckelmann there was also an attempt to rediscover elements of the past in the present, the emphasis was unequivocally upon the past. In *Levante* this appears also to be the case especially until Chapter VIII, which compares earlier Greeks favourably with their modern counterparts. However, the subsequent chapters, whilst they clearly have a comparative component, centre on the modern world, especially its politics and trade (with the exception of Chapter XI), reflecting the balance struck in Riedesel's life, of which only a part was dedicated to history and a good deal more to the modern world. The sentence with which the above quotation ends, praising Albanian surgical skill, serves to confirm the dichotomy of ancient and modern interests in Riedesel. A passage which might have contained a lyrical farewell to Athens is in fact taken up with an account of an operation, of which the above sentence is only part. Clearly ancient art was, in Riedesel's scheme and indeed in that of many contemporary travellers, in competition with a number of rival interests. These serve to undermine the accounts of the arts and prove that the exclusive artistic focus required by Winckelmann is absent here. The general interests, which were also present in *Sizilien*, have now grown in importance and interestingly it is in fields outside the arts that we see Riedesel using a vigorous style which would indicate engagement with the subject-matter. He reveals more of himself in his treatment of politics than he does in the arts.

In his introduction to the history of Athens Riedesel admits that he got carried away: 'Ich bin ein wenig abgekommen von Athen durch meine Betrachtungen!' (*Levante*, 106) In essence he was reflecting on the transience of the great moments of Greek history and culture; these had been founded in a desire for fame and immortality, but ironically proved to be subject to time like all other cultures. If we look at the way this subject is discussed we see that it does not take the form of casual remarks (*Levante*, 104–6). The section is framed by quotations which refer to the central theme. His text has a rhetorical opening. In the first sentence we see excitement at his arrival in Athens, reflected in an exclamation mark. In the second sentence the excitement is undermined by the question of how much is left of earlier glories. In the third sentence that question is answered in the negative with the extent of his disappointment driven home with an exclamation mark. The central elements of his experience of Athens are neatly concentrated into three sentences. He then offers a subtle analysis of the reasons for the greatness of Athens and its subsequent fall. The irony was in the fact that a desire for fame and immortality, whilst the source of greatness, could also be a source of disaster. The Ancient Greeks simply used better means to achieve their immortality than many other societies. Having established this principle he illustrates it amusingly, in a manner which makes the basic irony clear. The desire for praise inspired everyone since 'vom Helden bis zum Lastträger, vom Genie eines Gesetzgebers, der einen neuen Staat schafft, bis zum bescheidenen Schneider, der eine neue Kleidung erfindet, streben alle nach demselben Ziel'. All of these examples are, however, positive and he replaces them with more controversial examples, more representative of his views. On the one hand it inspired Alexander to put the world to the torch: on the other hand it inspired the culture 'im schönen Zeitalter der Griechen', under Pericles. This is not just neutral praise of the best period. It also implies that the subsequent collapse of Greek culture, under leaders such as Alexander, was caused by the same instinct to seek immortality which helped raise them to greatness. As if to reinforce the superiority of earlier Greek culture he devotes the largest part of the passage to it. However, this is not unfocused praise. Their achievements are always mentioned in connection with the desire for immortality, thus stressing the unity of his argument. The achievements in the arts and sports were meant to guarantee praise and immortality, as is suggested by numerous words and phrases in the account: 'Ehrungen', 'das Gedächtnis des Siegers zu verewigen', 'Ehrgeiz', 'unsterbliche Helden', 'berühmt', 'unnachahmlich', 'Bewunderung', 'Beifall', 'Kronen'. This amounts to a powerful illustration of the force of an 'Urleidenschaft'. It also serves to make the subsequent question of the collapse of the culture—which is repeated at the end of the introduction to Athens—seem more poignant. The question echoes the opening description of Athens as the 'Heimat von so viel großen Männern, Wissenschaften und Künsten!' Now he asks 'was ist heute dieses Griechenland, einst die Amme der Künste und Wissenschaften, die fruchtbare Mutter von Philosophen, Gesetzgebern und Helden?' The personification underlines the sense of loss and also reminds us of his belief in the organic connection between environment and culture. The highly developed culture belongs to Greece like a child to its mother; the health of the one is tied to the other. The passage ends with generalization of the problem, comparing the decay of Greece to that of Carthage and even of Rome.

I dealt with this passage at some length in order to show that Riedesel's language need not necessarily be flat. Given suitable stimulation he could formulate arguments clearly and even colourfully. Whilst

JOHANN HERMANN VON RIEDESEL

he largely restricted himself to brief notes on what he saw, he did not always do so. He would suspend his usual concision in order to give vent to his responses to specific objects or situations. We have elsewhere an appeal for tolerance of other cultures and particularly an attack on people who have black-and-white opinions about the Turks (*Levante*, 143–4). We also have a passionate statement on the subservience of the Greeks under Roman rule (*Levante*, 112). He also showed a degree of enthusiasm for landscape (*Levante*, 92, 122). The introduction to the text contains a powerful statement of his political and religious credentials (*Levante*, 65). In dealing with art there is, however, no sign of a change of register. He provides notes on art and most other matters, emphasizing variety and novelty rather than depth of interest.

7. THE PRIVATE LETTERS

Only a small part of Riedesel's correspondence with his cousin Diede has been published. This concerns Riedesel's trip to the British Isles in 1770–1, but comprises only five letters.[90] Both Becker and Rehm's accounts are based upon examination of the full correspondence, which they include in their publications in fragmentary form. Because the original correspondence was not available to me, I have to make use of these imperfect sources. The situation is made particularly difficult by the fact that the fullest version of the letters, in the Jena edition, appears not to be complete. Becker, in the introduction to the *Levante*, cites at length a letter of July 1770 concerning Lady Glenorchy. The same letter is reproduced in the Jena edition but passages critical of Methodism have been removed.[91] Nevertheless the treatment of Scotland and parts of Northern England, and particularly Scottish landscapes, appears to be consistent in all versions and these will form the basis of my discussion.

(*a*) These few letters contain very little in the way of observations on politics, economics, or religion and those comments that are present certainly do not form a systematic whole. However, there are indications

---

[90] Johann Hermann von Riedesel, *Reisen des Freiherrn Johann Hermann Riedesel zu Eisenbach durch Sizilien, Großgriechenland, den Archipelagus nach Constantinopel und durch Großbritannien in den Jahren 1767, 1768 und 1770 in Briefen an seinen Freund Winckelmann, seine Schwester die Gräfin Degenfeld geb. Riedesel zu Eisenbach und seinen Vetter den Freiherrn Diede zum Fürstenstein* (Jena, 1830), 244–9. All subsequent references to British travel by Riedesel are taken from the same five pages of this text. No further indication of their provenance is given in the body of the text.
[91] Compare Riedesel, *Reisen*, 246 with *Levante*, 36.

that Riedesel's favourite themes, including religion, had not changed. In his view the Scots 'sont spéculatifs en tout, mais surtout en matières de religion, et le méthodisme, dont les principes sont tous mystiques, y fait plus de progrès que nulle part'. This sort of commentary corresponds very closely with the critical attitude towards organized religion present in his two publications.

His interest in the economy also surfaces briefly. He remarks on developments in Newcastle, 'cette ville enfumée et rouillée, riche, peuplée et opulente, rien de plus ressemblant à Liège! les mines de charbon, les machines à feu, tout cela est fort curieux et intéressant pour un voyageur et utile pour les habitans!' His interest in economic development meant that he also mentioned agriculture, canal-building, and other aspects of the local economies.[92] Furthermore he seemed sceptical about the value of the ordinary man's faith in his local aristocrat in a manner which we know from *Sizilien* and *Levante*. He also recommended to his cousin a publication by his new acquaintance James Stuart, entitled *Political Economy*. Of course, he shared political interests with his cousin, who like him became a diplomat.[93]

(*b*)–(*c*)–(*d*) There is practically no treatment of the visual arts in these letters. Edinburgh harbour 'est une belle pièce d'architecture, mais pas également solide'. Otherwise no visual art-form is mentioned. Correspondingly there is no attempt to account for the production and quality of art, or his response to it.

He did, however, discuss literature and music. He listened to 'les anciens airs celtes' and mentioned that 'tout le monde chante les poëmes de *Fingal*'. This interest in folk music and the Fingal sagas (he does not actually mention his son Ossian) would seem more characteristic of the Romantic movement and so would mark another point of divergence in Winckelmann and Riedesel's approaches. But Winckelmann's own taste in literature was also occasionally at odds with his tastes in the visual arts.[94] And at least the production theory was still being applied even if to radically different objects of study. The local poems offered the perfect reflection of the Romantic landscapes inhabited by Fingal and still present in Scotland. Riedesel himself walked 'près de montagnes couvertes de chênes plantés du tems de Fingal'. He reported the Romantic nature of poetic inspiration in Scotland through the example of an

---

[92] Cf. Riedesel, *Reisen*, 245 (agriculture), 246 (canals), 247–8 (local economy).
[93] Cf. *Levante*, 34.
[94] For example his interest in Geßner, even when it was, in contemporary terms, conventional. Cf. *Briefe*, ii. 407 f.

uneducated mountain poet. He read 'un poëme composé par une femme montagnarde, qui ne sait ni lire ni écrire, rustre, grossier il est vrai, mais rempli d'idées et d'imagination. On a des chants pour toutes choses dans ces pays, pour la pêche, pour la chasse, pour la guerre, chaque quartier en a un particulier'. But for the reader of Winckelmann this is a new type of artistic production, even if it is consistent with its environment. Even if we see this woman poet as more representative of ancient than modern Scottish culture—as a leftover from the time of Fingal—we still have evidence of an outlook contradicting some of Winckelmann's assumptions about art. Winckelmann, and with him Riedesel, had seen good art as the product of a highly developed culture. Their theory envisaged, on the basis of an examination of Greek culture, artists as products of that culture, concerned to guarantee their immortality in works with a high philosophical content. The sort of Scottish folk art described above, of whatever period, simply does not comply with these norms and there can be little doubt that Winckelmann would have rejected any claims for its greatness. We cannot imagine Winckelmann being interested, for example, in a song about fishing, composed by an illiterate. Even if the Fingal sagas could be seen as a parallel undertaking to Homer's works—and people did think them similar: he was the Homer of the North—they were rooted in a radically different culture. Any art was indeed a product of its environment but the very environment of Fingal would, for Winckelmann, have excluded great art.

As if to mark still further his departure from Winckelmann, Riedesel enumerated the qualities of the physical landscape which were attractive to him: they were, of course precisely those that repelled Winckelmann (see n. 24 above). Interestingly, these descriptions are couched in aesthetic terms—but not the terms of Winckelmann's aesthetic. He used the language of Rousseau and Burke rather than that of Winckelmann.[95] He was attracted by the sublime impact of the landscape, although his enthusiasm for the horribly beautiful was moderated slightly by his pleasure at seeing gentle, cultivated land also. He liked to see in the countryside the evidence of 'l'agrément mêlé à l'avantage'. This meant that he liked to see 'une campagne bien cultivée, quelquefois des rochers et du sauvage', or 'tantôt du sauvage, tantôt la main de l'agriculteur'. In fact these could be descriptions of the landscape in parts of Greece. However, the Romantic northern landscape was clearly most important. The following passages give a clear indication of his inspiration:

[95] Cf. Rehm, 'Riedesel', 243–5.

A *Hakfull* j'ai trouvé, tout ce que Salvador Rosa a jamais pu imaginer de romanesque et beau dans le grand et le sauvage; les plus belles cascades, des arbres touffus, des rocs, un ruisseau coulant ses eaux limpides sur des pierres innombrables, des ruines sur le sommet d'une montagne, une solitude mélancholique enfin, qui plaît tant quand on est triste et qui paraît soulager des regrets, que trop de desirs et de sensibilité ont pu faire naître.

. . . il faudrait copier cet endroit [Lockenhouse]; il est sauvage mais beau . . .

Nous avons vu les plus belles situations, des cascades superbes, tout ce que les déserts ont d'horriblement beau.

Je vous écris d'un paradis terrestre caché dans les montagnes d'Ecosse, et habité par les plus aimables personnes du monde.

Dans cette charmante solitude, je respire depuis trois jours, sur les bords d'un lac et d'une rivière délicieuse, sous les tilleuls plus beaux que ceux des Tuileries, près de montagnes couvertes de chênes plantés du tems de Fingal, du sommet desquelles deux cascades précipitent leurs flots argentés dans ce petit océan. Chaque pas que l'on fait offre une nouvelle vue, chaque vue surpasse l'autre en beauté et majesté. Tantôt du sauvage, tantôt la main de l'agriculteur, tantôt la musette et les troupeaux du berger tranquille frappent la vue et l'oreille.

. . . j'ai passé un jour à *Inverary*, l'endroit le plus singulier, le plus sauvage, le plus horriblement beau, que l'on puisse voir . . .

Le pays est sauvage, mais beau dans ce genre, et surpasse tout ce que l'on trouve de beau, dans les Alpes, et les Apennins.

Rehm argues that Riedesel found in Scotland what he had been looking for in Greece, namely 'Andres, Nichtkultiviertes, nicht französisch Bestimmtes, also Urwüchsiges, Unberührtes'.[96] Riedesel did indeed search for traces of the earlier Greek appearance and character on his journeys in Southern Europe. The fact that he indicates at points that Scotland would be the place for Scipio, Aristides, Homer, and Virgil would suggest that he was on a similar search in Northern Europe. However, if Riedesel's wishes correspond with Rehm's assertion then they mark a point of divergence from Winckelmann. In Greece it looked as if Riedesel was trying to confirm aspects of Winckelmann's theories about the nature of the Greeks, and only the Greeks. Other cultures were examined only to provide counter-examples. The whole point of the undertaking, which Riedesel supported particularly in *Sizilien*, was to prove the superiority of Greek culture and identify the factors which contributed to it. They were looking for a very specific 'Urwuchs', to use Rehm's term, and hoping to provide a very specific answer to French

---

[96] Rehm, 'Riedesel', 244.

cultural hegemony. The probability of finding a substitute in Scotland was impossibly low since none of the environmental factors, physical or otherwise, which produced the Greek character were present there. If Riedesel believed that he had found one then he had either fundamentally misunderstood Winckelmann's intentions or chosen to ignore them. He would appear to be searching for the primitive rather than the polite and not for the Greek as opposed to the non-Greek: these are oppositions of radically different kinds. Riedesel was introducing new criteria in establishing Homer and Ossian together in opposition to dominant French culture. Winckelmann's interest in Homer—which was profound—was based on his essential Greek nature.[97]

If we take the aesthetic terminology given above and imagine applying it to works of art we gain some idea of the extent of the divergence. Winckelmann's noble simplicity simply cannot accommodate the sublime, as it is presented by Riedesel. The calm associated with noble simplicity would be shattered by such horrible impressions. The range and extremity of emotions and aesthetic effects characteristic of the sublime (in Riedesel's landscape descriptions) stands in contrast to the simple, unified effects that Winckelmann admired. Whilst Winckelmann, and Riedesel with him, felt sad at the passing of Greek culture this was compensated by the uplifting, spiritual effect of exposure to their art. The final effect was one of elevation rather than melancholy—the Greek ruins Winckelmann could imaginatively reconstruct. Through this process the ancient world could be brought to life and the sadness of the destruction of the objects and the culture that produced them overcome. However, for the Romantic the ruin (again part of Riedesel's Scottish landscape) was itself the object of reverence: it provoked melancholy reverie.

By embracing what appears to be a Romantic manner of seeing Riedesel has clearly moved very far from Winckelmann. This brief glimpse at his letters confirms the impression that developed in my reading of *Levante*, namely that immediately Winckelmann's direct influence was removed, Riedesel began to adopt other approaches. In *Levante* the departure was not as radical since the 'new' theories were closely related to those which informed Winckelmann's work. However, the object had changed since the arts were only of secondary interest. In the Scottish letters both the manner of seeing and the objects of interest have changed.

[97] Cf. Konrad Kraus, *Winckelmann und Homer* (Berlin, 1935) and Wolfgang Schadewaldt, *Winckelmann und Homer*, Leipziger Universitätsreden, 6 (Leipzig, 1941).

8. CONCLUSION

In this chapter I have shown that Riedesel's early education corresponded broadly with Winckelmann's expectations of his pupils, although in some areas we lack specific confirmative evidence. He had the wealth and the freedom of movement which Winckelmann saw as necessary (1(a)–(b)). He was also young but perhaps lacked the good looks which Winckelmann associated with the ability to appreciate beauty. However, Winckelmann's own statements and those of others indicate that he had the required sensibility (1(c)–(d)). The only reservation would be that he was praised largely for his thoroughness rather than for his engagement with art. Goethe saw a lack of poetry in his responses.

On this basis a firm friendship developed. On the surface their private correspondence did not differ from many of Winckelmann's other correspondences. The apparent familiarity of the forms of address in fact emerges as largely formulaic (2(a)). However, other evidence suggests that this was a particularly warm friendship. The range of topics covered in the letters would indicate a close understanding of one another's interests (2(b)). To this extent most of Winckelmann's requirements for a successful aesthetic education were in place.

In his treatment of the visual arts Riedesel showed a large degree of dependence on Winckelmann. The limited discussion of the arts in the private correspondence revolves around new discoveries but there are some indications that their discussions of art were based upon shared theoretical assumptions. In particular it seems that elements of the production theory and the pattern of Winckelmann's historical and qualitative judgements of art were familiar to him (3(b)–(c)). A sort of shorthand for the quality of a work of art seems to have been operating. It is used in the letters by Winckelmann, whose side of the correspondence survives. Riedesel was to use a similar shorthand in his own publications. Like Winckelmann's method it was based on indicating the degree of similarity of the given work to the best Greek art, which provided absolute criteria for quality. These letters naturally provide no indication of engagement with art in the Winckelmannian manner because they contain none of his own statements (3(d)). Winckelmann does, however, refer to the 'Empfindung' for art of his pupil.

The *Sendschreiben von der Reise eines Liebhabers der Künste nach Rom* also gives us some indication of the education that Riedesel underwent. Interestingly no element of the production theory is to be found in this incomplete text. It concentrates on the stylistic history of architecture and certain of the guidelines here are taken over directly into Riedesel's other publications (4(c)). It also contains no reference to high aesthetic engagement since it was aimed at people at an early stage in their aesthetic education.

Riedesel's two publications naturally provide the fullest evidence of his debt to Winckelmann. It is most apparent in *Sizilien*. Even in the matter of general political or religious discussion Riedesel appeared to espouse views which were close to those of Winckelmann (5(a)). In the treatment of the arts the relationship was obviously much closer and parts of Riedesel's text appear to contain direct answers to problems raised in Winckelmann's texts (5(b)–(c)). He also constantly referred to Winckelmann himself and asked for guidance in solving archaeological problems. The relationship was so close that many people have supposed that Winckelmann took a major editorial role in order to make the text conform with his expectations. Numerous elements of the production theory were applied to discoveries in Sicily and it was also used to account for the lack of artistic production in contemporary Sicily. The stylistic/historical criteria according to which works of art were judged also bear a very close resemblance to those which we know from Winckelmann. In particular the dismissal of the Middle Ages and the concentration of the search on noble simplicity in art were hallmarks of Winckelmann. In fact it is arguable that Winckelmann's effect on the work was inhibitive since he imposes a number of prejudices which prevent Riedesel from assessing works of art objectively. However, even when he found great works there is no evidence that he engaged himself with them. For Riedesel works of art appear to be historical artefacts rather than sources of inspiration (5(d)). His characteristic attitude towards art was passive and he felt most at home with architecture which could be explained in mathematical terms. It has been argued that, for example, the fact that these were only letters and then written in his second language would account for the dryness of the accounts. There is, however, evidence that even writing in German Riedesel could express enthusiasm and interest. He appears only to have done this when the subject was not art.

Of course, a constant problem when dealing with the production/historical aspects of *Sizilien* is the fact that many of Winckelmann's theories were themselves derivative. It does, however, seem reasonable to suggest that Winckelmann was at least the latest and most direct source of, for example, the production theory which could be traced back through Montesquieu into antiquity. The constant explicit and implicit references to Winckelmann would support this case. However, in *Levante* the argument appears to be undermined. Riedesel refers directly to Rousseau and, particularly, Montesquieu in his account. This can be explained by the very different nature of the texts. *Levante* is not concerned primarily with the arts: it is a wide-ranging account, covering politics, religion, and anthropology. As such it is appropriate to return to the similarly wide-ranging Montesquieu for inspiration. Whereas Winckelmann used theories such as his to a specific end, namely to account for aspects of art history, Montesquieu was concerned with a much broader spectrum of issues. It is therefore appropriate that when Riedesel moves away from a primary interest in the arts he should similarly see parallels between his observations and those of a more general historian and theorist (6(a)–(b)–(c)). Interestingly there is some evidence of colourful style and rhetorical use of language in his account but again the stimulus is political rather than artistic (6(d)). The fact that Riedesel appears to have drifted away from Winckelmann's influence during *Levante* has profound implications for our assessment of the success of his aesthetic education.

In the Scottish letters Riedesel not only shows general, rather than artistic interests, but also a wholly different manner of seeing (7). In particular the language of his landscape descriptions owes more to Rousseau and Burke than to Winckelmann. His aesthetic expectations are wholly different in these letters when compared to those in *Sizilien* and *Levante*. The setting in part determined this change but the fact that there was such a profound change indicates that the hold of Winckelmann's aesthetic was not as firm as he would have hoped.

Even if we look at the best parts of Riedesel's work—viewed from a Winckelmannian perspective—we see only the scholarly component and not the whole aesthetic of his teacher. There is no evidence that Riedesel experienced the transformative power of art in the way that Winckelmann did. Perhaps because of this he was distracted towards more general interests. He thought in historical terms rather than aesthetic terms, and in historical terms a new agricultural method was as likely to be significant as a new work of art. He seems to have been insensitive to aesthetic potential, even in the Scottish landscapes which he loved. Describing the area around Stirling he says:

Comme habitant bourgeois de cette ville, il faut que j'en fasse les éloges et si j'étais poëte, je dirais que ce vallon est si beau, que la rivière a peine à s'en arracher et par mille détours prend plaisir à prolonger son cours, mais ne l'étant pas, je vous dirais en bonne prose, que la distance d'un village, qui n'est que 4 milles par terre, devient celle de 24 par eau.

He had similar difficulties in coming to terms with the 'poetry' of art, as Goethe had suspected.[98] Unlike Winckelmann he was unable, or unwilling, to come to terms with art by writing about his experience of it. Winckelmann appears to have operated according to a variant of the artistic adage: 'dessiner, c'est connaître'. For him the experience of writing about art was his way of getting to know it. Riedesel was deprived of this rewarding level of acquaintance.

It is very easy to drift into a negative critical tone when examining a pupil's work in the light of a more eminent teacher's achievements. Riedesel's work inevitably seems less interesting than that of Winckelmann. But we must be cautious: we may not be comparing like with like. Riedesel's work was subject to practical and generic constraints of a kind not experienced by Winckelmann. Winckelmann, after all, determined the scope of and time available for his work; there was room for innovation as he created his own field of study. Riedesel appears not to have enjoyed that sort of freedom, even if one assumes a will to have done so. And the reader of Riedesel who is seeking a particular Winckelmannian manner of seeing is also haunted by a problem of proof, mentioned earlier. How could he prove beyond doubt the presence or absence of a particular brand of aesthetic insight? We have literary evidence of Winckelmann's insight but it is not possible to argue on that basis that aesthetic understanding is necessarily connected with the ability to articulate that understanding in writing. It does not follow that all aesthetes will be able to write up their experiences, indeed Winckelmann himself (as we saw in Chapter 2) was preoccupied with the pitfalls of self-expression. On that basis it is not really suprising, and least of all disappointing, that Riedesel should not emerge as a new poet of the visual arts. The comparison of Winckelmann with Riedesel, far from clarifying the process of aesthetic education, could be said to obscure it. On the basis of literary evidence can we prove the development of an improved sensibility? In some cases, if not in Riedesel's, such evidence might at least suggest it. Riedesel's writing, which to be fair is the only substantive evidence available to us, seems to point in a different direction. And on the grounds of fairness we should perhaps side with

---

[98] Cf. *Levante*, 96. Here he tries to imagine that stalactites form in the shape of human beings—because other spectators insist that they can see human features there—but he does not succeed. Imagination was not his strength.

Winckelmann and assume the best of Riedesel for want of definitive proofs otherwise.

If the pathways of aesthetic education seem complex in the case of Riedesel then they become more so when we deal with J. J. Volkmann, whose life and works were subject to a whole new series of constraints.

4
Johann Jacob Volkmann

JOHANN JACOB VOLKMANN'S position in literary history is broadly similar to that of Johann Hermann von Riedesel. He is largely known by association with Goethe since in Goethe's luggage for his Italian journey, alongside a copy of Riedesel's *Sizilien*, were the three volumes of Volkmann's *Historisch-kritische Nachrichten von Italien*. This text marks one of the many direct connections between Winckelmann and Goethe, alongside Oeser and Riedesel. In the latter case we have seen how a text, produced by a Winckelmann pupil, not only marks a chance personal connection between Winckelmann and Goethe but also paves the way for a (limited) degree of ideological continuity between the two men. Even if the vision and insight which I identified in Winckelmann was lacking in Riedesel's texts they reproduced some of the basic tenets of his historical approach, albeit whilst reminding us of the French writers whose work informed Winckelmann's. Goethe's reading of *Sizilien* will inevitably have (re-)exposed him to this version of Winckelmann as art historian. In part this chapter will be concerned to answer the question whether, and if so to what extent, Volkmann's *Nachrichten* could have transmitted Winckelmann's thinking to another generation of readers and in particular whether it reproduces anything more than his art history.

Of course, Volkmann's text is very different in nature from Riedesel's. It was intended as a handy but at the same time comprehensive guidebook, kept down to a reasonable size by means of a focus on the visual arts, at least when compared with more conventional itineraries.[1] This focus on the arts might appear to offer some promise in the search for elements of Winckelmann's *Gedankengut*. However, numerous aspects of the text undermine it. By its very nature the guidebook would appear to offer little space for serious discussion of the arts. Any comments are likely to be introductory, or superficial in nature. Breadth of coverage is likely to be preferred to depth of investigation. Eighteenth-century guidebooks had not yet reached the stage of offering marks or stars for

---

[1] The normal range of interest in travel literature is indicated by the itinerary reproduced in Ch. 1.

quality but they did operate on the basis of key words which would indicate the degree to which a given work of art conformed to contemporary expectations of quality. Some of the most potent key words for the late eighteenth century were 'nobility', 'simplicity', or 'grandeur', words which are very strongly associated with Winckelmann. To that extent we may find in Volkmann evidence of the transmission of Winckelmannian ideology but any feeling of success is likely to be offset by the vulgarization of that ideology which reduces it simply to a number of code words. The problem of vulgarization which we saw in Riedesel was not as far-reaching as it was in contemporary guidebooks, which offered their authors even less space for exhaustive coverage of the arts than there was in a brief personal travelogue in the form of letters. This generic difficulty is compounded by the fact that the greatest part of Volkmann's work was not in fact his own. The *Nachrichten* consist in essence of a translation of Lalande's *Voyage d'un François en Italie* supplemented by translations of Richard and Cochin's guides where they contribute fresh insights.[2] Despite the formulaic assertion to have seen everything himself, Volkmann's own contribution is restricted to a number of brief interjections, the addition of a small amount of supplementary information, and the introduction of some personal notes (not least in connection with Winckelmann). Despite these evident problems, I was drawn to the text by the fact that it was produced by one of Winckelmann's long-term pupils, and by a man who had most of the qualifications expected by Winckelmann. That such a pupil should then produce works which do little justice to his teacher is itself of interest. In the same way that for a scientist an experiment with no result can be as productive as any other, so Volkmann's failure to produce Winckelmannian insights has an intrinsic interest. Volkmann's guidebook almost operates as an antidote to Winckelmann's efforts. Whilst Winckelmann was complaining about the unqualified people who were making their way to Rome Volkmann was providing them with a guidebook.[3] His work was a publishing success and because of its authoritative tone may have hindered more profound preparations for a visit to Italy, envisaged by Winckelmann. In bringing together a number of respected authors in one work Volkmann may have given his readers the impression that here was all you needed to

---

[2] Wherever Volkmann uses material taken directly from these sources I indicate this in the body of the text. Typically a passage cited from Volkmann will be followed by a parenthetic bibliographical reference in the form: (*Nachrichten*, vol. and page = (e.g.) Lalande, vol. and page).

[3] Winckelmann complained directly to Volkmann about poorly prepared travellers (*Briefe*, ii. 131).

know. He in fact claimed that his work could supplant the 'cicerone' or 'antiquario' for most travellers (see below). Certainly we have the impression that Volkmann's publications were demand led. The increasingly broad travelling public was his goal—and indeed his own presence in Rome, as a middle-class gentleman rather than an aristocrat, was a sign of the changing times which his publications exploit. Winckelmann's approach was, to put it crudely, product led. He sought people who would be in a position to do justice to the works of art, rather than attempting what Volkmann and others clearly achieved, that is to bring works of art closer to the people.

Of course, there exist sketches for guides by Winckelmann himself. They do not have the range of Volkmann's publications but they also differ in other more important ways. They are tailored to individuals or groups of individuals, offer advice on preparation, and are aimed in the first instance at developing a clear historical sense through systematic treatment of few objects. Their scope was limited but then they were to be supplemented by the personal involvement of Winckelmann himself as tutor and provider of the enthusiastic treatment of individual works. Volkmann's texts are the antithesis of this intimate approach and most significantly they contain nothing of the author himself. In as far as his texts have an educational function they have a very different, or at least more limited one than Winckelmann's programme offered. They provide conclusions about works of art rather than preparation for personal insight. And those conclusions are not necessarily based upon Volkmann's observations and so to that extent they contradict that most fundamental of Winckelmann's instructions: 'Geh hin und sieh!' (KS 233). Volkmann uses other people's insights in his translation, although he occasionally corrects errors of fact. There could scarcely be a clearer departure from Winckelmannian expectations; even Riedesel was an empiricist, went to Sicily, saw and measured works of art, and wrote his own account. Volkmann's guidebook could be seen as a microcosmic representation of the fate of Winckelmann's ideas in general, of the manner in which they became subject to vulgarization and absorbed into the mainstream of art criticism with only a few phrases reminding us of their original aesthetic impact. Of course, we return here to our core problem of proof: how can we be sure that art had no aesthetic impact on Volkmann? There may be no measurable literary evidence but that need not mean that art had no impact on him. It may yet prove a dangerous enterprise to try to measure pupils' achievements in Winckelmann's terms.

However, if we look at Volkmann's guidebook on its own terms it is quite clearly a success, a fact which is reflected in its reception. But these are not the terms of this book, and indeed not terms which Winckelmann could have appreciated. Perhaps it was always optimistic to look for a Winckelmannian manner of seeing in a guidebook since the genre seems unlikely to encourage it. Its presence would be exceptional—but then we are clearly looking for something exceptional. Even contemporary art-historical writing reveals little engagement of the Winckelmannian sort; Winckelmann's interest was exceptional and redefined the boundaries of art history. Volkmann did not contribute as much to the genre of guidebook since the *Nachrichten* is a very conservative text.[4] To that extent he has not fully absorbed Winckelmann's teaching. Volkmann's text achieved what he meant it to achieve; it was a very good 'Handbuch'. Interestingly Winckelmann said that when writing the *Geschichte der Kunst* he too was aiming to write a 'Handbuch'. In a letter to Volkmann, however, he reported how this limited scheme had been altered. His 'Handbuch' had become a 'Werk' (*Briefe*, ii. 129). The difference is not merely one of scale and in part this chapter is concerned to identify the features which made the *Nachrichten* stop at being a handbook.

1. THE PREPARATION FOR THE VISIT TO ITALY

As we have seen, Winckelmann identified four factors which could significantly affect the prospects of aesthetic education. They were (*a*) wealth, (*b*) location, (*c*) youth, and (*d*) sensibility. The picture which emerges in connection with Volkmann is not as positive as that which we had of Riedesel, although in part this is due to lack of information. None the less, Winckelmann thought him a worthy pupil—they spent over a year in close contact in Rome and Florence—even if his background was, in Winckelmannian terms, not conventional.

(a) Wealth

Volkmann came from a family of independent means, but those means were not derived from the benefits of aristocracy. The Volkmanns were a very successful middle-class family. According to the *Allgemeine*

[4] Cf. W. E. Stewart, *Die Reisebeschreibung und ihre Theorie im Deutschland des 18. Jahrhunderts* (Bonn, 1978).

deutsche Biographie Johann Jacob's father was a 'Licentiat der Rechte' and his maternal grandfather had been Mayor of Hamburg. Johann Jacob and his brother Peter looked set to continue this middle-class tradition. Johann's studies included law and his brother became a respected doctor and later a 'Senator'.[5] The family wealth was sufficient to cover their periods of study and subsequently to fund extensive periods of travel for both men. Their family history points to an interesting transitional phase in European social history where the bourgeosie was becoming increasingly dominant, especially through its control of the money supply, the prime determinant of freedom. The fact that we should be dealing with Volkmann in the context of the previously aristocratic preserve of the Grand Tour only serves to confirm this impression of an increasingly ambitious middle class.[6] It is also interesting to contrast Riedesel's occasional financial troubles and the very limited amount of land under his control with Volkmann's decision in 1764 to buy the 'Ritter- und Mannlehengüter' at Zschortau and Biesen in Saxony. His ability to buy these properties before his publishing successes and before he had been able to earn significantly after his most important travels is a firm indication of the wealth of the family and the aspirations of his class generally. Interestingly he, like Riedesel, did not take to running the estates himself and soon let them out so that he could concentrate on his writing. There is every reason to believe that earlier, namely during the period preceding and during his time with Winckelmann, Volkmann enjoyed this same sort of freedom to study based upon family wealth. This was, of course, in accordance with Winckelmann's wishes for his pupils. There remains the question of whether Volkmann's studies were of the disinterested kind envisaged by Winckelmann. The *Biographie universelle* suggests that his writing was inspired by the money on offer. It notes that 'très-avide d'argent, il ne cessa de travailler jusqu'à sa mort'.[7] However, it seems unlikely that his royalties would have made a very significant contribution to his private wealth, which was guaranteed by his status as eldest son in the family. The quotation also suggests a rather cynical attitude towards the value of work. Certainly much of his writing was not based on original research and was basically translation, but this does not make it unimportant. If he

[5] All biographical information was taken from the *Allgemeine deutsche Biographie*, 56 vols. (Leipzig, 1875–1912), xl. 237, except where I indicate otherwise.

[6] There is, of course, other pertinent anecdotal evidence of this trend in the travels of Johann Wolfgang Goethe and earlier his father Johann Caspar. Cf. Ch. 5 below and J. C. Goethe, *Reise durch Italien im Jahre 1740 (Viaggio per l'Italia)*, ed. and trans. A. Meier (Munich, 1986). [7] *Biographie universelle*, xliv. 58.

was unable to provide original research himself he could at least make the work of others available to a wider public. Such work is not necessarily inspired by the prospect of financial gain.

Volkmann's social and financial profile must have appeared to Winckelmann to be broadly equivalent to those of the many aristocrats whom he met. They met in fact through the Count Firmian. Winckelmann was responsible for introducing him to (von) Stosch and at home he was in contact with (von) Berg (*Briefe*, i. 403–4, 603, iv. 91). At one point Winckelmann even refers to him as 'Hr. von Volkmann' in a letter to Caspar Füssli, and even if this is more a reflection of his desire to be seen mixing in the highest social circles, it still suggests that Volkmann could have passed for a nobleman (*Briefe*, i. 400). There is therefore little to suggest that in this respect at least he was not an ideal pupil, albeit without a title.

(b) Location

The most important place for Winckelmann's pupils to be was in proximity to great works of art. If disadvantaged at home Volkmann was very fortunate to be able to afford to travel, apparently at will. These travels could, according to Winckelmann, compensate for the natural disadvantages for the student of art of living in Northern Europe. Of course, for Winckelmann the only true destination was Italy. Volkmann was aware of the importance of Italy and he spent a large period of time there, most importantly in 1758. During the summer of that year he was in Rome and in almost daily contact with Winckelmann.[8] They met again in Florence later that year. To that extent he was not one of the many travellers who made only fleeting visits to the most important sites. His relationship with Winckelmann was of very significant proportions and measured by duration alone would place him alongside other important pupils such as Riedesel. The Italian journey was a serious undertaking for Volkmann, but in the context of his later travels its significance seems to diminish. He travelled to and wrote about a number of countries and his publications about these rival cultures are at least as substantial as that on Italy.[9] If that is not enough to qualify our

---

[8] Both the *Allgemeine Deutsche Biographie* and Daßdorf's introduction to *Winckelmanns Briefe an seine Freunde* suggest daily contact with Winckelmann.

[9] Cf. J. J. Volkmann, *Neueste Reisen durch Frankreich*, 3 vols. (Leipzig, 1787); *Neueste Reisen durch Spanien*, 2 vols. (Leipzig, 1785); *Neueste Reisen durch England*, 4 vols. (Leipzig, 1781–2); *Neueste Reisen durch die Vereinigten Niederlande* (Leipzig, 1783); *Neueste Reisen durch Schottland und Irland* (Leipzig, 1784); *Italienische Bibliothek*, 2

impression of his interest in Italy then we need only look at the period immediately after his departure from Rome. Volkmann in fact left for France, where he completed his university education in the form of a doctorate at Lyon. Winckelmann consistently objected to the dominance of French culture (despite his own debt to it) and we can assume that Volkmann was aware of his objections. It is therefore striking that he should immediately move there; his formal education almost appears to act as a counterbalance to the less formal aesthetic education which he had undergone in Italy. Volkmann had a less strict view of the value of location in education than Winckelmann. He clearly felt, if his actions reflected his feelings, that exposure to the maximum number of cultures was likely to have greater educational value than devotion to a single country. This devalued Italy for him but did not lead to its dismissal. The importance of Italy was sufficient for him to arrange for his brother to visit also, and indeed for him to meet the same teacher, Winckelmann. However, it was the same brother with whom he later travelled to Holland and England.

(c) Youth

There can be litle doubt that Volkmann met Winckelmann at the right time, in the latter's terms. He was born on 17 March 1732 and so was 26 during the period which they spent in close contact. His formal education was not yet complete and he was not forced to work in order to support himself. Although perhaps a little older than Winckelmann's ideal there is little to suggest that his age would have been a disadvantage for Winckelmann. It is, however, interesting that his publications on Italy do not follow on immediately from his experience of it. The *Nachrichten* were published in 1770–1, some twelve years after his period with Winckelmann and perhaps this gap could help to explain the rather dry nature of the text. His works seem more appropriate to the middle-aged author rather than the youthful enthusiast; they are the product of an author setting himself sensible, if limited goals, rather than trying to do justice to exciting aesthetic experience, although there can be little doubt that his earlier Italian journey provided the inspiration and some of the raw materials for the book.[10]

vols. (Leipzig, 1778–9). The editorial procedure is in each case similar to that employed in the *Nachrichten*.

[10] Cf. *Briefe*, ii. 415. Rehm here suggests that Winckelmann and Volkmann's discussions of travel writing reflect the beginnings of Volkmann's publishing plans in the 1750s and 1760s.

(d) Sensibility

We have very little evidence of Volkmann's likely responsiveness to the arts outside his texts. Winckelmann's letters to him contain, unlike those to Riedesel, no specific reference to his aesthetic sensibility. This represents a distinct omission. Winckelmann often used praise as a tool to manipulate people as well as to express his genuine feeling for them. The fact that such comments are missing on either count may therefore indicate a perceived failure. But it is beyond doubt that Winckelmann spent a lot of time and effort on Volkmann which would in turn suggest that the necessary sensibility was not absent. In a letter to Volkmann Winckelmann referred to 'die unweisen unberichteten jungen Gecken' circulating in Rome, and we can safely assume that he did not see Volkmann as one of these (*Briefe*, ii. 131). His recommendation of Volkmann to Stosch would also suggest that he saw him in a positive light, although it may have been a social or political move.

Daßdorf says in his introduction to Winckelmann's letters to Volkmann that the two men shared 'gleiche Lieblingsneigungen', pursued 'verwandte Studien', and showed 'wechselseitige Hochachtung und innige Werthschätzung'.[11] This may be true but Daßdorf does not give the evidence which enabled him to make this judgement. Indeed Daßdorf's whole editorial procedure means that we cannot be sure that we have the full picture of their relationship; we also know that some letters went missing during Volkmann's move to Saxony.[12] Our suspicion must be that Daßdorf is presenting Volkmann's view of the relationship. In a later passage in the same introduction Daßdorf appears to be citing Volkmann, presumably from a letter concerning the publication of the letters which does not itself survive. If true it shows that Volkmann was at least exposed to the sensibility which enabled true understanding of art:

> Herr *Volkmann* erinnert sich hierbey immer noch mit einem eigenen Vergnügen an den Enthusiasmus, womit ihn sein Freund die bekannte Beschreibung des *Torso* und des *Apolls* in Belvedere vorlas, so daß die Päpstlichen Aufseher immer mit offenem Munde ganz erstaunt da standen, und vielleicht dachten, daß die mal'aria ihm das Gehirn verrückt hätte.[13]

This account does not sound entirely positive. Whilst mocking the *Aufseher* it also manages to make Winckelmann's enthusiasm seem

---

[11] *Winckelmanns Briefe an seine Freunde*, ed. Daßdorf, ii. 173.
[12] Cf. *Briefe*, i. 464.
[13] *Winckelmanns Briefe an seine Freunde*, ed. Daßdorf, ii. 175.

manic. We sense that Volkmann did not fully understand what he was seeing.

The fact that he introduced Winckelmann to Geßner's work might suggest that there was a common strand of feeling (*Briefe*, ii. 113). Similarly his continued interest in the arts and the fact that he kept in contact with other aesthetes such as Weisse and Hagedorn would seem positive, although Winckelmann was not always an admirer of Hagedorn.[14] However, the reliance upon this sort of scant evidence can be dangerous. Later Volkmann translated Baltimore's travels into German. Are we to assume on that basis that his particular sensibility had disappeared? Winckelmann regarded Baltimore as one of the worst specimens of British aristocrat that he encountered.[15] We can only safely say that Volkmann's background and education at Leipzig and Göttingen (including ancient and modern languages as well as law) prepared him well for the trip, and that during it Winckelmann devoted a great deal of time to him.

2. THE RELATIONSHIP

The clearest aspect of the relationship between Winckelmann and Volkmann was its duration. After their period together in 1758 they maintained a correspondence at least until 1764. The last surviving letter to Volkmann from Winckelmann was sent in February 1764 although there are references to him in later letters, notably to P. D. Volkmann in 1766, which includes best wishes and expresses the hope of selling him a copy of the *Monumenti* (*Briefe*, iii. 18, 209). He is also mentioned (albeit negatively) in a letter to H. Füssli written in April 1767, although this letter does not indicate that the postal relationship between Volkmann and Winckelmann was still intact but merely that Volkmann still figured in his thinking (*Briefe*, iii. 252). Because of the missing letters it is difficult to be certain of the period over which the relationship endured in any significant form beyond the sixth year. Also, if the number of letters for the period 1758–64 truly reflects the state of their correspondence, it could not be described as a very intense one. As they stand the letters are punctuated by considerable gaps and Winckelmann writes mostly to summarize the events since the last letter.[16] The fact that

---

[14] Cf. *Briefe*, iv. 79, 81 for the connection with other aesthetes and *Briefe*, ii. 19 for Winckelmann's negative attitude to Hagedorn.   [15] Cf. Ch. 1 n. 8.

[16] *Briefe*, ii. 128 refers to a large gap. The letter dates from Mar. 1761. The previous surviving letter is from Dec. 1758 (*Briefe*, i. 439).

Winckelmann's summaries reach back so far gives a fairly clear idea that not many letters are missing from intervening periods since otherwise Winckelmann would surely have been repeating information that was already old hat. We might expect their correspondence to have been given something of a boost after five years of separation by the arrival in December 1763 (in the company of H. Füssli) of P. D. Volkmann (*Briefe*, ii. 466). However, by this stage the relationship had gone downhill and although Winckelmann's acceptance of the brother may have been based upon some residual affection for Volkmann, it seems to have been guaranteed by Füssli's presence since without this 'hätte ich ihm das schändliche Betragen seines Bruders empfinden laßen, und ich würde keinen Schritt für ihn gegangen seyn' (*Briefe*, iii. 253). The signs are then confusing—a long but not intense correspondence, maintained despite quite clear negative undercurrents. The duration of the relationship is not the clear positive indicator that we might have expected and the contradictions of their relationship will bear closer examination.

Winckelmann was able to talk about his private concerns to Volkmann in much the same way as he was later to do with Riedesel. The themes that emerge are the same. In one letter from December 1758 we hear about his 'eselsmäßige Arbeit', his sceptical attitude towards the Catholic Church, and the impending necessity 'Messe zu lesen'. We also hear about his finances (and the beginnings of his relationship with Albani) and about his loves, in this case the attractive 12-year-old dancer whom he had recently seen in the theatre, commenting: 'Ich glaube aber, es ist in ganz Paris keine solche Schönheit; allein, ich will nicht ungetreu werden'. Rehm does not comment on the last part of this sentence but it seems to suggest that Volkmann was aware of Winckelmann's preferences and knew who would be offended by any disloyalty. Winckelmann also refers to a freely written ending to the *Geschichte der Kunst* which he would include if he was sure that he was not going to return to Germany (and so which never appeared). The implication here is that Volkmann will have known and understood Winckelmann's attitude towards the contemporary political situation in Germany, even if it was difficult to express in the public realm (*Briefe*, i. 439–41).

The letters also have the common feature of Winckelmann's letters to friends, namely his pleas for practical/financial help. The most important task selected for Volkmann was to find a Hamburg publisher for the *Geschichte der Kunst*, a project which did not come to fruition but which was potentially a highly responsible one and a sign of a considerable degree of trust (*Briefe*, ii. 236–8, 458).¹⁷ In fact these basic features of the letters, plus the extended period of the correspondence, would lead us to think of Volkmann as Winckelmann's good friend were it not for the presence of more sinister undertones, mentioned earlier. Certainly Winckelmann could only hope for limited practical help from Volkmann, and he was unlikely to introduce him to major patrons, or finance a trip to Greece; it therefore seems likely that a degree of affection was present. He could have chosen to ignore Volkmann, as he did countless other travellers, and need not have accepted his brother, with or without Füssli. Some fundamental connection between the two men seems to have survived the very difficult period which saw Volkmann cursed for 'das schändliche Betragen' (*Briefe*, iii. 253). Sadly the exact nature of Volkmann's crime remains obscure, although it is referred to on a number of occasions. It concerned Volkmann's attitude towards Stosch but cannot be explained much further; Volkmann appears to have abused Winckelmann's introduction to Stosch by upsetting his host (*Briefe*, ii. 25). Winckelmann did not forget it easily (*Briefe*, ii. 85, iii. 253). And this rift may help to explain the obvious gap in the letters between 1758 and 1761, although once more the transmission of the letters leaves us in doubt.

Winckelmann does not refer to Volkmann's crime directly in his letters to him. His attitude is, however, noticeably cooler than that to Riedesel. In dealing with Riedesel I noted the effusiveness of the forms of address but was hesitant to make a value-judgement about them because of their largely formulaic nature. The Volkmann correspondence makes it clear that even these formulas can give an indication of the quality of a relationship. A correspondent can choose amongst the available formulas and Winckelmann chose rather cooler terms for Volkmann than for Riedesel. In the first letter he is 'mit aller Hochachtung und Freundschaft | Der Ihrige'. Later he says: 'Ich empfehle mich ihrer beständigen Freundschaft, und bin beständig | Der Ihrige' (*Briefe*, i. 441, ii. 130). Elsewhere: 'Ich bin, wie ich jederzeit seyn werde | Ihr ergebenster Freund und Diener' (*Briefe*, ii. 213, 238). Most passionate is the signing off: 'Er [Hagedorn] sey gebenedeyet in Ewigkeit! und auch Sie' (*Briefe*, iii. 19). But Volkmann is almost an accessory to the blessing here.

The terms in which he refers to Volkmann when writing to other

¹⁷ *Winckelmanns Briefe an seine Freunde*, ed. Daßdorf, ii. 201 discusses the arrangements for the publication of the *Geschichte der Kunst*. Apparently Volkmann was even prepared to pay for the plates in order to avoid further difficulties. Volkmann's letter explaining the problems to Winckelmann did not arrive and so the latter returned to his old publisher.

people are still cooler. The complaints about Volkmann's 'Streich' form the biggest group of references to him but even in other contexts he scarcely warrants a description other than as 'ein Hamburger' (*Briefe*, i. 400, ii. 113). The sort of praise that Winckelmann expressed for Riedesel is not present in any comparable form for Volkmann, even when there would appear to be opportunities. Volkmann and Winckelmann shared a very important trip to Pesto to visit the temples. In Winckelmann's letters concerning the trip Volkmann is mentioned only in passing. He introduced Winckelmann to Geßner and read aloud from his work; although this would appear to be a very significant contribution, the report is very matter-of-fact.[18] On board ship from Salerno the travellers reflected on the fate of their home country 'und der Hamb. Hr. von Volkmann sagte mir Stellen aus Hrn. Geßners Idyllen vor' (*Briefe*, i. 400). More positive is the account given to Geßner himself. Usteri had delivered to Winckelmann a copy of the *Idylls*, 'die ich nur aus Erzehlungen kannte, aber von jemand der dieselbe gelesen wie man das seltene unserer Zeit zu schätzen hat. Dieses war ein Hamburger, welcher mit mir die Reise nach Pesto that, und in dem Salernitanischen Meer-Busen sagte er mir Stellen aus den Idyllen vor' (*Briefe*, ii. 113). This is as close as we get to a statement on Volkmann's aesthetic sensibility.

Of course, all of the above judgements are Winckelmann's. Volkmann appears to have seen their relationship differently, less coolly. The surviving letters give us no evidence of a profound shared concern in the arts, since they are on the whole surveys of Winckelmann's own latest work. But Volkmann's report to Daßdorf suggests that the arts were indeed the focus of their relationship, offering a view of how they arranged their shared interests. As I noted earlier, we hear of their 'gleiche Lieblingsneigungen', 'verwandte Studien', and 'wechselseitige Hochachtung und innige Werthschätzung'. Winckelmann and Volkmann are described further as 'diese beyden aufgeklärten und nach Erweiterung ihrer Kunstkenntnisse so eifrig strebenden Männer' whose shared work at Pesto produced 'gemeinschaftliche Resultate', published in Winckelmann's *Baukunst der Alten*. Back in Rome they met almost daily 'weil ihre Neigung zu den Kunstwerken der Alten sie einander so werth und fast nothwendig machte'.[19] These comments are intriguing since they suggest a balance of interest, and indeed of talent, which bears no resemblance to reality. Are we to assume that all of Volkmann's novel ideas

---

[18] This may have inspired Winckelmann's correspondence with Geßner, according to Rehm at *Briefe*, ii. 407.

[19] All references from *Winckelmanns Briefe an seine Freunde*, ed. Daßdorf, ii. 173–4.

on the arts were miraculously absorbed by Winckelmann? Certainly there are no independent publications by Volkmann which would point to an original mind like Winckelmann's. Even if we allow for Daßdorf's need to flatter his correspondents and for Volkmann's rose-tinted view of his past, we still have a strange view of the pedagogical relationship. In this version we have a meeting of equal minds. They pursue similar studies, have mutual respect, are both similarly enlightened and ambitious and even necessary to one another. It is therefore not suprising that they produce results 'gemeinschaftlich'. However, only to a limited extent does this relationship bear resemblance to Winckelmann's educational scheme. Interest in the arts was clearly a necessity as was the intimacy between master and pupil. But he did not imagine discussion between equals but a master/pupil arrangement in which he was the source of the wisdom. Given Volkmann's relative immaturity it seems likely that this was the reality of their relationship and that any talk of shared insights was optimistic or simply a misunderstanding of the basic situation. Certainly his version of the relationship as projected by Daßdorf bears little resemblance to that which we would imagine on the basis of their correspondence, which contains no significant discussion of the arts, as might take place between equals, not even to the extent that it was present in the Riedesel correspondence. On the contrary we have the impression that Volkmann is picking up the latest titbits about Winckelmann. Even allowing for the fact that their relationship had been soured immediately upon Volkmann's departure, and so fundamentally changed in nature, we still have no sense of a meeting of minds. Clearly when we compare Winckelmann's later view of Volkmann with Volkmann's view of Winckelmann a discrepancy emerges. In a letter to Winckelmann Weiße mentions Volkmann 'der Ihr größter Verehrer ist' and whose letters are 'ganz voll von Ihnen' (*Briefe*, iv. 79, 449–50). Hagedorn writes in a similar vein: 'Aus Paris habe ich schöne Briefe von ihm [Volkmann] gesehen. Er lobt Sie nach Wunsch' (*Briefe*, iv. 81). Rehm also suggests that Volkmann's enthusiasm for Winckelmann may have caused him to write a poem in his honour. On closer examination this poem, which is found in Daßdorf's edition of the letters, appears to be by Daßdorf or, more likely, the poet Weiße about Hagedorn who died in the year of publication of the letters, 1780.[20] The impression that we have is that Winckelmann was more important to Volkmann than Volkmann was to

---

[20] Compare *Briefe*, iv. 496 and *Winckelmanns Briefe an seine Freunde*, ed. Daßdorf, ii. 210.

Winckelmann. The balance which Daßdorf suggests in the relationship was surely something of an illusion.

This and the preceding sections can do little more than suggest that during his period in Italy Volkmann fulfilled some of Winckelmann's expectations. The clearest indication that we have of Volkmann's suitability as a pupil is the amount of time that Winckelmann spent with him, even if the claim of daily contact is exaggerated. This fact cannot be altered by the subsequent rancour in their relationship and is a highly positive indicator given Winckelmann's promptly dimissive attitude towards inappropriate pupils.

3. THE TEXT

Volkmann's debt to Winckelmann can be examined in the same manner as Riedesel's. Despite the very different nature of the texts they have a common focus on the visual arts, and given the common strands in the aesthetic education of the two men, it is no suprise that they deal with many problems in similar ways. In dealing with Riedesel, I pointed out the pattern of art-historical thinking which he shared with his teacher. This covered accounts of artistic production and the link between environment, in the broadest sense, and art. It also included accounts of the quality of certain stylistic features of art and their importance for a historical account of a given work. Finally I dealt with degree of enthusiasm for art in the texts, measured against that seen in Winckelmann's great descriptions. The treatment of Volkmann will follow a similar pattern. In Volkmann's case as in Riedesel's I will deal with the extent to which ideas can reasonably be attributed to Winckelmann. A reading of Riedesel makes it increasingly clear that whilst on first sight an attribution of central art-historical notions to Winckelmann may be reasonable, many of them appear ultimately to have their roots in earlier French theory (not unrelated to Winckelmann's work), sources which Riedesel mentions freely after the death of Winckelmann. Riedesel was tapping into a mainstream of aesthetic theory to which Winckelmann belonged but which he advanced through his poetic treatment of individual works and of aesthetic experience. Volkmann, like Riedesel, restricts himself to the treatment of works of art as artefacts and does not attempt to express his aesthetic experience. To that extent his work also belongs firmly to a mainstream, a fact which is driven home by his near total dependence upon contemporary (or near-contemporary) French sources. The situation is, of course, made more complicated by the nature of the text, a matter mentioned earlier. But Volkmann does in fact find room for aesthetic, enthusiastic passages in his guide to Italy—passages taken directly from Winckelmann (albeit not in their full form (see below)). They could be accommodated whereas Volkmann's personal responses could not. Whilst like Riedesel he could repeat and reapply much of the methodology and many of the conclusions of contemporary art history, he does not offer any evidence of spiritual elevation through art. His work is informative rather than inspirational and to that extent shows little sign of the teacher. His real loyalty is to the least original aspect of Winckelmann's work, the art history. The fact that he should be perceived as a true disciple of Winckelmann, as Riedesel was also, again suggests that Winckelmann's aesthetic has been vulgarized. Winckelmann was more than a German representative of a well-established art-historical tradition.

The extent of Volkmann's dependence upon that tradition can be shown by a brief treatment of his approach to art history. There is no attempt to be original in this aspect of his work. He openly declares his sources—Lalande, Richard, Cochin in the first instance—and declares his intention of using their material in the most effective combination, with supplementary information drawn from parallel sources (including Winckelmann on specific works of art) and his own memories of travel in Italy. It does not take an art historian to predict the outcome of this sort of collective authorship on the treatment of art history. It produces a work which is generally conventional and whose central tenets, whatever their source, seem very familiar to the reader of Winckelmann. The parallels with the deceptively Winckelmannian passages of art history in Riedesel are quite clear. Whilst it may be reasonable to assume that Winckelmann could have provided the most recent reminder of this manner of dealing with art (although the case is stronger for Winckelmann's influence on Riedesel) much of the material is lifted directly from other sympathetic sources. If we look at some of the central commonplaces of contemporary art history we find many of them reproduced by Volkmann.

Both Winckelmann and Riedesel were interested in the genesis of works of art and the environmental conditions which were favourable to their production. This is also the case with Volkmann. Many of the comments in his work reflect similar concerns. The introduction to the guide is largely a translation of Richard, who was no stranger to such environmental theories. The equation central to the theory, namely that certain aspects of physical environment can determine the appearance and character of local inhabitants, was clearly familiar. He identifies a people of gentle character 'welcher viel ähnliches mit ihrem weichlichem Himmelsstriche hat' (*Nachrichten*, i. 73 = Richard, i. p. cviii). Perhaps more important than the effect of environment on character is that on appearance. Physical beauty was a crucial inspiration for the artist even in contemporary Italy. Nature could still provide this inspiration and so good taste could be maintained. For example 'derselbe Geschmack herrscht noch in Italien; die Natur, welche die ersten Muster dazu an die Hand gegeben, ist daselbst nicht ausgeartet, sie zeigt sich noch in ihrer frischen Blüthe, und mit allen Reichthümern' (*Nachrichten*, i. 31 = Richard, i. p. lxv). Not all aspects of environment need be natural. The arts of earlier periods could also inspire since 'der beständige Anblick der Meisterstücke großer Künstler, und das Anhören der trefflichsten Musiken, ist Ursache, daß ein glückliches Talent zur Malerey und Musik fast allen Ständen angeboren zu seyn scheint' (*Nachrichten*, i. 31 = Richard, i. p. lxv). On the same basis Volkmann/Richard can suggest that the arts in Britain will bloom because of the number of great works recently imported (*Nachrichten*, i. 128 = Richard, ii. p. lxvi).

Of course, it was not only absence or presence of beauty which determined the quality of art production. Volkmann/Lalande make a link between economic success and the flourishing of the arts. They mention Tuscany 'darinn Handlung und Künste geblühet haben' (*Nachrichten*, i. 447 = Lalande, ii. p. 141). The two things belong together in this view of history. The development of business was determined primarily by the ruling aristocracies. Precisely their failures as managers had preoccupied Riedesel in Sicily; political failures affected the economic health of the country and by extension the fate of the arts which required their support. Volkmann's political concerns follow a similar pattern. The ultimate aim was to establish 'der Geist der Freyheit', in the related spheres of politics, economics, and the arts in a way that had only rarely been achieved, most noticeably under the Greeks (*Nachrichten*, i. 639 = Lalande, ii. 568). As in the cases of Winckelmann and Riedesel the embracing of the principle of freedom, however loosely defined, led to some liberal views in the detail of politics. Volkmann insisted, with his source Richard, that the achievement of freedom depended upon the individual's enjoyment of his natural rights (*Nachrichten*, i. 20–1). Like Riedesel who was concerned by the unemployment caused by economic mismanagement in Sicily, Volkmann was made uneasy by poverty. He shows concern, for example, for the finances of a hospital and praises a legal aid scheme (*Nachrichten*, iii. 125). Implicit in this concern is criticism of the prevailing political order since it had failed to create the necessary atmosphere of freedom. This particular case is interesting because the political force which threatens the hospital finances is the church. Funds should in Volkmann's view be directed at the poor and ill rather than funnelled towards the building of a new church. The notion that the Church could work against freedom rather than as an agent for it is common to Riedesel and Winckelmann as well as Volkmann. And like most other subjects in which they were interested this one was clearly related to the visual arts. The misuse of funds suggested above was only one symptom of an illiberal streak in the Church. There were others. The Church's exploitation of the powers of superstition and ritual are favourite themes for Winckelmann and his pupils (*Nachrichten*, i. 10). Volkmann mocks not only the ritual of Catholicism but also the limiting, rather than liberating, effect of Protestantism for Northern European visitors to Italy. He criticizes those who parade their Protestantism as a badge and so cannot fully appreciate another culture. And orthodox faith does not only inhibit the normal citizen. Volkmann mourns the fact that many great artists were forced to produce religious paintings when they may more usefully have worked on historical themes (*Nachrichten*, i. 415 = Lalande, ii. 78).[21]

The whole complex of factors which could in Volkmann's view affect the quality of artistic production—his production theory—is then clearly very closely related to those to be found in both Riedesel and Winckelmann. Equally none of our three authors could reasonably be seen as the source of the ideas. Volkmann's case makes this particularly obvious since most of his material is lifted directly from alternative sources. Volkmann's adaptation of the introduction to Richard indicates the extent to which these ideas were already commonplaces. I pointed out a number of production theories which Volkmann took over from Richard; perhaps more importantly Volkmann left out a large amount of material concerning the environment in his version of Richard. Presumably he thought that the ideas had become almost self-explanatory and so not worthy of repetition. For the same reason the

---

[21] Winckelmann's art history suggests a preference for mythological rather than historical themes. It was he who revised the general assumption that most ancient art depicted historical themes, suggesting for his part that the key to an understanding of them lay in mythology. Cf. Himmelmann, 'Winckelmanns Hermeneutik' and Käfer, *Winckelmanns hermeneutische Prinzipien*. Volkmann has a different view on this fundamental Winckelmannian issue.

material relating to the production theory used above is spread throughout the text and not easy to locate. Whilst numerous statements allude to a production theory Volkmann rarely feels the need to explain art/environment theories fully. But there can be little doubt that these were live issues since they concerned the quality of art. For him as for Winckelmann art was not only to be studied historically in this way. In a telling extension of the production theory he points out that art could also determine environment as well as be determined by it. Art is seen to have a power to improve environment, to educate, and he points to a case where 'die Wiederherstellung der Künste und Wissenschaften hat die wilden Sitten verbessert' (*Nachrichten*, i. 30). This educational function for art, which could also improve behaviour which was not simply wild, is at the heart of Winckelmann's aesthetic. However, the nature of the improvement in Volkmann himself as a result of his aesthetic education is not yet clear. Thus far we can only suggest increased knowledge of art rather than spiritual refinement through it. This same pattern is repeated when we look at other aspects of Volkmann's treatment of art.

Winckelmann's assessments of artistic styles were not based upon objective evaluation of individual features of a work. Whilst these may all have been dutifully listed certain features were to his mind unequivocally good, others unequivocally bad. His view of the history of art was based upon certain key oppositions which may have had their source outside of the work itself (e.g. in his admiration for certain periods of Greek history), but which could also be relocated in the stylistic features of individual works. Hence the magnificent edifice of the political system in Periclean Athens, which might be characterized by the epithets 'noble' or 'manly', was seen to produce a brand of art which could be described in similar terms. The basic harmony of life during this period is reflected in an art which could also be assessed in terms of harmony, with its simple components combined pleasingly. By contrast other less harmonious times or individuals produced art which lacked the noble simplicity of the ideal Greek art. Winckelmann's whole value scheme in stylistics is based upon this sort of opposition. Quality was measured according to the degree of divergence from a very clearly defined stylistic norm.

There are very clear signs of a similar scheme in operation in Volkmann's *Nachrichten*. If we look for the key Winckelmannian epithets we are not disappointed. The degree of simplicity is a key measure of a work of art in whatever form. A bowl seen in Naples has the necessary qualities because 'die Form ist simpel und schön' (*Nachrichten*, iii. 65 = Lalande, vi. 180). Likewise Michelangelo's representation of Christ in

Maria sopra Minerva, Rome, has some key positive features because 'die Figur und Stellung sind edel und simpel' (*Nachrichten*, ii. 455 = Lalande, iv. 213). Elsewhere in Rome (S. Pietro in Vincoli) he saw a statue of Moses by the same artist and offered a more elaborate account of its simplicity, noting that 'die Stellung, Action und ganze Figur ist von einer edlen Simplicität; der Ausdruck im Kopfe vortrefflich und zugleich erhaben, und die Zeichnung nach der genauesten Schärfe' (*Nachrichten*, ii. 209 = Lalande, iii. 434–5). To this extent Michelangelo's work satisfied expectations derived from ancient Greek sculpture which contained an expression which was 'wahr und edel', contours which were 'rein und gefällig' and clothes with some variety but with that essential 'edle Einfalt'. All in all 'vermieden die Alten alles, was nicht wesentlich zu ihrem Gegenstande gehörte' (*Nachrichten*, i. 51 = Richard, i. p. lxxxvii).

The same principles applied, in a different manifestation, to architecture. Describing S. Maria Novella in Florence he notes that 'die Architektur der Kirche ist alt, aber von edler Einfalt' (*Nachrichten*, i. 516 = Lalande, ii. 310). Modern architects tended to move away from such simplicity in search of more powerful effects than those on offer in older masterpieces of architecture: 'Die vortreffliche Simplicität jener Meisterstücke ... scheinen ihnen vielleicht zu einförmig und bereits zu oft angebracht.'[22] Any movement away from the aim of noble simplicity is seen as a deviation which could be dangerous in its consequences. Buildings which reveal different architectural principles might corrupt good taste. The oratorio next to the Chiesa nuova in Rome had an arrangement of columns which posed precisely this threat for 'in der That läuft die ganze Erfindung aber wider die edle Einfalt der schönen Architektur, und ist ein gefährliches Muster zur Nachahmung für junge Künstler' (*Nachrichten*, ii. 387 = Lalande, iv. 103). This passage is based upon parallel statements in Lalande but differs in important ways. The danger of corruption is made less explicit in Lalande and he reports simply how many artists find the architectural features strange.

Significantly, the more didactic tone in Volkmann makes it tempting to see parallels with Winckelmann first. Volkmann apparently accentuated some of the stylistic value-judgements in Richard and Lalande on the basis of his own opinions. In an assessment of Michelangelo's work in Florence he includes a passage which is not in Richard or Lalande: 'Der Geschmack des Michael Angelo und der damaligen großen Meister zeigt sich hier besonders, ohne daß er so wie zu Neapel ins Gezierte und

---

[22] *Nachrichten*, i. 60 marks a departure from Richard. Again stylistic criteria sometimes appear more important to Volkmann than to his sources.

Lächerliche gefallen wäre.' (*Nachrichten*, i. 456) Whilst he might reasonably have called the style of other artists 'geziert', when he calls it 'lächerlich' he has introduced a value-judgement in a manner seen frequently in Winckelmann. Those works of art which do not satisfy certain basic criteria are dismissed and the language of dismissal is broadly similar to that used by Winckelmann. The artist whose work embodies all of the qualities disliked by Volkmann is Bernini who was, of course, regularly ridiculed by Winckelmann. Bernini's *Constantine* is assessed negatively, for 'es ist zwar viel Handlung darinn, aber alles übertrieben' (*Nachrichten*, ii. 53 = Lalande, iii. 51). Bernini's style is described as not aiming at nobility but rather at being 'reizend und gefällig' and consequently becoming 'maniert' and 'übertrieben' (*Nachrichten*, i. 50). Interestingly, Volkmann's source passage which is a description of Bernini's *St. Theresa* by Richard, is entirely positive, indeed in this version 'la statue ... est une pièce admirable qui a tout le charme possible de l'expression, & à laquelle je ne connois aucun antique que l'on puisse opposer' (Richard, i. p. lxxxvi). And whilst in his use of Lalande there appears to be less authorial intrusion this does not mean that he does not amend source material, perhaps in line with Winckelmannian expectations. It is enough for him to add the term 'Verzerrung' to a description of Bernini's *St. Theresa*, which is otherwise similar to that in Lalande, for us to glimpse the more clear-cut aesthetic principles which underlie Volkmann's work (*Nachrichten*, i. 174 = Lalande, i. 146). He also adds the Winckelmannian epithet 'theatralisch' to the Lalande description of the façade of Santa Croce in Rome and so by simple means suggests that it is not a great building (*Nachrichten*, ii. 190 = Lalande, iii. 398). Elsewhere his departures from Lalande can be quite extreme as, for example, in his description of Bernini's *Apollo and Daphne*. This work is, in his view, essentially a successful imitation of ancient statuary but this success is seen as an exception in Bernini's work for 'es wäre zu wünschen, er hätte sich beständig bey diesem richtigen Stil erhalten, und keinen eignen manierten und übertriebnen Stil angenommen, der in seinen Scholaren vollends ausartete' (*Nachrichten*, ii. 812).[23] This parting comment is entirely absent in the source texts. Bernini was naturally not alone in attracting such criticism and indeed his perceived rival Borromini was picked out as one of many other artists whose work offended key principles. He looked for dramatic effect but 'dadurch

---

[23] An equivalent passage is absent from the obvious locations, namely Lalande, v. 312 and Richard, vi. 199–200. There is, however, a similar comment by Winckelmann (KS 161–2).

verwildert der Geschmack, der Hang zum Sonderbaren bringt eigensinnige Anlagen, gehäufte und oft mit vielen Schnörkeln versehene gothische Zierathen, neue Säulenordnungen von bizarrer Zusammensetzung hervor' (*Nachrichten*, i. 60).[24]

The most powerful statements of Volkmann's preferences in art come when he compares directly those works which satisfy him with those which do not. Here the opposition that is at the centre of his aesthetic is stated most clearly. In Naples a public monument to Maria attracts his wrath because it is 'ein Monument von einem so barbarischen, gezwungenen, elenden Geschmack'. It causes him to reflect that 'wenn man an die edle Einfalt der römischen Obeliske gewohnt ist, und dieses Gemisch von gedrehten, krummen und geraden Linien, von plumpen Gliedern, von Basreliefs und andern Zierathen ansieht, so glaubt man nach China oder in die Türkey versetzt zu seyn. Die gothischen Monumente sind wirklich weit besser' (*Nachrichten*, iii. 84 = Lalande, vi. 218). Similarly the Gothic cathedral in Sienna suffers by comparison to ancient models, indeed 'Kenner, welche die edle Einfalt der alten Griechen und das Majestätische in der Architektur lieben, werden diesen übertriebenen ängstlichen Zierathen nie ihren Beyfall geben' (*Nachrichten*, i. 642 = Lalande, ii. 573). Since we all wish to see ourselves as 'Kenner' then we are invited also to accept the biased aesthetic judgements of Volkmann and his source, whose voice is in this case strikingly similar to Winckelmann's. However, this method for assessing art, of which I have shown only a representative part, is useful for more than determining the quality of a given work. It can help to determine the place of the individual work in the history of art. The general pattern perceived in art history is a corruption of the old through the new, seen as a movement away from stylistic simplicity. At times this can be as crude as the addition of inappropriate detail to earlier works. In the church of S. Chiara in Naples the old church has been spoiled by new décor since 'die Kirche ist groß und ein altes Gebäude, aber neu aufgeputzt, und mit Vergoldungen und Zierathen dermaßen überhäuft, daß der gute Geschmack dabey verliert' (*Nachrichten*, iii. 86).[25] Even when the decoration is not a crude addition but rather an intrinsic part of a design it can help us to locate the position of the work within the scheme of art history. The history of art is shown to move cyclically with highpoints reflected in a particular purity

---

[24] Again the passage is missing from sources. Winckelmann expresses similar views at *Werke*, ii. 471; vi. 73.
[25] Lalande, vi. 221 differs. In his version the church is 'ancienne mais très-ornée'. Volkmann's objects more strongly to the décor.

of taste. The highest point, against which all others are measured, is the art of Periclean Athens. According to this scheme the Theatre of Marcellus can be placed at a cultural highpoint because 'aus den wenigen Resten kann man zwar schließen, daß das Gebäude zur Zeit, da der Geschmack in der Architektur zu Rom am reinsten war, aufgeführt worden' (*Nachrichten*, ii. 595 = Lalande, iv. 464). A key indication of this high period can be found in the 'edle Verhältnisse' of the columns (*Nachrichten*, ii. 595). Likewise the supposed Temple of Romulus and Remus belongs to a period of high achievement as 'man sieht an diesem runden Tempel die alte Simplicität im höchsten Grade, indem fast alle architektonische Zierrathen fehlen' (*Nachrichten*, ii. 587 = Lalande, iv. 440–1). On the other hand the Arch of Janus betrays its origins since 'aus den Verzierungen erkennt man aber die Abnahme des guten Geschmacks und der Baukunst' (*Nachrichten*, ii. 591 = Lalande, iv. 452).

Volkmann then clearly has a number of stylistic prejudices in common with Winckelmann, and on the basis of these he also appears to apply a broadly similar scheme of historical stylistics. Even if the immediate source of this material is not Winckelmann we can at least suggest that the editorial process has taken place along Winckelmannian lines.[26] Some of Volkmann's enhancements of the judgements of Richard/Lalande would suggest that he was indeed editing in line with Winckelmann's views on some occasions. The parallels in the men's views go further than their views on history and style. Both men have a clear interest in the ideal nature of the greatest works of art. Great art, according to both views, refines the raw materials provided by nature. The manner in which this is done is explained fully by Volkmann in a passage taken from Richard concerning the reasons for the low grade of artistic production during certain periods:

Mit einem Worte, es gibt gewisse Zeiten, wo sich der Verstand und der Geschmack nicht genug aufklären kann, um die schönen Muster, welche uns die Natur darbietet, zu finden, die wahren Schönheiten derselben zu unterscheiden, und auf eine glückliche Art nachzuahmen. Raphael, Michael Angelo, Titian, Paul Veronese, Annibal Caracci und Guido hatten den Kopf mit erhabenen und reizenden Gedanken angefüllt, und wußten also, wenn sie einen Gegenstand ausführen wollten, denselben einen neuen Grad von Schönheit zu geben, der nur

[26] Naturally, in a work of this scale there are differences of opinion/emphasis when compared with Winckelmann. Most strikingly, he gives more time to painting than to statuary which contradicts Winckelmann's declared preference. Whilst it may have been a marketing necessity it also appears to reflect Volkmann's opinion. He takes over a passage from Richard celebrating 'diese herrlichen Werke des Genies, welche noch interessanter als die Statuen sind' (*Nachrichten*, ii. 19 = Richard, v. pp. xxviii–xxix).

allein aus ihrer Einbildungskraft kommen konnte, der aber zugleich so wahr, so natürlich, und der Sache so angemessen schien, das alle diejenigen, welche seine Empfindung genug besitzen, um ihre herrlichen Meisterstücke mit rechtem Auge zu betrachten, solche über die Natur setzen, oder als die verschönerte Natur ansehen. (*Nachrichten*, i. 36 = Richard, i. p. lxx)

This passage corresponds very closely to Winckelmann's theory of composite beauty, of taking the best from nature, enhancing it with artistic imagination, and so making it appealing to those with the necessary sensibility. Simple realism in art is, in his view, unsuccessful. In other passages we see how Carravaggio fails because 'die Figuren sind zwar nach der Natur, aber nach der niedrigen Natur' (*Nachrichten*, ii. 435 = Lalande, iv. 182).[27] The best model is provided by Raphael—Winckelmann's choice also—who took occasional aspects of beauty glimpsed in the real world and combined them to provide ideal beauties on canvas (*Nachrichten*, i. 42–3 = Richard, i. p. lxxviii). The aim is not to perfect a reproduction of nature in art but to produce in the imagination an ideal image which can be made into an artistic reality. Volkmann cites in support of this case du Quesnoy's response to the accusation that his work is unrealistic: 'Sie haben recht, erwiederte Quesnoy, weil sie das Original nicht sehen, ich habe solches aber in meinem Kopfe, und gebe mir alle Mühe, daß diese Kopie ihm ähnlich werde.' (*Nachrichten*, i. 43 = Richard, i. p. lxxxix) This notion of copying is closely related to the idea of 'Nachahmung' in Winckelmann's work which was also based upon capturing the spirit of great works of art or of ideal nature. The terms used in Volkmann's text for the ideal world are familiar to the reader of Winckelmann—'die simple Natur', 'die schöne Natur', or perhaps most tellingly 'die edle Einfalt der Natur' (*Nachrichten*, i. 50, 51, 44). In Volkmann's view, as in Winckelmann's, two groups have access to the ideal world, the artist and the viewer. In each case a particular sensibility is required. He gives some indication of how he imagines the artist's mind operating, collating and refining material drawn from nature. In the passage cited at length above Volkmann (with Richard) also suggests that a particular 'Empfindung' is required for the proper understanding of art; we have to be able to see 'mit rechtem Auge'. It is precisely this perception of the need for active response on the part of the observer which I see as the core of Winckelmann's aesthetic. But Winckelmann goes beyond the statement of the necessity of active participation to reveal the nature of his own participation in the experience of art. He not only tells us of the necessity of developing an appropriate sensibility but also

[27] Winckelmann had similar views. Cf. KS 2, 39.

shows us how his eye operates. Volkmann's statements, which are in the introduction to the text, are not then substantiated by his own experience of art. The parallels between his conclusions about art history and those of Winckelmann are clear, even where we cannot prove direct derivation from Winckelmann and can see other direct sources. These conclusions are not, however, the product of a special sensibility. They are rather produced by careful observation according to a strict art-historical scheme. This is purely a function of a critical intelligence working on a large body of data. The qualitative difference between such work and the aesthetic passages produced by Winckelmann (or indeed the creative work of the artist) is clearly great. Whilst Volkmann can report the presence of an ideal component in art he does not suggest in the *Nachrichten* that he is in this sense an idealist. Art remains for him essentially artefact, to be characterized largely through its physical appearance rather than its ability to inspire metaphysical speculation. He appears comfortable where he can analyse given artistic material but does not move on to the central aesthetic process of synthesizing ideal images. Volkmann, on the evidence of this text, does not experience God through art. Likewise Apollo does not come alive for him when he looks at a statue of him. If we look closely at Volkmann's direct use of material from Winckelmann (quotation of and reference to him rather than broad ideological correspondence of the type detailed above) we are given some idea of where he saw the limits of the experience of art. These passages have the additional benefit of marking departures from his other sources, none of which use Winckelmann's voice directly, and so they naturally provide the clearest evidence of debt to Winckelmann.

These passages fall into two categories. First, Volkmann uses reference to Winckelmann as a means of substantiating his own assertions about art. Bibliographical references to Winckelmann are used to add weight to views on art history and to confirm the importance of particular sites/works. Similarly, he uses the fact of his own relationship with Winckelmann as a means of lending authority to his publication. Secondly he uses Winckelmann to capture the greatness of individual works, something which he achieves by citing his famous descriptions at length.

The use of Winckelmannian views in passing references is particularly common in the second volume of the *Nachrichten*. For example, in his review of the Capitoline collection of the busts of the Caesars he introduces a dating of the bust of Nerva from Winckelmann, who believed the work to be substantially antique whereas Bottari thought it was in the manner of Algardi (*Nachrichten*, ii. 499 = *Werke*, vi. 248). He reinforces the quotation from Winckelmann with a stylistic assessment of some of the busts on display which also suggests a certain debt to Winckelmann, namely his view of later Roman art: 'An den folgenden bemerkt man, wie der gute Stil sich mit starken Schritten seinem Untergange nahet' (*Nachrichten*, ii. 499). Winckelmann is also mentioned in connection with the statue of Marcus Aurelius on the Capitol and as useful preparatory reading for an examination of the Egyptian parts of the collections there (*Nachrichten*, ii. 478, 491). The latter recommendation is made on the following basis: 'Um diese Sammlung mit rechtem Nutzen zu besehen, muß man das andre Kapitel in Winckelmann's Geschichte der Kunst, welches vom egyptischen Stil handelt, lesen. Man wird die Sachen alsdenn mit viel aufgeklärtern Augen ansehen.' The route to enlightened insight into art leads in Volkmann's view through a reading of Winckelmann. If his use of sympathetic sources like Lalande and Richard make it difficult to determine the precise pattern of Winckelmann's influence on Volkmann then such statements go a long way to clarifying the situation.

Whilst he was happy to use the material that was provided by Lalande and Richard he does not refer to their achievements in providing a systematic approach to the problems of art history. The framework is provided by Winckelmann and his precursors in systematic art history. This sort of reinforcing role is also in evidence in Volkmann's description of the Villa Medici, where we are offered his judgements on a supposed Cleopatra figure with a new head in support of observations otherwise taken directly from Lalande (*Nachrichten*, ii. 343–4 = *Werke*, iv. 266, 334, 394). We are also offered his view of the Niobe group although this provides more than an art-historical explanation and gives Volkmann an opportunity to express remotely the enthusiasm which can be generated by great art (*Nachrichten*, ii. 344–6). On a simpler level there are many references to matters of art-historical debate where Winckelmann is used to provide answers (*Nachrichten*, ii. 271, 820, 834). These do not only include works of art to be found in Rome. For obvious reasons Winckelmann is also introduced as an authority on the discoveries at Pompeii and Herculaneum and the collection of finds at Portici (*Nachrichten*, iii. 265, 267, 276, 279, 294, 330). No less reasonably Volkmann uses Winckelmann's account of their joint trip to Pesto, noting that 'die folgenden Nachrichten sind aus Winckelmanns Vorbericht zu den Anmerkungen über die Baukunst der Alten genommen, und diese sind in meiner Gegenwart aufgezeichnet. Ich hatte das Vergnügen, woran ich wegen des unglücklichen Endes von dem see. Winckelmann nie ohne Rührung gedenke, diese Reise in seiner Gesellschaft zu thun, da mir solche desto unterrichtender ward' (*Nachrichten*, iii. 333). Winckelmann's contributions appear to be used then as a sort of theoretical backbone to the work with the additional function as supplements where the original source material is found wanting. The personal relationship with Winckelmann clearly adds weight to Volkmann's statements on art; Volkmann is portrayed as having been at the source of the most important art-historical ideas of the period. In the text he is, however, more modest in his claims as an original thinker than he appeared to be in the Daßdorf edition of the letters. In an earlier reference to Winckelmann, inspired by his treatment of the Villa Albani, Volkmann moves away from his other sources to pay a very generous tribute to Winckelmann. He talks at first of 'der durch seinen unglücklichen Tod den Wissenschaften, und der Kunst entrissene Winckelmann' (*Nachrichten*, ii. 225). The footnote to the same passage contains still more praise:

> Kein Gelehrter hat mit so vielem Geschmack von den Alterthümern geschrieben: er zündete gleichsam ein neues Licht zur Betrachtung derselben an. Sein Auge drang in die Geheimnisse der Kunst, und war durch unaufhörliches Betrachten geübt. Voll von der Lektüre der Alten, trat er zu den Denkmalen hinzu, und fand sich dadurch imstande, die Monumente durch die Alten, und diese wieder durch jene zu erklären. Ein Genie, wie das seinige, wird vielleicht in hundert Jahren nicht wieder gebohren. Wer die Werke der Alten mit rechtem Nutzen besehen, und den Geschmack bilden will, kann nichts besseres thun, als Winckelmanns Geschichte der Kunst in Rom selbst lesen, und die Statuen darnach untersuchen. Seine Anmerkungen über die Baukunst der Alten, seine *Monumenti inediti spiegati*, werden die Reisenden auf Kenntnisse führen, die sie in allen andern Büchern vergebens suchen. (*Nachrichten*, ii. 225)

These passages are interesting for a number of reasons, but particularly for the description of Winckelmann's insight. The metaphors are familiar from Winckelmann himself. The examination of art as a journey into the light—towards enlightenment—and the business of seeing described in terms of revealing secrets, of getting beneath the surface of art correspond to passages in my analysis of Winckelmann's way of seeing. They also mark a stark contrast with Volkmann's treatment of the work of art as artefact. In Volkmann's treatment a work is important for its surface—which can be readily described—rather than for its innermost secrets. Volkmann decodes art in terms of its style and the allegory which it contains. He is well prepared and consequently has 'ein geübtes Auge' (*Nachrichten*, i. 40–1 = Richard, i. p. lxxv). But his work only shows evidence of a limited functioning of the eye when compared with Winckelmann.

He alerts us to the discrepancy himself. Volkmann identifies, in the above passage, the means by which Winckelmann achieved his level of insight. Many of the basic measures correspond to the prescriptions for aesthetic education laid down by Winckelmann. Winckelmann was *full* of ancient literature and this familiarity allowed him to decode the mysteries of ancient art. In a crude sense this was what he wanted from his pupils: they too should read ancient literature as a preparation for the study of the arts. Few of them, however, achieved the same degree of fullness. His was a saturation study of ancient culture, a complete absorption of it. In as far as it was possible he became a Greek. To be a Greek was, in any case, Winckelmann's dream; imaginatively, in his poetic descriptions, he walked the Elysian fields. It was also how Goethe saw Winckelmann, as an embodiment of the culture which he admired rather than as a source of knowledge about it. The image of fullness, of course, also reproduces the central metaphor in Winckelmann (and Goethe) for the business of aesthetic response. We saw Winckelmann complete or fill out works of art, on the basis of his absorption of the culture which created them. Winckelmann also reveals the educational product of exposure to a great culture: it fills out the student, makes him more complete.

One means to this sense of fulfilment was, I suggested in my analysis, interaction with works of art. Volkmann's description confirms the sort of interaction which was at the heart of Winckelmann's responses to art. He absorbed, was full of ancient culture, and then studied ancient art, finding himself 'dadurch im Stande, die Monumente durch die Alten, und diese wieder durch jene zu erkären'. This process of reciprocal illumination corresponds to the process of reciprocal concretization described in Chapter 2. Likewise it offers a clear parallel to Goethe's notion of conversation with the work of art (see Chapter 5 below). However, Volkmann's treatment of Winckelmann's manner of seeing differs importantly from that of the man himself. Winckelmann sought a particular sensibility in his students, but did not believe that this was such a great rarity once specific qualifications were in place. Volkmann, one of those pupils, sees the task as much more difficult. Winckelmann had, in Volkmann's view, a brand of intelligence or 'Genie' of a very exceptional nature, one which might only recur in one hundred years. Having made this point he goes on to describe a contrasting group of students who wish to study 'mit rechtem Nutzen' and so can usefully be 'led' by Winckelmann. They are portrayed as an earnest group reading the available literature but lacking the inspired insights of a Winckelmann. That Winckelmann should produce the insights missing in the other unnamed books again tempts us to describe his very particular talents in terms of genius. Volkmann's portrayal of the process of studying the visual arts in the wake of Winckelmann does not suggest that he and those like him were expecting to reproduce Winckelmann's genius but simply to profit from it. Interestingly Winckelmann's genius appears to be based upon the reconciliation of certain qualities generally seen in opposition to one another. He is described by Volkmann as a loss to both 'Kunst' and 'Wissenschaft'. He is an academic with intuitive taste. This rare brand of 'Genie' is, on the evidence of the *Nachrichten*, not reproduced by Volkmann, and this is in line with his own more limited expectation of following rather than achieving the same as Winckelmann. When he uses material taken directly from Winckelmann he mainly uses his academic/historical passages. The material mentioned so far in this chapter (with the exception of the Medici *Niobe*) employs, to use Stewart's term, statistical aspects of Winckelmann's work.[28] These passages complement those which he has written himself, or more likely borrowed from Lalande or Richard. He does, however, also make use of the poetic side of Winckelmann's work which stands out starkly from the surrounding material.

An early example of Volkmann's use of poetic material from Winckelmann comes in his treatment of the *Venus Medici*. Winckelmann's description of the statue in the *Geschichte der Kunst* reads:

Die medeceische Venus zu Florenz ist einer Rose gleich, die nach einer schönen Morgenröthe beim Aufgang der Sonne aufbricht, und die aus dem Alter, welches, wie Früchte vor der völligen Reife, hart und herblich ist, in ein Alter tritt, in welchem sich die Gefäße zu erweitern und der Busen sich auszubreiten anfängt, wie selbst ihr Busen meldet, welcher schon ausgebreiteter ist, als an zarten Mädchens. Bei dem Stande derselben stelle ich mir diejenige Lais vor, die Apelles im Lieben unterrichtete, und ich bilde mir ein, dieselbe so zu sehen, wie sie sich das erstemal vor den Augen dieses Künstlers entkleiden müßen. (*Werke*, iv. 147)

This brief assessment of the statue contains many of the hallmarks of Winckelmannian analysis. Earlier I discussed the difficulty which Winckelmann had in finding a language appropriate to the expression of aesthetic experience. This led him to combine strands of imagery and rhetorical techniques in order to do justice to a dynamic process. This description offers in its first line two strands of imagery—the metaphors

---

[28] Cf. Stewart, *Die Reisebeschreibung*, 9–28, 273–7 for a summary of historical developments in travel writing.

of roses and fruit. Within the same sentence he talks in anatomical terms. These combinations of imagery and observation in a sort of loose expressive alliance occur regularly in Winckelmann, as do the rather overstretched sentence structures which again suggest in their disjointedness a battle towards self-expression. Another feature of his great descriptions, present here in this cameo, is the bringing to life of the object. Winckelmann does not see a static female figure but a woman in the process of undressing herself. And not only does the dramatic moment or single image captured in the statue generate dramatic scenes and multiple images in Winckelmann's imagination it produces them at a very high quality. It is as if she was being seen for the first time. When we understand this then we can retrospectively understand the rather breathless quality of the syntax.

This brief analysis of Winckelmann's main description of the statue was not intended to suggest that he produces, in this case, poetry of the highest quality. But Winckelmann was certainly trying to do more than simply describe the work of art as an artefact. This particular concretization was available to Volkmann in the *Geschichte der Kunst*. Volkmann's interpretation of the same statue, based largely on Winckelmann's, is interesting for what it omits:

Man sieht hier die Natur in ihrer höchsten Schönheit. Eine gefällige, sanfte, bescheidne Miene bey der schönsten Blüthe der Jugend. Sie ist etwas fett gebildet, und das Fleisch so weich, daß man glauben sollte, es müsse der Hand nachgeben, wenn man es berühret. Winckelmann sagt, sie sey noch nicht völlig ausgewachsen, und ihr Busen gleiche einem noch nicht völlig reifen Mägdchen. (*Nachrichten*, i. 486)

The conclusions offered here are clearly those of Winckelmann. His preference for boys and girls in their early adolescent years and his praise of the gentler contours of their bodies, along with those of hermaphrodites and castrates, is well known. That the Venus Medici has many of these qualities guaranteed Winckelmann's approval and that of his pupils. However, this particular pupil expresses his approval differently. The metaphor in Winckelmann's description, which Volkmann must have known, is rolled back, although his conclusions are matched. The organic metaphors in Winckelmann are in a limited sense reproduced— Volkmann uses the terms 'Blüthe', 'ausgewachsen', 'reif'—but these are clearly more commonplace representatives of that family of metaphors. Volkmann does find himself drawn into imaginative speculation about the statue but of a very different sort to that seen in Winckelmann. He imagines touching soft skin himself whereas Winckelmann imagines seeing her through an artist's eyes. The quality of response is very different. Of course, Winckelmann listed the physical components of beauty very meticulously throughout his work and one of those was obviously the amount of flesh that covered the ideal body. However, at the moment of aesthetic experience of and interaction with a work of art (as opposed to artistic/stylistic evaluation) these technical prescriptions became less important than the need to express the greatness of the experience. Thus Winckelmann refers on numerous occasions to the physical qualities of the Venus Medici, even having reservations about the shape of her face, but these are cast aside when he attempts to do justice to the positive experience which he has of the statue.[29] On the evidence of this response Volkmann saw things differently.

Volkmann also used many of Winckelmann's more famous descriptions. Volkmann's treatment of the Belvedere collection owes more to Winckelmann than to any of the other sources (*Nachrichten*, ii. 128 f.). He uses the material very fully as if to acknowledge the difficulty of providing a version of Winckelmann in his own words. For the most part the descriptions are attributed to Winckelmann, although he does on one occasion use Winckelmann's voice without attribution (e.g. *Nachrichten*, ii. 135). These descriptions in their original form and context give us the fullest picture of Winckelmann's manner of seeing. Volkmann's use of them indicates very clearly how his perspective differed.

Volkmann uses the description of the Apollo Belvedere from the *Geschichte der Kunst*. The expression of anger in the nostrils is an idea which comes up separately from the main description in Winckelmann's text and Volkmann combines it in a slightly altered form with his main account (*Nachrichten*, ii. 135–6). This is directly parallel to Winckelmann's description. As such it contains a treatment of the ideal components of the statue, the meaning of the facial expression, the character of the god, etc. Volkmann's description ends with Apollo's divine hairstyle: Winckelmann's continues. More precisely the final part of Winckelmann's description deals with the nature of the effects of this work of art upon him as an observer. An important indicator of the nature of Winckelmann's treatment of the experience of art were such passages which showed the work of art operating upon him and not just his critical intelligence operating on the work of art. The omitted passage, which belongs to the same paragraph in Winckelmann's text, and which we have used before, reads:

---

[29] Cf. *Werke*, 172–3. KS 534 lists all references to the statue.

Ich vergesse alles andere über dem Anblike dieses Wunderwerks der Kunst, und ich nehme selbst einen erhabenen Stand an, um mit Würdigkeit anzuschauen. Mit Verehrung scheinet sich meine Brust zu erweitern und zu erheben, wie diejenigen, die ich wie vom Geiste der Weissagung aufgeschwellet sehe, und ich fühle mich weggerüket nach Delos und in die lycischen Haine, Orte, welche Apollo mit seiner Gegenwart beehrete: denn mein Bild scheinet Leben und Bewegung zu bekommen, wie des Pygmalions Schönheit. Wie ist es möglich, es zu malen und zu beschreiben! Die Kunst selbst müßte mir rathen, und die Hand leiten, die ersten Züge, welche ich hier entworfen habe, künftig auszuführen. Ich lege den Begrif, welchen ich von diesem Bilde gegeben habe, zu dessen Füßen, wie die Kränze derjenigen, die das Haupt der Gottheiten, welche sie krönen wollten, nicht erreichen konnten. (*Werke*, vi. 223).

This passage of Winckelmann's description is important for a number of reasons. We see the life-enhancing qualities of art. He does not simply see noble objects but experiences nobility; and the experience is so intense that it is best expressed in physical terms. Art forces him out of himself and into an imaginative world where the gods are alive again. But the life of the gods in this case depends on him like that of Pygmalion. Pygmalion provides the perfect metaphor for the aesthetic experience of art in Winckelmann; it expresses perfectly the interdependence of observer and work of art in Winckelmann's experience. It could, of course, seem rather extreme and it is perhaps on the basis of this part of the description that Volkmann observes that 'Winckelmann geräth über diese Statue fast in eine Begeisterung'. He does, however, acknowledge that 'seine Beschreibung ist zu schön, als daß der Liebhaber sie nicht mit Vergnügen in Rom gegen das Original halten sollte' (*Nachrichten*, ii. 135). We have already seen evidence of Volkmann's rather sceptical attitude towards Winckelmann's enthusiasm. He also misses the point that comparing the descriptions with the original statues is rather useless since they are as much a product of Winckelmann's imagination in response to the work as an account of the appearance of the statue. It was presumably whilst speaking in the enthusiastic manner of the passage cited above that Winckelmann could cause observers to believe that he was suffering from malaria, as Volkmann suggested earlier. In any case his omission of this passage is enough to suggest that Volkmann was not wanting to present, or perhaps did not understand, this side of aesthetic experience. The generic question cannot be raised as an explanation of Volkmann's omission of these high aesthetic passages. The book could easily have accommodated these few extra lines. And in removing them he removes any connection in his text between the work of art and personal aesthetic experience.[30] If he had retained the high aesthetic passages from Winckelmann he could have given an example of the inspirational value of art, even if the example was not his own. However, he clearly had more limited horizons in his study of art, which remains strictly statistical. Or perhaps it would be fairer to say that he had more limited expectations of his travel publications since we cannot exclude the possibility of personal aesthetic experience on his part outside the material presented in his texts. This helps us also to explain what at first appears a rather difficult passage in the *Nachrichten*, namely his rejection of the role of the 'cicerone' for visitors to Italy. Clearly he felt that his book could completely supplant the cicerone, which constitutes a complete failure to appreciate what his teacher and cicerone, Winckelmann, was trying to offer him over and above a course in basic art history. The introduction to the second volume of the *Nachrichten* contains an attack upon ciceroni and antiquarians who know nothing, give works of art wrong names, and call all things *cose stupende*, no matter what their real quality (*Nachrichten*, ii. 19–21). This same long passage contains a tribute to Winckelmann's published work, and echoes some of his views on preparation for a trip to Rome and the importance of contact with artists, but it also implicitly seems to contain criticism of the brand of 'Begeisterung' which some guides offer. He aims his criticism in the first instance at poor guides, but we also remember that on two occasions he appeared to have reservations about Winckelmann's enthusiasm, which was certainly not of a fraudulent kind designed to cover for ignorance. These statements also mark a rejection of the very brand of aesthetic education which he must have experienced under Winckelmann. Winckelmann specifically rejected the notion of lone study for his pupils in favour of personal contact with a tutor. Perhaps Volkmann's scholarly approach may have been more efficient in some respects, as far as the accumulation of information was concerned, but it left little room for aesthetic enthusiasms at least in as far as these can present themselves in texts. This does not make his book any less useful as an introductory guide but makes Goethe's criticism of it seem appropriate. At one point he noted that 'ich lese jetzt des guten, trocknen Volkmanns zweiten Teil' (iv. 8, 161). The dryness comes from the lack of obvious aesthetic engagement, a point which Stiller makes in a passing comparison of Volkmann with Goethe: 'Er [Goethe] wollte ja keinen zweiten Volkmann schreiben, nach dem andere reisen sollten, sondern lediglich

[30] The Belvedere Torso description is similarly edited. Compare *Nachrichten*, ii. 138 and KS 169–73.

zeigen, wie sich sein Kunstempfinden entwickelt, sein Geschmack gebildet hat.'[31] If Volkmann's feeling for art had developed over the years surely it would have made itself evident in his text, even if it was a text produced with a different intention. Stiller also offers specific criticism of Volkmann's views of art: 'Von dem künstlerischen Standpunkt des Verfassers zu reden, hiesse vielleicht ihm zuviel Ehre antun.'[32] Stiller is referring critically to Volkmann's dependence upon direct source material but at least his use of this material shows a certain editorial skill in combining compatible material and providing a reasonably consistent perspective on art.[33] The one perspective that seems to be missing is the aesthetic one. Volkmann gives no evidence that he is an 'Augenmensch'. Goethe suggests in his diaries that he will show how he has seen in Italy; Winckelmann similarly insists on a highly self-conscious approach to art. Volkmann provides a number of criteria for judging art but does not investigate the process of seeing. Correspondingly his approach to art seems passive and the passivity is not a precursor to the activity which we see in Winckelmann. Unlike Winckelmann and Goethe he does not attempt to overcome his initial fear that he will be unable to capture the beauty of an object and the aesthetic experience it offers. On the contrary he allows Winckelmann to do that work for him when he uses his most important descriptions to substitute for his own apparent absence of insight. We are reminded in this context of a passage in the *Gedanken*, and tempted to think of Winckelmann in the role of Nichomachus to Volkmann's 'Unwissender'. Winckelmann is stressing the necessity of an intimate relationship with the work of art: 'In solcher genauen Bekanntschafft wird man wie Nichomachus von der Helena des Zeuxis urtheilen: "Nimm meine Augen", sagte er zu einen Unwissenden, der das Bild tadeln wollte, "so wird sie dir eine Göttin scheinen." ' (KS 30). Sadly, insight cannot be transferred so easily. Volkmann does not see with Winckelmann's eyes, neither does he write in his hand.

4. CONCLUSION

Stewart suggests that the development of travel writing in the eighteenth century was broadly characterized by a move from the general itinerary

---

[31] O. Stiller, 'J. J. Volkmann, eine Quelle für Goethes *Italienische Reise*', *Programm*, 63 (1908), 1–15 (15). [32] Ibid. 6.
[33] Stiller, 'J. J. Volkmann' deals with some of the ways in which Volkmann sorted out inconsistencies between his various sources.

to the personal travelogue, a development which reflected increasing familiarity with the main foreign attractions on the part of an expanding travelling public, and consequently left authors free to concentrate upon their responses to travel rather than listing already familiar (whether from the literature or from actual visits) sites. If we accept this analysis and attempt to place Volkmann within the framework given then we are confronted by the conservative nature of the text. This can be explained as a clever marketing manœuvre, because the need for basic reference books inevitably remained; it was undoubtedly a very useful undertaking. It is, however, somewhat surprising given the nature of the aesthetic education undergone by the author with the premium which it set upon autopsy and personal experience. The analysis of Volkmann's editorial procedure, given above, shows how it almost excludes or at least submerges any significant development of an informed personal viewpoint. The determinants of this editorial style are in part generic, in part personal. There is no suggestion that the production of a guidebook excludes an aesthetic component; we can only suggest that Volkmann did not see it as part of his task to accommodate his aesthetic responses or that these were simply not present for him to record. Certainly he makes no attempt to stretch the generic limitations of the guidebook in the way that Winckelmann had expanded the boundaries of art history. The very conformity of Volkmann's text is a sign that the writer has not achieved the level of aesthetic insight which Winckelmann imagined possible, or at least was not able to express it. Indeed certain aspects of his work actively work against the type of aesthetic education which Winckelmann envisaged.

These observations, along with those on Riedesel in Chapter 3 lead us to the key question. The aesthetic core is missing in this work, as it had been in Riedesel's. How do we account for this absence in the works of two pupils who have apparently undergone the appropriate aesthetic education? There appear to be two possible responses to this question. First we can suggest that the aesthetic responses identified are absolutely unique to Winckelmann and the personal qualities which produced them simply not transferable. The mission was, according to this view, always impossible. The acceptance of the impossibility of an aesthetic education is not, however, helpful for an understanding of a man who clearly saw it as a possibility. It is more productive to allow for the possibility in an attempt to explain how specific aspects of Winckelmann's approach led to failure. Clearly many aspects of his teaching were effective. People learnt a lot from him, and in particular they developed a strong sense for art history. They did not on the other hand reproduce his manner of seeing, treating works of art as mere artefacts rather than entering into communion with them. The reason that he was successful as a teacher of art history is clear. He provided a systematic treatment of history which the pupils could with some effort reproduce. There was a simple method to be applied. He could list specific artistic phenomena, their historical meaning and their derivation. However, to use a distinction made by Ingarden, this understanding of *artistic* qualities of an artefact is not necessarily accompanied by an understanding of or response to the *aesthetic* qualities generated by the interaction of that artefact with a refined critical intelligence. To accept Winckelmann's historical explanation of the nobility of the Greeks is not the same as experiencing nobility through exposure to art, as he claims to have done.

The artistic elements of art are more easily dealt with than the qualities of the aesthetic object. Whilst Winckelmann's own writing gives us very clear insight into genuine aesthetics his programme for aesthetic education in fact offers little more than prescriptions for a degree of artistic awareness on a historical basis. The teacher appears to have failed to identify that which separated him from his contemporaries, his aestheticism. His programme would only allow for chance aesthetic responses and does not amount to a means for guaranteeing them. In fact as a programme for aesthetic education it falls at an early hurdle which should make it unsurprising that both Riedesel and Volkmann do not provide aesthetic insights. In my treatment of both men, and in line with Winckelmann's expectations, I spent a great deal of time dealing with their qualifications as pupils. Whilst interesting in their own right these qualifications prove to have no relationship to the quality of the texts (in aesthetic terms) produced by Riedesel and Volkmann. Winckelmann's starting-point in defining appropriate qualifications appears to have been to think of those things which would have made his own study of art easier. The obvious conclusion to which he comes is that he would, to put it crudely, have been better off as an aristocrat. This is, however, a long way from proving that such people necessarily make the best students, which is an essential claim of his. Similarly early exposure to ancient literature and history may be beneficial to a potential art historian. This is, however, not to say that there is a causal connection of the highest order between that reading and the quality of the eventual responses to art.

The factor which is omitted from Winckelmann's calculations—and which obviously has a causal relationship with the final attitude to art—is an analysis of his own brand of intelligence, his personal sensibility. His attempts to provide a system of aesthetic education lack a crucial element, namely a psychology of perception. Whilst his own descriptions bear witness to a highly sophisticated brand of response his prescriptions for his pupils indicate a rather crude assessment of their psychology. Such crude programmatic thinking does little justice to the complexity of aesthetic responses. In essence Winckelmann appears to have done little justice to his own perceptions in assuming that they would be reproduced in others. He was perhaps not the best judge of character himself, as his support for people such as von Berg might show. But the character which he misjudged most severely was perhaps his own. Whilst we have plenty of evidence of his personal struggle to express his aesthetic responses, in the various versions of the great descriptions, this fundamental difficulty is overlooked in producing a programme for others. My analysis provides only one new insight into the descriptions, but if we also take into account Zeller's and Koch's treatments of different aspects, we have a picture of some sophistication. When we look at the sections on qualifications in the wake of this picture of sophistication they seem simplistic and unconnected. Frankly, they have little relevance. The qualities upon which Winckelmann insisted are not of any significance for the possibility of aesthetic response, that is apart from the category of 'sensibility', which should perhaps have been the most specific but is in fact the most neglected. The other things—wealth, class, etc.—may be helpful but only if an aesthetic disposition is already present. This oversight, namely the failure to identify the real sensibility required, is interesting in a man who spent so much time coming to terms with his own responses. Winckelmann in fact only identifies useful external criteria which might conceivably encourage aesthetic response. He does not address, except implicitly in his own descriptions, the question of the internal, or psychological determinants of response. By extension his provision of a framework for the understanding of the history of art, which was the basis of his own aestheticism, becomes the core of his teaching on art for his pupils. It may have been a prerequisite for aesthetic response in his case but does not, as we have seen in the case of Volkmann, necessarily lead to it—or indeed guarantee the ability to express it if it is present. It is precisely the pathway which leads from accumulating information about art to responding to art and then expressing that response which is not explored. Winckelmann lists things which he found useful rather than explaining how he found them useful. He does not deal with the aesthete's required state of mind.

In this context the example of Goethe is illuminating. He was not exposed to Winckelmann's programme although he was in many respects qualified for it. His attitude to much of Winckelmann's systematic art-historical work was also ambivalent. Not only is there evidence to suggest that he did not read much of it but he also left the treatment of that part of his work to someone else when it came to writing a tribute to Winckelmann. Interestingly, he was concerned with the psychology of the man Winckelmann and this proved to be at least one basis for his high degree of responsiveness to art, indeed for an all-pervasive aestheticism which far surpasses that of the model pupils Riedesel and Volkmann. His greater distance from Winckelmann perhaps allowed him to understand the requirements more clearly. He appears to have identified some key elements of Winckelmann's aestheticism which are not dependent upon the strict syllabus which Winckelmann himself imagined to be the most effective means to arrive at aesthetic response.

5
Conclusion
Johann Wolfgang Von Goethe

IT requires an imaginative leap to see Goethe as Winckelmann's pupil. He belonged to a different generation and could scarcely have known Winckelmann personally. He could therefore not enjoy his personal supervision nor have his insights into art tested by the master. Many of the assumed preconditions for aesthetic education in the Winckelmannian manner were simply absent. But despite these biographical/historical difficulties there are compelling reasons for seeing Goethe as a follower of Winckelmann. Of course, there were many bridges between the generations, not least in the form of Riedesel's and Volkmann's publications; they were produced in part as a result of Winckelmann's teaching and used by Goethe in Italy.[1] We also know that Goethe read Mengs's work.[2] Many ideas now primarily associated with Winckelmann must then have been known to Goethe.[3] He also enjoyed a classical education which Winckelmann would have seen as appropriate to the potential student of art. A more direct stimulus to engagement with Winckelmannian ideas will have come through Adam Friedrich Oeser. Winckelmann lived with and studied under Oeser in Dresden in the 1750s and most importantly they spent a good deal of time together in the two years preceding Winckelmann's departure for Italy in 1755.[4] It has been

---

[1] Goethe's use of, and attitude towards, Riedesel and Volkmann is discussed in the chapters on those men. Cf. also A. Schultz, 'Goethe and the Literature of Travel', *Journal of English and Germanic Philology*, 48 (1949), 445–68 and Stiller, 'J. J. Volkmann'.

[2] A reading of Mengs's work is mentioned in a letter to Knebel on 26 Feb. 1782 (*Werke*, iv. 5. 282).

[3] Goethe was very well informed in the matter of the visual arts. In the Berlin edition of his works the publications on art for the period 1771–1808 occupy 714 pages of text, excluding notes. This very useful collection reveals familiarity with most of the major currents of contemporary art-historical thinking (including Winckelmann). Cf. Goethe, *Werke*, 22 vols. (Berlin, 1985), xix ('Schriften zur bildenden Kunst I'). We must also remember that his reading of philosophers, such as Spinoza, and of natural science affected his understanding of the process of seeing the essence of things. Whilst each of these strands of influence was important, and has been thoroughly researched, they only help us to understand his ideology and not the dynamic nature of his response to art. It is here that the parallel with Winckelmann is so inviting.

[4] He may have known Oeser since 1752, before his more extended stay in Dresden. Cf.

coherently argued that those aspects of Winckelmann's early writings which deal directly with the practical aspects of art owe much to Oeser.⁵ It is also likely that Oeser helped to convince Winckelmann of the value of classical art, although he was undoubtedly predisposed to like it as a result of his obsessive study of ancient literature and history. Winckelmann was never particularly ready to acknowledge debt to others but he did point out from Rome that Oeser knew, with regard to classical art, 'soviel man außer Italien wissen kann', even if he was lazy and not strict in his own application of ancient principles of painting (*Briefe*, ii. 307). Such knowledge was no doubt exploited fully by Winckelmann. It offered him access to the hitherto unexplored world of the visual arts, one which he was still having some difficulty in understanding. In one anecdote we hear that Winckelmann spent three days trying to understand a Raphael *Madonna*—which had recently been brought to Dresden—without success. On the following day Oeser accompanied him and was able to unravel the mysteries of the painting (*Briefe*, iv. 205).

Oeser seems to have played a similar role for Goethe, although this time in Leipzig. The latter was delighted 'aus derselben Quelle zu schöpfen, aus der Winckelmann seinen ersten Durst gestillt hatte'. His studio became a 'university' for Goethe—and he attended to his studies here rather more assiduously than elsewhere.⁶ In *Dichtung und Wahrheit* he summarizes some of Oeser's key ideas. Oeser's principle for the visual arts was 'die Einfalt in allem'. As a result he was 'ein abgesagter Feind des Schnörkel- und Muschelwesens'—he reviled the excesses of baroque art. Clearly these statements could be used to describe Winckelmann's outlook as well as Oeser's. Oeser's approach to the arts even encompassed the same contradictions as Winckelmann's. Like Winckelmann he was unable to cast off the influence of baroque art as completely as he would have liked. But also like Winckelmann he remained interested in allegory in the baroque manner—having what Goethe described as an 'eingewurzelte Neigung zum Bedeutenden, Allegorischen, einen Nebengedanken Erregenden'. Like Winckelmann Oeser was also a pedagogue with a

---

Briefe, i. 81, which suggests that whilst working for Bünau he had fallen into the company of artists, presumably including Oeser.

⁵ The extent of Winckelmann's debt to Oeser is difficult to assess, in the same manner as his debt to Mengs. The most successful attempts to confront the difficulty are to be found in the collection 'Johann Joachim Winckelmann und Adam Friedrich Oeser: Eine Aufsatzsammlung', ed. Max Kunze, *Beiträge der Winckelmann-Gesellschaft*, 7 (Stendal, 1977)

⁶ All of Goethe's comments on Oeser are taken from the eighth book of *Dichtung und Wahrheit* (*Werke*, i. 27. 153–222).

mission. Goethe remembered that 'er das Evangelium des Schönen, mehr noch des Geschmackvollen und Angenehmen auch uns unablässig überlieferte'. This early exposure to ideas related very closely to those of Winckelmann may not have had immediate consequences but was ultimately very important and it is interesting that his correspondence with Oeser carried on for some years afterwards.[7] Furthermore he was encouraged by Oeser to read about Winckelmann himself, to participate from afar in 'das hohe Kunstleben Winckelmanns in Italien' and ultimately to share in the tragedy of Winckelmann's death in 1768 (which he heard about as he was going to visit Oeser). He remarked that 'dieser ungeheure Vorfall that eine ungeheure Wirkung; es war ein allgemeines Jammern und Wehklagen, und sein frühzeitiger Tod schärfte die Aufmerksamkeit auf den Werth seines Lebens'. At the very least Goethe was armed with many of the basic precepts of Winckelmann's teachings on the visual arts when he left Leipzig. These were to be very useful to him when he later refocused his attention on them. In an interesting parallel to Winckelmann's difficulties in understanding Raphael, Goethe notes his own reaction to Raphael cartoons: 'Hier nun wurden alle Maximen, welche ich in Oesers Schule mir zu eigen gemacht, in meinem Busen rege.' These principles were driven home still further in Italy. He characterizes the effect of the Italian trip in the following terms: 'Ich habe viel gesehen und noch mehr gedacht: die Welt eröffnet sich mehr und mehr, und alles, was ich schon lange weiß, wird mir erst eigen' (IR 196). Amongst the things which he already knew were many ideas drawn from Winckelmann's publications, from texts related to Winckelmann's or from discussions with former friends of his. Reminders of Winckelmann abound. Goethe visited the estate of Wörlitz (near Dresden), owned by the dynasty of Anhalt-Dessau, one of whom famously visited Winckelmann in Rome with the designer of the estate, the architect Erdmannsdorf. In Rome Goethe came across Angelika Kaufmann, who had painted Winckelmann and worked with Tischbein. He knew Hamilton.[8]

But Goethe took from Winckelmann something rather different. Whilst many people—including Riedesel, Volkmann, Oeser, Mengs—accepted Winckelmann's theories of art production and many of his

---

[7] Winckelmann's last preserved letter to Oeser dates from Feb. 1767 (*Briefe*, iii. 238–40). However, their correspondence was not extensive and seems to have been suspended after 1758 (*Briefe*, iii. 525). Goethe was still in touch in 1769.

[8] Boyle offers the best treatment of Goethe's various meetings with important figures. Although he does not emphasize any connections with Winckelmann, he does give a strong sense of academic/aesthetic community. Cf. Nicholas Boyle, *Goethe: The Poet and the Age*, vol. i (Oxford, 1991).

characteristic critical epithets, Goethe remained obsessed with the act of seeing which is, in my opinion, central to Winckelmann's aesthetic and yet was consistently overlooked by his contemporaries. Whilst Winckelmann might have been less than pleased with Goethe's fluctuating attitudes towards different periods and styles of art, he would have been delighted with his dynamic approach to individual works—his desire to investigate the work at every possible level and to elicit a response from it. It was perhaps for this reason that he took such an interest in the personality of Winckelmann, reflected in his essay on him. Certainly, as Osterkamp has proved, he did not expend too much energy on his study of Winckelmann's art history.[9] Even in *Winckelmann und sein Jahrhundert* he allowed others to write about this aspect of Winckelmann's work.[10] His interest was in the development of Winckelmann's character and in the intense personal engagement with art which helped to shape it. In other words he was interested in the key educational components of aesthetic experience.

1. WAYS OF SEEING: A NEW QUALITY OF RESPONSE TO ART

The experience of art in Italy proved more problematic than the well-prepared Goethe might have expected. No basic appreciative skills abandoned him; it was as true as it had ever been that he could identify the historical, biblical, or mythological content of particular works of art.[11] Equally, the methods of formal appreciation learnt from Oeser were still reliable in their basic tenets. What proved problematic for him was the intensity of the experience; it affected him personally to an extent that he had not anticipated and no study provided adequate preparation for this. It was an experience with which he was at first unable to cope, a position reflected in a degree of hesitancy in his writing.

[9] In a paper to the German seminar in Oxford, given in Dec. 1989, Ernst Osterkamp showed how little Goethe could have read of Winckelmann's major art-historical publications. Goethe, according to his letters, left himself little time to read Winckelmann, and certainly not enough (if his page counts are to be believed) to ever finish the texts.

[10] Cf. *Winckelmann von Goethe*, ed. Howald (introd.), 9–21 for Heinrich Meyer's contribution on art history. Also Ernst Gombrich, 'Goethe and the History of Art: The Contribution of Johann Heinrich Meyer', *Journal of the English Goethe Society*, 60 (1979), 1–19.

[11] These abilities were the product of Goethe's early education, following the modern principles adopted by his father, which are detailed in the early books of *Dichtung und Wahrheit* (*Werke*, i. 26, *passim*).

To begin with Goethe did not allow the fact that he was in Rome to affect his scholarly approach to art; indeed he accelerated and concentrated his efforts in this direction. His work as an artist and his study of the practical aspects of the visual arts were advanced under the tutelage of Tischbein and Hackert.[12] Furthermore his attempts to become an artist in his own right added particular intensity to his efforts to understand the workings of art. He spent a large part of his time in artists' workshops and exposed to a 'Künstlergesellschaft', broadly of the type recommended by Winckelmann. In his study he concentrated on understanding technique rather than on coming to terms with his own overwhelming response, which is our central interest. This emphasis may have contributed to the fact that he came to regard much of his art study as fruitless, although an understanding of the practical side of the visual arts was clearly useful in its own right.[13]

His background knowledge (in the matters of history and mythology) continued to expand not least in the context of his own literary work, which drew upon a wide range of source material. The fact that he was in Italy also reawakened his interest in classical authors. But this aspect of his development has been fully discussed by others.[14]

His renewed engagement with the arts and the themes which informed them did not, however, have the desired effect; he did not yet feel at ease with art. Certainly, he was as well armed to deal with art as many of the Grand Tourists of his age and many of these had had no hesitation in publishing their findings on ancient art even where their knowledge of thematic content and formal expression was limited. However, Goethe was, for his part, acutely aware that these Tourists had not done justice to the work which they described. He aspired to an insight into art which was qualitatively different from that of his contemporaries. He was dismissive of those writers who attempted to produce serious works on

---

[12] Goethe's relationship with both artists is traced by Boyle in *Goethe: The Poet and the Age*. He also indicates the body of art theory (e.g. Sulzer/Gottsched through Hackert) to which he will have been exposed by them. This note, with n. 9, might suggest only a very limited debt to Winckelmann. This is true in the matter of general principles of art. But more important than these are the dynamic properties of Goethe's responses to art, which are closely related to Winckelmann's.

[13] This sort of initiation into the technical aspects of art mimics that experienced by Winckelmann. Although the latter had no ambition to be an artist, his works, beginning with the *Gedanken über die Nachahmung*, indicate a high degree of technical awareness.

[14] Cf. Humphrey Trevelyan, *Goethe and the Greeks* (Cambridge, 1941) for an account of his use of historical and literary source material during his Italian period. Again Boyle in *Goethe: The Poet and the Age* provides an excellent account of the relationship between Goethe's reading, experience, and publications.

Italy and failed to produce works which lived up to the reality. Archenholz was one victim of his criticism:

> Zufällig hab ich hier Archenholzens Italien gefunden. Wie so ein Geschreibe am Ort und Stelle zusammenschrumpft, ist nicht zu sagen. Eben als wenn man das Büchlein auf Kohlen legte, daß es nach und nach braun und schwarz würde, die Blätter sich krümmten und im Rauch aufgingen. Er hat die Sachen gesehen, aber zu der großthuischen, verachtenden Manier, besitzt er viel zu wenig Kenntniße und stolpert lobend und tadelnd. (*Werke*, iv. 8, 76)

Goethe was particularly suspicious of those people who were ready to leap to conclusions, and dispense praise and criticism on the basis of little knowledge, as was the case with Archenholz. This was perhaps only possible for those people who had a fixed idea of what they were going to see. Many travellers were critically overprepared and had effectively prejudged the art they saw. Goethe did not wish his predisposition to enjoy the great works, nurtured by years of study, to interfere with the actual experience of art in Rome. His expectations were not allowed to colour his immediate reactions—or, at least, this was his declared intention. Circumstances conspired to help him resist the desire to prejudge art:

> Jeder denckt doch eigentlich für sein Geld auf der Reise zu genießen. Er erwartet alle die Gegenstände von denen er so vieles hat reden hören, nicht zu finden, wie der Himmel und die Umstände wollen, sondern so rein wie sie in seiner Imagination stehen und fast nichts findet er so, fast nichts kann er so genießen. Hier ist was zerstört hier was angekleckt, hier stinckts, hier rauchts, hier ist Schmutz &c, so in den Wirtshäusern, mit den Menschen &c. (*Werke*, iii. 1, 231)

But he did not rely entirely on chance to help him remain critically alert; he formulated his desire to avoid merely confirming inherited views most clearly in his *Italienische Reise*, where he was able to assess his stance with the benefit of hindsight. He conceived of his task in Italy as a willed reaction against traditional expectations: 'Und nun dringe ich nur darauf, daß mir nichts Name, nichts Wort bleibe. Was schön, groß, ehrwürdig gehalten wird, will ich mit eignen Augen sehn und erkennen' (IR 340). As well as implicitly attacking the status of some received views on art in this passage, Goethe also casts doubt on the fundamental ability of language to capture aesthetic experience. He shared both of these impulses with Winckelmann. Winckelmann, as we have seen, distrusted the contemporary 'word' on aesthetics and indeed doubted any word's ability to capture visual impressions. The only way to overcome one's frustration at this situation was to return to the work of art itself. Goethe, like Winckelmann, wanted to activate his knowledge of art through repeated acts of seeing, noting that 'in der Kunst muß ich es so weit bringen, daß alles anschauende Kenntnis werde, nichts Tradition und Name bleibe, und ich zwinge es in diesem halben Jahre, auch ist es nirgends als in Rom zu zwingen' (IR 361). The opposition between 'Tradition/ Name/Wort' and 'anschauende Kenntnis/mit eignen Augen sehn und erkennen' is maintained throughout his reports on Rome:

Ich will auch nicht mehr ruhen, bis mir nichts mehr *Wort und Tradition*, sondern *lebendiger Begriff* ist. (IR 327–8) [My emphasis throughout this chapter.]

Auf *den ersten sichern Blick* kommt alles an, *das übrige* gibt sich, und durch *Schrifft und Tradition* hat man keinen sichern Blick. (*Werke*, iv. 8. 106)

In the above quotations he hinted at a new critical language based on 'lebendige Begriffe' rather than empty 'Worte' but elsewhere he took a more extreme stance, suggesting that words should play no part in aesthetic appreciation. Art existed 'daß man sie *sehe*, nicht davon *spreche*, als höchstens in ihrer Gegenwart' (IR 346). Any critical commentary is seen as an empty activity, akin to the 'Kunstgeschwätz' which he disliked in others (IR 346). He posited an alternative to the conventional scholarly processing of the visual arts—a learning apart from the account of the conventional student, who would draw on his literary experience and impose certain limited formal criteria. He did not follow their lead for 'es ist alles schon so durch beschrieben, so durch dissertirt, daß man nur erst die Augen aufthun, erst lernen muß' (*Werke*, iv. 8. 66).

Neither description nor scholarly analysis (which I take to be the import of the verb 'dissertiren') has been able to express adequately the experience of art, despite repeated efforts ('durch . . . durch'). He opposed the repetitiveness and fruitlessness of this striving with the immediacy of his own experience. (I am thinking of the opposition 'durch/durch' with 'erst/erst'). Lengthy intellectual processes ('beschreiben/dissertiren') are replaced in his scheme by a simple physical act ('die Augen aufthun'). Whilst the description of aesthetic education as merely a matter of opening the eyes is patently a simplification which strategically omits the functions of the 'Kenntnis' and 'Begriffe', central to the appreciation of art, it does emphasize the immediacy of the experience. A second glance at some of the phrases cited above confirms a sense of urgency:

dringen
muß ich es so weit bringen
zwingen
nicht mehr ruhen
erster Blick
lernen *müssen*

Like Winckelmann he felt that he was fulfilling his natural calling, and even on the basis of the limited examples given above we have the impression that he was helpless to resist this urge (note the repetition of the verb 'müssen'). This urgency was reflected in a very concrete manner in his actions in Rome; his work schedule was full and his energy in visiting galleries was almost boundless. I say almost boundless because he did, at points, feel relieved to be getting away from art, such was his overexposure.[15] There was no question of scholarly 'Prätension' in his approach to the subject (*Werke*, iv. 8. 50). He responded to its 'Gegenwart' and so maximized his time in the presence of art.

But in examining Goethe's responses we are not dealing with a wholly naïve observer. His claim to have cast aside any inherited expectations of art was clearly to be distrusted. Even his 'erster Blick' must inevitably have been coloured by assumptions brought with him from Germany and developed in Italy. It was not possible to suspend one's 'Kenntnis' or the 'Begriffe' used to articulate it at the moment when one observed a work. Goethe's formulations—such as 'anschauende *Kenntnis*' 'lebendiger *Begriff*'—acknowledge this fact. But crucially he qualifies his particular set of *traditional* expectations ('Tradition' = Kenntnis') and the *words* ('Wort/Name' = 'Begriff') used to express them. They are activated in the act of seeing, becoming 'anschauend' or 'lebendig'; these terms suggest that knowledge and its allied 'Begriffe' somehow comes to life in the process of aesthetic experience. Knowledge (in the form of 'Kenntnisse' or 'Begriffe') did not represent an end in itself but, as the adjectives suggest, was part of a living process of response. Indeed this process necessarily involved both the work and its observer in the manner of Winckelmann's reception of art. Knowledge was not the ultimate product of our rational faculties but rather had to be seen as a means at the disposal of the aesthetic faculty which Goethe (rather simplistically) calls the eye. He posited, as a result of this shift in focus, a new brand of learning, dependent above all else on opening one's eyes—'mit eignen Augen sehn und *erkennen*' (IR 340) or 'die Augen aufthun ... *lernen*' (*Werke*, iv. 8. 66). This process of learning is a very dynamic one.

The above formulations are a neat way of capturing the immediacy of response which Goethe regarded as the essence of art experience. However, we must look more closely at the fate of Goethe's store of conventional knowledge and at the impact upon his expectations of the

---

[15] We hear of his need to relax (*Werke*, iii. 1. 295), the pressure to which he felt himself exposed (*Werke*, iv. 8. 221) and the sheer difficulty of dealing with some works (IR 505).

presence of great works. Was he able to adhere to the maxim which he offered his friend Seidel on the matter of inherited opinion versus experience: 'Nur mußt du immer deine Meynung geringer halten als dein Auge' (*Werke*, iv. 8. 313)?

On a number of occasions Goethe referred to the effect of Rome upon his expectations of art. It provided, at the very least, a broader context for the information already at his disposal. Works could be given their appropriate place in his value scheme (or that inherited from Oeser/Winckelmann/Piranesi and many others) and those works whose value had become exaggerated in his imagination during the long years when he had not been able to see them could find a more realistic place in his personal hierarchy of art achievement:

An der Architecktur geh ich denn immer so hin, mit meinem selbstgeschnitzten Maasstab und reiche weit, freylich fehlt mir viel, indeß wollen wir damit vorlieb nehmen und nur brav einsammeln. Die Hauptsache ist daß alle diese Gegenstände, die nun schon über 30 Jahre auf meine Imagination abwesend gewürckt haben und also alle zu hoch stehn, nun in den ordentlichen Cammer und Haus Ton der Coexistenz herunter gestimmt werden. (*Werke*, iii. 1. 227)

This passage is deceptive in many ways. Certain phrases suggest that any new insights were achieved almost incidentally. He portrays himself as wandering ('geh ich denn immer so hin') and his description of his attempt to accumulate knowledge makes him sound like a schoolboy collector ('brav einsammeln'). The evidence of his programme of study in Italy, on the contrary, suggests a much more purposeful approach. The passage is also unusual in devaluing his personal benchmarks for the appreciation of beauty (he appears to have little faith in his 'selbstgeschnitzter Maasstab') and in casting doubt upon the workings of his imagination. His mind is cluttered with assumptions about art which cannot simply be cast off but are gently 'herunter gestimmt' by exposure to ancient art. Rome provided a relativizing context in which to assess the value of art and qualify the workings of an imagination deprived of exposure to great works. The fixed criteria for quality provided by contemporary art-historical theory—not least Winckelmann—had an important role in leading the imagination astray and increasingly Goethe saw historical study as inhibiting rather than liberating:

Hätt ich nicht den Entschluß gefaßt den ich jetzt ausführe, so wär ich rein zu Grunde gegangen und zu allem unfähig geworden, solch einen Grad von Reife hatte die Begierde diese Gegenstände mit Augen zu sehen in meinem Gemüth erlangt. Denn ich konnte mit der historischen Erkänntnis nicht näher, die

Gegenstände standen gleichsam nur eine Handbreit von mir ab waren aber durch eine undurchdringliche Mauer von mir abgesondert.

Denn es ist mir wirklich auch jetzt so, nicht als ob ich die Sachen sähe, sondern als ob ich sie wiedersähe ... Auch weiß ich daß ich wenn auch einen unvollständigen, doch gewiß einen ganz klaren und wahren Begriff mit fortnehme. (*Werke*, iii. 1. 290–1)

Again a firm distinction is made between the act of seeing with one's own eyes ('mit Augen zu sehen') and any other approach to art. In this case the attempt to develop 'historische Känntnis' precludes any close contact with the work of art. The 'Gegenwart' of the work is shut out by a wall and so the all-important interaction with the work is ruled out. Whilst the works are now physically present they are effectively rendered absent by this 'undurchdringliche Mauer'. This wall could be seen as built upon the foundations of 'Wort' and 'Tradition', described above. He is applying an inherited historical method in an attempt to come to terms with substantially new experiences. The tension between these different ways of seeing is reflected in numerous statements but, although there is increasing insistence upon immediacy of experience, historical study of art is never devalued. As he points out, even this is difficult enough for 'es ist eine ernsthafte Sache um die Kunst, wenn man es ein wenig streng nimmt, und *sogar die Kenntnis* ist schon ein Metier, welches man doch kaum glauben mag' (*Werke*, iv. 8. 261–2).

Breaking down or climbing over the wall of 'Kenntnis' (historical or otherwise) to establish immediate contact with a work of art was clearly very difficult and even when you achieved it the outcome could be puzzling. Indeed 'es ist alles, wie ich mir's dachte, und alles neu' (IR 119; *Werke*, iv. 8, 38). Are we not dealing here with the tension 'Tradition/Wort/Name' and 'Gegenwart/Leben', discussed earlier? But there is a sense of progress. Talking of his 'ideas' of art, in the same passage, he notes that 'die alten sind so bestimmt, so lebendig, so zusammenhängend geworden, daß sie für neu gelten können'. It was clearly an important point in the development of Goethe as an observer when his ideas were 'rejuvenated'; this is the key testimony that Goethe had discovered the dynamic nature of aesthetic experience.

On balance Goethe's assessment of his Roman experience is dominated by images suggesting that a live/dynamic experience of art is preferable to a degree of intellectual satisfaction at accounting for the history or style of a work. And yet there are really rather few references to the dynamic nature of aesthetic experience. Indeed references to his intellectual curiosity towards art (i.e. in its history, theories of production, methods of working) outnumber those to other ways of seeing. He also shows a parallel interest in the scientific investigation of the world which confirms the 'intellectual' aspect of Goethe's personality and its importance in the Roman context. The two sides of the man were not in opposition. But there is a qualitative difference between the two ways of seeing. Immediate responses to art have a dynamic impact on the observer; he is moved by art. We have the impression that there is an exchange between the life in art and the life in the observer, whereas as a 'mere' art historian he simply imposes his system of thought onto a work. Whilst Goethe's art-historical opinions, his knowledge of technique acquired through Mengs and his anti-baroque inclinations, inherited from Oeser, may have been confirmed in Italy—his system worked—he could have had only a limited idea of the impact which individual works of art would have on him. Experiences in Mannheim and Strasbourg may have offered him some impression of things to come but they did not prevent him from feeling uneasy in dealing with many works in Italy, at least in the first instance.[16] He sought a new brand of knowledge of art:

> Ich fühle nur auch jetzt wie weit ich in diesen Kenntnißen zurück bin, doch es wird rücken, wenigstens weiß ich den Weg. Palladius hat mir ihn auch dazu und zu aller Kunst und Leben geöffnet. Es klingt das vielleicht ein wenig wunderlich, aber doch nicht so paradox, als wenn Jakob Böhme bey Erblickung einer zinnernden Schüssel über das Universum erleuchtet wurde. (*Werke*, iii. 1. 261)

The difficulties in this passage begin with the claim that there is a path, founded on 'Kenntnisse' which leads towards a complete ('zu *aller* Kunst') understanding of art. Goethe was apparently aware of the dubiousness of this claim, describing it as potentially 'wunderlich' or even 'paradox'. But what is more important is the fact that he was hoping not merely for an understanding of art. His new ambition (and it is particularly associated with Italy) is a form of understanding which can embrace 'Kunst und Leben' and, by extension even 'das Universum', since he has more promising raw materials than Böhme as the basis of his study. And it is indeed his use of the example of and implied comparison with Böhme which gives us a clue that he is looking for something rather more than a large stock of 'Kenntnisse', which can account for art. Böhme experienced a moment of extraordinary insight which enabled him to understand the workings of the universe; this insight was not the

---

[16] See n. 21. Goethe's difficulties in dealing with art in Mannheim pre-date similar problems in Italy.

product of extended analysis and discussion (remember 'beschreiben/ dissertiren') but of revelation. The study of art then was more a matter of generating the right state of mind to enable moments of inspiration and insight than of accumulating information. Although Goethe was not a mystic in the manner of Böhme, and for that matter not even in the manner of Winckelmann, the experience of art was clearly revelatory for him—he has found the path to true understanding and insight ('Erleuchtung'). In comparing his brand of insight with Böhme's he makes clear how much the heightened state of the viewer (as mystic) contributes to the moment of insight. The work of art itself only forms part of the complex of aesthetic experience; to extend Goethe's example it would be false to attribute too much significance to the bowl's role in shaping Böhme's view of the universe.[17]

There is some evidence to suggest that what we might call Goethe's aesthetic mode, based on dynamic personal response, had a role to play in his perception of aspects of life unrelated to the visual arts. In the following passage he is discussing the unlikely topic of trade patterns in Bolzano. The tone is highly familiar and the terminology has been only subtly altered from that which we know from his aesthetics—for 'Wort und Tradition' read 'Buch und Bild' or 'Wissenschaft und Kenntnis':

Doch ist das mein Trost, alles das ist gewiß schon gedruckt. In unsern statistischen Zeiten braucht man sich um diese Dinge wenig zu bekümmern, ein andrer hat schon die Sorge übernommen, mir ists nur jetzt um die sinnlichen Eindrücke zu thun, die mir kein Buch und kein Bild geben kann, daß ich wieder Interesse an der Welt nehme und daß ich meinen Beobachtungsgeist versuche, und auch sehe wie weit es mit meinen Wissenschaften und Kenntnissen geht, ob und wie mein Auge licht, rein und hell ist, was ich in der Geschwindigkeit fassen kann und ob die Falten, die sich in mein Gemüth geschlagen und gedruckt haben, wieder auszutilgen sind. (*Werke*, iii. 1, 175)

It is significant that the very 'drucken' is repeated at two different points in this passage. In the first instance it is used to refer to the range of printed material available to the traveller. In the second instance it is used to refer to the creation of troublesome creases in the mind which impede

---

[17] The parallel with Böhme is not as far-fetched as it may seem. In his introduction to a selection of Böhme's work, in particular in the section on 'Das mystische Urerlebnis', Charles Waldemar emphasizes the links forward to Pietistic writings and back to Platonic/Neoplatonic philosophy, both brands of thinking which were crucially important to both Winckelmann and Goethe. Cf. *Jakob Böhme: Der schlesische Mystiker*, ed. and sel. Charles Waldemar (Munich, 1959), 5–34 (14–19).

the operation of the 'Beobachtungsgeist' and the 'Auge'.[18] Were published texts responsible for the restricted operation of his mind? He rejected the use of material provided by others (not strictly true since he used guidebooks and continued to buy theoretical works etc.) and insisted on developing his own ('ich', 'mein') insight into the world. It is interesting that he should use the term 'statistical' to describe the spirit of the age. It is precisely the term used by critics to describe the nature of most of the eighteenth-century travel literature in the manner, for example, of Volkmann. In suggesting that the recording of information was not an end in itself even when the issue was trade—and certainly only an intermediate stage in the treatment of the visual arts—Goethe appears to be pointing to some of the difficulties which we identified in Riedesel and Volkmann's texts which seem to overvalue basic information and undervalue impressions. To that extent Goethe appears to have more in common with Winckelmann than with his pupils.

2. THE INITIAL STAGES OF AESTHETIC RESPONSE: THE GROUNDS FOR HESITATION

Goethe's reports do not have the set-piece descriptions of individual statues found in Winckelmann. It is, however, possible to derive from his many observations on the nature of the experience of art, a probable pattern of reception. This pattern of reception shares many common features with that observed in a more concentrated form in Winckelmann.

In travelling to Italy Goethe was responding to a calling. He also hoped for a period of recovery from a malaise brought on by isolation from Italy and the works of art stored there.[19] In the simplest formulation 'es war Zeit' (*Werke*, iii. 1. 147). However, it proved more difficult to answer this calling than he expected. To return to the terms used in the previous section the conversion of 'Tradition' and 'Wort' into 'lebendige Begriffe' was more awkward than he anticipated. As he noted: 'ich muß erst mein Auge bilden, mich zu sehen gewöhnen' (*Werke*, iii. 1. 206). And he wished to do this even if it meant that 'ich lauffe und dencke mich müd und matt' (*Werke*, iv. 8. 177). But even if there was a will there was not always a way. On the one hand Goethe felt himself inadequately

---

[18] This passage perhaps refers to the ageing process. As such it marks an extreme contrast with the images of rebirth and rejuvenation discussed later.

[19] Cf. *Werke*, iv. 8. 40. Again the image of illness contrasts with the new life on offer.

equipped to deal with art but on the other he suggested that somehow the works of art were resisting his attention. He had a sense that 'vieles will mir gar nicht ein' (*Werke*, iii. 1. 153). Or else 'es will mir nicht in die Augen' (*Werke*, iii. 1. 340). The suggestion that the works of art have a will of their own is one that is often repeated in Goethe's statements on that subject. The interaction between the trained eye and the resistant, though eventually yielding, work of art was at the core of his aesthetic experience; it was productive in the same manner as Winckelmann's reception of art in as far as it promoted imaginative engagement. In the cases of both men we have an impression of a difficult early courtship of the work of art. And the problem began afresh with each new work, as the wide range of the above quotations (written at different times of different places) might suggest.

In his sense of initial uncertainty Goethe was not dissimilar to the many other travellers who visited Rome but could not make any sense of the vast number and high quality of the works confronting them. It is perhaps ironic that he should express pity for such people, since he seems to have suffered a version of the same fate: 'Recht bedauerlich waren mir einige Reisende die ich habe kennen lernen, die jung und unvorbereitet und doch mit Eifer und Ernst unter der Last von Begriffen die auf sie zudrangen gleichsam erlagen' (*Werke*, iv. 8. 169). The terms 'Eifer' and 'Ernst' were particularly associated in Goethe's mind with the Germanic (or Northern European) approach to learning; people from those parts were thorough without necessarily having profound insights. He also used the latter term to describe negatively Winckelmann's art-historical studies since he felt that they were the product of 'Fleiß', which was a quality which he did not consider promising in its own right.[20] He referred to 'der ehrwürdige deutsche Fleiß, der mehr auf Sammlung und Entwickelung von Einzelheiten als auf Resultate losging' (*Werke*, i. 28. 134). In Italy he pursued 'results'—deeper insights—more substantial than the accumulation of information, and yet ironically his own approach was in many respects similar to that implicit in the above statements; and he had the same sense of doing battle with the work of art. The passage cited above continues: 'Ich habe nun *überwunden* und bin nun täglich mit mehr Lust und Freude da; besonders wird eine kleine Abwesenheit das Anschauen nur mehr auffrischen' (*Werke*, iii. 8. 170). This sort of 'engagement' clearly had serious implications for the

---

[20] But Goethe also describes his writing and working in *Winckelmann von Goethe*, ed. Howald, pp. 126–8. Here he emphasizes the constant revision of the texts as Winckelmann's insight improves, surely a positive brand of assiduity.

observer. On the one hand there was the pleasure of victory ('Lust und Leben', 'auffrischen'), on the other the bewilderment of defeat ('unter der Last von Begriffen erliegen'). The rewards of victory were clearly sufficient to offset the prospect of defeat; the observer was offered an apparent rejuvenation through art, described in a terminology of renewal, or even of rebirth. But the rewards were not guaranteed and Goethe often felt himself inhibited by great works of art; this affected not only his appreciation of these particular works but also his attempts to produce works in their spirit for 'ich hatte schon Angst ich würde von dem Anschauen der großen Kunstwerke erdruckt werden, und mich nicht getrauen ein Bleystift anzusetzen' (*Werke*, iv. 8. 181). The verb 'erdrucken' echoes the verb 'drucken', discussed above. It also suggests an intermediate stage to the verb 'erliegen' and so offers little prospect of an aesthetic victory. His inability to draw also mirrors his doubts about the ability to write about art, and by extension Winckelmann's fears regarding the adequate expression of aesthetic experience. This fear of being crushed by the burden of art was realized on a number of occasions and Goethe found himself wandering clueless in the midst of all of these great works. The following description shows a state of excited confusion similar to that which Goethe described in connection with his first significant encounter with ancient art (or its reproductions) in Mannheim.[21]

Die erste Zeit eines hiesigen Aufenthalts geht ohnedies unter Staunen und Bewundrung hin, biß man nach und nach mit den Gegenständen bekannter und sich selbst gleichsam erst gewahr wird. Alsdann lernt man erst sondern, beurtheilen und schätzen. (*Werke*, iv. 8. 196)

But the initial state of 'Staunen und Bewundrung' is not unproductive; it encourages the observer to acquaint himself with art and prevents him from making hasty judgements. Noticeably the verb 'schätzen' marks the last stage of art appreciation described above and even then any judgement can only be partial; he makes this point in the continuation of the passage where he pointed out that many travellers failed to do art justice because 'die Masse des zu Betrachtenden [bleibt] allzugroß'. One cannot have a complete overview and therefore must abandon any claim to total insight. The portrayal of the relationship of the viewer to the work of art as a productive 'Bekanntschaft' ('mit den Gegenständen bekannter werden') is important. It is not simply a matter of knowing more about art; Goethe conceives of a relationship in which the student

[21] Cf. Goethe's account at *Werke*, i. 28. 85–7.

comes to know more about himself ('sich selbst gewahr werden') through the experience of art. The educational function of art is not merely informative. Genuine interaction with the work of art results in the fullest activation of the critical intelligence, whose three main components are isolated above—'sondern, beurtheilen und schätzen'. One grows into the task of art appreciation and attunes oneself to the greatness of the works of art in question, moving from the passivity suggested by the nouns 'Staunen' and 'Bewunderung' towards active discrimination of the properties of a given work. To that extent it is rather like coming to terms with life. First you watch things happen, as in Rome:

> Es dringt eine zu grose Masse Existenz auf einen zu, man muß eine Umwandlung sein selbst geschehen laßen, man kann an seinen vorigen Ideen nicht mehr kleben bleiben, und doch nicht einzeln sagen worinn die Aufklärung besteht. (*Werke*, iv. 8. 139)

The educational phenomenon of 'Aufklärung' is Goethe's aim and it is something that can be achieved through the study of art. Even if the pathways to this enlightenment are not clear in detail the first movement has to be to open yourself to new impressions. You have to allow the 'Unwandlung' to take place and abandon any preconceptions that you might have of art (i.e. 'vorige Ideen', 'Wort und Tradition'). The works of art must be allowed to operate on the receiver.

The clearest statement of this approach comes in his description of a visit to the Sistine Chapel and St Peter's with Tischbein. His reaction to the latter is interesting since, although he did not particularly appreciate the building (it did not perhaps conform to his expectations), he none the less tried to keep an open mind and take the work of art on its own terms:

> Dann gingen wir in die Sixtinische Capelle, die wir auch hell und heiter, die Gemälde wohl erleuchtet fanden. Das jüngste Gericht und die manigfaltigen Gemälde der Decke von Michel Ange theilten unsre *Bewunderung, Ich konnte nur sehen und anstaunen*. Die innre große Sicherheit und Männlichkeit des Meisters, seine Großheit geht *über allen Ausdruck*. Nachdem wir alles wieder und wieder gesehn, verließen wir dieses Heiligthum und gingen nach der Peterskirche, die von dem heitern Himmel das schönste Licht empfing und in allen Theilen hell und klar war. Wir *ergötzten* uns als *genießende* Menschen, an der Größe und Pracht, ohne durch allzueklen und zu verständigen Geschmack uns dies mal irre machen zu laßen und unterdrückten jedes schärfere Urtheil. Wir *erfreuten* uns des erfreulichen. (*Werke*, iv. 8. 63)

In this passage the work operates upon the receiver in two radically different ways. In the first case 'Bewunderung' is called forth by the sheer power of the impression made by the art. The receiver is powerless and 'konnte nur sehen und anstaunen'. He has no means to express the profound impact made by the work since it is 'über allen Ausdruck', but he chooses a familiar terminology in the attempt. We hear of 'innre große Sicherheit und Männlichkeit', 'Großheit'. In this case then Goethe was in some sense unequal to the task of appreciation set by the work. In the second case, St Peter's, the observer maintains an open mind in order to make the most of a work to which he does not intuitively respond. The experience of 'Großheit' is replaced by a simpler pleasure—'ergötzen/ genießen/erfreuen'. The inexhaustible pleasure of looking at the Sistine Chapel is contrasted with the limited pleasure of looking at St Peter's, a pleasure which could, in fact, only be maintained by suspending critical instincts. We sense that a 'schärferes Urteil' would have been forthcoming if Goethe had not chosen to focus on the superficial appeal of the building. Only in the first case given above was pleasure allied to its natural companion (according to the aesthetic adage), instruction. The Sistine Chapel offers the prospect of 'Großheit' whilst St Peter's only has 'Größe'—here physical size—on its side. The Sistine Chapel embodies some key aesthetic principles—'Sicherheit/Männlichkeit/Großheit'— and it is not just incidentally a 'Heiligthum'. There is something present in the art to which the observer can aspire; its impact is not merely superficial or decorative as was the case with St Peter's. Works which belong to the first category clearly have the greater appeal to Goethe since they demand that the viewer be somehow improved ('instructed') in order to appreciate them.[22] Hence even when Goethe is at his most uncertain in dealing with works of art his uncertainty is made more tolerable by the awareness that he will eventually be improved by the attempt to understand the work: 'Im Pallaste Giustiani steht eine Minerva die meine ganze Verehrung hat. Winckelmann gedenckt ihrer kaum, wenigstens nicht an der rechten Stelle, und ich fühle mich nicht würdig genug über sie etwas zu sagen' (Werke, iv. 8. 130). It is, of course, interesting that Goethe should turn to Winckelmann as a source of information when his own critical insight is insufficient. However, the most important point is the improvement in the viewer which is, implicitly, necessary to do justice to such works. There are echoes here of Winckelmann's claim to have felt improved by the experience of art; this sensation was

[22] This indicates Goethe's independent thinking. He did not feel obliged to reproduce the views of others on individual works of art, even when he agreed with their general principles. Here he differs from Winckelmann, who saw St Peter's as one of the few great works of architecture produced in the modern period.

so strong in Winckelmann that he felt that the works were having an almost physical impact upon him, causing his chest to expand and his posture to become more dignified, as well as making him feel enlightened spiritually. Schiller needed a similar improvement in himself in order to cope with the collection at Mannheim, which as we have seen caused Goethe such difficulties.[23] Goethe is suggesting that he has to become more 'worthy' in order to appreciate fully the 'Würde' of the statue and in saying this he has clearly identified the central impulse towards aesthetic education. Goethe frequently refers to the difficulty in understanding the pathways which enable such improvement. The following two quotations indicate that this difficulty exists from the moment of initial exposure to a work and accompanies any more profound investigation. In a discussion of 'first impressions', he says:

Doch muß man auf alle Fälle wieder und wieder sehn, wenn man einen reinen Eindruck der Gegenstände gewinnen will. Es ist ein sonderbares Ding um den ersten Eindruck, er ist immer ein Gemisch von Wahrheit und Lüge im hohen Grade. ich kann noch nicht recht herauskriegen wie es damit ist. (*Werke*, iii. 1. 228)

However, close and extended study is no guarantee of clear perception. Talking of Rome in general, he notes 'wie man die See immer tiefer findet ie weiter man hineingeht; so geht es auch mir in Betrachtung dieser Stadt' (*Werke*, iv. 8. 146). This pattern of imagery is familiar from Winckelmann's works and is a strong indication that the two men were confronted by parallel aesthetic dilemmas.[24] They experienced an aesthetic baptism and were, to use Winckelmann's image, offered access to the 'Quelle' of great art. As Goethe said of Rome: 'Es ist mir sehr gesund in einem solchen Elemente mich erst recht zu baden und zu waschen, das Einölen soll nach Ihrem Recepte in Neapel vor sich gehn' (*Werke*, iv. 8. 178). Art has healing and purifying properties and we remember that Goethe described the visit to Italy as a necessary recuperation from an illness brought about by underexposure to ancient art and culture.

Opening oneself up to art can help to give one's life substance, a

[23] Cf. the *Brief eines reisendenden Dänen* in the *Sämtliche Werke*, ed. G. Fricke and H. G. Göpfert, 5 vols. (Munich, 1958), v. 879–84.

[24] Winckelmann's sea imagery is introduced in the *Gedanken*, where we are shown the calm depths of Laocoön's soul. The related image of the source was also important. Cf. Koch, 'Sprache und Kunstwerk', 100–2. Both images are characteristic of the language of Pietism and Platonic philosophy, where they serve to express both mystery and power. Goethe knew this and was aware of their importance to Winckelmann. Thus when, as we saw earlier, he talks of drawing from the same well as Winckelmann, he acknowledges the shared provenance of many of their ideas.

progression which is recorded in appropriate imagery. We hear, for example, that Goethe's life in Italy has taken on a certain solidity and substance. Talking in general terms, he says: 'Meine Existenz hat nun einen Ballast bekommen, der ihr die gehörige Schweere giebt[;] ich fürchte mich nun für denen Gespenstern nicht mehr, die so oft mit mir gespielt haben' (*Werke*, iv. 8. 151). He uses a number of verbs to describe this taking on of ballast at various points in his reports. He refers to his accumulation of knowledge with the following verbs—'aufpacken' (iv. 8. 41), 'aufladen' (iii. 1. 306), 'ausstatten' (iii. 1. 221). As a result he has become 'wohl ausstaffirt' (iv. 8. 26) and 'solid' (iv. 8. 48). These verbs give the impression of a certain confidence on Goethe's part—he is making the most of himself, filling himself to the brim with information and above all impressions. However, it frequently becomes apparent that he is unable to accommodate certain impressions of art. He may be more complete through the experience of art but he is not yet complete in the manner which we have seen in Winckelmann, whose life was also given substance through art. In some cases it is simply that he has seen too much and is unable to keep a grasp on it all. In his own terms he is in these cases 'überfüllt' (iv. 8. 93). Otherwise the impression may be too strong; the mind cannot do justice to it. At its simplest we have an experience such as the following. Goethe is describing the Colisseum which is 'so groß daß man das Bild nicht in der Seele behalten kann, man erinnert sich dessen nur kleiner wieder' (iv. 8. 53). How then can the soul be improved to accommodate more of the beauty of art? How can the student of art achieve more substantial responses to art? How can he learn to express his responses less hesitantly?

3. THE PRODUCTIVE ASPECTS OF THE PASSIVE ATTITUDE

Although there was undoubtedly a degree of hesitation in Goethe's dealings with art this did not preclude enjoyment of it. Passivity was not always equated in his mind with feelings of inadequacy as an art critic. Passivity also enabled pleasure in a world 'wo *sich* denn wohl *dem Auge* ein einzig Schauspiel *darstellt*' (*Werke*, iii. 1. 249) (he is talking about Naples and the view from a tower).

History and, in particular, ancient history was no longer merely of academic interest to him but was brought alive, especially through the study of art. Goethe talks again of the 'spirit' of history present in Rome, but in this case such spirits hold no fear for him:

Hundertfältig *steigen* die Geister der Geschichte *aus dem Grabe*, und *zeigen mir* ihre wahre Gestalt. Ich freue mich nun auf so manches zu lesen und zu überdencken, das mir in Ermanglung eines sinnlichen Begriffs unerträglich war. (*Werke*, iii. 1. 310)

Life, and, in particular, art appear to have opened themselves to him; he portrayed himself as a happy recipient of all that they could offer him. In an early letter from Italy to his friends in Weimar he describes this pleasant state of affairs. Again his attitude was essentially passive; he claimed merely to have opened his eyes and to have absorbed impressions:

Ich bin nun zehen Tage hier und nach und nach *thut sich vor mir der allgemeine Begriff dieser Stadt auf*. Wir gehen fleißig auf und ab, ich mache mir den Plan des alten und des neuen Roms bekannt, betrachte die Ruinen, die Gebäude, besuche ein und die andre Ville, alsdann nehmen wir die größten Merckwürdigkeiten ganz langsam, *ich thue nur die Augen auf und sehe und gehe und komme wieder*. Der Menschen wird auch nicht vergeßen und *so macht sich's nach und nach*. Denn gewiß man kann sich nur in Rom auf Rom bereiten. (*Werke*, iv. 8. 44)

Goethe sees his insights developing independently ('machen sich') and presenting themselves to him ('sich vor mir thun'). His only act was to open his eyes, a metaphor (as well as a fact), which, as was suggested earlier, does little justice to the complexities of aesthetic reception. Goethe, however, continued to insist upon this 'explanation'. Such is the formative power of art that it could even affect the quality of the eye itself:

Noch einige Gebäude hab ich besehn und mein Auge *fängt sich gut an zu bilden*, ich habe nun Muth dem Mechanischen der Kunst näher zu treten. Was mich freut ist daß keine von meinen alten Grundideen *verrückt und verändert wird, es bestimmt sich nur alles mehr, entwickelt sich und wächst mir entgegen*. (*Werke*, iii. 1. 229)

The phrase 'mein Auge fängt sich gut an zu bilden' suggests that it was developing independently; its development allowed him to approach the work of art with freshly discovered 'Muth'. His hesitation appeared to be disappearing. But even when he had this proximity to the work of art the aesthetic energy appears to stem from the work. It provides the impulse to change, fix, develop, or nurture ideas; they stem from the work of art and grow towards the receiver.

There is a calm on the part of the receiver which contrasts with the state of uncertainty and hesitation described in other cases. Various instances of this state of calm can be found elsewhere. We are offered, for example, the following descriptions of his state of mind:

Ich gehe nach meiner Gewohnheit nur so herum, sehe alles *still* an, und *empfange und behalte einen schönen Eindruck*. Nur eins nach dem andern. (*Werke*, iii. 1. 194)

We hear, in a different context, the related statement:

Ich habe endlich das Ziel meiner Wünsche erreicht und lebe hier mit einer *Klarheit und Ruhe*, die Ihr Euch denckt weil ihr mich kennt. Meine Übung alle Dinge wie sie sind zu sehen und zu lesen, *meine Treue das Auge Licht seyn zu laßen, meine völlige Entäusserung von aller Prätension*, machen mich hier höchst *im Stillen* glücklich. (*Werke*, iv. 8. 50)

Or, specifically of people-watching, he says:

Ich habe das alles mit einem *stillen feinen Auge* betrachtet und mich dieser grosen Existenz gefreut. (*Werke*, iii. 1. 245)

It was, according to the scheme suggested above, only necessary to keep a calm eye or steady focus in order to achieve results. The aesthetic faculties had to be allowed to operate—or, rather, be operated upon—unimpeded, and the receiver had to remain 'frei von aller Prätension', which I take to mean abandoning the 'Wort und Tradition' discussed above. To return to the terminology used earlier the 'result' consisted in the experience of pleasure ('Glück' and 'Freude' implicit in above statements); pleasure is, in turn, derived from beauty (a 'schöner Eindruck' presumably stems from exposure to a beautiful object). Their effects were wholly positive and did not stop at simple pleasure. Elsewhere Goethe talked in terms of illness in connection with his negative state of mind before his departure for Italy. Things soon changed. On leaving Rome for Naples he looked forward to the new experience 'mit offnen und *gesunden* Augen' (*Werke*, iv. 8. 194). He aimed to maintain this healthy condition by controlled exposure to the arts. Importantly, the crucial aspect of this diet of the arts was the maintainance of a state of calm in his soul for 'ich lebe sehr diät und halte mich ruhig damit die Gegenstände keine erhöhte Seele finden, sondern die Seele erhöhen' (*Werke*, iii. 1. 227). He is suggesting here that a potential impediment to the understanding of art is a predisposition to enjoy it. If one had an 'erhöhte Seele' in anticipation of the experience of art then one was unlikely to enjoy the actual moment of spiritual elevation in the presence of the work, a danger as great as that of adhering to 'Wort und Tradition'. Goethe insisted that such presuppositions and predispositions had to be removed before exposure to art; if this were not the case then the observer would be too active in his initial appreciation of the work.

In Goethe's portrayal of his experience of art he shows himself ruling out such interference in the aesthetic process. He arrives naturally at the 'lebendige Begriffe' of art to which he aspired. As if to prove that the 'Begriffe' are indeed 'lebendig' they are shown by Goethe to have a life of their own since 'meine Begriffe von Welt weiten sich nun gar schön aus' (*Werke*, iv. 8. 181). More generally, 'man muß nur sehen, wenn man Augen hat und alles entwickelt sich' (*Werke*, iii. 1. 276). This development of 'Begriffe' is not, however, unlimited. For the mind to be able to process the experience of art it has to be able to impose order upon it. Nevertheless, such was Goethe's adherence to the notion of pure and uninhibited insight, that he insisted that the organization, or rationalization, of aesthetic information took place of its own accord without conscious input on his part. At a given point 'schon fängt das Gesehene an sich zu ordnen und das unendlich scheinende schließt sich in Gränzen' (*Werke*, iv. 8. 125). Or else 'man meynt man sähe alles, alles reiht sich' (*Werke*, iv. 8. 109). Indeed Goethe consistently devalued his contribution to the act of seeing. He portrayed himself as being led towards an understanding of art and life, saying that 'es ist unglaublich was mich diese acht Wochen auf Haupt und Grundbegriffe des Lebens sowohl, als der Kunst geführt haben' (*Werke*, iii. 1. 315).

This is interesting since Goethe suggested that on arrival in Italy he lacked the 'Mittelbegriffe' let alone the 'Grundbegriffe' for understanding art.[25] Perhaps the final indication that he felt himself to have been passive in his appreciation of art came when he considered the idea of another visit. In that case he would return 'mit geöffneten Augen' (*Werke*, iii. 1. 303). This phrase implies an agent which opened his eyes—and in Rome the most powerful of the potential agents was art. Even when he accepted that he had made some contribution to his experiences of Rome any changes in his 'Sinn' were still attributed to the power which Italy and art brought to bear on him for 'dem denckenden und fühlenden Menschen *geht* ein neues Leben, ein neuer Sinn *auf*, wenn er diesen Ort betritt, ja allen Menschen, jedem nach seinem Maase' (*Werke*, iv. 8, 81).

Predictably, the change brought about in Italy was associated with images of rebirth and fresh insight.[26] The final parenthetical phrases, however, suggest that the environment (and in our case most particularly the art) does not wholly determine the quality of the traveller's responses. Everyone responds but 'jeder nach seinem Maase'. The

---

[25] Cf. e.g. *Werke*, iv. 8. 221 ('Mittelkenntniße').
[26] The most exhaustive treatment of the theme of rebirth is provided by Klaus H. Kiefer, *Wiedergeburt und neues Leben: Aspekte des Strukturwandels in Goethes 'Italienische Reise'* (Bonn, 1978).

intrinsic quality of the observer would be reflected in the quality of his response. We are reminded of Goethe's reference, discussed earlier, to his 'selbstgeschnitzter Maasstab'; this benchmark proved a little unreliable but presumably it was amended during his time in Italy and came to be a more reliable measure of art. The particular qualities of his individuality inevitably coloured his responses as they would any other traveller's. Even when he felt himself to have been transformed by Italy, this transformation still left him—almost paradoxically—unchanged in his essence for 'ob ich gleich noch immer derselbe bin; so meyn ich biß aufs innerste Knochenmark verändert zu seyn' (*Werke*, iv. 8. 72).

It is the *essential* contribution of Goethe's to the business of aesthetic reception which is to be the focus of the remaining part of this chapter. Whilst he reflected on how 'sie [die Reise] mich aufgeklärt und mich erheitert hat' (*Werke*, iv. 8. 225)—i.e. operated upon him as a passive observer—I wish to investigate his often submerged contribution to the process of self-enlightenment.

Goethe struggled to find expression for his immediate experience of art. Where does one find a language appropriate to aesthetic experience and able to encapsulate '*lebendige* Begriffe' which by their nature appear to be elusive? He formulated this difficulty in the following way: 'Man müßte Jahre hier bleiben um den Begriff recht lebendig zu haben, ich fühle nur die verborgnen und halbsichtbaren Punckte' (*Werke*, iv. 8. 52). Even these half-formulated 'lebendige Begriffe' were difficult to explain; it was difficult to give expression to something which one sensed but could not see clearly. 'Begriffe' remained elusive for as long as they were 'lebendig'; for those 'Begriffe' to become fixed or fully explicable they had to be reduced to the status of mere 'Begriffe' or 'Worte', which in Goethe's terms meant having the life drained out of them. Words did nevertheless have a potential which his pejorative use of the word 'Wort' might conceal. Whilst they may have proved inadequate as a means of capturing truths about art they could *express* some aspects of the experience of art. There is a good deal of evidence that Goethe, at various points, overcame his hesitation in dealing with art. In the quotation which follows Goethe is discussing his reluctance to attempt to draw the human figure; this reluctance is rooted in the familiar hesitation when faced with a powerful impression:

Gegen Ende Ottobers kam ich wieder in die Stadt und da ging eine neue Epoche an. Die Menschengestalt zog nunmehr meine Blicke auf sich und wie ich vorher, gleichsam wie von der Glanz der Sonne meine Augen von ihr weggewendet, so konnte ich nun mit Entzücken sie betrachten und auf ihr verweilen. Ich begab mich in die Schule, lernte den Kopf mit seinen Theilen zeichnen und nun fing ich erst an die Antiken zu verstehen. (*Werke*, iv. 8. 329)[27]

Here the idea of a new beginning ('neue Epoche') through the experience of art is closely linked to activity on the viewer's part. One could no longer turn away from powerful impressions but had to face them and actively investigate the phenomenon with which one was confronted. He was not prepared, in this state of mind, to 'bescheiden sehen und erwarten was sich mir in der Seele bildet' as had happened on a number of occasions (*Werke*, iv. 8. 76). At its most effective the reception of art (as well as nature, life) was conceived of as an act of communication. When Goethe was hesitant or passive this act of communication was a one-sided affair since 'es spricht eben alles zu mir und zeigt sich mir an' (*Werke*, iii. 1. 150). However, at its most productive it could be described as a conversation. It is important to notice, once more, the stress laid upon the presence of the work of art:

Ich gehe nur immer herum und herum und sehe und übe mein Aug und meinen innern Sinn... Du weißt was die Gegenwart der Dinge zu mir spricht und ich bin den ganzen Tag in einem Gespräch mit den Dingen. (*Werke*, iii. 1. 219)

We can see here how 'lebendige Begriffe' are generated; we see a live exchange between the viewer and the work of art, which is itself imagined as living. The conventionally inanimate—'Dinge'—is brought to life. Such conversations are the basis of the 'Bekanntschaft' which he claimed to have with art—a notion developed more fully later. At his most enthusiastic he even suggested that the independent 'lives' of the viewer and the work of art had fused into a state of 'Mitleben'. In the following quotation he describes progressive improvement in insight parallel to that suggested in this and the preceding two sections of this chapter:

Ich fange nun an die besten Sachen zum zweytenmal zu sehen, wo denn das erste Staunen sich in ein Mitleben und näheres Gefühl des Werthes der Sachen auflöst. (*Werke*, iv. 8. 100)

We must now look at this idea of interaction, or 'Mitleben', in more detail. What further evidence is there of reciprocity in his relationship with art?

---

[27] There is a powerful link here to the notion introduced at the end of Ch. 3, namely that 'dessiner c'est connaître'. To draw objects, even in words, demands a greater degree of familiarity with objects than that achieved by the mere observer.

4. THE DEVELOPMENT OF AN ACTIVE APPROACH: ENTHUSIASM

Goethe was always aware of the inadequacies of conventional critical language as a means to express aesthetic experience. Art was something which could be 'gefühlt' or equally 'erkannt' and so the critic was forced to find a language which could accommodate both the sensuous and intellectual sides of the experience (*Werke*, i. 29. 115). Such was the difficulty that Goethe frequently refused to engage in discussions of works of art in his letters to friends. He awaited the moment when he would be able to describe his experiences to these people in person: 'Von Kunstsachen mag ich gar nicht reden und von der Nation wird mir auch schweer etwas zusammen zu faßen, in der Folge, oder am besten mündlich, wird das schon beßer kommen' (*Werke*, iv. 8. 90). Why did Goethe insist on this? Conversation does not normally allow the considered responses which one might expect from a written exchange. However, the spoken word, supported by facial expression and other gestures, is likely to convey successfully the immediacy of the reported experience. This advantage outweighed in Goethe's mind the disadvantage of less consideration.

There is here an interesting parallel with Winckelmann's efforts to capture his own enthusiasm for art. As part of the meticulous preparation of his writings on art Winckelmann, perhaps suprisingly, retained a number of 'körnicht' phrases, unusual in an academic work. These clearly formed part of his attempt to provide a lively account of art. His use of German, and indeed of dialect German, could also be seen as attempts to break the academic mould to some extent in works which are otherwise highly academic. The sentence structures in Winckelmann's writing often owed more to conversation than scholarly exposition and were clearly aimed at breaking down the distance between critic and audience and establishing a degree of intimacy. We are also reminded of his major occupation in Italy as a cicerone, which depended upon his ability to convey enthusiasm for as well as basic information about the arts. Arguably, this impression of enthusiasm conveyed through both the spoken and written word was the key to Winckelmann's success. It was the means to inspire others.

But it seems strange that Goethe should have such difficulties in expressing himself. After all he did not hesitate to describe himself as having 'eine schnelle Fassungskraft' in his youth (*Werke*, i. 29. 137). There is no evidence that this talent diminished with age and in Italy he seems to have been concerned to test its limits by exposing it to the visual arts. His success in understanding art was not immediate but he made vigorous efforts to overcome this difficulty. In a letter to Carl August he promises to devote himself to 'der Landes Administration' fully on his return, in the same way as he has devoted himself to the study of art in Italy. Talking particularly of his administrative duties but implicitly of his attitude to the arts before Italy, he says 'ich habe lange getappt und versucht, es ist Zeit zu *ergreifen* und zu *würcken*' (*Werke*, iv. 8. 242). Art demanded this degree of engagement if the observer was to derive any benefit from his studies. Real enjoyment of the visual arts came only after extensive exposure and profound contemplation. Goethe aimed to fulfil both of these conditions for enjoyment and he was always amused by those who claimed deep insights into art on the basis of no experience:

Sie erlauben mir, ja Sie fordern mich auf Ihnen öfter zu schreiben, ich will es mit Freuden thun, wenn mir vergönnt ist auf das Papier zu setzen was der Tag und die Stunde giebt, dass denn nicht immer das bedeutendste seyn möchte; der großen Resultate sind so wenig und je länger man Gegenstände betrachtet desto weniger getraut man sich etwas allgemeines darüber zu sagen. Man möchte lieber die Sache selbst mit allen ihren Theilen ausdrucken oder gar schweigen.

Ich muß immer heimlich lachen wenn ich Fremde sehe, die beym ersten Anblick eines großen Monumentes sich den besondern Effekt notiren, den es auf sie macht. Und doch wer thuts nicht? und wie viele begnügen sich nicht damit? (*Werke*, iv. 8. 292)

In contrast to many of his fellow travellers Goethe was active in his attempts to understand art. Despite his modesty when faced with great works the position represented by the above quotation marks a considerable advance from the attitude of fear and nervous hesitation towards art indicated in other passages. In the first paragraph he alludes to his wish to understand fully individual works ('mit allen ihren Theilen') and make observations of more general import ('etwas allgemeines darüber sagen'). Individual, immediate responses to art ('der besondere Effekt') are of limited interest; Goethe appeared to be searching for objective criteria for the assessment of the value of art and at this stage he can still imagine achieving 'große Resultate'. In the following quotation he describes this process as a search for the 'Begriff' which could unlock an understanding of art. Importantly, he distinguished himself from many of his fellow travellers because he searched for the 'Begriff'; he chose not to apply principles inherited from others as a time- and energy-saving way to understand art:

Aber so sollte es mir immer ergehen, daß ich durch Anschauen und Betrachten der Dinge erst mühsam zu einem Begriffe gelangen mußte, der mir vielleicht nicht so auffallend und fruchtbar gewesen wäre, wenn man mir ihn überliefert hätte. (*Werke*, i. 28. 83)

This quotation indicates the degree of 'Mühe', or *activity*, necessary to bring 'Begriffe' alive. He gradually developed a 'Prinzip' which helped him to understand art for 'meine Kunststudien gehen sehr vorwärts, mein Prinzip paßt überall und schließt mir alles auf' (IR 365). Even if we ignore temporarily the precise nature of this 'Prinzip' or the associated 'Begriffe' we can see that there is a more active aesthetic principle in play. Earlier, I focused on a passage from a letter in which Goethe described how 'das Gesehene . . . schließt sich in Gränzen' and even 'ordnet sich'. The observer is in these cases essentially passive. But here he is actively sorting out art in his mind: 'Meine Liebschaften reinigen und entscheiden sich, und nun erst kann mein Gemüt den Größeren und Echtsten mit gelassener Teilnahme sich entgegen heben' (IR 161). The reflexive verb-forms in the first phrase do echo many of those used by Goethe in his more passive moments, indicating that changes were taking place within him that he did not control; the final verb, on the other hand, indicates a much more positive approach. I noted earlier how Goethe felt at one point that he was being 'auf Haupt und Grundbegriffe . . . der Kunst *geführt*' and at another that an understanding of art '*wächst mir entgegen*'. In the above quotation he portrays himself as calmly ('mit gelassener Teilnahme') rising to an understanding of the greatness and truth in art. This condition was very different to the hesitant and passive state typical of Goethe in his initial response to works of art. It is at this point that Goethe begins to locate the improvement in his own aesthetic faculties which was the educational benefit of the study of art. This was part of a more general improvement which he attributed (retrospectively) to his Italian journey, during which 'ich bin fleißig und nehme von allen Seiten ein und wachse von innen heraus' (IR 326).[28] In the field of the arts the basic improvement consisted in the confidence to put more of himself into the process of art appreciation.

[28] On first examination the references to the published version of the *Italienische Reise* may appear to sit uneasily alongside the passages from the earlier diaries and letters. Whilst they may lack spontaneity they do, however, provide considered views on art and a cool retrospective assessment of an aesthetic education. On the whole there is little difference in the conclusions offered earlier and later, at least in the matter of aesthetic education, although individual formulations may differ. I have largely restricted myself to use of the *Italienische Reise* in cases where no similar lucidity is provided in the original accounts. I have used *Dichtung und Wahrheit* in a similar manner, as befits its shared genesis with the *Italienische Reise*.

He had greater faith in his own insights into art and life in Italy; the most obvious consequence of this positive outlook was a speedier understanding of fresh material. He did not always feel the need to be patient and to wait for objects, as it were, to inform him. He would interpret positively new experiences rather than persevere in the hope of eventual understanding. He summarized his outlook thus: 'Nicht sowohl das Beharren als ein schnelles Auffassen muß jetzt mein Augenmerk sein. Hab' ich einem Gegenstande nur die Spitze des Fingers abgewonnen, so kann ich mir die ganze Hand durch Hören und Denken wohl zueignen' (IR 203).

The image which Goethe uses to express this method is significant. It is an image of reconstruction, and in that respect provides a striking parallel with the process which I located at the core of Winckelmann's descriptions of works of art. Furthermore this is not an isolated use of such an image; he refers elsewhere to the 'Restaurationstalent' needed to appreciate the remnants of ancient art (IR 275). The implication contained in these images is clear: given a clue as to the nature of an object (in nature or in art—the first quotation is not specific) Goethe provided his own concretization of it. The whole hand he imagined is, to use my critical terminology, an aesthetic object—a projection on the part of the observer and on the basis of his particular interpretative skills. We are reminded of Winckelmann's description of the Belvedere Torso; the statue was incomplete and yet, in Winckelmann's interpretation, was depicted as whole and alive. The gaps between the incomplete work of art and the complete aesthetic object were filled by the observer's imaginative input. 'Hören und Denken' are the means to stock that imagination. We noted earlier that Goethe rejected the mere application of other people's principles and methods as a means of understanding art. We do, however, inevitably collect knowledge and information which we can use productively when we combine it with out own independent thought; the aim is a more embracing understanding of the individual object of the type envisaged by Goethe when he said that 'ich thue die Augen auf so weit ich kann und greife das Werck von allen Seiten an' (*Werke*, iv. 8. 135).

The reward for such active response was the establishment of a dialogue with a given object. There were precedents for this experience before Goethe arrived in Italy, although it took on particular importance there. In his autobiography he relates a discussion in which he was involved about the disposition of the towers of Strasbourg Cathedral. Goethe makes the unexpected observation that the one tower built was not complete and should have been taller:

Als ich diese Behauptung mit gewöhnlicher Lebhaftigkeit aussprach, redete mich ein kleiner muntrer Mann an und fragte: Wer hat Ihnen das gesagt?—der Thurm selbst, versetzte ich. Ich habe ihn so lange und aufmerksam betrachtet, und ihm so viel Neigung erwiesen, daß er sich zuletzt entschloß, mir dieses offenbare Geheimnis zu gestehn. (*Werke*, i. 28. 82)

On this evidence Goethe saw the business of art appreciation as depending upon a reciprocity between the work of art and the observer. He does not simply guess at the design of the spire; his intuition is only one part of an equation balanced by a corresponding input on the part of the tower itself. This relationship between observer and aesthetic object was not self-explanatory—particularly to Goethe's listener—and had something of a mysterious source, suggested by the noun 'Geheimnis'. Of course, Winckelmann also saw his task as an aesthetician as exploring the mysterious ontological status of the work of art; and he too thought that he knew the secret. But the extent of both men's engagement with art could cause confusion in third parties who were not privy to the secret, like the man in Strasbourg. We remember that even Volkmann confused Winckelmann's aesthetic rapture with malaria; the wife of the 'Kustode' of a gallery in Italy could only understand Goethe's fascination with a Minerva statue by supposing that it reminded him of a lover:

Da ich auch von der Statue nicht weg wollte, fragte sie mich, ob ich etwa eine Schöne hätte, die diesem Marmor ähnlich sähe, daß er mich so sehr anzöge. Das gute Weib kannte nur Anbetung und Liebe, aber von der reinen Bewunderung eines herrlichen Werkes, von der brüderlichen Verehrung eines Menschengeistes konnte sie keinen Begriff haben. (IR 150)

There is clearly an erotic element in this relationship with the work of art, despite Goethe's denials. It reminds us of the erotic aspects of Winckelmann's aesthetic. But on a theoretical level, and in keeping with the theoretical teachings of Winckelmann, Goethe insisted upon the disinterested nature of his observations and denied any sexual interest in the figure. According to this view, the study of art, at its best, consists in a communion of spirits—those of the creating artist and the observer through the medium of the work of art. One could develop a relationship with the artist and with the work which he created; he often used the noun 'Bekanntschaft'—in the sense of acquaintance, rather than knowledge—to describe this relationship:

Doch immer sind mir noch diese herrlichen Gegenstände, wie neue Bekanntschaften, man hat mit ihnen nicht gelebt, sie nicht genug verglichen. Einige reißen einen mit Gewalt an sich, daß man eine Zeitlang gleichgultig, ja ungerecht gegen andre wird. (*Werke*, iv. 8. 75)

There is clearly an element of passion here; and, given that one of the works cited as producing this effect is the Apollo Belvedere, we naturally think of Winckelmann's passionate involvement with art. Elsewhere he is less passionate and describes the development of an understanding of art in terms which would be appropriate to describe the growth of a relationship. Things are difficult 'biß man nach und nach mit den Gegenständen bekannter und sich selbst gleichsam erst gewahr wird' (*Werke*, iv. 8. 196). The idea that the observer is improved through the experience of art is one that will be discussed more fully later. It is not suprising that a view of art as an intimate 'Bekanntschaft' should call for close proximity to the works of art at all times. This condition could be fulfilled most easily in Rome where 'wohin ich gehe find ich eine Bekanntschaft in einer neuen Welt' (*Werke*, iv. 8. 38). Goethe's appreciation of art was dramatically improved by the opportunity to view great works at first hand and in the original form rather than in plaster copies or etchings. However, this proximity was not important simply because it allowed him to be more accurate in his analysis of the formal properties and historical character of the works in question; close contact with the works meant contact with the energy, or 'presence', emitted by them. In Padua he saw some works by Mantegna and Titian which had this force:

Was in den Bildern [von Mantegna] für eine scharfe sichre Gegenwart ist läßt sich nicht ausdrucken, von dieser ganzen, wahren, (nicht scheinbaren, Effektlügenden, zur Immagination sprechenden) derben reinen, lichten, ausführlichen gewißenhaften, zarten, umschriebenen Gegenwart, die zugleich etwas strenges, emsiges, mühsames hatte gingen die folgenden aus wie ich gestern Bilder von Titian sah und konnten durch die Lebhafftigkeit ihres Geistes, die Energie ihrer Natur, erleuchtet von dem Geiste der Alten immer höher und höher steigen sich von der Erde heben und himmlische aber wahre Gestalten hervorbringen. Es ist das die Geschichte der Kunst und jedes der einzelnen grosen ersten Künstler nach der barbarischen Zeit. (*Werke*, iii. 1. 240)

Goethe goes to some lengths to capture the intensity of aesthetic experience. The impression left by the works is 'scharf', 'sicher', 'ganz', and 'wahr'; nine further adjectives are used to pin down other aspects of this experience. Interestingly, it would be difficult to gain any clear impression of the style of the paintings from this description, a similar dilemma to the one which confronts the reader in Winckelmann whose descriptions often contain little external detail but convey a strong impression of his response to the work. Goethe insisted upon the reality of this 'presence' even though it may be a brand of reality which we have not experienced. The attempt to characterize the 'Lebhafftigkeit' of a work of art, or describe the 'Energie' which it transmits was difficult, as the above passage proves. Nevertheless it was of central importance to Goethe (alongside attempts to understand the history of the work or its formal composition independently of its impact on the observer) because it was only through this attempt that one could contact that which was 'himmlisch' or 'wahr' in art. This could only be achieved through contact with the ancients, in this case by proxy through the imagination of artists working in their spirit. The essence of aesthetic experience could in this light be described as communion with the spirit of ancient art by means of an indescribable 'Energie' to which certain observers are sensitive. Goethe acknowledged the 'abstract' nature of this exchange at various points:

Der Genuß auf einer Reise ist wenn man ihn rein haben will, ein abstrackter Genuß, ich muß die Unbequemlichkeiten, Widerwärtigkeiten, das was mit mir nicht stimmt, was ich nicht erwarte, alles muß ich bey Seite bringen, in dem Kunstwerk nur den Gedanken des Künstlers, die erste Ausführung, das Leben der ersten Zeit da das Werk entstand *heraussuchen* und es wieder rein in meine Seele *bringen*, abgeschieden von allem was die Zeit, der alles unterworfen ist und der Wechsel der Dinge darauf gewürckt haben. Dann habe ich einen reinen bleibenden Genuß und um dessentwillen bin ich gereißt, nicht um des Augenblicklichen Wohlseyns oder Spases willen. (*Werke*, iii. 1. 232)

This certainly demanded a high degree of activity and engagement on the part of the observer. In this respect it was more difficult to understand than nature. It was, he argued, relatively easy to understand the beauty and perfection of nature, whereas art required a more complex study; its ontological status was more complex:

Ein Kunstwerck hingegen hat seine Vollkommenheit ausser sich, das 'Beste' in der Idee des Künstlers, die er selten oder nie erreicht, die folgenden in gewissen angenommnen Gesetzen, welche zwar aus der Natur der Kunst und des Handwercks hergeleitet, aber doch nicht so leicht zu *verstehen* und zu entziffern sind als die Gesetze der lebendigen Natur. Es ist viel Tradition bey den Kunstwercken, die Naturwercke sind immer wie ein erstausgesprochnes Wort Gottes. (*Werke*, iv. 8. 97)

Art was not seen as giving easy answers or 'Resultate' (to echo a term used earlier); the observer was forced to pursue an abstract idea through the work of art. Goethe was seeking to understand an idea which was to be found outside, or beyond the work of art itself. The work was a means for him to establish a dialogue with the creative artist; there was an aesthetic exchange. He dismissed or doubted the value of simple academic investigation, based on a systematic approach, because of the obscurity of the system of principles which ruled artistic production.[29] The ability to get beyond the work of art and towards the ideas of the artist (the aesthetic realm) could not be learnt.

To those observers sensitive to the energy, described above, the experience of art is so powerful that the figures represented in the works of art are brought to life in the observer's mind and appear to take on a concrete existence. In this connection it is not suprising that Goethe should appeal to the Pygmalion myth as an illustration of his experience. He was talking of the powerful impact made by works which he had only seen previously in copies and comparing the impact of these on him with Pygmalion's suprise at what he had created:

Da Pygmalions Elise, die er sich ganz nach seinen Wünschen geformt, und ihr soviel Wahrheit und Daseyn gegeben hatte, als der Künstler vermag, endlich auf ihn zukam und sagte: ich bins! wie anders war die Lebendige, als der gebildete Stein. (*Werke*, iv. 8. 38)

A situation is described here in which the artist implants the potential for life and the observer releases it (though in Pygmalion's case they are the same person). This interaction between the creating and the receiving mind is central to both Winckelmann's and Goethe's portrayals of aesthetic experience. And we remember that in one of Winckelmann's most powerful evocations of the nature of aesthetic experience he too drew upon the Pygmalion myth as an appropriate analogue; this myth apparently embodied many of the magical and simultaneously erotic elements of aesthetic experience.[30]

The idea that the artist and the observer were interdependent or complementary, was a crucial element of both men's analyses of aesthetic response. Indeed: 'Dem Dilettanten [the observer] ist die Nähe des Künstlers unerläßlich, denn er sieht in diesem das Complement seines eignen Daseyns; die Wünsche des Liebhabers erfüllen sich im Artisten' (*Werke*, i. 29. 169). This meeting of minds often had very direct and disturbing consequences; at times Goethe was unable to maintain a 'disinterested' stance when faced with art. He described a family scene on a grave in Verona in the following terms:

---

[29] Of course, Winckelmann thought that he could see rules which determined historical developments but high aesthetic engagement could not be reduced to such simple principles.

[30] We remember Winckelmann's use of the Pygmalion myth, in a similar context, in his discussion of the Apollo Belvedere (see Ch. 2 above).

Mir war die *Gegenwart* der Steine höchströhrend, daß ich mich der Thränen nicht enthalten konnte. Hier ist kein geharnischter Mann auf den Knien, der einer fröhlichen Auferstehung wartet, hier hat der Künstler mit mehr oder weniger Geschick immer nur die einfache *Gegenwart* der Menschen hingestellt, ihre *Existenz* dadurch fortgesetzt und bleibend gemacht . . . Die Kupfer nehmen das offt weg, sie verschönern, aber der Geist verfliegt. (*Werke*, iii. 1. 200)

The artist captures a particular brand of 'Existenz' and in doing so makes it immortal. Through the artist's work the viewer has access to this existence, he can understand the 'einfache Gegenwart' of the people represented. The adjective 'einfach' is not without significance in connection with Winckelmann, who saw the most essential human qualities—and therefore those most suitable for artistic representation—as 'einfach'. This was, as the above passage suggests, one element of the 'spirit' of art which was highly volatile and so likely to evaporate. A work exhibited poorly could lose its 'Gegenwart' (*Werke*, iii. 1. 236). Or, as Goethe noted above, the act of copying a work was often enough to destroy its essential beauty. In copying, one could 'verschönern', i.e. make the work appear superficially more attractive, but its essential beauty was lost. This is a distinction made very clearly by Winckelmann between mere external beauty and essential or inner beauty; in his terms only few observers of art had 'den inneren Sinn' which enabled one to appreciate essential beauty and only few (ancient) works call upon it, in any case.[31] Goethe insisted on both of these points. He distinguished between those works which appealed superficially and those with a more profound appeal. In the following passage he makes his preference clear in a context familiar from Winckelmann—an attack on superfluity in art:

So verhaßt waren mir immer die Willkürlichkeiten. Der Winterkasten auf Weissenstein, ein Nichts um Nichts, ein ungeheuer Confekt Aufsatz und so mit Tausend andern Dingen. Was nicht eine wahre innre Existenz hat, hat kein *Leben* und kann nicht *lebendig* gemacht werden, und kann nicht gros seyn und nicht gros werden. (*Werke*, iii. 1. 327)

If a work of art lacks the essential quality it cannot be made to appear significant. To use the term which Goethe added to this argument in the *Italienische Reise* the work has been 'totgeboren' (IR 114). The contrast with the promise of rebirth through aesthetic education, mentioned earlier, could not be more stark. Implicit in the above passage is also a criticism of those judges who would insist that a work is great even when it lacks inner life. For his part he could not bring it to life or insist that it is

---

[31] Winckelmann had a similar notion of 'inner sense'. Cf. KS 218–19 and Ch. 2.

great; he merely responded to the life which was already present in the work. However, only few spectators had 'den innern Sinn' or the talent of 'poetisches Anschauen' which we see in Goethe (*Werke*, i. 29. 168; i. 28. 99). Few people had themselves an 'inner life' to match that in the works which they were viewing; if the viewers did not radiate a certain energy then the works in question would appear dead. He pointed out the various benefits of Rome for the serious student and the dangers of not taking art seriously, in a manner which illustrates this point:

und so wird Rom für einen der sich appliciren will eine wahre hohe Schule; dagegen es andern Fremden gar bald traurig und *todt* vorkommen muß, deßwegen auch die meisten schnell nach Neapel, dem Orte des Lebens und der Bewegung, eilen. (*Werke*, iv. 8. 286)

The sort of life offered to most tourists in Naples was radically different from the inner life in which Goethe was primarily interested. Dynamic exchanges (with other artists) and the intellectual and imaginative activity stimulated by art were not of a kind with the social 'Bewegung' sought by most travellers in Naples.

This rewarding exposure to art was not a bonus for Goethe as it might have been for other travellers; it was essential to his purpose in travelling to Italy. And again there is an inviting parallel with Winckelmann who, as we have seen, also saw Rome as a 'hohe Schule für alle Welt' and was similarly serious in his purpose. Its importance to Goethe was reflected in the metaphors of nourishment which he used to describe his Italian experiences: 'Aber es ist eine Lust in einem so großen Elemente zu leben, wo man für viele Jahre Nahrung vor sich sieht, wenn man sie auch nur für den Augenblick mit den äussersten Lippen nur kosten kann' (*Werke*, iv. 8. 86). Art, in particular, provided the intellectual and imaginative sustenance which he required; his inner life was supported by it. He frequently referred to the ways in which he felt improved by the experience of art. Broadly speaking, he felt his life to have gained substance or to have been 'filled out' through his exposure to art, the new element. He portrayed himself as immersing himself in art and finding that he was absorbing 'das Kunstelement':

Wie eine Flasche sich leicht füllt, die man oben offen unter das Wasser stößt, so kann man hier leicht sich ausfüllen, wenn man empfänglich und bereit ist; es drängt das Kunstelement von allen Seiten zu. (IR 356)

The important qualification for this experience is that one should be 'open', 'receptive', and 'ready'; this condition is parallel to the 'passive' state which I described as typical of Goethe's early stages of response to art. The following stage depends on 'immersion'; in immersing himself Goethe proved his engagement with art and the reward was to be able to absorb the 'Kunstelement'. Indeed he becomes merely a container for it; his baptism in art is complete. He has proved his faith through physical effort and imaginative engagement; the reward is to be at one with art. What benefits did this bring?

5. THE TRANSFORMATIVE POWER OF ART

We have talked, so far, about the ways in which the critical intelligence and imagination of an observer become engaged with a work of art. Further, we have discussed the ways in which that engagement could be regarded as a response to stimuli provided by the work; potentially the work can, it appears, provide access to the mind of the creating artist and the world in which he was creating (a very 'live' form of art history akin to that practised by Winckelmann). We must now discuss the benefits which the observer felt that he was deriving from such engagement and interaction with art. In a treatment of the impact of particular artistic environments upon artists Goethe (in line with Winckelmann and many others) asserted that differences in the former could account for the uneven distribution of good artists for 'es ist offenbar, daß sich das Auge nach den Gegenständen bildet, die es von Jugend auf erblickt' (IR 82). The same principle could be applied to account for the improvement in the eye brought about by exposure to great works of art in Italy; this experience provided fresh criteria for the evaluation of works of art as well as making greater demands upon the eye itself and stretching its faculties. However, Goethe felt that the Italian journey would have less specific, but perhaps more important benefits since 'ich mache diese wunderbare Reise nicht, um mich selbst zu betriegen, sondern um mich an den Gegenständen kennen zu lernen' (IR 43). Through art one could come to know oneself. Indeed one could say that it was literally true when Goethe described the process of finding his feet in Italy in the following terms: 'Nach und nach find ich mich' (*Werke*, iii. 1. 193). In improving the eye—and implicitly the critical mind and the imagination—one is, of course, altering some fundamental parts of one's make-up or self.

Goethe remarked on his mission of self-discovery through art on numerous occasions. He justifies his absence from Germany to Charlotte von Stein as follows:

Übrigens habe ich glückliche Menschen kennen lernen, die es nur sind weil sie ganz sind, auch der Geringste wenn er ganz ist kann glücklich und in seiner Art Vollkommen seyn, das will und muß ich nun auch erlangen, und ich kanns, wenigstens weiß ich wo es liegt und wie es steht, ich habe mich auf dieser Reise unsäglich kennen lernen. (*Werke*, iv. 8. 231–2)

Not only does he repeat the desire to know himself but he compares himself with people who have apparently completed the process of self-discovery and achieved happiness. His wish to emulate them appears quite natural, but what is more important for us is the terminology which he uses to describe their achievement. They have become 'whole' and 'complete'. These terms are part of a complex of similar terms related to gaining substance and shape which Goethe used to describe his own development as a person. For example, he described the experience of Italy in the following terms (introduced provisionally earlier in this chapter):

Was aber das größte ist und was ich erst hier fühle; wer mit Ernst sich hier umsieht und Augen hat zu sehen muß *solid* werden, er muß einen Begriff von Solidität faßen der ihm nie so lebendig ward. Mir wenigstens ist es so als wenn ich alle Dinge dieser Welt nie so richtig geschätzt hätte als hier. (*Werke*, iii. 1. 48)

... denn ich bin wirklich umgeboren und erneuert und *ausgefüllt* ... (IR 359)

Schon fühl ich in meinem Gemüth, in meiner Vorstellungsart gar mercklichen Unterschied und ich habe Hofnung einen wohl ausgewaschnen, *wohl ausstaffirten* Menschen wieder zurück zu bringen. (*Werke*, iv. 8. 26)

Ich werde bis dahin noch einige Schaalen aus dem grosen Ocean geschlürft haben und mein dringendstes Bedürfniß wird befriedigt seyn. Ich bin von einer ungeheuren Leidenschafft und Kranckheit geheilt, wieder zum Lebensgenuß, zum Genuß der Geschichte, der Dichtkunst der Alterthümer geneßen und habe Vorrath auf Jahrelang *auszubilden und zu kompletiren* (*Werke*, iv. 8. 119)

These terms may seem a perfectly natural means of expressing a sense of improvement; they are also very familiar in the context of this book, which, in its basic tenets depends upon modern reception theory. We have talked frequently of the manner in which an observer concretizes a work of art creating an aesthetic object. The observer in this scheme of things 'fills out' impressions gained from that work which cannot be regarded as complete without his contribution. The metaphors used above by Goethe to describe his own development are very similar to the terminology of reception theory. 'Solid' equals 'concrete'—'ausfüllen' is the verb used by reception theorists to describe the filling out of 'Unbestimmtheitsstellen'. But what we have here is precisely the reverse of the process which the reception theorists were attempting to explain. They talk about completing the work of art; here it is the observer who is transformed by exposure to art. Whilst the details of the process of transformation may be vague, Goethe's description provides evidence of the reciprocity between the work of art and its observer; art cannot be fully realized without the receiver; and, on the above evidence, the observer cannot be himself without art, since it contributes substantially to the process of his personal development. The feeling of reciprocity is enhanced by other images which Goethe uses to describe his altered state. He imagined himself being knocked into shape or being given form; the terminology is familiar from the arts and in that respect further confirms that the experience of art is a two-way process. Both man and art are shaped in the experience of art. The shaping took place when he became able to enjoy the new experiences offered in Italy: 'Ich habe in der Welt nichts zu suchen als das Gefundne, nur daß ichs genießen lerne, das ist alles warum ich mich hier noch mehr *hämmern* und *bearbeiten* laße' (*Werke*, iv. 8. 116). This reformation of Goethe's character, as he described it, could be seen as a part of a larger process of 'Bildung'. It is appropriate that the German noun for 'education' should be drawn from the idea of giving form. Apparently the business of aesthetic education, as Goethe experienced it, was indeed based upon giving form to his life and thinking. He cast off his old shell to emerge as a new person in Italy. He described the beginnings of this metamorphosis in the following terms:

Ich hab Zeither eine Pause im Sehen gemacht um das Gesehne würcken zu lassen. Nun fang ich wieder an und es geht trefflich. Das gesteh ich aber auch daß ich mich aller alten Ideen, alles eignen Willens entäussere um recht wiedergebohren und *neu gebildet* zu werden. (*Werke*, iv. 8. 108)

It is only a small step from this image to the images of rebirth mentioned earlier. It appears that Goethe like Winckelmann—who only counted his age from the date of his arrival in Rome—had his life effectively begin again in Italy. His mind was radically transformed through the medium of art which offered him a whole new range of existential criteria and a new intensity of experience. Despite their differences in personality, sexuality, and even in their views on individual works of art, Winckelmann and Goethe show a remarkably similar brand of aesthetic engagement, even down to the terminology used to express it. It demanded an openness to fresh impressions, a refusal to accept inherited theories of art and so an insistence upon the development of an individual method for dealing with art. It balanced activity and passivity in the response to a given work generating a dynamic interchange between the work and the student, which could best be described as a conversation, or even a love. On this basis both men felt themselves to have been transformed or reborn through aesthetic experience. We can now understand Goethe's insistence that in studying Winckelmann one did not learn anything but rather 'became something' (see below).

I suggested above that Goethe's manner of seeing had a number of characteristics reminiscent of Winckelmann. These are not chance parallels. Goethe was acutely aware of the mechanisms of aesthetic response and did not only investigate the way in which he himself responded to art but also undertook other case-studies (see n. 3). Winckelmann was one important case. In his essay in *Winckelmann und sein Jahrhundert* Goethe reflects on Winckelmann's responses to art; and, tellingly, those things which he most admires are exactly those to which we see him aspire in his account of Italy.

Winckelmann is seen in this essay as someone who has reached the ultimate stage of aesthetic insight. We remember how Goethe hoped to achieve the stability and substance—to feel more complete—through exposure to art. Winckelmann is portrayed as someone who had the required substance. Goethe sees Winckelmann as a complete man, using a terminology which corresponds neatly to his descriptions of his own experience and to the terminology of reception theory:

Wenn die Natur gewöhnlichen Menschen die köstliche Mitgift nicht versagt, ich meine jenen lebhaften Trieb, von Kindheit an die äußere Welt mit Lust zu ergreifen, sie kennen zu lernen, sich mit ihr in Verhältnis zu setzen, mit ihr verbunden ein Ganzes zu bilden, so haben vorzügliche Geister öfters die Eigenheit, eine Art von Scheu vor dem wirklichen Leben zu empfinden, sich in sich selbst zurückzuziehen, in sich selbst eine eigene Welt zu erschaffen und auf diese Weise das Vortrefflichste nach innen bezüglich zu leisten.

Findet sich hingegen in besonders begabten Menschen jenes gemeinsame Bedürfnis, eifrig zu allem, was die Natur in sie gelegt hat, auch in der äußeren Welt die antwortenden Gegenbilder zu suchen und dadurch das Innere völlig zum Ganzen und Gewissen zu steigern, so kann man versichert sein, daß auch so ein für Welt und Nachwelt höchst erfreuliches Dasein sich ausbilden werde.

Unser Winckelmann war von dieser Art.[32]

Goethe describes a very positive way of being in the world. All of the key elements of the Winckelmannian manner of seeing are identified as the

[32] *Winckelmann von Goethe*, ed. Howald, p. 91.

most important guarantors of quality of life. It is dynamic ('lebhafter Trieb', 'Lust', 'ergreifen', 'eifrig', 'suchen') and dependent upon an intimate relationship with the external world ('Verhältnis', 'verbunden'). Whilst this relationship with the external world is an intellectual/aesthetic one, it is so powerful that it is best described in terms of a human relationship. Winckelmann may be looking for the confirmation of ideas in the external world but we are given the impression of a conversation with that world ('antwortend'), an image which Goethe used of his own relationship ('Gespräch') with art. The part of the external world which provided the appropriate responses to Winckelmann's questions was art; it provided the sensation of wholeness and certainty for which we saw Goethe searching in Italy. Goethe later uses the familiar terminology of art in his description of the type of character who might achieve this level of insight. They must have a character which 'als ein Ganzes wirkt' and their feelings may not be 'zerstückelt' or their minds 'zerstreut'.[33] This is the terminology used by Winckelmann in his rejection of Baroque art with its emphasis upon detail at the expense of noble simplicity, and as such constitutes scarcely disguised praise for Winckelmann whose life appears to satisfy his own aesthetic criteria. Goethe's introduction to his essay contains similar praise. The treatment of Winckelmann's life and work from different perspectives in *Winckelmann und sein Jahrhundert* produces a work which has 'das Verdienst der Mannigfaltigkeit und der Einheit', primary characteristics of great works of art.[34] Winckelmann's biography is here paid the ultimate tribute—it has become an aesthetic object itself. And these are the surest signs of the intimacy of Winckelmann's relationship with art, as seen by Goethe. He can in some meaningful sense become a work of art because of his absorption by art. He opened himself to the impressions offered by art and was sensitive to beauty and so 'sie [die Schönheit] kam ihm aus den Werken der bildenden Kunst persönlich entgegen'.[35] In Rome he could 'sich innig mit dem dortigen Dasein ... verweben', an image which suggests that Winckelmann became part of the substance of the place.[36] He was a Roman, as he was for Goethe also a Greek.[37] And these intimate relationships clearly have some of the 'wissenschaftlicher Eros' identified by Howald.[38] Ideas take on life, and so offer the possibility of relationships, above all in Rome where 'verkörpert stehn seine Ideen um ihn her' in the form of works of art.[39] And an added

[33] Ibid. 95, 96.   [34] Ibid. 89.   [35] Ibid. 102.   [36] Ibid. 104.
[37] Ibid. 93–7 discusses Winckelmann in precisely those terms.   [38] Ibid. 63.
[39] Ibid. 109.

dynamism came, according to Goethe, from the constant addition to the stock of art provided by new discoveries:

> Traurig ist es, wenn man das Vorhandene als fertig und abgeschlossen ansehen muß. Rüstkammern, Galerien und Museen, zu denen nichts hinzugefügt wird, haben etwas Grab- und Gespensterartiges; man beschränkt seinen Sinn in einem so beschränkten Kunstkreis, man gewöhnt sich, solche Sammlungen als ein Ganzes anzusehen, anstatt daß man durch immer neuen Zuwachs erinnert werden sollte, daß in der Kunst, wie im Leben, kein Abgeschlossenes beharre, sondern ein Unendliches in Bewegung sei.[40]

How different is the attitude of a Riedesel or a Volkmann for whom the world of art was full of static artefacts! How different from this celebration of new discoveries and the life that they embody and the fresh intellectual impetus which they provide! Although Winckelmann's basic view of art did not alter radically it was subject to constant refinement. And it was not, according to Goethe, simply a matter of accumulating information.[41] It was a question of coming to terms with individual moments of aesthetic experience which could best be done through writing for 'so lernte er im Entwerfen und Schreiben'.[42] This was, as my earlier chapters suggested, also a dynamic process, since:

> Wir finden ihn immer in Tätigkeit, mit dem Augenblick beschäftigt, ihn dergestalt ergreifend und festhaltend, als wenn der Augenblick vollständig und befriedigend sein könnte, und eben so ließ er sich wieder vom nächsten Augenblick belehren.[43]

This seems the perfect explanation of Winckelmann's motivation for attempting to capture the beauty of objects in words. A moment of insight is something so beautiful that it inspires a person's attempt to fix it in an appropriate form, to make it timeless. The imagery of capture ('festhalten', and in that context 'ergreifen') gives some impression of the urgency of the need. But sadly it is in the nature of such experiences to be transitory; and so the hope then is for another moment which will allude to an ultimate condition in which things are perfect and satisfying. In other words the search goes on. And the search is aided by the reciprocity between him and the work of art. His activity is portrayed as productive and positive; but according to this passage he must also allow himself *to be taught* by the next significant moment. This confirms another statement in the essay to the effect that in developing his judgement 'die

[40] Ibid. 124–5.   [41] Ibid. 111–14.
[42] Ibid. 127. There is a another connection here with the idea of learning through writing/drawing: 'dessiner c'est connâitre'.   [43] Ibid. 127.

bildende Kunst und das Leben kräftig einwirkend zu Hilfe kamen'.[44] The function of such interactions in refining insight into art and life is something which we have seen in both Winckelmann and Goethe.

Unsurprisingly, Goethe celebrates Winckelmann's search for meaning in life through art:

> Und so ist alles, was er uns hinterlassen, als ein Lebendiges für die Lebendigen, nicht für die im Buchstaben Toten geschrieben. Seine Werke, verbunden mit seinen Briefen, sind eine Lebensdarstellung, sind ein Leben selbst. Sie sehen, wie das Leben der meisten Menschen, nur einer Vorbereitung, nicht einem Werke gleich. Sie veranlassen zu Hoffnungen, zu Wünschen, zu Ahnungen; wie man daran bessern will, so sieht man, daß man sich selbst zu bessern hätte; wie man sie tadeln will, so sieht man, daß man demselbigen Tadel, vielleicht auf einer höhern Stufe der Erkenntnis, selbst ausgesetzt sein möchte: denn Beschränkung ist überall unser Los.[45]

This passage gives a very clear idea of the educational function of Winckelmann's life and work. In presenting his hopes, wishes, and intuitive insights he inspires his readers and friends to try to attempt to improve themselves. But there is an irony here. In his own scheme for aesthetic education Winckelmann was hoping to present less nebulous concepts. He was hoping to provide a clear programme which would lead to insight into art. Those students whose work we have examined preferred certainty in their dealings with life and art to vague 'Ahnungen' of something greater. He could provide such students with his art-historical scheme, even if it was subject to some revision and elaboration, and this enabled them to deal with art to a considerable extent. But a degree of art-historical understanding did not lead automatically to the personal growth described in the above passage. It did not mean that you would have the glimpse of the ideas which inspired Winckelmann's hopes and wishes. Winckelmann appears not to have seen this difficulty, at least in connection with his chosen pupils.[46] Goethe also sees another fundamental difficulty which did not present itself to Winckelmann. The latter could believe, perhaps idealistically, that it was possible to identify ideals through art. It was also possible to achieve an ideal state in your personal development on that basis. Put simply, in looking at the Apollo Belvedere you could take on some of his properties. Whilst Goethe does not deny the possibility of growth and self-improvement, he does not imagine that it can ever be complete; the process of improvement is the

---

[44] Ibid. 131.   [45] Ibid. 128.

[46] He did disqualify many pupils but, as the introductory sections of Chs. 3 and 4 show, on a rather different basis to that envisaged by Goethe.

crucial thing. We have to confront the fact that our life's work will never be complete. But this philosophical difference did not cause Goethe to devalue Winckelmann's life and work for 'von seinem Grabe her stärkt uns der Anhauch seiner Kraft und erregt in uns den lebhaften Drang, das, was er begonnen, mit Eifer und Liebe fort- und immer fortzusetzen'.[47] This quotation is vital because it gives an unequivocal impression of the quality which Goethe saw as most important in Winckelmann's life and work: energy. He talks in terms of a transfer of power which produces a drive towards finding the Truth in art and life. This is presumably the final manifestation of that energy which we located at the core of Winckelmann's dynamic responses to works of art. It is the energy which fuels insight. In 1816 Goethe wrote that 'seit Winckelmanns und seiner Nachfolger Bemühungen ist Philosophie ohne Kunstbegriff einäugig' (*Werke*, iv. 26. 221). With one eye an observer can never get beyond the surface of a work of art; his view must lack perspective, depth. This was clearly not true of Winckelmann or Goethe. Sadly, less perceptive followers of Winckelmann's work, including Volkmann and Riedesel, appear to have been blinkered in a way which robbed them of any depth of vision; and ironically one of the reasons for this may have been Winckelmann's own teaching, which seemed so authoritative. Goethe was lucky enough not to have been so close to Winckelmann. From his perspective he could see the growth and development in Winckelmann's ideas and personality, to see what set him apart from mainstream art historians. Because he was aware of the process involved it was less likely that he would succumb to the apparent authority of particular statements on the arts. Hence Goethe's own taste in art does not match that of Winckelmann; it is for one thing less exclusive. He leaves the business of dealing with Winckelmann's art history to others because it does not interest him to the same extent. But this does not exclude the possibility that he could learn to see from Winckelmann, or at least become more aware of his own manner of seeing, by examining that of another aesthete.

Aesthetic education is shown to be a real possibility, even if it does not follow the planned course. Certainly, Goethe was blessed, in contrast to Riedesel and Volkmann, with the ability and desire to record his own subtle responses to art in a subtle manner. This certainly enables the critic to be more confident in his assertions about the presence or absence of a 'good' eye. Indeed one could argue—although it may be

---

[47] *Winckelmann von Goethe*, ed. Howald, p. 147.

slightly ungenerous—that it is above all in the area of expression that Winckelmann and Goethe distinguish themselves from more conventional students of art such as Riedesel and Volkmann. They offer us evidence enough of aesthetic insight, and evidence of a quality which the others could not reproduce, either because they had no such gift or because of the type of work they produced. We inevitably contrast the growth of their insights and even personalities with the picture of relative stasis offered by Riedesel and Volkmann whose opinions on art change largely in response to fashion. The picture of aesthetic education offered by Winckelmann and Goethe is extensive, subtle, complex, and informs our sense of their development as aesthetes. In the cases of Riedesel and Volkmann the evidence is less reliable, at times even negative; we have a strong sense that they may not have satisfied Winckelmann's aspirations for them. And there is the rub; were those aspirations ever fair? Can a programme for aesthetic education ever be designed by one individual for another? If we accept that possibility then we must then ask whether Winckelmann's flawed scheme could ever produce results? And what would those results be? Can we expect poetic expression of the personal experience of God, as Winckelmann might have wished for his pupils? If not then which intermediate goals might be acceptable? The establishment of 'good taste' among the general public? It seems almost a matter of chance that we should have found in Goethe someone operating in the spirit of Winckelmann. However, the chance correspondence between these spirits would seem to make a very shaky foundation for any programme of aesthetic education. It is perhaps Goethe who points out most successfully the fundamental difficulty in establishing a scheme for aesthetic education. If, as he suggests (p. 247), the study of art and the associated personal growth are ongoing processes—where the process itself is more important than the promise of completion—then it will be difficult to design an appropriate curriculum. Winckelmann's will to self-completion perhaps blinded him to this difficulty; his untimely death provides us with an abrupt reminder of the force of Goethe's case.

Bibliography

PRIMARY SOURCES

Winckelmann manuscripts

Pariser Nachlaß, Paris, Bibliothèque nationale, fonds allemands, 56–67.
Handschriftlicher Nachlaß Winckelmanns in der Staats- und Universitätsbibliothek Hamburg (photographic repr.), Winckelmann-Sammlung, Stendal.
Handschriftlicher Nachlaß Winckelmanns in Montpellier (Faculté de Médecine) (photographic repr.), Winckelmann-Sammlung, Stendal.
Handschriftlicher Nachlaß Winckelmanns in der Società Colombaria, Florenz (photographic repr.), Winckelmann-Sammlung, Stendal.
Handschriftlicher Nachlaß Winckelmanns in Savignano sul Rubico (photographic repr.), Winckelmann-Sammlung, Stendal.
Handschriftlicher Nachlaß Winckelmanns in der Bibliotheca Nazionale Centrale, Rom (photographic repr.), Winckelmann-Sammlung, Stendal.

Winckelmann publications (in order of importance)

Sämtliche Werke: Einzige vollständige Ausgabe, ed. Joseph Eiselein, 12 vols. (Donauöschingen, 1825–9; repr. Osnabrück, 1965).
Kleine Schriften, Vorreden, Entwürfe, ed. Walther Rehm (Berlin, 1968).
Briefe, ed. Walther Rehm, 4 vols. (Berlin, 1952–7).
Geschichte der Kunst des Altertums, ed. Ludwig Goldscheider (Vienna, 1934).
Winckelmanns Briefe an seine Freunde, ed. Karl Wilhelm Daßdorf, 2 vols. (Dresden, 1777–80).
Kleine Schriften und Briefe, ed. Wilhelm Senff (Weimar, 1960).
Gedanken über die Nachahmung der griechischen Werke in der Malerei und Bildhauerkunst: Sendschreiben: Erläuterung, ed. Ludwig Uhlig (Stuttgart, 1969).
Johann Joachim Winckelmann: Unbekannte Schriften, ed. Sigrid von Moisy, Hellmut Sichtermann, and Ludwig Tavernier, Abhandlungen der Bayerischen Akademie der Wissenschaften: Philosophisch-Historische Klasse, NS 95 (Munich, 1987).
Meisterstücke aus Winckelmann's Werken nebst Goethes Aufsatz über Winckelmann, ed. Wilhelm Kunze (Berlin, 1879).
Edle Einfalt und stille Grösse: Eine mit Goetheschen und Herderschen Worten eingeleitete Auswahl aus Johann Joachim Winckelmanns Werken, ed. Walter Winckelmann (Berlin, 1909).

Description des pierres gravées du feu-baron de Stosch (Florence, 1760).
Monumenti antichi inediti spiegati ed illustrati (Rome, 1767).

Contemporary writing on travel and art

ADAM, JAMES (misattributed to Robert Adam), 'Journal of a Tour in Italy', *Library of the Fine Arts*, 2/9 (Oct. 1831), 165–78 and 2/10 (Nov. 1831), 235–45.
ADAMS (sic), ROBERT, *The Ruins of the Palace of the Emperor Diocletian at Spalatro in Dalmatia* (London, 1764).
ADDISON, JOSEPH, 'Remarks on Several Parts of Italy', in *The Miscellaneous Works of Joseph Addison*, ed. A. C. Guthkelch, 2 vols. (London, 1914), ii. 13–235.
AKENSIDE, MARK, *The Pleasures of the Imagination* (London, 1744).
ASCHENBRENNER, KARL, and HOLTHER, WILLIAM B. (eds. and trans.) (contains original text), *Reflections on Poetry: Alexander Gottlieb Baumgarten's 'Meditationes philosophicae de nonnullis ad poema pertinentibus'* (Berkeley and Los Angeles, 1954).
BARRY, JAMES, *An Inquiry into the Real and Imaginary Obstructions to the Acquisition of the Arts in England* (London, 1775).
BERNOUILLI, JOHANN, *Zusätze zu den neuesten Reisebeschreibungen von Italien nach der in Herrn D. J. J. Volkmanns historisch kritischen Nachrichten angenommenen Ordnung zusammengetragen*, 2 vols. (Leipzig, 1777–8).
BÖHME, JAKOB, *Jakob Böhme: Der schlesische Mystiker*, ed. and sel. Charles Waldemar (Munich, 1959).
BOSWELL, JAMES, *Letters*, ed. Chauncey Brewster Tinker, 2 vols. (Oxford, 1924).
—— *Journal of a Tour to Corsica and Memoirs of Pascal Paoli*, ed. M. Bishop (London, 1951).
BREVAL, JOHN DURANT, *Remarks on Several Parts of Europe*, 2 vols. (London, 1726).
CALVERT, FREDERICK (Lord Baltimore), *A Tour to the East with Remarks on Constantinople and the Turks; also Select Pieces of Oriental Wit, Poetry, and Wisdom* (London, 1767).
—— *Gaudia Poetica; Latina, Anglica et Gallica Lingua composita* (Augsburg, 1770).
—— *Celestes et Inferi* (Venice, 1771).
—— 'The Calvert Papers', *Maryland Historical Society Fund Publications*, 28 (1889), 34 (1894), 35 (1899).
CHÉNIER, ELISABETH, *Lettres grècques*, ed. Robert de Bonnières (Paris, 1879).
CLÉRISSEAU, CHARLES LOUIS, *Antiquités de la France* (Paris, 1778).
CLUVER, PHILIPP, *Sicilia antiqua; cum minoribus insulis ei adjacentibus* (n. p., 1619).

COCHIN, CHARLES-NICHOLAS, *Voyage pittoresque d'Italie, ou Receuil de notes sur les ouvrages de peinture et de sculpture, qu'on voit dans les principales villes d'Italie*, 3 vols. (Paris, 1751).
—— *Observations sur les antiquités d'Herculanum* (Paris, 1757).
COOPER, ANTHONY A. (Earl of Shaftesbury), *Characteristics of Men, Manners, Opinions, Times, etc*, ed. John M. Robertson, 2 vols. (London, 1900).
—— *Second Characters, or The Language of Forms*, ed. Benjamin Rand (Cambridge, 1914).
—— *Several Letters written by a Noble Lord to a Young Man at the University* (London, 1716).
DUBOS, JEAN BAPTISTE, *Réflexions critiques sur la poésie et sur la peinture*, 2 vols. (Paris, 1719).
DU FRESNOY, CHARLES ALPHONSE, *The Art of Painting*, trans. John Dryden (London, 1695).
GOETHE, JOHANN CASPAR, *Reise durch Italien im Jahre 1740 (Viaggio per l'Italia)*, ed. and trans. Albert Meier (Munich, 1986).
GOETHE, JOHANN WOLFGANG VON, *Werke*, 142 vols. (Weimar, 1887–1919).
—— *Winckelmann von Goethe*, ed. Ernst Howald (Erlenbach, 1943).
—— *Italienische Reise*, ed. Peter Sprengel (Munich, 1986).
GUYS, PIERRE AUGUSTIN, *Voyage littéraire de la Grèce ou lettres sur les Grecs anciens et modernes, avec un parallèle de leurs mœurs*, 2 vols. (Paris, 1771).
HERSANT, YVES, *Italies: Anthologie des voyageurs français aux xviiie et xixe siècles* (Paris, 1988).
HOGARTH, WILLIAM, *The Analysis of Beauty* (Menton, 1971) (repr. of 1753 edn.).
—— *The Analysis of Beauty*, ed. Joseph Burke (Oxford, 1955).
HOME, HENRY (LORD KAMES), *Elements of Criticism*, 3 vols. (Edinburgh, 1762).
HURD, R., *Dialogues on the Uses of Foreign Travel: Considered as Part of an English Gentleman's Education between Lord Shaftesbury and Mr. Locke* (London, 1764).
HUTCHESON, FRANCIS, *An Inquiry into the Original of our Ideas of Beauty and Virtue* (London, 1725).
KNOX, VICESIMUS, *Liberal Education: Or a Practical Treatise on the Methods of Acquiring Useful and Polite Learning* (London, 1781).
LALANDE, JERÔME DE, *Voyage d'un françois en Italie*, 8 vols. (Venice, 1769).
LASSELS, RICHARD, *The Voyage of Italy* (London, 1670).
MENGS, ANTON RAPHAEL, *Opere*, 2 vols. (Venice, 1783).
NUGENT, THOMAS, *The Grand Tour*, 3rd edn., 4 vols. (London, 1778).
ORVILLE, JACOBI PHILIPPI D', *Sicula, quibus Siciliae veteris rudera* (Amsterdam, 1764).
OSTERKAMP, ERNST (ed.), *Sizilien: Reisebilder aus drei Jahrhunderten* (Munich, 1986).

PANCRAZI, GIUSEPPE MARIA, *Antichità siciliane*, 2 vols. (Naples, 1751).
PILES, ROGER DE, *The Art of Painting and the Lives of the Painters* (London, 1706).
—— *The Principles of Painting* (London, 1743).
REYNOLDS, JOSHUA, *Discourses on Art*, ed. Robert B. Wark (New Haven, 1975).
RICHARD, JEAN-MARIE, *Description historique et critique de l'Italie*, 6 vols. (Paris, 1766).
RICHTER, JEAN PAUL (ed.), *The Literary Works of Leonardo da Vinci*, 3rd edn., 2 vols. (New York, 1970).
RIEDESEL, JOHANN HERMANN FREIHERR VON, *Reise durch Sicilien und Großgriechenland* (Zürich, 1771).
—— *Travels through Sicily and that Part of Italy called Magna Graecia*, ed. and trans. J. R. Forster (London, 1773).
—— *Johann Hermann Riedesels Freiherrn zu Eisenbach Sendschreiben über seine Reise nach Sizilien und Großgriechenland*, ed. Kasimir Edschmid (Darmstadt, 1939).
—— 'Johann Hermann von Riedesels Reise durch Sizilien und Großgriechenland', ed. Arthur Schulz, *Jahresgabe der Winckelmann-Gesellschaft, 1964* (Berlin, 1965).
—— *Remarques d'un voyageur moderne au Levant* (Amsterdam, 1773).
—— *Bemerkungen auf einer Reise nach der Levante*, ed. and trans. C. W. Dohm (Leipzig, 1774).
—— *Randbemerkungen über eine Reise nach der Levante 1768*, trans. L. M. Schultheis, ed. E. E. Becker (Darmstadt, 1940).
—— *Un viaggiatore tedesco in Puglia nella seconda metà del sec. xviii: Lettere di I. H. Riedesel a J. J. Winckelmann*, ed. and trans. Luigi Correra (Bari, 1913).
—— *Reisen des Freiherrn Johann Hermann Riedesel zu Eisenbach durch Sizilien, Großgriechenland, den Archipelagus nach Constantinopel und durch Großbritannien in den Jahren 1767, 1768 und 1770 in Briefen an seinen Freund Winckelmann, seine Schwester die Gräfin Degenfeld geb. Riedesel zu Eisenbach und seinen Vetter den Freiherrn Diede zum Fürstenstein* (Jena, 1830).
SCHILLER, JOHANN CHRISTOPH FRIEDRICH VON, *Brief eines reisendenden Dänen*, in *Sämtliche Werke*, ed. G. Fricke and H. G. Göpfert, 5 vols. (Munich, 1958).
SMOLLETT, TOBIAS, *Travels through France and Italy*, ed. Frank Felsenstein, The World's Classics (paperback series) (Oxford, 1981) (first pub. Oxford, 1979).
STERNE, LAURENCE, *'A Sentimental Journey' with the 'Journal to Eliza' and 'A Political Romance'*, The World's Classics (paperback series) (Oxford, 1984).
TEMPLE, LANCELOT (pseudonym for John Armstrong), *A Short Ramble through some Parts of France and Italy* (London, 1771).

VOLKMANN, JOHANN JACOB, *Historisch-Kritische Nachrichten von Italien*, 3 vols. (Leipzig, 1770–1) (2nd edn. Leipzig, 1777–8).
—— *Italienische Bibliothek*, 2 vols. (Leipzig, 1778–9).
—— *Neueste Reisen durch England*, 4 vols. (Leipzig, 1781–2).
—— *Neueste Reisen durch die Vereinigten Niederlande* (Leipzig, 1783).
—— *Neueste Reisen durch Schottland und Irland* (Leipzig, 1784).
—— *Neueste Reisen durch Spanien*, 2 vols. (Leipzig, 1785).
—— *Neueste Reisen durch Frankreich*, 3 vols. (Leipzig, 1787).
WEBB, DANIEL, *An Enquiry into the Beauties of Painting; and into the Merits of the most Celebrated Painters, Ancient and Modern* (London, 1760).
WRIGHT, EDWARD, *Some Observations made in Travelling through France, Italy etc in the Years 1720, 1721, and 1722*, 2 vols. (London, 1730).
YOUNG, EDWARD, *Conjectures on Original Composition in a Letter to the Author of Sir Charles Grandison* (London, 1759).

Reception theory

INGARDEN, ROMAN, *Untersuchungen zur Ontologie der Kunst* (Tübingen, 1962).
—— *Das literarische Kunstwerk* (Tübingen, 1965).
—— *Vom Erkennen des literarischen Kunstwerks* (Tübingen, 1968).
—— *Erlebnis, Kunstwerk und Wert: Vorträge zur Ästhetik 1937–1967* (Tübingen, 1969).
—— *Gegenstand und Aufgaben der Literaturwissenschaft: Aufsätze und Diskussionsbeiträge 1937–1964*, ed. Rolf Fieguth, Konzepte der Sprach- und Literaturwissenschaft, 19 (Tübingen, 1976).
—— *Selected Papers in Aesthetics*, ed. Peter J. McCormick (Munich, 1985).
ISER, WOLFGANG, *Walther Pater: Die Autonomie des Ästhetischen* (Tübingen, 1966).
—— (ed.), *Immanente Ästhetik: Ästhetische Reflexion* (Munich, 1966).
—— *Der implizite Leser* (Munich, 1972).
—— *Der Akt des Lesens* (Munich, 1976).
JAUSS, HANS ROBERT, *Ästhetische Erfahrung und literarische Hermeneutik*, 2 vols. (Munich, 1977).

SECONDARY LITERATURE

ALBRECHT, HERMANN, *Winckelmann contra Rembrandt als Erzieher oder unsere künstlerische Selbsterziehung* (Leipzig, 1895).
ALER, JAN, 'Winckelmann bei Schelling oder zur Frage nach der Wahrheit der Kunst', in *Über Literatur und Geschichte*, Festschrift für Gerhard Storz (Frankfurt am Main, 1973), 185–221.

Allgemeine deutsche Biographie, 56 vols. (Leipzig, 1875–1912).
ALSCHER, LUDWIG, 'Die Bedeutung der griechischen Plastik für Werk und Wirkung Winckelmanns', *Schriften der Winckelmann-Gesellschaft*, 1 (1973) ('Beiträge zu einem neuen Winckelmannbild'), 47–51.
ALTHAUS, HORST, *Laokoon: Stoff und Form* (Berne, 1968).
ARNHEIM, RUDOLF, *Art and Visual Perception: A Psychology of the Creative Eye*, the new version (Berkeley, 1974) (first pub. 1954).
ARON, ERICH, *Die deutsche Erweckung des Griechentums durch Winckelmann und Herder* (Heidelberg, 1929).
ATKINS, STUART, 'Italienische Reise and Goethean Classicism', in *Aspekte der Goethezeit*, ed. S. A. Corngold, M. Curschmann, and T. J. Ziolkowski (Göttingen, 1977), 81–96.
BAC, FERDINAND, *Le favori du cardinal Albani (Jean-Joachim Winckelmann), 'le père de l'archéologie' 1717–1768* (Paris, 1929).
BADEN, HANS JÜRGEN, 'Winckelmann oder Die griechische Sehnsucht', in *Das Abenteuer der Wahrheit: Platon, Pascal, Winckelmann, Oetinger* (Hamburg, 1946), 27–39.
BAEUMER, MAX L., 'Winckelmanns Formulierung der klassischen Schönheit', *Monatshefte für deutschen Unterricht, deutsche Sprache und Literatur*, 65/1 (Spring 1973), 61–75.
—— 'Winckelmanns Auffassung republikanischer Freiheit und sein Einfluß auf die Kunst der Französischen Revolution', *Beiträge der Winckelmann-Gesellschaft*, 16 (1986) ('Beiträge zur internationalen Wirkung Winckelmanns'), 18–34.
BAGNANI, GILBERT, 'Winckelmann and the Second Renascence', *American Journal of Archaeology*, 59/2 (Apr. 1955).
BARASCH, MOSHE, *Theories of Art from Plato to Winckelmann* (New York, 1985).
BATTEN, CHARLES L., *Pleasurable Instruction: Form and Convention in Eighteenth-Century Travel Literature* (Berkeley, 1978).
BEARDSLEY, MONROE C., *Aesthetics from Classical Greece to the Present: A Short History* (New York, 1966).
BECHTLE, RICHARD, 'Der Freiherr von Riedesel als Freund Winckelmanns in Griechenland', in id., *Wege nach Hellas: Studien zum Griechenlandbild deutscher Reisender* (Eßlingen, 1959), 9–23.
BENZ, RICHARD, 'Goethes Glaube an die klassische Kunst', *Goethe-Kalender* (1941), 36–77.
BERGER, ARNOLD E., 'Der junge Herder und Winckelmann', in *Studien zur deutschen Philologie: Festschrift der germanischen Abteilung der 47. Versammlung deutscher Philologen und Schulmänner in Halle* (Halle, 1903), 83–168.
BERGER, JOHN, *Ways of Seing* (London, 1972).
BERGMANN, ERNST, 'Das Leben und die Wunder Johann Winckelmanns', in

Festschrift für Johannes Volkelt (zum 70. Geburtstag dargebracht) (Munich, 1918), 229–64.
BERINGER, J. A., 'Winckelmann und Goethe: Zu Winckelmanns 150. Todestag am 8. Juni', *Reclams Universum*, 34 (1918), 603–4.
BERLIN, ISAIAH, *The Age of Enlightenment: The Eighteenth-Century Philosophers* (Oxford, 1979).
BEUTLER, ERNST, 'Die *Italienische Reise*', in id., *Wiederholte Spiegelungen: Drei Essays über Goethe* (Göttingen, 1957), 31–54.
BIEDRZYNSKI, RICHARD, 'The Eagerness to See and Observe', in T. W. Gaehtgens (ed.), *Johann Joachim Winckelmann 1717–1768* (Hamburg, 1986), 40–56.
BLÄTTNER, FRITZ, 'Winckelmanns deutsche Sendung', *Deutsche Vierteljahresschrift*, 21 (1943), 23–66.
—— 'Goethes *Italienische Reise* als Dokument seiner Bildung', *Deutsche Vierteljahresschrift*, 23 (1949), 449–71.
BOARDMAN, JOHN, *Greek Art* (London, 1964).
BODE, WILHELM, *Goethes Ästhetik* (Berlin, 1901).
BÖHLER, MICHAEL J., *Soziale Rolle und ästhetische Vermittlung: Studien zur Literatursoziologie von A. G. Baumgarten bis F. Schiller* (Berne, 1975).
BOEHLICH, WALTER, 'Winckelmanns Sudelbuch in Montpellier', *Neue Schweizer Rundschau*, 9 (Jan. 1953), 531–48.
BOENIGK, OTTO FREIHERR von, 'Winckelmanns Abstammung', *Beiträge zur Geschichte, Landes- und Volkskunde der Altmark*, 2/6 (1909), 380–6.
BÖSCHENSTEIN, BERNHARD, 'Winckelmann, Goethe und Hölderlin als Deuter antiker Plastik', *Hölderlin-Jahrbuch* (1967–8), 158–79.
BOLLERT, MARTIN, 'Johann Joachim Winckelmann als Bibliothekar des Grafen Bünau', in *Festschrift für G. Leidinger* (Munich, 1930), 19–24.
—— 'Joh. Joach. Winckelmann und Joh. Mich. Francke', in *Otto Glauning zum 60. Geburtstag*, vol. i (Leipzig, 1936), 11–17.
—— 'Winckelmann als Bibliothekar', *Zentralblatt für Bibliothekarwesen*, 53 (1936), 482–9.
BOLTON, ARTHUR T., *The Architecture of Robert and James Adam (1758–1794)*, 2 vols. (London, 1922).
BORINSKI, KARL, 'Winckelmann und Mengs: Winckelmann und Lessing', in id., *Die Antike in Poetik und Kunsttheorie vom Ausgang des klassischen Altertums bis auf Goethe und Wilhelm von Humboldt*, 2 vols. (Darmstadt, 1965), ii. 203–34 (first pub. Leipzig, 1924).
BOSSHARD, WALTER, *Winckelmann: Aesthetik der Mitte* (Zürich, 1960).
—— *Dasein in der Mitte: Zur Äesthetik Winckelmanns*, publication of doctoral thesis (Einsiedeln, 1960).
BOYLE, NICHOLAS, *Goethe: The Poet and the Age*, vol. i (Oxford, 1991).
BRETT, R. L., *The Third Earl of Shaftesbury: A Study in Eighteenth-Century Literary Theory* (London, 1951).

BREYSIG, KURT, 'Winckelmanns Geschichte der Kunst des Altertums', in id., *Die Meister der entwickelnden Geschichtsforschung* (Breslau, 1936), 138–66.
BRITSCH, TODD ADAM, 'Winckelmann and Romanticism: A Study of the Eighteenth-Century Shift in Aesthetic Sensibility', (part of doctoral thesis requirement, University of Florida, 1966).
BUSCH, ERNST, 'Das Erlebnis des Schönen im Antikenbild der deutschen Klassik', *Deutsche Vierteljahresschrift*, 18 (1940), 26–60 (27–31).
BUTLER, E. M., 'Goethe and Winckelmann', *Publications of the English Goethe Society*, 10 (1934), 1–22.
CART, THÉOPHILE, *Goethe en Italie*, publication of doctoral thesis, University of Lausanne (Lausanne, 1881).
CASSIRER, ERNST, *Die Philosophie der Aufklärung* (Tübingen, 1932).
CASTLE, EDUARD, 'Winckelmanns Kunsttheorie in Goethes Fortbildung', *Zeitschrift für die österreichischen Gymnasien*, 59 (1908), 1–17.
CHOUILLET, JACQUES, *L'Esthëtique des lumières* (Paris, 1974).
CHRISTOFFEL, ULRICH, *Der schriftliche Nachlaß des Anton Raphael Mengs: Ein Beitrag zur Erklärung des Kunstempfindens im spätern 18. Jahrhundert*, publication of inaugural dissertation, University of Munich (Basle, 1918).
CLARK, KENNETH, *The Nude* (London, 1956).
CLARK, WILLIAM H., 'Wieland and Winckelmann: Saul and the Prophet', *Modern Language Quarterly*, 17 (1956), 1–16.
—— 'Wieland *contra* Winckelmann', *The Germanic Review*, 34/1 (1959), 4–13.
COHEN, HERMANN, 'Winckelmann', in id., *Kants Begründung der Aesthetik* (Berlin, 1889), 37–62.
COLLINGWOOD, R. G., *The Principles of Art* (Oxford, 1982) (first pub. 1938).
CONSTANTINE, DAVID, *Early Greek Travellers and the Hellenic Ideal* (Cambridge, 1984).
CRISTOFANI, M., 'Winckelmann a Firenze', *Prospettiva*, 25 (1981), 24–30.
CURTIUS, LUDWIG, 'Goethes Künstlerauge', in id., *Humanistisches und Humanes: Fünf Essays und Vorträge* (Basle, 1954), 63–80.
—— 'Winckelmann', in id., *Humanistisches und Humanes: Fünf Essays und Vorträge* (Basle, 1954), 39–62.
—— 'Johann Joachim Winckelmann 1717–1768', in T. W. Gaehtgens (ed.), *Johann Joachim Winckelmann 1717–1768* (Hamburg, 1986) 5–19.
DANTON, GEORGE A., 'Winckelmann in Contemporary German Literature', *Germanic Review*, 9 (1934), 173–95.
DANZEL, T. W., 'Goethe und die Weimarischen Kunstfreunde in ihrem Verhältnis zu Winckelmann', *Blätter für literarische Unterhaltung*, 282 (1846), 1125–7, 1129–31, 1133–5, 1137–9, 1141–3, 1145–7, 1149–51, 1153–4.
DAVIES, JOHN K., *Das klassische Griechenland und die Demokratie* (Munich, 1986) (first pub. as *Democracy and Classical Greece* (London, 1978)).

DEETZ, MARIA, 'Anschauungen von italienischer Kunst in der deutschen Literatur von Winckelmann bis zur Romantik', *Germanische Studien*, 94 (1930).

DIMOFF, PAUL, 'Winckelmann und André Chénier', *Revue de littérature comparée*, 21 (1947), 321–3.

DOLBERG, GLEN A., *The Reception of Johann Joachim Winckelmann in Modern German Prose Fiction*, Stuttgarter Arbeiten zur Germanistik, 31 (Stuttgart, 1976).

DOVER, K. J., *Greek Homosexuality* (London, 1978).

DOWDEN, EDWARD, 'Goethe in Italy', *Publications of the English Goethe Society*, 3 (1888), 1–23 (repr. from *The Fortnightly Review*, July 1888).

DÜPPENGIESSER, ADOLF, 'Der "gründlich geborne Heide": Religion, Theologie und Kirche bei Winckelmann' (inaugural dissertation, University of Passau (Passau, 1981)).

DUMMER, J., 'J. J. Winckelmann und der griechische Tempel: Versuch eines Plädoyers', *Beiträge der Winckelmann-Gesellschaft*, 8 (1977) ('Griechische Tempel: Wesen und Wirkung'), 103–111.

EBERLEIN, KURT KARL, 'Winckelmann und Frankreich: Zur Geschichte des deutschen Kultureinflusses im französischen Klassizismus', *Deutsche Vierteljahresschrift*, 11 (1933), 592–610.

EDSCHMID, KASIMIR, 'Riedesel in Apulien', *Goethe-Kalender* (1941), 170–92.

—— *Italien* (Stuttgart, 1969).

EINEM, HERBERT VON (ed.), *Beiträge zu Goethes Kunstauffassung* (Hamburg, 1956).

EPHRAIM, CHARLOTTE, *Wandel des Griechenbildes im achtzehnten Jahrhundert: Winckelmann, Lessing, Herder*, Sprache und Dichtung: Forschungen zur Sprach- und Literaturwissenschaft, 61 (Berne, 1936).

ERMISCH, H., 'Winckelmann und Sachsen', *Neues Archiv für sächsische Geschichte und Altertumskunde*, 39 (1918), 52–83.

EVERS, HANS GERHARD, 'Studien zu Winckelmanns Stil' (doctoral thesis, University of Göttingen (Göttingen, 1924)).

FALK, EUGENE H., *The Poetics of Roman Ingarden* (Chapel Hill, NC, 1981).

FEIST, PETER H., 'Winckelmanns Theorie im Verhältnis zur klassischen deutschen Kunst und zum Realismus', *Schriften der Winckelmann-Gesellschaft*, 1 (1973) ('Beiträge zu einem neuen Winckelmannbild'), 56–60.

FINSLER, GEORG, *Homer in der Neuzeit* (Leipzig, 1912).

FISCHER, BERNHARD, 'Kunstautonomie und Ende der Ikonographie: Zur historischen Problematik von "Allegorie" und "Symbol" in Winckelmanns, Moritz' und Goethes Kunsttheorie', *Deutsche Vierteljahresschrift*, 64 (1990), 247–77.

FISCHER, K., 'Johann Joachim Winckelmann und Halle', *Hallesches Monatsheft*, 6 (1958), 300–4.

FLAVELL, M. KAY, 'Winckelmann and the German Enlightenment: On the Recovery and Uses of the Past', *Modern Language Review*, 74 (1979), 79–96.

FLEISCHER, VICTOR, 'Winckelmann', *Die Zukunft*, 81 (1912), 260–9 (from the introd. to edn. of the *Geschichte der Kunst* by Fleischer (Berlin, 1913)).

FLEMING, JOHN, *Robert Adam and his Circle in Edinburgh and Rome* (London, 1962).

FLITTNER, ANDREAS, 'Das Basler Winckelmann-Portrait' (Werner Kaegi zum 70. Geburtstag), *Deutsche Vierteljahresschrift*, 45 (1971), 757–72.

FONTIUS, MARTIN, 'Winckelmann und die französische Aufklärung', *Sitzungsberichte der deutschen Akademie der Wissenschaften zu Berlin, Klasse für Sprache, Literatur und Kunst*, 1 (1968), 1–27.

FRANCISCUS, H. de, 'L'esperienza neopolitana del Winckelmann', *Cronache Pompeiane*, 1 (1975), 7–24.

FREDE, L., 'Winckelmanns Tod', *Zeitschrift für die gesamte Strafrechtswissenschaft*, 81/2 (1969), 329–44.

FRIED, MICHAEL, *Absorption and Theatricality: Painting and Beholder in the Age of Diderot* (Berkeley, 1980).

FRIEDLÄNDER, LUDWIG, 'Winckelmann und seine Nachfolger', *Preußische Jahrbücher*, 2 (1858), 303–32.

FRIEDRICHS, C., *Winckelmann: Ein Vortrag gehalten am 22. Februar 1862 im wissenschaftlichen Verein zu Berlin* (Hamburg, 1862).

FRY, ROGER, *Vision and Design* (Oxford, 1981) (first pub. London, 1920).

FUHRMANN, MANFRED, 'Winckelmann, ein deutsches Symbol', *Neue Rundschau*, 83 (1972), 265–83.

GAEHTGENS, THOMAS W. (ed.), *Johann Joachim Winckelmann 1717–1768*, Studien zum achtzehnten Jahrhundert, 7 (Hamburg, 1986).

GERHARD, MELITTA, 'Die Redaktion der *Italienischen Reise* im Lichte von Goethes autobiographischem Gesamtwerk', in id., *Leben im Gesetz: Fünf Goethe-Aufsätze* (Berne, 1966), 34–51.

GIESECKE, ALBERT, 'J. J. Winckelmann und Adam Friedrich Oeser', *Lemberger Zeitung*, 13 June 1943, no pp.

GIRAUD, RAYMOND, 'Winckelmanns Part in Gautier's Perception of Classical Beauty', *Yale French Studies*, 38 (1967), 172–82.

GIRNUS, WILHELM, 'Winckelmann und das Problem der Schönheit', *Schriften der Winckelmann-Gesellschaft*, 1 (1973) ('Beiträge zu einem neuen Winckelmannbild'), 61–6.

GOMBRICH, E. H., 'Goethe and the History of Art: The Contribution of Johann Heinrich Meyer', *Journal of the English Goethe Society*, 60 (1979), 1–19.

—— *The Image and the Eye: Further Studies in the Psychology of Pictorial Representation* (Oxford, 1982).

GREENHALGH, MICHAEL, *The Classical Tradition in Art* (London, 1978).

GRIEP, WOLFGANG, and JÄGER, HANS-WOLF (eds.), *Reise und soziale Realität am Ende des 18. Jahrhunderts*, Neue Bremer Beiträge, 1 (Heidelberg, 1983).

—— —— (eds.), *Reisen im 18. Jahrhundert*, Neue Bremer Beiträge, 3 (Heidelberg, 1986).
GUNDOLF, FRIEDRICH, 'Winckelmann', in *Anfänge deutscher Geschichtsschreibung von Tschudi bis Winckelmann*, ed. Edgar Wind (Amsterdam, 1938), 166.
GURLITT, J., *Biographische und literarische Notiz von Johann Winckelmann* (Magdeburg, 1797).
HÄSLER, BERTHOLD, 'Winckelmanns Verhältnis zur griechischen Literatur', *Schriften der Winckelmann-Gesellschaft*, 1 (1973) ('Beiträge zu einem neuen Winckelmannbild'), 39–42.
HAFEN, HANS, 'Studien zur Geschichte der deutschen Prosa im 18. Jahrhundert' (doctoral thesis, University of Zürich (Olten, 1952)).
HAILE, H. G., *Artist in Chrysalis: A Biographical Study of Goethe in Italy* (Urbana, Ill. 1973).
HAMANN, RICHARD, 'Winckelmann und die kanonische Auffassung der antiken Kunst', in id., *Krieg, Kunst und Gegenwart* (Marpurg, 1917), 39–61.
HAMM, HEINZ, *Der Theoretiker Goethe: Grundpositionen seiner Weltanschauung, Philosophie und Kunsttheorie* (Berlin, 1975).
HAMPSON, NORMAN, *The Enlightenment* (Harmondsworth, 1968).
HANTZSCH, ADOLF, 'Johann Joachim Winckelmann' (Hervorragende Persönlichkeiten in Dresden und ihre Wohnungen, no. 114), *Mitteilungen des Vereins für Geschichte Dresdens*, 25 (1918), 100–1.
HARRIS, JOHN, *Headfort House and Robert Adam: Drawings from the Collection of Mr. and Mrs. Paul Mellon* (London, 1973).
HASKELL, FRANCIS, and PENNY, NICHOLAS, *Taste and the Antique: The Love of Classical Sculpture 1500–1900* (New Haven, 1981).
HATFIELD, HENRY CARAWAY, *Winckelmann and his German Critics 1755–1781: A Prelude to the Classical Age*, Columbia University Germanic Studies, 15 (New York, 1943).
—— 'Winckelmann: The Romantic Element', *The Germanic Review*, 28 (1953), 282–9.
—— 'Schiller, Winckelmann and the Myth of Greece', in id., *Aesthetic Paganism in German Literature* (Cambridge, Mass., 1964), 1–23.
HECKER, JUTTA, *Flammendes Leben: Sehnsucht, Erfüllung und Katastrophe im Leben J. J. Winckelmanns* (Weimar, 1956).
HEIDRICH, ERNST, 'Winckelmann', in id., *Beiträge zur Geschichte und Methode der Kunstgeschichte* (Basle, 1917), 28–49.
—— 'Winckelmann', *Jahresgabe der Winckelmann-Gesellschaft*, 1958, 42–57.
HEISE, WOLFGANG, 'Winckelmann und die Aufklärung', *Schriften der Winckelmann-Gesellschaft*, 1 (1973), 32–8.
HEITZ, CAROL, 'Un nouveau portrait de Winckelmann', *Études germaniques*, 16 (Jan.–Mar. 1961), 26–30.
HENNING, HANS, *Aus dem Briefwechsel Johann Michael Franckes: Neue*

Mitteilungen zu Franckes Biographie und über Winckelmann, Gellert und Gottsched (Weimar, 1960).

HENNING, HANS, 'Winckelmann-Bibliographie: Folge 3', Jahresgabe der Winckelmann-Gesellschaft, 1967 (Berlin, 1967).

HENNINGS, W. (ed.), 'Winckelmann', Deutscher Ehren-Tempel 7 (1825), 1–32.

HÉRENGER, ALEXANDRE, Goethe en Italie d'après son journal et ses lettres (Paris, 1931).

HERES, G., 'Winckelmann, Bernini, Bellori: Betrachtungen zur "Nachahmung der Alten" ', Forschungen und Berichte, 19 (1979), 9–16.

HERTZ, M., Zum Säculargedächtnisse an Winckelmanns Eintritt in Rom und an Johann Georg Zoega (Greifswald, 1856).

HETTNER, HERMANN, Geschichte der deutschen Literatur im 18. Jahrhundert, ed. Georg Witkowski, 2 vols. (Leipzig, 1929) (first pub. 1864).

HEYDEMANN, HEINRICH, Ellas ed asia sul vaso dei Persiani nel Museo Nazionale di Napoli, Estratto dagli Annali dell'Instituto di corrispondenza anno 1873 (Rome, 1873).

HIBBERT, CHRISTOPHER, The Grand Tour (London, 1969).

HIGHET, GILBERT, The Classical Tradition: Greek and Roman Influences on Western Literature (Oxford, 1949).

HIMMELMANN, N., 'Winckelmanns Hermeneutik' (doctoral thesis, University of Mainz (Mainz, 1971)).

HOLTZHAUER, HELMUT, 'Winckelmann und Goethe', Neue Museumskunde, Year 11, 4 (1968), 389–91.

—— 'Winckelmann und die deutsche Klassik', Schriften der Winckelmann-Gesellschaft, 1 (1973), 52–5.

HOLUB, ROBERT, C., Reception Theory: A Critical Introduction (London, 1984).

HONOUR, HUGH, Neoclassicism (Harmondsworth, 1968).

HUSAR, IRENE, 'Die Idee der Vergottung des Menschen bei Johann Joachim Winckelmann', Schriften der Winckelmann-Gesellschaft, 1 (1973) ('Beiträge zu einem neuen Winckelmannbild'), 67–74.

IRMSCHER, JOHANNES, 'Winckelmann und Byzanz', Revue des études sud-est européennes, 9 (1971), 433–42.

—— 'Dreißig Jahre Winckelmann-Gesellschaft: Winckelmann-Pflege gestern und heute', Das Altertum, 17 (1971), Book 2, 110–19.

—— 'Johann Joachim Winckelmann und die Kirchenväter', in Epektasis: Mélanges patristiques offerts au cardinal Jean Daniélou, ed. J. Fontaine and Charles Kannengiesser (Paris, 1972), 661–75.

—— 'Das Winckelmann-Bild Franz Mehrings', Schriften der Winckelmann-Gesellschaft, 1 (1973) ('Beiträge zu einem neuen Winckelmannbild'), 88–92.

—— 'Johann Joachim Winckelmann und die Altertumswissenschaft heute', Schriften der Winckelmann-Gesellschaft, 1 (1973) ('Beiträge zu einem neuen Winckelmannbild'), 21–31.

—— 'Antikebild und Antikeverständnis in Goethes Winckelmann-Schrift', *Goethe-Jahrbuch*, 95 (1978), 85–111.

—— (ed.), 'Antikerzeption, deutsche Klassik und sozialistische Gegenwart', *Schriften der Winckelmann-Gesellschaft*, 5 (Berlin, 1979).

JACOBS, JÜRGEN, 'Der "Winckelmannische Faden": Zeitlosigkeit und Historizität in der Kunstanchauung des italienischen Goethe', *Wirkendes Wort*, 6 (1987), 363–73.

JAHN, OTTO, *Winckelmann: Eine Rede gehalten am 9. December 1843 in der Akademischen Aula zu Greifswald* (Greifswald, 1844).

JEDIN, HUBERT, *Die deutsche Romfahrt von Bonifatius bis Winckelmann* (Krefeld, 1951).

JERSCH, HILDEGARD, 'Untersuchungen zum Stile Winckelmanns mit besonderer Berücksichtigung der *Geschichte der Kunst des Altertums*' (doctoral thesis, University of Königsberg (Calw, 1939)).

JESSEN, HANS B., 'Zur deutsch-griechischen Begegnung', *Forschungen und Fortschritte*, Year 30, 9 (Sept. 1956), 283–6.

JOLLES, MATHIJS, *Goethes Kunstauffasung* (Berne, 1957).

JUCKER, HANS, 'Winckelmann und die sardischen Bronzen', *Neue Zürcher Zeitung*, 7 Feb. 1954, no. 229.

JUSTI, CARL, *Winckelmann und seine Zeitgenossen*, 3rd edn., 3 vols. (Leipzig, 1923) (first pub. as *Winckelmann, seine Werke und seine Zeitgenossen* (Leipzig, 1866–72).

KÄFER, MARKUS, *Winckelmanns hermeneutische Prinzipien*, Heidelberger Forschungen, 27 (Heidelberg, 1986).

KAMPHAUSEN, ALFRED, 'Winckelmann und sein Dienst an der Heimat', *Beiträge zur Geschichte und zur Landes- und Volkskunde der Altmark*, 7/3 (1940), 197–208.

KARO, GEORG, 'Johann Joachim Winckelmann', *Mitteldeutsche Lebensbilder*, 5 (1930), 130–62.

KASSEL, RUDOLF, 'Heilung einer Textverderbnis in Winckelmanns *Abhandlung von der Fähigkeit der Empfindung des Schönen in der Kunst, und dem Unterrichte in derselben*', *Euphorion*, 56 (1962), 417.

KELLER, HEINRICH, *Goethe und das Laokoön-Problem*, Wege zur Dichtung: Zürcher Schriften zur Literaturwissenschaft, 21 (Frauenfeld, 1935).

KELLER, R. E., *The German Language* (London, 1978).

KIEFER, KLAUS H., *Wiedergeburt und neues Leben: Aspekte des Strukturwandels in Goethes 'Italienische Reise'* (Bonn, 1978).

KIRBY, PAUL FRANKLIN, *The Grand Tour in Italy 1700–1800* (New York, 1952).

KLEINERT, JOCHEN, *Winckelmann und seine Vaterstadt: Zeugnisse, Erinnerungen, Gedanken* (Stendal, 1988).

KLEMM, WALTHER, 'Sieben Zeichnungen zum Leben J. J. Winckelmanns', *Jahresgabe der Winckelmann-Gesellschaft*, 1952–3 (Stendal, 1957).

KOCH, HANNA, 'Johann Joachim Winckelmann: Sprache und Kunstwerk', *Jahresgabe der Winckelmann-Gesellschaft, 1956–7* (Berlin, 1957).

KOCH, HERBERT, *Winckelmann und Goethe in Rom*, Die Gestalt, 20 (Tübingen, 1950).

KÖSTER, ALBERT, 'Johann Joachim Winckelmann: Aus einer Festrede zur zweihundertesten Wiederkehr seines Geburtstages', *Zeitschrift für bildende Kunst*, 53 (1918), 75–82.

KOHLSCHMIDT, WERNER, 'Winckelmann und der Barock', in id., *Form und Innerlichkeit: Beiträge zur Geschichte und Wirkung der deutschen Klassik und Romantik* (Berne, 1955), 11–32.

KRAUS, KONRAD, *Winckelmann und Homer: Mit Benutzung der Hamburger Homer-Ausschreibungen Winckelmanns* (Berlin, 1935).

KRECH, A., *Erinnerungen an Winckelmann* (Berlin, 1935).

KREUZER, INGRID, 'Studien zu Winckelmanns Aesthetik: Normativität und historisches Bewußtsein', *Jahresgabe der Winckelmann-Gesellschaft, 1959* (Berlin, 1959).

KRUFT, HANNO WALTHER, 'Studies in Proportion by J. J. Winckelmann', *Burlington Magazine*, 114 (Mar. 1972), 165–70.

KÜHN, ERICH, 'Vom Schustersohn zum Sänger: Die Sendung Johann Joachim Winckelmanns', *Hamburger Fremdenblatt*, 30 Oct. 1944, no pp.

KÜNTZEL, HEINRICH, *Essay und Aufklärung: Zum Ursprung einer originellen deutschen Prosa im 18. Jahrhundert* (Munich, 1969).

KUNZE, MAX (ed.), 'Archäologie zur Zeit Winckelmanns', *Beiträge der Winckelmann-Gesellschaft*, 2 (Stendal, 1975).

—— (ed.), 'Italia und Germania: Deutsche Klassizisten und Romantiker in Italien', *Beiträge der Winckelmann-Gesellschaft*, 3 (Stendal, 1976).

—— (ed.), 'Winckelmann und Nöthnitz: Eine Aufsatzsammlung', *Beiträge der Winckelmann-Gesellschaft*, 4 (Stendal, 1976).

—— (ed.), 'Adam Friedrich Oeser: Freund und Lehrer Winckelmanns und Goethes', *Beiträge der Winckelmann-Gesellschaft*, 6 (Stendal, 1976).

—— (ed.), 'Beiträge zum antiken Realismus', *Schriften der Winckelmann-Gesellschaft*, 3 (Berlin, 1977).

—— (ed.), 'Johann Joachim Winckelmann und Adam Friedrich Oeser: Eine Aufsatzsammlung', *Beiträge der Winckelmann-Gesellschaft*, 7 (Stendal, 1977).

—— (ed.) with Jürgen Dummer, 'Antikerezeption, Antikeverhältnis, Antikebegenung in Vergangenheit und Gegenwart', *Schriften der Winckelmann-Gesellschaft*, 6 (Stendal, 1983).

—— (ed.), 'Christian Daniel Rauch: Beiträge zum Werk und Wirken', *Beiträge der Winckelmann-Gesellschaft*, 10 (Stendal, 1980).

—— (ed.), 'Pompeji 79–1979: Beiträge zum Vesuvausbruch und seiner Nachwirkung', *Beiträge der Winckelmann-Gesellschaft*, 11 (Stendal, 1982).

—— (ed.) with Jürgen Kraeft, 'Karl Friedrich Schinkel und die Antike: Eine Aufsatzsammlung', *Beiträge der Winckelmann-Gesellschaft*, 12 (Stendal, 1985).

—— (ed.), 'Antikerezeption heute: Protokoll eines Kolloquiums', *Beiträge der Winckelmann-Gesellschaft*, 13 (Stendal, 1985).

—— (ed.), 'Christoph Martin Wieland und die Antike: Eine Aufsatzsammlung', *Beiträge der Winckelmann-Gesellschaft*, 14 (Stendal, 1986).

—— *Winckelmann-Bibliographie: Folge 4* (Stendal, 1988).

KUPKA, PAUL, 'J. J. Winckelmanns Stendaler Zeit', Special issue of the *Montagblatt: Wissenschaftliche Wochenbeilage der 'Magdeburgischen Zeitung'*, 26 (1912), 8 pp.

LAMBERT, R. S., *Grand Tour: A Journey in the Tracks of the Aristocracy* (London, 1935).

LANGEN, AUGUST, *Anschauungsformen in der deutschen Dichtung des 18. Jahrhunderts: Rahmenschau und Rationalismus* (Jena, 1934).

—— 'Die Wechselbeziehungen zwischen Wort- und Bildkunst in der Goethezeit', and 'Verbale Dynamik in der dichterischen Landschaftsschilderung des 18. Jahrhunderts', in *Gesammelte Studien zur neueren deutschen Sprache und Literatur*, ed. K. Richter et al. (Berlin, 1978).

LANGLOTZ, E., 'Winckelman heute', in *Griechische Kunst in heutiger Sicht* (Frankfurt, 1973).

LEES-MILNE, JAMES, *The Age of Adam* (London, 1947).

LEPPMANN, WOLFGANG, *J. J. Winckelmann: Eine Biographie* (Frankfurt am Main, 1971).

LEWIS, LESLEY, *Connoisseurs and Secret Agents in Eighteenth-Century Rome* (London, 1961).

LUKÁCS, GERHARD, 'Johann Joachim Winckelmann in unserer Gegenwart', *Schriften der Winckelmann-Gesellschaft*, 1 (1973) ('Beiträge zu einem neuen Winckelmannbild'), 9–20.

LULLIES, R., 'Ein Bildnis J. J. Winckelmanns von Anton Graf', *Jahrbuch der Hamburger Kunstsammlungen*, 11 (1966), 53–60.

MARX, HARALD, 'Winckelmanns Verhältnis zur Antikenrezeption in der Kunst des Barock: Unter besonderer Berücksichtigung von Werken Louis de Silvestres', *Sächsische Heimatblätter*, Year 19, 2 (1973), 57–62.

MASON, EUDO C., 'Heinrich Füßli und Winckelmann', in *Unterscheidung und Bewahrung: Festschrift für Hermann Kunisch*, ed. K. Lazarowicz and W. Kron (Berlin, 1961), 232–58.

MATUSCHEK, STEFAN, ' "Le bon goût" und "der gute Geschmack": Ein Versuch, Winckelmann nach Voltaire zu lesen', *Germanisch-Romanische Monatsschrift*, 71 (NS 40) (1990), 230–4.

MAUGHAM, H. NEVILLE, *The Book of Italian Travel* (London, 1903).

MAYER, HANS, 'Winckelmanns Tod und die Enthüllung des Doppellebens', in id., *Außenseiter* (Frankfurt am Main, 1977), 198–206 (first pub. Frankfurt am Main, 1975).

MEAD, WILLIAM EDWARD, *The Grand Tour in the Eighteenth Century* (Boston, 1914).

MEINECKE, FRIEDRICH, *Die Entstehung des Historismus*, 2 vols. (Munich, 1936).
MEUSEL, J. G., *Das gelehrte Teutschland oder Lexicon der jetzt lebenden teutschen Schriftsteller*, 12 vols. (Lemgo, 1796–1806).
MICHAUD, L. G., *Biographie universelle*, A New Edition, 42 vols. (Paris, 1842–65).
MIEHE, O., 'Der Mord an Winckelmann', *Nachrichten der Akademie der Wissenschaften in Göttingen, Philologisch-Historische Klasse*, 8 (1968), 209–30.
MIGNER, KARL, *Werner Bergengreuen 'Die Letzte Reise': Betrachtung der Novelle im Rahmen der Klassik* (Munich, 1961).
MORGENSTERN, CARL, *Johann Winckelmann: Eine Rede* (Leipzig, 1805).
MORRIS, JOHN G., 'The Lords Baltimore', *Maryland Historical Fund Publications*, 8 (1874), 56–61.
MÜLLER, CURT, *Die geschichtlichen Vorraussetzungen des Symbolbegriffs in Goethes Kunstanschauung*, Palaestra, 211 (Leipzig, 1937).
—— 'Die geschichtlichen Vorraussetzungen des Symbolbegriffs bei Winckelmann' (inaugural dissertation, Friedrich-Wilhelm's University, Berlin (Grafenhainchen, 1937)).
NAMOWICZ, TADEUSZ, 'Johann Joachim Winckelmann und der Aufklärungsklassizismus in Polen', *Beiträge der Winckelmann-Gesellschaft*, 5 (1976).
—— 'Die aufklärerische Utopie: Rezeption der Griechen auffassung J. J. Winckelmanns um 1800 in Deutschland und Polen' (unpublished dissertation, University of Warsaw, 1978).
NEUMANN, WILHELM, 'Die Bedeutung Home's für die Ästhetik und sein Einfluss auf die deutschen Äesthetiker' (unpublished inaugural dissertation, University of Halle/Wittenberg, 1894).
NIKLEWSKI, GÜNTHER, *Versuch über Symbol und Allegorie: Winckelmann, Moritz, Schelling* (Erlangen, 1979).
NISBET, H. B., 'Laocoön in Germany: The Reception of the Group since Winckelmann', *Oxford German Studies*, 10 (1979), 22–63.
NIVELLE, ARMAND, *Les Théories esthétiques en allemagne de Baumgarten à Kant* (Paris, 1955).
NOACK, FRIEDRICH, *Italienisches Skizzenbuch*, 2 vols. (Stuttgart, 1900).
—— *Deutsches Leben in Rom 1700 bis 1900* (Berne, 1971) (repr. of the edn. pub. Stuttgart, 1907).
—— *Das deutsche Rom* (Rome, 1912).
—— *Das Deutschtum in Rom seit dem Ausgang des Mittelalters*, 2 vols. (Stuttgart, 1927).
OSBORNE, HAROLD, *Aesthetics and Criticism* (London, 1955).
OSTERKAMP, ERNST, 'Zierde und Beweis: Über die Illustrations prinzipien von J. J. Winckelmanns *Geschichte der Kunst des Altertums*', *Germanisch-Romanische Monatsschrift*, 70 (NS 39) (1989), 301–25.
PANOFSKY, ERWIN, *Idea: Ein Beitrag zur Begriffsgeschichte der älteren Kunsttheorie*, Studien der Bibliothek Warburg, 2nd edn. (Berlin, 1960).

PATER, WALTER, 'Winckelmann', in id., *The Renaissance: Studies in Art and Poetry*, a new edition (London, 1910), 177–232.

PATZER, FRANZ (ed.), *Reiseführer im Wandel der Zeit*, 196 Wechselausstellung der Wiener Stadt- und Landesbibliothek (Vienna, 1982).

PÈDIO, TOMMASO, *Johann Hermann von Riedesel: nella Puglia del'700 (lettera a J. J. Winckelmann)*, Itinerari Meridionali, 3 (Lecce, 1979).

PELZEL, THOMAS O., 'Mengs and his German Critics', in *Goethe in Italy, 1786–1786*, ed. G. Hoffmeister (Santa Barbara, Calif., 1988), 95–113.

PIECHOTTA, HANS JOACHIM (ed.), *Reise und Utopie: Zur Literatur der Spätaufklärung* (Frankfurt am Main, 1976).

PIEPER, PAUL, 'Zu Carl Justis Winckelmann', *Boreas: Münstersche Beiträge zur Archäologie*, 5 (1982), 259–65.

PODRO, MICHAEL, *The Critical Historians of Art*, 2nd edn. (New Haven, 1986).

POTTS, ALEX, 'Winckelmanns Construction of History', *Art History*, 5/4 (1982), 377–407.

PRANG, H., 'Goethe als Benutzer von italienischen Reiseführern', *Goethe-Kalender* (1936), 222–7.

—— *Goethe und die Kunst der italienischen Renaissance*, Germanische Studien, 198 (Berlin, 1938).

PREIME, EBERHARD, 'Winckelmann und das deutsche Schicksal', typewritten MSS in Winckelmann-Sammlung, Stendal, dated spring 1934.

REED, T. J., 'Goethe and Happiness', in *Goethe Revisited*, ed. E. M. Willoughby (London, 1984), 111–31 (first pub. New York, 1983).

REHM, ELSE, 'Briefe von und über Winckelmann', *Arcadia*, 2 (1967), Book 3, 305–19.

REHM, WALTHER, 'Winckelmann and Lessing' and 'Johann Hermann von Riedesel: Freund Winckelmanns, Mentor Goethes, Diplomat Friedrich des Großen', in id., *Götterstille und Göttertrauer: Aufsätze zur Deutsch-Antiken Begegnung* (Berne, 1951), 183–247.

—— *Griechentum und Goethezeit: Geschichte eines Glaubens*, 3rd edn. (Berne, 1952).

—— 'Winckelmanns Lebensform und Selbstbildnis in seinen Briefen', *Jahresgabe der Winckelmann-Gesellschaft* (1958), 9–41.

RICHTER, GERHARD, 'Der berühmte Winckelmann', *Mitteldeutsches Land*, 3 (1957), 171–82.

—— 'Winckelmanns Tod', *Unsere Heimat*, 1/6 (1959), 209–14.

—— 'Lebendiger Winckelmann', *Unsere Heimat*, 2/2 (1960), 41–6.

ROBSON-SCOTT, WILLIAM DOUGLAS, *The Younger Goethe and the Visual Arts*, Anglica Germanica, ser. 2 (Cambridge, 1981).

RÖNNEFAHRT, J. G., *Johann Joachim Winckelmann* (Stendal, 1859).

ROSETTI, D., *Joh. Winckelmanns letzte Lebenswoche: Ein Beitrag zu dessen Biographie* (Dresden, 1818).

ROSSI, G. G. de, *Vita di Angelica Kaufmann, pittrice* (Florence, 1810).

ROSTEUTSCHER, JOACHIM, *Das ästhetische Idol im Werke von Winckelmann, Novalis, Hoffmann, Goethe, George und Rilke* (Berne, 1956).
RÜDIGER, HORST, 'Eine gescheiterte Winckelmann-Biographie', *Neue Zürcher Zeitung, Beilage für Literatur und Kunst* (Fernausgabe), 25 (1952), 3.
—— 'Winckelmann und seine Zürcher Freunde', *Neue Zürcher Zeitung*, 4 Aug. 1955, pp. 1–2.
—— *Winckelmann und Italien: Sprache, Dichtung, Menschen*, Schriften und Vorträge des Petrarca-Instituts Köln, 8 (Krefeld, 1956).
—— '*Pura et illustrus brevitas*: Über Kürze als Stilideal', *Konkrete Vernunft* (1958), 345–72.
—— (ed.), *Winckelmanns Tod: Die Originalberichte* (Frankfurt am Main, 1959).
—— 'Winckelmanns Geschichtsauffassung: Ein Dresdener Entwurf als Keimzelle seines historischen Denkens', *Euphorion*, 62 (1968), 99–116.
—— 'Winckelmann's Personality', in *Winckelmann 1768–1968* (Bad Godesberg, 1968), 20–39.
—— 'Das Urteil eines Sachverständigen: Winckelmann über Clelands Still', *Arcadia*, 7 (1972), Book 2/3, 272–3.
—— 'Zur Komposition von Goethes *Zweitem römischen Aufenthalt*', in *Aspekte der Goethezeit*, ed. S. A. Corngold and others (Göttingen, 1977), 97–114.
RUPPERT, HANS, 'Winckelmann-Renaissance', *Geistige Arbeit*, 9/1 (1942), 1–2.
—— 'Ergänzungen zur Winckelmann-Bibliographie für die Jahre 1942–1955', *Jahresgabe der Winckelmann-Gesellschaft* (1956), 7–17.
SAUER, BRUNO, 'Zu Winckelmanns Ehren', *Neue Jahrbücher für das klassische Altertum*, 20/39 (1917), 577–86.
—— 'Johann Joachim Winckelmann geboren 9. Dezember 1717', *Westermanns Monatshefte*, 62/123 (1917), 482–7.
—— 'Winckelmann und Wagner', *Bayreuther Blätter*, 41/4–7 (1918), 176–9.
SCHADEWALDT, WOLFGANG, *Winckelmann und Homer*, Leipziger Universitätsreden, 6 (Leipzig, 1941).
—— (with Walther Rehm), 'Winckelmann als Exzerptor und Selbstdarsteller', in id., *Hellas und Hesperien: Gesammelte Schriften zur Antike und zur neueren Literatur* (Zürich, 1960), 637–57 (first pub. 1954).
—— 'Winckelmann und Rilke: Zwei Beschreibungen des Apollon' (Pfullingen, 1968).
SCHEFOLD, K., 'Winckelmanns neue Sicht der antiken Kunst', in id., *Wort und Bild: Studien zur Gegenwart der Antike* (Basle, 1975).
SCHEVEN, FRIEDRICH, 'Joh. Joachim Winckelmann und seine Strelitzer Freunde und Schüler', *Das Carolinum*, 30/41 (1964/5), 3–35.
SCHMIDT, VALENTIN HEINRICH, *Rede bei der am Geburtstage Johann Joachim Winckelmanns von den Altmärkern veranstalteten Feier* (Berlin, 1828).

SCHMITT, GERHARD, 'Winckelmanns Ästhetik: Untersuchungen zum Verhältnis von Kunstauffassung, Geschichte und Menschenbild in seinen Schriften' (dissertation as part of teaching qualification, Free University of Berlin (Berlin, 1978)).
SCHÖMANN, G. F., *Winckelmann und die Archäologie* (Greifswald, 1845).
SCHUDT, LUDWIG, *Italienreisen im 17. und 18. Jahrhundert*, Römische Forschungen der Bibliotheca Hertziana, 15 (Vienna, 1959).
SCHULTZ, A., 'Goethe and the Literature of Travel', *Journal of English and Germanic Philology*, 48 (1949), 445–68.
—— ' "Ehrwürdiger Mensch, unerreicht als Bibliothekar!": Johann Michael Francke—Freund Winckelmanns?', in *Festschrift Johannes Jahn zum xxii. November mcmlvii* (Leipzig, 1957), 287–92.
SCHULZ, ARTHUR, 'Die Bildnisse Johann Joachim Winckelmanns', *Jahresgabe der Winckelmann-Gesellschaft, 1953* (Berlin, 1953).
—— 'Gedenkblätter auf Winckelmann', *Jahresgabe der Winckelmann-Gesellschaft* (1954–55), 57–72.
—— *Wie stehen wir heute zu Winckelmann* (Stendal, 1956).
—— 'Ce charmante enthousiaste de Winckelmann', *Das Altertum*, 3/1 (1957), 52–60.
—— 'Plastische Rundbildnisse Winckelmanns', *Jahresgabe der Winckelmann-Gesellschaft* (1958), 58–68.
—— 'Winckelmann und seine Welt', *Jahresgabe der Winckelmann-Gesellschaft, 1961* (Berlin, 1962).
—— (ed.), 'Die Kasseler Lobschriften auf Winckelmann', *Jahresgabe der Winckelmann-Gesellschaft, 1963* (Berlin, 1963).
SCHULZ, EBERHARD WILHELM, 'Winckelmanns Schreibart', in *Studien zur Goethezeit: Erich Trunz zum 75. Geburtstag*, ed. Hans-Joachim Mähl and Eberhard Mannack, Beihefte zum Euphorion, 18 (Heidelberg, 1981), 233–55.
SCHULTZE, WERNER, 'Winckelmann und die Religion', *Archiv für Kulturgeschichte*, 34/3 (1952), 247–60.
SCHWEIZER, NIKLAUS RUDOLF, *The Ut pictura poesis Controversy in Eighteenth-Century England and Germany*, European University Papers (Frankfurt am Main, 1972).
—— *Ästhetik als Philosophie der sinnlichen Erkenntnis* (Basle, 1973).
SEEBA, HINRICH C., 'Zur Wirkungsgeschichte eines "unhistorischen" Historikers zwischen Ästhetik und Geschichte', *Deutsche Vierteljahresschrift*, 56 (special Issue) (1982), 168–210.
SEGELKEN, HEINRICH, *Winckelmann 1717–1768: Ein Lebensbericht zum 200. Gedenktage seiner Geburt* (Stendal, 1917).
SHEPPARD, ANNE, *Aesthetics: An Introduction to the Philosophy of Art* (Oxford, 1987).
SMIDT, H., 'Johann Joachim Winckelmann', in id., *Deutsche Romfahrer von*

Winckelmann bis Böcklin: Ein Jahrhundert römischen Lebens in Tagbuchblättern und Briefen (Leipzig, 1913), 1–6.
SPENGLER, W. E., *Der Begriff des Schönen bei Winckelmann: Ein Beitrag zur deutschen Klassik* (Göppingen, 1970).
STAFFORD, BARBARA MARIA, 'Beauty of the Invisible: Winckelmann and the Aesthetics of Imperceptibility', *Zeitschrift für Kunstgeschichte*, 43 (1980), 65–78.
STARK, C. B., *Johann Joachim Winckelmann, sein Bildungsgang und seine bleibende Bedeutung* (Berlin, 1867).
—— 'Johann Joachim Winckelmann 1717–1768', in *Systematik und Geschichte der Archäologie der Kunst* (Leipzig, 1880), 193–5.
STEWART, WILLIAM E., *Die Reisebeschreibung und ihre Theorie im Deutschland des 18. Jahrhunderts*, Literatur und Wirklichkeit, 20 (Bonn, 1978).
STILLER, OTTO, 'J. J. Volkmann, eine Quelle für Goethes *Italienische Reise*', *Programm*, 63 (1908), 3–15.
STOCKHAUSEN, HANS-ADALBERT VON, 'Zeitgeschmack und Geschichtsurteil bei Winckelmann', *Geistige Arbeit*, 5/5 (1938), 3.
STÖCKER, HELENE, 'Zur Kunstanschauung des xviii. Jahrhunderts von Winckelmann bis Wackenroder' (inaugural dissertation (part), University of Berne (Berlin, 1902)).
STOLL, HEINRICH ALEXANDER, 'Winckelmann seine Verleger und Drucker', *Jahresgabe der Winckelmann-Gesellschaft, 1960* (Berlin, 1960).
—— 'Winckelmann und seine Drucker', in *Renaissance und Humanismus in Mittel- und Osteuropa*, ed. J. Irmscher, 2 vols. (Berlin, 1962), i. 261–71.
—— (ed. and trans.), 'Mordakte Winckelmann: Die Originalakten des Kriminalprozesses gegen den Mörder Johann Joachim Winckelmanns', *Jahresgabe der Winckelmann-Gesellschaft, 1965* (Berlin, 1965).
—— *Tod in Triest: Leben, Taten und Wunder Johann Joachim Winckelmanns* (Berlin, 1973).
—— (with G. Löwe, eds.), *Entdeckungen in Hellas: Reisen deutscher Archäologen in Griechenland, Kleinasien und Sizilien* (Berlin, 1979).
STORBECK, LUDWIG, 'Winckelmann und Stendal', *Montagsblatt: Wissenschaftliche Beilage der Magdeburger Zeitung*, 70/27, 2 July 1928, 209–212.
—— 'Johann Joachim Winckelmann, ein Stendaler Kind', *Heimatkalender für die Altmark* (1935), 66–72.
SUMMERSON, JOHN (ed.), *Drawings by Robert and James Adam from the Collection in Sir John Soane's Museum* (London, 1953).
SWARBICK, JOHN (ed.), *The Works in Architecture of Robert and James Adam* (London, 1959).
SWEET, DENIS MARSHALL, 'An Introduction to Classicist Aesthetics in Eighteenth-Century Germany: Winckelmann's Writings on Art' (Part of Ph.D. requirement, University of Stanford (Stanford, Calif., 1978)).

—— 'Die Grenzen der Aufklärung: Winckelmann im englischen Sprachraum', *Beiträge der Winckelmann-Gesellschaft*, 16 (1986) ('Beiträge zur internationalen Wirkung Winckelmanns'), 5–17.
SYBEL, LUDWIG VON, 'Zum neunten December', *Deutsche Rundschau*, 57 (1888), 481–9.
SZAROTA, ELIDA MARIA, 'Winckelmann und Hölderlins Herkulesdeutung', *Schriften der Winckelmann-Gesellschaft*, 1 (1973) ('Beiträge zu einem neuen Winckelmannbild'), 75–87.
SZONDI, PETER, *Poetik und Geschichtsphilosophie I: Antike und Moderne in der Ästhetik der Goethezeit: Hegels Lehre von der Dichtung* (Frankfurt am Main, 1974).
TEASE, GEOFFREY, *The Grand Tour* (London, 1967).
TIBAL, ANDRÉ, *Inventaire des manuscrits de Winckelmann déposés à la Bibliothèque nationale* (Paris, 1911).
TÖWE, CARL, 'Winckelmann und Goethe', *Das Lyzeum*, 2 (1915), 227–33.
TREVELYAN, HUMPHREY, *Goethe and the Greeks* (Cambridge, 1941).
TUZET, HÉLÈNE, *La Sicile au XVIIIe siècle vue par les voyageurs étrangers* (Strasbourg, 1955).
TYTLER, A. F. (Lord Woodhousely), *Memoirs of the Life and Writings of the Honourable Henry Home of Kames*, 2 vols. and suppl. (London, 1807–9).
UHLIG, L., 'Klassik und Geschichtsbewußtsein in Goethes Winckelmannschrift', *Germanisch-Romanische Monatsschrift* 62 (1981), 143–55.
VALENTIN, V., 'Zu Goethe und Winckelmann', *Goethe-Jahrbuch*, 16 (1895), 213.
VALLENTIN, BERTHOLD, *Winckelmann* (Berlin, 1931).
VIËTOR, KARL, 'Goethe in Italien', *Germanic Review*, 7 (1932), 123–9.
WAETZOLDT, WILHELM, *Tiefe—Großheit—Einfachheit* (Halle, 1943).
WARNING, RAINER (ed.), *Rezeptionsästhetik: Theorie und Praxis*, 2nd edn. (Munich, 1979).
WARRY, J. G., *Greek Aesthetic Theory: A Study of Callistic and Aesthetic Concepts in the Works of Plato and Aristotle* (London, 1962).
WEBER, HERMANN J., 'Sprachliche Studien zur Ästhetik Winckelmanns', *Publications of the Modern Language Association of America*, 25/4 (NS 28/4) (1910), 568–607.
WEGENER, MAX, *Goethes Anschauung antiker Kunst* (Berlin, 1944).
WEILGENNY, HEDWIG (ed.), *Winckelmann und Goethe: Ausstellung zum 200. Todestag Johann Joachim Winckelmanns* (Weimar, 1968).
WELLBERRY, DAVID E., *Lessing's Laocoön: Semiotics and Aesthetics in the Age of Reason*, Anglica Germanica, 2 (Cambridge, 1984).
WELLEK, RENÉ, *Four Critics: Croce, Valéry, Lukács, and Ingarden* (Seattle, 1981).
WHEELER, KATHLEEN M., *German Aesthetic and Literary Criticism: The Romantic Ironists and Goethe* (Cambridge, 1984).
WIEHLE, MARTIN, 'Johann Joachim Winckelmann als Bibliothekar: Gelehrte

als Bibliothekare im Zeitalter der deutschen Klassik', *Der Bibliothekar*, 22/6 (1968), 632–5.

WIESNER, J. C., 'Winckelmann und Hippokrates: Zu Winckelmanns naturwissenschaftlich-medezinischen Studien', *Gymnasium*, 60 (1953), 149–67.

WILL, FREDERIC, 'Winckelmann and Cousin', *Symposium*, 10 (1956), 60–74.

WOHLGEMUTH, JOSEF, 'Henry Homes Ästhetik und ihr Einfluß auf deutsche Ästhetiker' (inaugural dissertation, University of Rostock (Berlin, 1893)).

WOLF, SIEGMUND A., 'Johann Joachim Winckelmanns Vorfahren', *Montagsblatt: Wissenschaftliche Beilage der Magdeburgischen Zeitung*, 80/36, 5 Sept. 1938, 281–3.

ZAZOFF, P. and ZAZOFF, H., *Gemmensammler und Gemmenforscher: Von einer noblen Passion zur Wissenschaft* (Munich, 1983).

ZBINDEN, W., *Winckelmann* (Berne, 1935).

ZELLER, HANS, *Winckelmanns Beschreibung des Apollo im Belvedere*, Zürcher Beiträge zur deutschen Literatur- und Geistesgeschichte, 8 (Zürich, 1955).

—— HANS and STEINMANN, ULRICH, 'Zur Entstehung der Winckelmann-Büsten von Friedrich Wilhelm Doell', *Jahresgabe der Winckelmann-Gesellschaft* (1954–5), 18–46.

ZIMMERMANN, KONRAD (ed.), 'Die Dresdener Antiken und Winckelmann', *Schriften der Winckelmann-Gesellschaft*, 4 (Berlin, 1977).

ZIMMERMANN, MAX, *Winckelmann, der Klassizismus und die märkische Kunst* (Leipzig, 1918).

ZINSERLING, GERHARD, 'Winckelmann und die Kunst der Gegenwart', *Schriften der Winckelmann-Gesellschaft*, 1 (1973) ('Beiträge zu einem neuen Winckelmannbild'), 93–112.

ZINSERLING, VERENA, 'Winckelmann als Begründer von Archäologie und Kunstgeschichte', *Schriften der Winckelmann-Gesellschaft*, 1 (1973) ('Beiträge zu einem neuen Winckelmannbild'), 43–6.

—— 'Ausstellung: "Winckelmann in Rom 1755–1768" ', *Schriften der Winckelmann-Gesellschaft*, 1 (1973), 113–117.

Index

Adam, J. 18
Adam, R. 9–19
Addison, J. 6
aesthetic experience:
   nature/consequences of 45–68, 101–2, 133–48, 155–9, 160–4, 192–205, 209–48
   preconditions for 37–45, 69–80, 172–7, 206–9
   see also friendship
Africa 115
   see also Egypt
Agrigento 107, 115, 124–6, 127, 128, 154
Albani, Cardinal Alessandro 5, 15, 18, 37, 85, 178, 194
Alexander the Great 158
Algardi, A. 192
America 119, 120
Anhalt-Dessau, F. F., Prince of 90, 208
Apollo Belvedere 48, 56, 63–8, 101, 129, 134, 142, 144, 198–200, 235, 246
Archenholz [sic]—Archenholtz, J. W. von 211
Archimedes 118
Archinto, Governor Alberigo 5
architecture *passim* esp. Ch. 3
Aristides 162
art:
   content of 24–30
   formation of beautiful images 30–1, 190–1
   historical stylistics 23–4, 31–3, 100–1, 102–3, 121–33, 153–5, 160–4, 186–201, 209–18
   reception, *see* aesthetic experience
   theories of production 20–3, 112–21, 150–3, 160–4, 184–6
Athemius 154
Athens 109, 110, 112, 113, 114, 149, 150, 151, 154, 155, 156, 157, 158, 186, 190

Barletta 126–7
Belvedere Torso 48, 56–62, 101, 141, 142, 156, 233
Benedict XIV 5

Berg, F. R. von 37, 39, 40, 41, 42, 80, 83, 84, 93, 94, 174
Bernini, L. 130, 188
Bianconi, L. 66
Biscari, Prince 88, 128, 130
Böhme, J. 216–7
Bolzano 217
Borromini, F. C. 188–9
Bottari 192
British Isles (and Britons) Ch. 1 *passim*, 38, 114, 136, 154, 159–64, 175, 177
   see also under individual family name
Bünau, H., Graf von 38, 67
Burke, E. 161

Calabria 110
Calvert, F. (Lord Baltimore) 38, 177
Caracci, A. 190
Castellani, N. 92–3, 94
Castello 85
Catania 116, 128, 130, 141
Cheroffini, C., Countess 5
China 189
Chytraeus, N. 2
Cicero 31
cicerone 9, 11, 15, 16, 17, 19, 35, 171, 200, 230
Clement XII 5
Clérisseau, C. L. 9, 15, 16, 17, 18, 28
Cochin, C.-N. 6, 170, 183
Constantinople 96, 97, 154
Cooper, A. A. (Lord Shaftesbury) 22–3, 24–5, 26–7

Da Vinci, L. 27
Daedalus 24
Diede, C. D. 73–4, 80, 159–64
Dieffenbach, A. G. 73–4
Diodurus 124, 140, 142
Du Fresnoy, C. A. 20, 27, 30
Du Loir, le Sieur 150

Egypt 88, 114, 116, 193
Elysium 135, 195
England, *see* British Isles

Erdmannsdorf, F. W. von 208
Erlangen 74, 76
Etna (Mount) 108, 116, 117, 144

Fingal 160–1
Firmian, K. J., Graf von 174
Florence 76, 92, 99, 100, 101, 174, 187, 196
France (and the French) Ch. 1 *passim*, 104, 150–3, 162–3, 174–5, 182–3.
 see also under individual family name/city
Francke, J. M. 87, 102
friendship 37–45, 80–102, 177–182.
 see also aesthetic experience (preconditions for)
Fröhlich, H. 74
Füßli, C. 80, 85, 174
Füßli, H. 83, 85, 177, 178

Gaghini (usually Gagini), D. 130, 131
Genoa 76
Germany 114
 see also under individual towns
Geßner, S. 49, 80, 177, 180
Girgenti 79, 121, 123, 124, 129, 130
Glenorchy, Lady 156
Goethe, J. W. von 2, 36, 69, 78, 84, 85, 136, 164, 167, 169, 195, 200–1, Ch. 5 *passim*
Göttingen 73–4, 88, 177
Greece (ancient and modern) *passim*
 see also under individual locations

Hackert, P. 210
Hagedorn, C. L. von 177, 181
Hakfull 162
Hamilton, Sir W. 75, 85, 92, 208
Hegel, G. W. F. 45
Herculaneum 8, 193
Herder, J. G. 112
Hogarth, W. 32, 95
Home, H. (Lord Kames) 22, 23, 29
Homer 161, 162, 163
homosexuality 39, 77, 92–5, 197
 see also friendship
Hope, C. 15
Horace 54, 119
Humboldt, W. von 9
Hurd, R. 12, 13, 14
Hutcheson, F. 28

Idstein 74

Ingarden, R. Ch. 2 *passim*
 see also aesthetic experience
Isodorus 154
Italy *passim*
 see also under individual location
itineraries 2–3, 102–3, 169–172, 201–2

Kaufmann, A. 208
Knox, V. 13, 14

Lalande, J. de Ch. 4 *passim*
Laocoön 33, 67, 101, 142
Lassels, R. 13, 14
Lausanne 72
Le Bruyn 150
Lecce 107, 118, 127
Leipzig 177, 207, 208
Lessing, G. E. 45, 60
Locke, J. 14
Lyons 75

Magna Graecia *passim*
 see also under individual locations
Malta 107, 117, 144
Mann, Sir H. 84
Mannheim 216, 220, 223
Mantegna, A. 235
Marseilles 75
Martanna 126
Mazzara 126
Mechel, C. von 83
Mecklenburg-Strelitz, Prince of 90, 91
Mengs, A. R. 11, 17, 39, 44, 49, 78, 80, 87, 206, 208, 216
Messina 106, 127
Michelangelo 31, 186, 187–8, 190
Middle Ages:
 art of the 96, 120–1, 126, 127, 165, 189
Milan 76
Misson 6
Monreale 127
Monte di Trapani 114, 126
Montesquieu, C. de 150, 151, 152, 165, 166
Muzel-Stosch, W., Baron von, *see* Stosch, P., Baron von
Mylne, R. 124

Naples 6, 85, 91, 92, 94, 112, 119, 127–8, 148, 186, 189, 239
Nettuno 85
Nicomachus 201
Nugent, T. 16–7

INDEX

Oeser, A. F. 11, 44, 85, 87, 169, 206–9, 214, 216
Ossian 160, 163
  see also Fingal

Padua 235
Palermo 106, 126, 130
Pancrazi 124
Paris 75, 181
Paros 153
patriotism 79, 95
  see also friendship
Pericles 21, 109, 112, 113, 156, 186, 190
  see also Athens
Pesto (Paestum) 143, 180, 193–4
Piles, R. de 21, 23, 24, 27, 29, 30, 31
Pindar 39
Piranesi, G. 9, 17, 18, 214
Plato 2, 7, 41, 45, 63–8, 105
  see also aesthetic experience
Pliny 24, 124
Plotinus 67
Polybius 113
Polycrates 155
Pompeii 8, 92, 193
Portici 92, 193
Praxiteles 101
Pygmalion 64, 237
Pythagoras 155

Raphael 30, 42, 190, 207, 208
rebirth 62, 64–8, 220, 227, 238, 240–8
  see also aesthetic experience
Regensburg 75
Reiffenstein, J. F. 84, 85
Religion:
  church 104–5, 108, 185
  Vatican *passim*
  see aesthetic experience
Reni, Guido 190
Revett, N. 150
Richard, J.-M. Ch. 4 *passim*
Riedesel, J. H. von *passim* esp. Ch. 3
Romanticism 160–8
Rome *passim*
Rousseau, J. J. 151, 152, 161
Rubens 21

Samos 155
Sandrart, J. von 6
Saxe-Weimar-Eisenach, C. A., Duke of 231
Saxony 99

Scaliger, J. J. 31
Schiller, F. von 214
Schlabbrendorf, Graf von 80
Scipio 162
Segestus 143
Seidel, P. 214
Selinus 128
Sicily *passim*, esp. Ch. 3
  see also under individual locations
Sienna 189
Smollett, T. 10–11, 12, 13, 14, 15, 17, 18
Socrates 28
Spon, J. 6, 150
Stein, C. von 240–1
Sterne, L. 6–7
Stilo 127
Stosch, P., Baron von 80, 92, 122, 174, 176, 179
Strasbourg 75, 216, 233, 234
Stuart, J. 150, 160
Stuttgart 75
Syracuse 118, 142

Taormina 123, 124
Testoni 118
Theocrites 118
Thirty Years War 7
Tischbein, J. H. W. 85, 208, 210, 221
Titian 190, 235
Tournefort, J. P. de 149, 150
travel:
  danger 1–2, 9
  expectations 1–19, 71–80, 172–7
  literature (general) 6–19, otherwise Chs. 1, 3, 4, 5 *passim*
  see also itineraries
Turin 76
Turkey 149, 159, 189

Usteri, L. 93
Usteri, P. 83

Vatican *passim*
Venice 76
Verona 237
Veronese, P. 190
Vesuvius (Mount) 85, 144
Vienna 75
Virgil 162
Vitruvius 124
Volkmann, J. J. *passim* esp. Ch. 4
Volkmann, P. D. 173, 177, 178
Voltaire 151

INDEX

Walther, G. C. 88, 95
Webb, D. 20, 21-2, 24, 28, 29, 31
Weiße, C. F. von 181
Wheler, Sir G. 150
Wiedewelt, H. 80
Wilkes, J. 89
Wille, G. 80

Wörlitz 208
Wright, E. 13
Württemberg, E., Prinz von 77

Young, E. 20-1

Zürich 85, 99